G000111549

The
All-Ireland
Dream

Séamus McRory was born in the parish of Lissan in South Derry. A former chairman of his native club, with whom he played football in the 1960s and 1970s, he currently represents his adopted club, Longford Slashers, on Longford County Board. Over the past number of years, Séamus, a primary school teacher, has contributed many articles to various GAA publications. He is also the author of *The Voice from the Sideline: Famous GAA Managers* (1997) and *The Road to Croke Park: Great GAA Personalities* (1999).

Educated at St Patrick's College, Armagh, Séamus continued his education at St Joseph's College of Education and Queen's University, Belfast. He lives in Abbeycartron just outside Longford town with his wife Olive and family Mairéad and Diarmuid.

To Olive, Mairéad and Diarmuid.
With sincere thanks for their constant help and encouragement.

And to the following who have made my life more meaningful:
My late father, Dominic, and my late father-in-law, Harry D'Alton.
My mother, Margaret, and my mother-in-law, Mary Frances.
My sister Sheila and my brother Brendan.
The extended McRory and D'Alton families.
The late John Barry, who was such an integral part of my two previous books.
The late Hugh Shannon, with whom I, happily, shared so many Ulster final days.

The
All-Ireland
Dream

OVER 25 INTERVIEWS WITH GAA GREATS

Séamus McRory

WOLFHOUND PRESS

Published in 2005 by Wolfhound Press
An Imprint of Merlin Publishing
16 Upper Pembroke Street
Dublin 2, Ireland
Tel: +353 1 676 4373
Fax: +353 1 676 4368
publishing@merlin.ie
www.merlinwolfhound.com

Text © 2005 Séamus McRory
Editing, Design and Layout © 2005 Merlin Publishing
Cover Photographs © Lynn Group Publications, Kells, Co. Meath
Internal Photographs © of the individuals and institutions noted under
each image.

ISBN 0-86327-936-8

All rights reserved. No part of this book may be reproduced or utilised
in any form or by any means electronic or mechanical, including
photocopying, filming, recording, video recording, photography, or by
any information storage and retrieval system, nor shall by way of trade
or otherwise be lent, resold or otherwise circulated in any form of
binding or cover other than that in which it is published without prior
permission in writing from the publisher.

A CIP catalogue record for this book is available from the British
Library.

10 9 8 7 6 5 4 3 2 1

Typeset by Gough Typesetting Services
Cover Design by Graham Thew Design
Printed and bound by J. H. Haynes & Co. Ltd., Britain

*The publishers have made every reasonable effort to contact the copyright
holders of photographs reproduced in this book. If any involuntary
infringement of copyright has occurred, sincere apologies are offered and the
owner of such copyright is requested to contact the publisher.*

Contents

Acknowledgements

I would like to thank, most sincerely, all those who have contributed to the production of this book. In particular, I wish to express my deep appreciation to the following:

All the staff at Wolfhound Press, especially Managing Editor Aoife Barrett and Managing Director/Publisher Chenile Keogh, as well as freelance copy editor Aideen Quigley, for their courtesy and support throughout the whole process; the GAA personalities themselves for sharing with me their lifetime experiences and their views on the future of Gaelic Games – their spirit of generosity and friendly co-operation greatly simplified my work; Eugene McGee for so willingly and so ably writing a much appreciated Foreword; Tom McGuinness for his lovely poem *as Gaeilge* and for his most valuable proofing contribution; Fr Aodh Turbitt PP, Edgeworthstown; Seán Stakelum, Longford; Martin Jennings, Longford; Pat Lynch, Longford; Christy Delaney, Longford; Kevin Scully, Longford; Brendan McRory, Lissan; and Seán Murphy, Limerick, for their wide-ranging research; Danny O'Kane, Dungiven; Francis Stockwell, Tuam; and John Murray, Knockcroghery, for the use of photographs; Raymond Donlon, Longford, for his photographic scanning facilities; my daughter Mairéad, for her word-processing skills and editing expertise; my son Diarmuid, for his meticulous research and general advice; Noel Melia, Kildare, for his computer efficiency and constant help; Joe Hunt, Legan, for the thoroughly efficient manner in which he undertook the arduous task of proofing; John Patrick Conway, Managing Director, Meteor Electrical Ltd, Cookstown, Co. Tyrone; Noel O'Connor, Newsround, Longford; Tim Shanley, Business Manager, Ulster Bank, Longford; Tony Keenan, Manager, Bank of Ireland, Longford; Seán Duffy, Manager, Permanent/TSB, Longford; and Betty Martin, Area Manager of the Educational Building Society, Longford, for their kind contributions to the personal preparation of this book.

A particular word of gratitude is especially due to the publishers of the leading GAA magazine *The Hogan Stand*, both for the use of photographs and their comprehensive research material.

I would also like to record my sincere appreciation to Eamonn Brennan, Longford, for his invaluable suggestions and detailed research.

Most of all, I thank my wife, Olive, not only for her computer expertise but also for her patience, advice and constant availability. No one worked harder to ensure that the book progressed from my All-Ireland Dream to that of final production.

Foreword

The GAA is indeed a very wide canvas when we try to analyse its place in Irish life at the start of the 21st century – from the schoolchildren battling it out for Cumann na mBunscol titles in early summer to the big stars competing for the Sam Maguire Cup in September and from the ordinary club members competing in the Scór competitions on winter nights to the very successful elite clubs who contest the finals of the club championships on St Patrick's Day.

While every section of GAA activity plays an important role in the local community in which it operates, there is no doubt that the section which gives the organisation its special appeal all over Ireland is that involving inter-county teams. It is from the small rural parishes that the big heroes emerge, and their inter-county achievements make them national sporting icons.

Great sportsmen and women all over the world evoke tremendously strong emotions among their followers; generally, it must be said, for the better. The fans love to watch these folk heroes, always want to talk about them and have an insatiable appetite to learn more about them and find out who is the *real* person behind the public face.

In writing this book, Séamus McRory is responding to that need in a special way. Having written several books in a similar vein, he has perfected the art of portraying great GAA personalities with style and accuracy through the printed word. This latest book will surely add to those achievements. A glance through the list of famous football and hurling stars featured shows the depth of material available in the GAA when it comes to profiling great heroes of the playing fields.

Nowadays there is very extensive media coverage of the GAA like never before, so that many media people have themselves become part of the fabric of the games. It is fitting therefore that several commentators of GAA games are also profiled, and that referees and GAA officials have their important roles acknowledged in the book.

The GAA is a huge family whose members often give out about each other but all of whom have the same love of the games and a desire to see them presented and performed to the highest standards. The 26 people dealt with in Séamus McRory's book have done more than their share in this regard in enhancing the profile of the GAA over the past 60 years or so. There can hardly be a GAA person in the country who will not get great satisfaction out of *The All-Ireland Dream*.

Eugene McGee

Introduction

It was All-Ireland Sunday in Croke Park and the crowds had been gathering since early morning. One of the first into the Hogan Stand was a man who had presented two tickets on arrival. With only five minutes to go before the senior match, the seat beside him remained unoccupied. This aroused the curiosity of the person on his other side. 'Are you waiting on someone?' he inquired. 'Ah, no,' replied the man, 'we had a death in the family since I bought the tickets. In fact, to tell you the truth, it was my wife that died.' 'I'm very sorry for your trouble,' said the other, 'but could you not get anyone else from the family to come along with you?' 'Yerrah, not at all, sure they wanted to go to the funeral!'

The above fictitious story is a humorous reference to the indelible impact the GAA makes on our national consciousness. As an organisation, it has performed a pivotal role in creating, in all of us, a deep sense of patriotic pride. Irish social and cultural life has been considerably enhanced by the GAA's unique Irishness and its phenomenal ability to penetrate the whole country, from Antrim to Cork, from Galway to Dublin. First and foremost, the GAA is about the many thousands of players who have graced the playing fields of Ireland since its formation in 1884. Added to that are the large numbers of devoted voluntary workers and enthusiastic supporters who have always, selflessly, promoted Gaelic games.

The Association is multi-faceted in its structures and all-embracing in the totality of its magnificent contribution to Irish society. Three GAA stakeholders, in particular, deserve unstinting praise for making it such an integral part of what we are as a people. Administrators, match officials and media personnel have all helped immensely in the popularisation of our games.

As in many other sports, GAA referees never seem to have many friends when the actual games are taking place. Very often, the better and the more impartial a referee is, the more subject he is to unfair appraisal. This is, in essence, not so much a reflection on the referees' own integrity, but rather a commentary on the spectators' individual prejudices while watching a game. In all sections of the media the GAA have been blessed with a host of perceptive, incisive and talented commentators who, invariably, portray Gaelic games as a beautiful representation of our heritage.

The Gaelic games personalities featured in this book have all relentlessly pursued their own individual All-Ireland dreams. Many of these have already been fulfilled. May the remainder achieve theirs in the not too distant future.

Séamus McRory, August, 2005

ONE

Brian Corcoran—Cork

THE MAN WHO CAME BACK

Watching the 2003 All-Ireland senior hurling final between Cork and
Kilkenny, Brian Corcoran was not only deeply engrossed in the game
itself but also engaged in an intense, personal meditative process. He
started to ask himself some perplexing questions as the game gradually
unfolded. After a discouraging first-half performance, Cork rallied
strongly, and by the 55th minute they had edged into a one-point lead
but, again, they seemed to lose their way and the Cats eventually won
the contest by 1–14 to 1–11. Kilkenny were not all that convincing,
but they were made to look good by Cork's self-destructive streak.
Apart from their wayward shooting, Cork were also experiencing
difficulties when they attacked the heart of the Kilkenny defence, where
full-back Noel Hickey was magnificent.

Corcoran still cannot pinpoint the exact nature or precise moment
of his inexplicable change of heart. One thing he did know, however,
was that he wanted to return to what he had always done best. He
wanted to once again hurl with the élan of a master hurler and to
reinvent himself as a commanding talismanic figure on the hurling
fields of Ireland. If things worked out as he planned, he would end his
self-imposed retirement from hurling, which he had announced two
years earlier, in 2001, at the age of 28.

Unassuming by nature and too modest to announce his plans to a
wider audience, Brian's sole confidante about his future plans was his
wife, Elaine. From the week after the All-Ireland final until Christmas,
Brian took part in a personal, rigorous fitness programme in the gym
in the Silver Springs Hotel on the outside of Cork city. He trained
four times per week and for two hours per session. His first target was
to shed the excess weight which he had put on since he retired from
both club and county activity, after Cork were eliminated by Limerick
in the 2001 Munster championship.

As his training progressed, the anticipated buzz that is in every great hurler's heart gradually returned. By February, he took up the camán again with his club, Erin's Own. Sparkling club performances at centre half-forward soon came to the notice of the Cork manager, Donal O'Grady. Like other coaches and managers, Donal himself had tried to persuade Brian to return during the previous two years. The answer had always been a definite, though very polite, 'no'. At first, Brian's wife could hardly believe his change of heart. When she realised his determination to give it another go, she became very supportive.

On the first Saturday of April 2004, Donal O'Grady rang to ask Brian the obvious question. Both set up their stalls, like the consummate professionals they were. Brian wanted to play in the forward line as opposed to the defence where he had been a commanding figure for so long. Donal agreed to this without, naturally, specifying any particular position. Instinctively, and without saying so, it can be taken as read that both manager and prospective player knew who would be wearing the Cork No. 14 jersey 'when the hay had been saved and the shortest day of the year had passed', as the saying goes. All Cork hurling followers could not wait for the 2004 championship year to start.

After a mixed National League campaign, the Rebels opened their championship season with a comfortable win over Kerry. For the first time in almost three years, Brian Corcoran returned to his favourite colours when he came on as a second-half substitute. Their first serious test came against Limerick in the Munster semi-final at the revamped Gaelic grounds in Limerick. The home side made a dream start when Seán O'Connor goaled in the seventh minute. Cork fought back to restore parity before a Niall Moran point gave Limerick a slender 1–5 to 0–7 interval advantage.

After the shaky first-half showing, Cork recognised the need to improve, and by the 50th minute they had opened up a five-point advantage, thanks to a fortuitous goal from a Ben O'Connor long-range free. The game was heading for its predictable outcome, until a second goal from Seán O'Connor in the sixth minute gave Limerick renewed hope. When Patrick Tobin followed up with a point, just a goal separated the sides, but Cork held on for a 1–18 to 2–12 win. Again Corcoran made an appearance as a substitute. Connoisseurs of the game could now see that all the old skills were starting to resurface in the Erin's Own man's repertoire, as he gained full match fitness.

The Munster final was a repeat of the previous year's decider when a stunning second-half performance gave Cork victory over Waterford, but the Decies exacted sweet revenge to secure a rare Munster title at Cork's expense. A Garvan McCarthy goal handed the Rebels the early initiative, but they were unable to maintain the momentum. After scoring three of Waterford's first four points, Dan Shanahan fielded a high ball over Diarmuid O'Sullivan's head before despatching it to the net in the 25th minute. When Ken McGrath and Paul Flynn added further points, they were back in the game. At the break, the challengers were just three points in arrears.

Waterford's hopes appeared to suffer a fatal blow when John Mullane received his marching orders just after the restart. To their immense credit, the Decies responded positively with some massive individual contributions, especially from Flynn and McGrath. Inspired by Flynn's cheeky 51st minute goal, from a free, which put them in front for the first time, Waterford made all the running. They were, however, still clinging on to a one-point lead when a high ball dropped in the middle of the Waterford half-back line, deep into injury time. Heroically, Ken McGrath fielded it and won a free. And that was it. The game was over, with Waterford winning by the narrowest of margins, 3–16 to 1–21. Though disappointed with the result, Brian Corcoran was reasonably happy with his own performance. He had made his first inter-county start since 2001 and in the process he had scored 0–2. His playing rehabilitation was now fully underway.

Stung by the criticism they received in the wake of the Munster final defeat, Cork bounced back to see off the challenge of old rivals Tipperary by 2–19 to 1–16, in an exciting All-Ireland qualifier at Killarney. Again Brian fielded from the beginning and, as the game wore on, he became the natural fulcrum of Cork's attacking options. At the interval of that game, the signs did not look good for Donal O'Grady's charges, as they trailed by 0–8 to 0–7. In the second half they showed a dramatic improvement. The game's turning point came five minutes into that period, when impressive substitute Timmy McCarthy goaled to give Cork the lead for the first time since the eighth minute. While an Eoin Kelly-inspired Tipperary got back on level terms, a second goal from the outstanding Niall McCarthy, eight minutes from the end, put the result beyond doubt.

By the time Cork met Antrim in the All-Ireland quarter-final, there was a settled look to O'Grady's team. Tom Kenny and Jerry O'Connor formed a new midfield partnership, with John Gardiner reverting to wing-back, while Ben O'Connor had switched to wing-forward. Brian Corcoran was the new target man at full-forward. There was now an All-Ireland winning look about the team. The build-up to the Antrim match was dominated by comments made by Antrim manager Dinny Cahill about the Cork players. However, his remarks came back to haunt him as Cork cruised to a 2–26 to 0–10 victory in Croke Park. A wonderful display of superb technique and controlled aggression, highlighted by two goals of sublime quality from Brian Corcoran, left the Glensmen in a state of shock. The game was over as a contest at half-time with Cork leading by 2–13 to 0–3. The second half provided manager Donal O'Grady with a chance to try out some of his fringe players, ahead of the All-Ireland semi-final.

Standing between Cork and a place in the All-Ireland final was Wexford, who had shocked Kilkenny en route to winning the Leinster title. The Slaneysiders had taken Cork to a replay in the corresponding game twelve months earlier and were expected to pose a serious threat to Cork's All-Ireland ambitions. Nevertheless, it did not pan out like that and Cork produced another devastating performance to record a comfortable victory. With Timmy McCarthy and the O'Connor twins in sparkling form, the Rebels had established a 0–10 to 0–3 lead before Tom Kenny soloed through the whole Wexford defence to score the only goal of the game. At the interval, the Munster men led 1–13 to 0–4, and it continued to be one-way traffic following the changeover. Joe Deane, Niall McCarthy, Jerry O'Connor and Kevin Murphy added excellent points to give the Rebels a landslide 1–27 to 0–12 victory. The man whose watching of the 2003 All-Ireland was the catalytic spark which re-ignited his desire to return to hurling was destined to play in his third All-Ireland senior hurling final, twelve years after his first. Just as on the previous occasions, the Cats of Kilkenny were again to provide the opposition.

Over the years Cork and Kilkenny have been the most common pairing of them all. Still, the 2004 final managed to capture the public's imagination for a variety of reasons. One was Kilkenny's bid for three-in-a-row All-Ireland successes. The fact that both counties were locked together on 28 All-Ireland title wins added further spice to the meeting of the old rivals. In conditions that were far from suitable for hurling, the final failed to live up to expectations. This hardly bothered Cork, who turned in a fantastic second-half display to emerge triumphant on a scoreline of 0–17 to 0–9. Although the sides were level after twelve minutes, the Rebels were slow to settle and they had to wait until the 32nd minute for Brian Corcoran to register their only point from play in the opening half. Fortunately for Cork, Kilkenny were not firing on all cylinders either, and were just 0–7 to 0–6 in front at the interval, despite playing with a strong wind advantage.

After the break, Kilkenny's challenge gradually and surprisingly petered out. The Cork defence, with Seán Óg Ó hAilpín in especially inspiring form, took control after Henry Shefflin had twice given the Cats the lead. Niall McCarthy put over a marvellous equaliser to show that Cork were not going to collapse as they had done in the previous year's final.

Goalkeeper Donal Óg Cusack came to Cork's rescue in the 56th minute with a crucial save from the continually marauding Henry

Shefflin. This inspired Cork to produce a storming final quarter of power hurling, as they pulled away with unanswered points from Joe Deane, Ben O'Connor and Tom Kenny. Fittingly, Brian Corcoran had the final say when he split the posts from near the corner flag to seal a memorable triumph. 'I was very happy that I had returned to inter-county hurling when the final whistle went and we had won. Even if we had lost, I would still have been satisfied, because I was involved with a fantastic group of guys and a really magnificent managerial team. The hurt suffered by the previous year's final defeat was what motivated the whole team. In the last few minutes of the 2004 final there was a little more scope to enjoy ourselves than in the 1999 final. Our lead appeared safe in 2004, whereas it was touch and go right up to the final whistle in 1999,' Brian told me when I met him in the Silver Springs Hotel in Cork.

Brian Corcoran was born in the parish of Glounthaune, which is situated in a rural hinterland not far from Cork city. Both his parents were great GAA people and his paternal grandfather had been the founding chairman of the parish's GAA club, Erin's Own. Brian's older brother John had won All-Ireland medals with the Rebel County at both minor and U-21 levels. In addition, he had represented the county at senior level in the 1993 National League but had never played senior championship hurling. Young Brian's interest developed further when he won a Rice Cup medal with Midleton C.B.S. in 1987 — the same year that he first represented his county at U-14 level. In 1988, at 15 years of age and playing at right corner-back, Brian won a Harty Cup medal. For the next four years he played for the county minor hurlers, winning provincial championships in 1988 and 1990. The 15-year-old actually played at midfield for the Rebels when Kilkenny beat them in the 1988 All-Ireland minor final. Amongst his opponents were Pat O'Neill, Adrian Ronan, Charlie Carter and a certain Denis Joseph Carey — all of whom he would become familiar with in the years ahead.

At the same time, the multi-talented Erin's Own player was also playing football at both club and county levels. In 1991 he won both Munster and All-Ireland minor football medals. This was his third year with the under age footballers and he produced a brilliant display at full-back in the decider against Mayo. His performance prompted Cork's joint football coach, Fr Donncha Mac Carthaigh, to say: 'He gave the best defensive exhibition I have ever seen since I first became involved with the minors eleven years ago.'

That same year, 1991, also saw his progression in the county's hurling team. Though he had a disappointing minor hurling season when they were beaten by Tipperary, he impressed at centre half-forward on the Rebels' U-21 team, which beat Limerick in the final. On this occasion he was marked by another future colossus of hurling, Ciarán Carey. As a result of his under age exploits, Brian won his way onto the senior panel for the Munster final replay against Tipperary, in Thurles, but he was not brought on.

He actually made his senior debut in the first round of the National League against Dublin in October 1991, while still only 18. Playing in the forward line, his next outing was against Waterford in the league. In that game he displayed the type of skill and power in his play that we have come to associate with him, and he scored three points in the process. In the next game he was switched to right full-back, where he remained for most of his first full senior championship season of 1992. This was the year that the sporting nation at large became aware of Brian Corcoran's enormous talent. In Cork's Munster semi-final victory over Tipperary, Corcoran stamped his authority in a manner that earned him rave notices in the national press. If there had been any doubting Thomases, he proved his ability all over again in the provincial final against Limerick and, subsequently, in the All-Ireland final against Kilkenny. During that campaign Corcoran played like a wily veteran, totally blotting out such key marksmen as Pat Fox of Tipperary and Eamonn Morrissey of Kilkenny. It had been a roller-coaster year for Brian, though the Cats' victory in the final blighted his enjoyment. 'Even though I was selected as Texaco Hurler of the Year, I would gladly have exchanged it for an All-Ireland senior medal. Once again, Kilkenny, with Pat O'Neill and D.J. on board, had thwarted me.'

At club level, 1992 was also an historic year when Erin's Own won their first Cork county senior hurling title. Corcoran scored 10 points of his team's total of 1–12 — five from frees, five from play — three of those points off his right side and two off his left. In Erin's Own's five championship matches, he scored 44 points, although at various times, in some of their games, he would have been at midfield or centre half-back.

Between 1992 and 1999, Cork hurlers suffered the continual disappointment of being knocked out in the early stages of the Munster championship. This allowed Brian to concentrate on football. In 1994 he won an U-21 football All-Ireland medal while he also annexed three successive Munster senior football medals in 1993, 1994 and 1995. In 1993 Cork reached the All-Ireland senior football final, only to be beaten by first-time winners Derry. In that game Brian had the unenviable task of marking Derry's effervescent corner-forward, Joe Brolly. 'We could have won the game. Tony Davis was harshly sent off and we conceded a soft goal. However, Derry had a lot of tremendous footballers and thoroughly deserved their victory,' added Brian. Cork's lack of hurling championship honours at senior level since they won the 1990 All-Ireland against Galway had been attributed to an absence of accomplishments at minor level. That was to change, however, in 1995 when minor manager Jimmy Barry Murphy successfully steered the Rebel County to a 2–10 to 1–2 win over Kilkenny. This was their first national minor success since 1985.

So, after that 1995 triumph, a total wave of emotion ran through Cork, almost begging Jimmy to take on the task of Cork's hurling saviour. As a result, he agreed to manage the side, initially bringing in former colleagues Tom Cashman and Tony O'Sullivan as selectors. 'Jimmy was a very popular choice and possessed great man-management skills in his own quiet, efficient manner.'

To say that Jimmy had a rough first managerial year would be an understatement. Firstly, they suffered the utter humiliation of relegation in the National Hurling League. Secondly, and much more significantly, they lost their first-round Munster championship game to Limerick by the incredible margin of sixteen points. Worse still, this was Cork's first home defeat to Limerick in over 70 years of championship hurling. In 1997, defeat was again the Rebels' lot when they succumbed to a four-point defeat to Clare in the semi-final of the Munster championship. However, by the end of that season, Brian Corcoran and his colleagues were optimistic on two fronts. Their Munster conquerors, Clare, had gone on to record a resounding All-Ireland win and, more significantly from a Cork perspective, their U-21 team scored a highly impressive victory over Galway in the All-Ireland final. In spite of those limited successes, the supporters were bemoaning the fact that Cork had not been in an All-Ireland senior final since 1992. The fact that they had not even reached a Munster final for five years was an even greater bone of contention.

As Cork entered the 1998 season, the management team knew that Cork would have to achieve something of importance if they were to retain their credibility. Thanks to a magnificent display by Brian Corcoran and his team-mates, Cork overwhelmed Clare in the league semi-final before easily defeating Wexford in the final. But again, the Leesiders disappointed in the championship. Though they narrowly defeated Limerick in the first round, they once again suffered the ignominy of defeat as Clare convincingly beat them in the provincial semi-final.

Jimmy Barry Murphy faced a do-or-die scenario, as Cork faced the rigours of a fourth championship under his stewardship. With this in mind, the management boldly decided to introduce many younger players. The fact that Cork had won the minor and U-21 All-Ireland titles in 1998 was a huge psychological boost, as they embarked on this brave but imaginative youth policy. Cork played well in their first outing, defeating the men from the Decies by six points and thus reaching their first Munster final in seven years.

The previous three years' untimely exits were forgotten as they diligently prepared for the Munster final against Clare. Though Clare had to field without the injured Jamesie O'Connor, they played magnificently, only to be beaten by a superior and hungrier Cork side, 1–15 to 0–14.

The All-Ireland semi-final against Offaly was a thoroughly exciting and keenly contested encounter, with the midlanders leading by two points as the game entered its last ten minutes. Then Cork, inspired by a truly wonderful centre half-back display by Brian Corcoran, upped the tempo considerably. In the last seven minutes they scored five points, without reply, to run out winners by 0–19 to 0–16.

In the final, Cork were pitted against Kilkenny for the 18th time in a decider. Their record in finals against the Cats was not very impressive, as they had won only seven of those contests. In the view of many pundits, Cork, though possessing players of immense skill, were too light in build and too inexperienced in big-time situations. Furthermore, as the game approached, it was clearly apparent that the weather conditions were going to deteriorate. This development also appeared to lessen the hopes of the Rebel County. Despite speculation to the contrary from some quarters, the management team kept faith with their young players. That meant that all six championship debutantes, Donal Óg Cusack, Wayne Sherlock, Mickey O'Connell, Timmy McCarthy, Neil Ronan and Ben O'Connor, were retained.

Cork opened the scoring in the final with a point by captain Mark Landers in the eighth minute. Two other points by impressive right half-forward Timmy McCarthy closely followed this. Kilkenny scored their first point in the 20th minute, courtesy of a Henry Shefflin free. Then Kilkenny midfielder Andy Comerford and Cork corner-forward Joe Deane exchanged points to leave the score 0–4 to 0–2. Kilkenny, who clocked up an incredible eight wides in the first half, then scored three unanswered points to lead at the interval by the minimum of margins, 0–5 to 0–4.

When the game restarted, Cork's Alan Browne, who had replaced the out-of-form Neil Ronan, scored a neatly taken point with his first touch of the ball, to leave the sides level. Despite this encouraging start by Cork, it was Kilkenny who proceeded to dominate the game, with Andy Comerford being particularly prominent in the centre of the field. The net result of this period of Kilkenny control was that the Cats led by 0–9 to 0–5 with just sixteen minutes of the second half gone. After this, Mark Landers, who had not been fully fit entering the game, was replaced by Kevin Murray, who scored a very valuable point just after he entered the fray. During the next five minutes the sides exchanged two points each to leave the score 0–11 to 0–8 in Kilkenny's favour with 57 minutes gone. The defining moment, in many viewers' opinions, of the 1999 senior hurling final had come three minutes earlier. Kilkenny's Charlie Carter found himself in front of the goals with only the goalkeeper to beat. Instead of going for a goal, which would have clinched the game, he elected to take his point. Encouraged by this, Cork upped their own performance and displayed a tremendous resolve to focus on the task in hand. Two players in particular played key roles in the Rebels' revival. Timmy McCarthy, who had moved to midfield to break the stranglehold that Andy Comerford had been exercising, now played terrific hurling. Likewise, livewire wing-forward Seán McGrath, who had been inconspicuous in the first half, found his true form. His electrifying pace and soloing skills continually tormented the Kilkenny defence. For the next eight minutes Cork played brilliantly, McGrath twice, Ben O'Connor and Joe Deane, with two pointed frees, all scored to leave the Rebels leading 0–13 to 0–11. Three minutes from the end, the hardworking Shefflin pointed a free to reduce the arrears to a single point. The closeness of the scoring, with the possibility of a Kilkenny goal, kept the packed stadium on tenterhooks as the minutes ticked away. When the final whistle eventually sounded, there had been no more scores. For the first time in nine years, Cork were All-Ireland senior hurling champions.

As in all the games during the 1999 campaign, it was Cork's ability to display, in the final ten minutes, a great fighting spirit that swung the game in their favour. Diarmuid O'Sullivan and John Browne in the full-back line kept the much-vaunted and talented Kilkenny full-forward line of Ken O'Shea, Henry Shefflin and Charlie Carter at bay. Wayne Sherlock, Brian Corcoran and dual star Seán Óg Ó hAilpín increasingly imposed their will on proceedings as the game progressed. In the forward line, centre half-forward Fergal McCormack (a nephew of Mick O'Connell of Kerry football fame) put in an industrious 70 minutes. Timmy McCarthy, first of all at wing forward and later at midfield, made an especially telling contribution with his fetching and incisive runs. This gaining of vital possession, especially in the second half, allied to the intricate skills and penetration of Seánie McGrath, ultimately paved the way for Cork's success.

However, when that 1999 triumph is recalled, the performance of one player stood out above all others. Throughout the game Brian Corcoran strode the pitch like a proverbial colossus and deservedly received the Man of the Match award. 'After having been beaten by Kilkenny three times before that, at different levels, it was nice to defeat them. More importantly it was a good feeling of relief that at last we had won a senior All-Ireland,' Brian told me.

Meeting this hugely talented yet self-effacing individual was a most pleasant experience, as he commented on players, managers, the game of hurling and associated matters.

1. 'D.J. Carey is a supreme hurling artist. Eoin Kelly of Tipperary is playing terrific hurling, as is Henry Shefflin. Henry is so strong — very skilful and versatile. He is totally at home in any position in the forward line. The best individual performance I ever saw was Niall McCarthy's in the All-Ireland qualifier against Tipperary in 2004. When a player was needed to lift our game, he stood up and was counted. To crown it all, he scored a fantastic goal that really won the game for us.'

2. 'All the managers and management teams that I have played under have been superb. Donal O'Grady really got us back to the basic hurling skills for our 2004 success. I never met anyone so passionate, committed and competent as Billy Morgan. He also was a very persuasive football manager, as was Larry Tompkins. Hurling was always really my first love, even though I had many good games in football. I just think it is impossible to devote oneself totally to both games.'

3. 'I watch very little TV, except for the big GAA matches and golf. Golf to me is a fantastic game and I love following Tiger Woods and Fred Couples when they are playing. Otherwise, I would much prefer to be playing with my two young children on a sunny afternoon.'

4. 'The GPA should become an official part of the GAA. Only for players, there would be no GAA and therefore we should look after our players. When the GPA began, the GAA selected their own players' committee, so they must have seen the need for such a group. From the GAA's point of view, the original fear seemed to be that players would soon be looking to get paid for playing. The GPA has consistently denied this, so there should not be any problem. If the GPA became a fully integrated part of the GAA, it would create harmonious relationships all round.'

After the 2004 All-Ireland senior hurling final, Brian Corcoran was unanimously accepted by all sports-loving people as being the real embodiment of a true hurling legend. When Cork lost the 1992 All-Ireland against Kilkenny, their 19-year-old prodigy was selected as

Hurler of the Year. The then corner-back became only the second person to receive this award without winning the championship in the same season — the first to have that honour was the one and only Christy Ring. In 1999, the now centre half-back excelled in a Man of the Match performance when Cork regained the Liam McCarthy Cup after an absence of seven years. Popularly acknowledged as the best centre-back of his generation, Brian also scooped the Hurler of the Year honour as we headed for the new millennium.

In 2001, the whole hurling world was completely devastated when the Erin's Own star announced his retirement from both county and club at the age of 28. Fortunately, during the autumn of 2003, the magnetism of the clash of the ash and the burning desire of once again wielding the camán returned. By the summer of 2004, he once more fascinated us with his skill, accuracy, vision and strength. From his new role as full-forward, he scored two magical points as Liam McCarthy returned to the banks of the Lee. Like all great artists, he carries his talent ever so lightly, ever so unobtrusively. May his second coming last as long as his first.

BRIAN CORCORAN — FACT FILE

Native Place:	Glounthaune, Co. Cork
Date of Birth:	March 23, 1973
Club:	Erin's Own
College Honours:	Midleton C.B.S. Rice Cup 1987 Harty Cup 1988 White Cup 1988 Dean Ryan Cup 1989
Third Level	Cork R.T.C. Freshers' All-Ireland Hurling – 1991
Honours:	Freshers' All-Ireland Football – 1991
Club Honours:	U-14 East Cork Hurling Championship – 1986 U-16 East Cork Football Championship – 1989 U-16 Cork Hurling Championship – 1989 U-21 East Cork Hurling Championship – 1991 Cork Senior Hurling Championship – 1992 Cork Junior Football Championship – 1994 Cork Senior Hurling League (2) – 1996, 2004

County Honours:	National Hurling League (2) – 1993 (Captain), 1998
	All-Ireland Senior Hurling Championship (2) – 1999, 2004
	Munster Senior Hurling Championship (3) – 1992, 1999, 2000
	Munster Senior Football Championship (3) – 1993, 1994, 1995
	All-Ireland U-21 Football Championship – 1994
	Munster U-21 Football Championship – 1994
	Munster U-21 Hurling Championship (2) – 1991, 1994
	All-Ireland Minor Football Championship – 1991
	Munster Minor Football Championship – 1991
	Munster Minor Hurling Championship (2) – 1988, 1990
Other Honours:	Railway Cup Hurling – 1996
Awards:	All Star (3) – 1992, 1999, 2004
	Player of the Year (2) – 1992, 1999
	Texaco Hurler of the Year (2) – 1992, 1999
	Cork Team of the Millennium
	RTÉ Man of Match Awards:
	(a) 1992 Munster semi-final v. Tipperary
	(b) 1998 National Hurling League final v. Waterford
	(c) 1999 All-Ireland Senior Hurling semi-final v. Offaly
	(d) 1999 All-Ireland Senior Hurling final v. Kilkenny
	Various weekly/monthly awards
Occupation:	IT business analyst
Family:	Married to Elaine (née Walsh), Cork
Children:	Kate, Edel

Two

Trevor Giles–Meath

THE VISIONARY ROYAL LEADER

Growing up in Skryne in County Meath, Trevor Giles was destined to be centrally involved in the GAA. His father, Eamon, had played both football and hurling for Meath, and Eamon's own father, Ned, had represented the Royal County as an outstanding hurler. When Meath defeated their near neighbours and fierce rivals Dublin in the 1975 National Football League final, their captain was one Ronan Giles, uncle of Trevor. Trevor's maternal grandfather, Packie Mooney, had also represented the Royal County in football. So it would be fair to say that the young Trevor was steeped in a Gaelic tradition, which was further enhanced when one considers that his parish club team, Skryne, were always a very prominent club side. Even though they had not won the Meath senior football championship since 1965, they were never too far away from doing so.

The football curriculum vitae of Trevor Giles was further established when he won three Meath county championships with his primary school team. It was, however, when he commenced his secondary school education at that great nursery school of college football, St Patrick's Classical School, Navan, that the emerging star's football career flourished spectacularly. 'Ray Mooney, who was secretary and a selector with the Skryne club team, was our coach in first year. Under his expert guidance, we won the Meath county secondary school first year competition. For the remaining four years in St Patrick's we had another fantastic coach in Padraig Nolan, who is now the Kildare senior football manager. During that period, we won Leinster colleges senior titles at all levels. In fact, we reached the All-Ireland colleges final in 1991, only to be beaten by St Fachtna's, Skibbereen, in Croke Park. St Fachtna's had two powerful midfielders, Fachtna Collins and Pat Hegarty. They, along with their goalkeeper Kevin O'Dwyer, went on to win All-Ireland minor football medals that year when Cork defeated Mayo in the final.'

Simultaneously with Giles's personal football development at St Patrick's, another huge contributory factor to his burgeoning Gaelic interest was occurring. Prior to the appointment of Seán Boylan as Meath football manager, Meath's football was at an all-time low. However, a combination of Seán's own man-management skills and greater co-ordination and organisation at County Board level, as well as the adoption of new and more varied training techniques, improved matters considerably. By 1984, Meath had won their first senior competition title for many years when they won the Centenary Cup, which was a special open draw competition, inaugurated to commemorate the founding of the GAA a hundred years earlier in 1884. In 1986, boosted by talented players such as Robbie O'Malley, Bernard Flynn and Brian Stafford, Meath defeated Dublin in the Leinster final. This had been their first senior provincial success for sixteen years.

The seeds were now sown for a rich harvest of Gaelic football achievement in Meath. When the side progressed to win successive All-Ireland senior titles in 1987 and 1988, the whole county and their totally dedicated supporters were euphoric. They had built a tradition of football excellence, coupled with an unyielding 'never say die' attitude. More than that, the young people had real heroes, local and accessible icons that everyone wanted to emulate. Trevor Giles was lucky in that two of Meath's most prominent heroes were Skryne men whom he knew so well from infancy. Those players, Colm O'Rourke and Liam Hayes, were both All-Stars who played central roles in those successive triumphs over Cork when Meath annexed those titles. Trevor Giles now knew what he wanted. 'I, like so many other young boys from every county in Ireland, had a dream of playing for my county in Croke Park. Now, having seen Meath attain success and with my own progress, I knew that with hard work and a bit of luck that dream could turn into reality.'

In 1992, Trevor's dream progressed further when he was a star member of the Meath minor team, which defeated Armagh in the All-Ireland minor final, thanks to a dramatic last-minute goal by full-forward Peter O'Sullivan. That Meath side included only two players who would subsequently win All-Ireland senior medals in 1999 — Trevor Giles and Paul Shankey, who came on as a substitute in that decider. Goalkeeper Brendan Murphy, who shortly afterwards emigrated to England, has now returned and is currently the substitute goalkeeper on the present Meath senior team. 'That team did not possess any outstanding individuals but we were all very physically and mentally strong. We worked very hard for our success. In contrast, Armagh had some very talented players who went on to make their mark at senior level. Players like Barry O'Hagan, Paul McGrane, Diarmuid Marsden, Des Mackin and substitute Andrew McCann fall into this category. Actually our minor team, which reached the following year's All-Ireland minor final, were a more talented combination. We were unlucky to meet a powerful Cork side which had outstanding performers like Eoin Sexton and Martin Cronin. As well as myself, that Meath minor side had Hank Traynor, Paddy Reynolds, Darren Fay, Ollie Murphy and Barry O'Callaghan, who all were destined to achieve senior success on All-Ireland final day.'

Meanwhile, at club level, Trevor was putting in consistent sterling performances with his beloved Skryne. Playing at centre half-forward, his reputation as a magnificent playmaker, whose radar-evading passes unhinged the tightest of defences, enlightened the whole Meath club scene. With the evergreen and the ever-brilliant Colm O'Rourke as target man at full-forward, Skryne won successive Meath senior championships in 1992 and 1993. Unfortunately, Trevor's other boyhood idol, Liam Hayes, was not able to participate in those victories. The strapping, speedy midfielder had broken his arm in five places and thus missed Skryne's double triumph.

In the winter of 1993, Meath selector and 1988 All-Ireland winning captain Joe Cassells phoned Trevor to tell him that he was being called into the Meath senior panel. In February 1994, he made his debut as a substitute at left half-forward against Fermanagh and was in that position when Meath defeated Armagh in the National Football League final. Later on that year, Giles made his championship debut for the Royal County in a very tough match against Laois. With Tommy Dowd outstanding, Meath came from behind to score an emphatic win. In the Leinster semi-final Wexford were easily overcome, and Meath marched to another Leinster final meeting with their oldest rivals, Dublin. On the day that the bottom tier of the new Cusack Stand was opened for the first time, Meath once again showed their renowned fighting spirit in the face of adversity. With just seven minutes to go, Meath were trailing by six points. An impressive Meath rally, inspired by the outstanding Graham Geraghty, produced 1–2 but, unfortunately for Meath, time ran out and they lost the game by the minimum of margins. For Trevor Giles, the final whistle brought the curtain down on twelve months of football, during which he had experienced a whole spectrum of varying emotions. 'First of all, in the Leinster final itself I had a poor game, missing some very scoreable frees. Momentarily, negative thoughts crossed my mind and I began to question myself with regards those frees and whether or not I was to blame for this defeat. Overall, the previous twelve months had been a happy learning experience for me. I had won an All-Ireland U-21 medal when I came on as a substitute against Kerry in August, before winning another county club championship medal with Skryne a few weeks later. I was selected for the combined Universities team and made my inter-county debut before winning a National League medal. Perhaps one of the most significant developments in my career was the fact that regular and deadly accurate free-taker Brian Stafford broke his thumb during the early stages of the league campaign. I was then given the role of the team's free-taker. Though Brian was a much superior scorer than I was, the fact that you would score six or seven points a game was a tremendous boost to your confidence.'

In 1995, Meath easily accounted for Offaly, Longford and Wicklow en route to another final meeting with their metropolitan archrivals. Again, defeat was Meath's lot as they slumped to a ten-point drubbing by Dublin. Despite Herculean performances by the tigerish corner-back Colm Coyle and a mercurial swansong display by the retiring Colm O'Rourke, Meath inexplicably collapsed in the final quarter. What made the final result even more incredible was the fact that Meath were actually a point ahead ten minutes into the second half.

Seán Boylan's tenure as Meath manager was now under threat as some supporters within the county reckoned that a fresh managerial approach was required. After thirteen years in charge, he just survived opposition to his re-appointment. After the politics were over, Seán set about the task of reinvigorating a strong Meath challenge for the 1996 championship. When the two outgoing selectors, Mick Lyons and Joe Cassells, opted out, the Dunboyne man caused a major surprise when he selected their replacements — Frank Foley and Eamon O'Brien. Frank, who was from Trim, was a member of the All-Ireland winning panels of 1987 and 1988. Eamon had won a National League medal in 1975 and was regarded as the central figure behind Walterstown's five Meath senior championship successes. Though there were initial surprises at these appointments because of their low profiles, subsequent events were to prove them as inspired choices by the Dunboyne herbalist.

Giles was very impressed with Boylan's fresh approach. 'Everything was different. We had new selectors. Our training was relocated to Gormanston College where there were great outdoor and indoor facilities and the whole approach to training was very forward-thinking. Even though we were beaten by Mayo after a very poor performance in a league quarter-final in Roscommon, we were still relishing the challenge of a new championship campaign.'

In the opening round of the Leinster championship, Carlow were easily accounted for, and when Laois were beaten after a tough game in the semi-final, Dublin again awaited them in the Leinster final.

This was a make or break occasion for Meath as they simply could not afford to lose to the old enemy for the third successive year. In a terrible game, played in dreadful conditions, Meath scraped to an impressive two-point win. Giles himself was not concerned about the quality of the match. 'It was an important psychological boost for us. I was happy with my own performance and really looking forward to meeting back-to-back Ulster champions Tyrone in the All-Ireland semi-final.'

Tyrone, who had comprehensively beaten Meath several times in challenge games over the previous two years, raced into a three-point lead after a few minutes. Then the Royal County asserted control and when Graham Geraghty scored an excellent goal, the teams went in at half-time level. It now appeared that Meath were going to win the game, especially as Tyrone's ace forward, Peter Canavan, suffered badly torn ankle ligaments after fifteen minutes' play. And so it came to pass, with John McDermott and Jimmy McGuinness continuing to dominate the midfield exchanges for the Meath men. Meath scored the first points of the second half, and though Tyrone's young star, Gerard Cavlan, who had a terrific game, replied for the O'Neill County, the Tyrone side seemed to uncharacteristically lose their way. Then Meath, in a magnificent last quarter of football brilliance, scored seven points without reply. In the final minutes, the superb Graham Geraghty, with a terrific burst of speed and judicious anticipation, set up Barry O'Callaghan for his first championship goal. In the end, Meath coasted to a convincing victory on a 2–15 to 0–12 scoreline.

However, the jury was out on how good Meath really were, because three of Tyrone's most dangerous forwards, Brian Dooher, Ciarán McBride and Peter Canavan, were injured prior to Meath's totally dominant period. In the eyes of Tyrone supporters and indeed many neutral observers, Tyrone were very much in the game before the injuries. In addition, they felt that Meath had adopted at least a modicum of over-physical play. On the other hand, Meath supporters felt that this conclusion did not do justice to what was essentially a tremendous team performance by the Royal County.

In the All-Ireland final, Meath were pitted against their league conquerors and Connacht champions, Mayo. The first half of the game was uneventful, with Mayo appearing to be the much stronger side. With ten minutes gone in the second half, Mayo's Ray Dempsey notched an opportunist goal to put the westerners six points ahead. Meath were playing very badly at this stage and it seemed inevitable that Mayo were about to win their first senior All-Ireland title since 1951. Then Meath, with imminent defeat apparently staring them in the face, showed once again their renowned fighting spirit and, with sixteen minutes left in the game, they had halved the deficit. When

Trevor Giles pointed a free, the margin was reduced to two points. Three minutes from the end, Brendan Reilly's point left the minimum between the sides. The incredible tension was clearly palpable as Mayo defended desperately against incessant Meath attacks. With time almost up, the magnificent Colm Coyle sent a long, probing kick towards the Mayo goalmouth. The defence hesitated to attack the ball, which bounced high off the hard surface and went over the bar for a dramatic equaliser. When the final whistle sounded immediately afterwards, Meath were the happier side, as they had drawn a game in which they could have, and probably should have, lost.

When the replay came around, the Meath management decided to make their first team alteration since the championship began. Right corner-forward Evan Kelly was replaced by the talented Colm Brady, who was unfortunately plagued by injury and who, subsequently, had to retire prematurely from football. Shortly after the game began, Meath full-back Darren Fay appeared to be struck by an opponent and within seconds all hell broke loose, with almost twenty players from both sides involved in disgraceful scenes. As a consequence, the referee dismissed Meath's Colm Coyle and influential Mayo midfielder Liam McHale. Thereafter, the game stabilised and, as in the first game, Mayo initially played the much superior football. In the tenth minute, and after the fracas, James Horan opened the score for the Mayo men. With their clever inter-passing style of combination football, Mayo controlled the exchanges for almost the remainder of the first half. Even though Giles himself scored a well-struck penalty when Tommy Dowd was brought down just one minute before the interval, Mayo went in at half-time leading by four points.

At the beginning of the second half, captain Dowd and Giles added points to narrow the Mayo lead to two points. The momentum was now with the Royal County, and when Dowd added another minor, three minutes later, the odds were on a Meath victory. However, Mayo reasserted their dominance and, with ten minutes left, were leading by two points. Then, suddenly, and very much against the run of play, Mayo conceded easy possession at centre-field and the ball broke to Graham Geraghty, who was fouled. He took a quick free to Dowd, who duly planted the ball in the net. For the first time in the two games, Meath edged ahead on a 2–8 to 1–10 scoreline. Still, gallant Mayo were not to be outdone and James Horan equalised. Extra time loomed as the game entered its final minute. It was then a case of cometh the hour, cometh the man. Trevor Giles, who had been brilliant all through, cleverly intercepted a Mayo pass and passed to Brendan Reilly in the corner. With a marvellous kick, from a very acute angle, the defender-turned-attacker sent the ball over the bar for what proved to be a sensational winning point. When the final whistle sounded, Meath had won the Sam Maguire Cup for the sixth time in all and for the first time since 1988.

Throughout the whole championship, Meath had fabulous performers in Mark O'Reilly, Darren Fay, Martin O'Connell, Enda McManus and Colm Coyle, in defence. John McDermott and Jimmy McGuinness had been simply superb at centre-field, Tommy Dowd and Graham Geraghty had provided greet leadership in attack, whilst Brendan Reilly's transfer to the forward line had been a resounding success. However, one man stood head and shoulders above the rest. That man, Trevor Giles, was the architect supreme who orchestrated and unified the team into a fantastic winning combination. It would not be an exaggeration to say that Meath would not have been Leinster or All-Ireland champions but for the truly majestic efforts of the retiring Skryne man.

'When the final whistle ended the game, and I realised we were All-Ireland champions, I was totally elated. I thought of my dream as a child playing in the back garden and how it had actually come true. It was a lovely, very satisfying feeling. Because of the suspensions meted out afterwards and because of the unseemly brawl in the game, it was a few months before we really enjoyed the full fruits of victory. That Mayo side were a very good team, with an excellent full-back and a very strong midfield,' added Giles when I met him, at his parental home, in historic Tara.

Of all the great characteristics of Meath teams over the last 35 years, two pertinent attributes stand out: the number of outstanding footballers they have produced and, more importantly, the utter determination and sheer competitiveness they possess, especially when faced with adversity. How often have we seen Meath teams trailing by huge margins or down a man and still coming back to achieve either parity or snatch a dramatic victory. Some examples of this were against Cork in the 1987 All-Ireland final; against Donegal in the All-Ireland semi-final of 1990; against Dublin on four occasions in 1991 and almost against Down in the 1991 final. When you add in their last-minute minor victory against Armagh in 1992, not to mention their various 'lucky' escapes against Westmeath many times in recent years, one gets a very clear picture of their 'never say die' attitude. Trevor Giles was very emphatic and logical when I put it to him that there was something special in the Meath psyche which enabled them to perform so many 'Houdini' acts. 'Firstly, Seán Boylan keeps reminding each successive generation of players of the great feats that the Meath sides have performed in the past. Secondly, Seán's own positive attitude always instils in one's consciousness that, regardless of what is happening on the field of play, the game is never over until the final whistle goes. This attitude encourages a tremendous resolve, both physically and mentally, within each player. Lastly, and probably most fundamentally, Meath have always had team leaders and ball winners in every line. They constantly have had at least two brilliant scoring forwards who will transfer the outfield superiority onto the scoreboard. This builds up a great sense of confidence in the whole team.'

The next two years were non-eventful in Giles's county career, as the Royal County slumped to successive Leinster final championship defeats to Offaly and Kildare respectively. From the beginning of 1999, however, Meath were being touted by reputable pundits as potential All-Ireland champions. With new captain Graham Geraghty playing the best football of his career, and Giles doing likewise, having recovered from injury, the expectations greatly increased when Wicklow and Offaly were easily beaten en route to another Leinster final date with Dublin. Again, an impressive performance secured another provincial title. In the All-Ireland semi-final, Armagh, who had won their first provincial title in seventeen years, were their opponents. After a bright opening, the Ulstermen succumbed to a dominant Meath, who easily secured their passage to an All-Ireland final joust with Cork, their fourth such meeting in thirteen years. Giving a fabulous exhibition of flowing, direct football, the Royal County defeated Cork to secure their seventh All-Ireland title, on the fiftieth anniversary of their first in 1949. As in 1996, Giles's contribution to the Meath success was again immense, and when he was unanimously selected as Texaco Footballer of the Year, all Gaeldom, justifiably, acclaimed his greatness. Though Meath reached the league final in 2000, only to be beaten by Derry after a replay, it would be 2001 before they would again make a championship impact at national level.

Trevor Giles is universally acknowledged as one of the great footballers of the last ten years. Two All-Ireland senior medals, three All-Star Awards and the Texaco Footballer of the Year Award bear testimony to that. To be selected for one's country is the greatest national honour of all, and Trevor achieved that when he was selected to play for Ireland against Australia in the International Rules series in 1999, 2000 and 2002. Though he had the honour of captaining the 2000 Irish team, it was the 1999 series which received the highest accolade from him. 'Both sides fielded their strongest sides that year, so the standard of play in the games was exceptionally high. It was an especially great occasion for me as there were three Skryne club men involved: Colm O'Rourke was manager, John McDermott was captain and I was a team member. It was very exciting to play with top-quality Gaelic footballers from other counties: Séamus Moynihan (Kerry), Anthony

Tohill (Derry), Peter Canavan (Tyrone), Jarlath Fallon and Michael Donnellan of Galway would fall into that category.'

When Trevor Giles hurt his back in the 2000 series, little did he realise that a persistent disc problem would hinder his 2001 All-Ireland championship campaign. Still, with Giles now installed as team captain, Meath won the Leinster title again and reached the All-Ireland final against Galway. In the semi-final they were very impressive in overcoming a Kerry side by the unbelievable margin of fifteen points — one of the most astounding results in the history of Gaelic football. Just as Kerry flopped to Meath, the Royal County did likewise to Galway, who romped to an easy Pádraic Joyce-inspired victory. This was to provide Trevor Giles with his greatest disappointment.

Nevertheless, as he looks back on his career to date, Giles has to be very pleased with what he has achieved at club, county and national levels. Indeed, one must never forget his outstanding display for UCD when they won the Sigerson Cup in 1996 by defeating the Garda College in the final at Limerick. The then physiotherapy student had made history two years earlier in 1994, when he was awarded the first ever GAA scholarship at UCD. He also thinks of the many talented sporting opponents he faced during the last ten years. 'Funnily enough, three Dublin players and three Derry defenders were my most difficult opponents. Paul Curran's (Dublin) display in the 1994 Leinster final was the best individual performance I have seen. Two other Dublin half-backs — Keith Barr and Eamon Heery — were terrific players. Seán Lockhart (Derry) is a fantastic man-marker. I would also rate his fellow county men Henry Downey and Kieran McKeever as fabulous players who knew how to defend and attack. Downey had a great dominating influence.'

When Trevor looks forward to the future, there are four specific changes he would like to see emerge on the GAA scene:

1. 'All counties should have a proper floodlit venue, allowing a majority of games to be played on a Friday night in the league. This would have the additional benefit of allowing players to have a social life as well as freeing up a congested fixture list for club activity.'

2. 'Regarding the rules of the game, I would suggest that they do not need any major restructuring. After all, the physical aspect of the game is an integral part of Gaelic football. What the game does require is a better administration of the existing rules. I am of the opinion that we should introduce two referees, as per the International Rules system. Refereeing is a very difficult task and referees take an awful lot of unnecessary verbal abuse. If we had

much younger referees, trained at a much earlier age, specifically for both inter-county and indeed club games, and paid them a generous match fee, I have no doubt that we would have higher standards overall.'

3. 'The present system whereby the unofficial players' representative body, the GPA, remains officially outside the GAA should be changed. Instead, the GPA should be a central part of the main organisation and have an official representative on the GAA's Central Council. Likewise, at County Board level a players' representative should be elected at Annual conference and sit on the executive of the County Board. That would be a much fairer system and allow every sector of the GAA to have a real voice in the decision-making process.'

4. 'I would love to see Croke Park being opened up for rugby and soccer internationals, especially during the time that Lansdowne Road is being redeveloped. We are all sports people. GAA players support our rugby and soccer internationals and many of those two codes support their GAA county team. The opening up process would be great for the image of the GAA and I have no doubt it would generate a lot of goodwill across the whole sporting fraternity.'

Trevor did not consider any Meath player when selecting his respective sides.

Leinster (1994–2005)

John O'Leary
(Dublin)

Brian Lacey	Paddy Christie	Joe Higgins
(Kildare)	(Dublin)	(Laois)

Paul Curran	Glen Ryan	Finbarr Cullen
(Dublin)	(Kildare)	(Offaly)

Ciarán McManus   Ciarán Whelan
(Offaly)   (Dublin)

Ross Munnelly	Stefan White	Paul Barden
(Laois)	(Louth)	(Longford)

Vinnie Claffey	Dessie Farrell	Dessie Dolan
(Offaly)	(Dublin)	(Westmeath)

Rest of Ireland (1994–2005)

Mickey McVeigh
(Down)

Kenneth Mortimer	Séamus Moynihan	Tony Scullion
(Mayo)	(Kerry)	(Derry)

Seán De Paor	Henry Downey	Kieran McGeeney
(Galway)	(Derry)	(Armagh)

Anthony Tohill   Dara Ó Sé
(Derry)   (Kerry)

Eamon O'Hara	Jarlath Fallon	Michael Donnellan
(Sligo)	(Galway)	(Galway)

Mickey Linden	Peter Canavan	Colm Cooper
(Down)	(Tyrone)	(Kerry)

In 1997 Trevor graduated from UCD with an honours degree in physiotherapy. For the next three years, the North Eastern Health Board employed him as a physiotherapist. In 2000, he set up his own private practice, at his parents' house, before marrying Caroline Deacy in November 2003. They live in Clonee. Trevor is still recognised as a vital cog in a Meath team which is now very much in transition mode.

He and his only sibling, his sister Judith, play a lot of golf, but it is as a Gaelic footballer that he wishes to be known for years to come. 'Ideally I would love to play county football for another few years, while concentrating for a further two years with my club. But all things being equal, I do not see myself leaving the GAA scene. It is something I was born into, enjoyed and continue to enjoy. I would like to pass on that tremendous feeling of GAA satisfaction, in either a coaching or managerial capacity, in the years to come.'

TREVOR GILES – FACT FILE

Native Place:	Tara, Co. Meath
Date of Birth:	February 19, 1975
Club:	Skryne
Primary School:	Skryne National School Meath Schools' Division 3 winners 1984 and 1986
Colleges' Honours:	St Patrick's Classical School, Navan Leinster Colleges 'A' Juvenile Championship – 1989 Junior Football Championship – 1990 Senior Football Championship – 1991 All-Ireland Colleges 'A' beaten finalists – 1991
University College Dublin:	Sigerson Cup – 1996 Represented combined Universities 1994 and 1996
Club Honours:	Skryne U-12 Division 2 Championship – 1984 U-17 Division 2 League Championship (2) – 1990 and 1991 Minor League Championship – 1991 U-21 Championship – 1995 Senior Football Championship (4) – 1992, 1993, 1999, 2004
County Honours:	Leinster Minor Championship (2) – 1992, 1993 All-Ireland Minor Championship – 1992 All-Ireland Minor runners-up – 1993 Leinster U-21 Championship – 1996 (Captain) All-Ireland U-21 Championship 1993 Leinster Senior Football Championship (3) – 1996, 1999, and 2001 All-Ireland Senior Football Championship (2) – 1996, 1999 All-Ireland Senior Football runners-up – 2001 National Football League – 1994 National Football League runners-up – 2000
Other Playing	Railway Cup: Represented Leinster in 1997, 2000
Honours:	International Rules: 1999, 2000 (Captain), 2002. Won the 1999 series.

Awards:	All Stars (3) – 1996, 1997, 1999
	GAA Writers' Footballer of the Year – 1996, 1999
	Players' Footballer of the Year – 1996, 1999
	Texaco Footballer of the Year – 1999
	Meath Footballer of the Year – 1996, 1999
	Meath Young Footballer of the Year – 1993
	Skryne Player of the Year – 1999
	First ever GAA Scholarship (UCD) – 1994
	Irish Independent Sports Star of the Week – September 1996
Wife:	Caroline (née Deacy) from Glenties, Co. Donegal
Family:	Parents – Eamon and Mary
	Sister – Judith

THREE

James McCartan–Down

THE KING OF A MOURNE DYNASTY

Down made their All-Ireland senior football semi-final debut in Croke Park against Galway in 1959. Down were two points up in two minutes, but gradually Galway imposed their will on the game and ran out easy winners in the end, 1–11 to 1–4. James McCartan, centre half-back for Down, was totally disconsolate as he sadly made his exit from the famous stadium after the game. A year that had started with so much promise had ended in abject failure. To compound James's state of frustration, his father, Brian, was scathing in his comments about James's own performance as well as the inept team display. James was so fed up with his father's annoyance as they journeyed home together that he decided there and then that 1960 would be a different year: 'When we arrived home in our yard in Donacloney, I told my father, "I'll bring Sam Maguire home next year, should I steal it!"'

To put the importance of Down's search for the Holy Grail into context, one has to go back three years earlier, to 1956, when the Town Clerk of Downpatrick, Maurice Hayes, was elected Secretary of the Down County Board. He immediately brought to the post a new sense of order, innovation, imagination and professionalism. Coincidentally, that was the year that 18-year-old James McCartan made his senior debut with the county team, at right full-back in a McKenna Cup game. A few months later he lined out at full-forward in his first championship game against Armagh, whose famed full-back Jack Bratten was his direct opponent. Hayes, meanwhile, organised collective and regular training sessions, introduced the concept of tactical awareness and arranged challenge games with the top teams in the country. Through their outstanding displays in these friendly games, Hayes convinced his players that they were as good as any team in the country. When Down, minus the suspended Paddy Doherty (he was banned for playing soccer) and James McCartan, whom the taximan failed to collect, were trounced by Donegal in the 1957 Ulster championship, the players were totally disillusioned. They really believed at this stage that Hayes's ideas were falsely based.

Hayes, on the other hand, was not to be deterred and in the immediate aftermath of that Donegal defeat, he revealed his master plan. Down, he told them, with proper physical preparation and a positive mental attitude, would win an All-Ireland senior title within the next five years. 'If you do what we say, we will ensure that medically, socially and workwise, we will look after you. There will be regular training throughout the year and indoor training when the nights are short and the weather unsuitable,' he told the astounded players. Danny Flynn was appointed trainer, Barney Carr was selected as team manager and Martin Walsh became the first doctor, on a permanent basis, of the senior county football side. Down's thorough preparation began to bear fruit when they convincingly defeated Donegal in the first round of the 1958 Ulster championship. In the semi-final they deprived Tyrone of a possible third-in-a-row Ulster title when they defeated them by 1–9 to 0–2. Down were now in their first Ulster final since 1942. It took a Herculean display by Derry midfielder Jim McKeever to ensure a four-point victory for the Oak Leaf County. Down, though disappointed, were far from being despondent. They had started to combine excellently as a team and they now had Doherty restored to their ranks. He was adding that vital scoring power in the forward line. In addition, the Down minor team of 1958 had a potentially great senior player in a brilliant youngster called Seán O'Neill (McCartan's first cousin). Year one of the Hayes five-year plan had been very satisfactory.

The following year, in the annual Wembley GAA tournament, Down showed the first glimpses of greatness when they overcame Galway in a splendid encounter. Down, in that year's Ulster championship, defeated Antrim and Tyrone (after a replay) to reach their second successive Ulster final, against the province's traditional kingpins, Cavan. In a fabulous display of individual skill and terrific teamwork, the Mourne men crushed the Breffni challenge on a 2–16 to 0–7 scoreline. Although, as stated at the outset, Down subsequently lost to Galway in that 1959 All-Ireland semi-final, Hayes and company were not unduly perturbed. They reasoned that the defeat was part of the natural learning process and that, after all, Down had progressed another rung on the ladder to ultimate glory. However, that is not a prognosis that the straight-speaking McCartan is fully in agreement with: 'We left home at one o'clock on the previous day to go to Butlins, where we were staying for the night. We had beans and toast for our tea, before retiring for the night, with nothing else to eat. They told us if we went to second Mass the following morning we would get our breakfast on our return. When we came back from Mass, breakfast was over and we went to play an All-Ireland semi-final totally weak from the hunger. In fact, none of us had eaten since the previous day. That is why we lost and now I knew, with different preparation, we would do much better the following year.'

Be that as it may, certain more pertinent factors were now to play an increasingly important role in Down's development as a potent football force. With Seán O'Neill now a vital additional cog in the forward line and McCartan himself switched to being chief playmaker at centre half-forward, the concept of playing as a cohesive unit became vital to Down's future strategy. What is now known as 'total football' would replace the 'catch and kick' style favoured by so many counties. 'There never was any pre-planning regarding style of play or team tactics outlined to us by any member of the management team. Our game just evolved because of the natural skill and intelligence of all the players,' James explained.

Prior to the 1960 Ulster championship, Down had a fantastic league run, which culminated in the defeat of Kerry in the semi-final and Cavan in the final. Down had now won their first major national title. They easily coasted through the Ulster championship, again defeating Cavan in the final. The All-Ireland semi-final would be a much more difficult proposition, however. Their opponents, Offaly, played superbly in the first half of that game to go in at the interval leading by 2–4 to 0–3. Then, in the second half, Paddy Doherty showed the huge crowd his true worth when he, time and again, ran at the hard-pressed defence, creating scoring opportunities both for himself and his colleagues. With eight minutes to go, the deficit had been reduced to three points. The pendulum of fate then swung decidedly in Down's favour. They were awarded a controversial penalty when the surging McCartan, now playing at full-forward, was fouled in the square. The tension was unbearable as many Offaly supporters voiced their disapproval. Unperturbed, the ice-cool Paddy Doherty sent the ball crashing to the net. Though both sides exchanged further points, the sides were level when the full-time whistle blew. James himself is in no doubt about the validity of the penalty: 'I was standing on the edge of the square when I got the ball, then I took one step forward and the defenders pulled me around. I was now facing outfield when the referee blew for the penalty. The photographs of the incident prove this. Offaly people said I was charging goalwards. If this had been true, I would have been facing the net. It was a definite penalty.'

Before the replay, former Meath All-Ireland winning captain Peter McDermott addressed the Down players. He had written to a Down friend pointing out flaws which he had observed in Down's performance in the first game. In a formal coaching session the Meath great illustrated the need for more astuteness and team tactics. This instilled a greater confidence in Down and, thanks to a fantastic performance by midfielder Joe Lennon, they deservedly overcame the midlanders by two points in the replay.

The All-Ireland final was to see Down face the might of Kerry, who had, down through the years, set such high standards for others to emulate. They were seeking their twentieth title and Down were aiming for their first. Playing scintillating combination football at a blinding pace, Down controlled the first half and went in at the interval leading by 0–9 to 0–5. After the resumption, however, Kerry fought back to draw level. With the outcome now delicately poised, the moment of destiny that was to change the course of Gaelic football had come. Down's captain, Kevin Mussen, passed the ball to James McCartan forty yards out from the Kerry goal. The Kingdom's goalkeeper, Johnny Culloty, allowed McCartan's lob to slip through his fingers to give the Ulster champions a three-point advantage. Shortly afterwards, the mercurial Doherty raced goalwards and was pulled down in the square. For the second time in six weeks, the Ballykinlar man calmly slotted the resultant penalty to the net. Down were now on their way to an historic triumph. Now six points ahead, the men from the 'Wee Six' were about to create one of the greatest outpourings of euphoria ever witnessed in Croke Park. As Doherty's kick nestled in the net, Down supporters threw scarves, hats and coats into the air, in a combined gesture of unbridled joy. Looking around at their excited supporters spurred the Mourne men to display the full repertoire of their exquisite skills. They seemed to score at will, with the immaculate Doherty forcing the white flag to be raised thrice. Luckily, the spectators were forced back and when the long whistle sounded, Down had won their first senior All-Ireland title, inflicting upon Kerry their heaviest ever-final defeat until then, on a 2–10 to 0–8 scoreline.

By this victory, Down had not only won a national football title, they had also brought a new sense of hope and instilled in 'lesser' GAA counties a new confidence and self-belief. Maurice Hayes's dream had been realised two years ahead of schedule, but no one was complaining, certainly not James McCartan! 'First of all, I was relieved when the whistle sounded, because I feared that the game could have been abandoned when the crowd rushed onto the pitch. Then a feeling of tremendous satisfaction came over me as I watched Kevin Mussen raising the Sam Maguire Cup. That was the culmination of all our dreams. For almost an hour, the whole pitch was totally packed with Down supporters and well-wishers from all over Ireland. Kerry were very sporting in defeat. I was particularly impressed with defenders

Seán Murphy and Jerome O'Shea. Murphy was a very stylish player and O'Shea was a great fielder of the ball. One thought above all others dominated my feelings as I tried to take in the wonder of it all. I had to see my father. Then, when we had togged in, I wandered out into the street outside and there he was, surrounded by exultant fans and crying his eyes out. When I shouted at him, he ran towards me, totally overcome with happiness, and he said, "You kept your promise, Jimmy boy!" That was the best moment of my life.'

'The whole journey home from Dublin, right up to the border, was just incredible. After we reached the border at Killeen customs post, we all got out of the team bus and openly declared the name and the priceless nature of our newfound friend — Sam Maguire. The whole team then walked with the Cup into our native county. To be the first team from the six counties to win the All-Ireland made the whole occasion really magical. For the next few weeks we went on tour to every club, village and town in the county and we got a tremendous reception everywhere. There was a civic reception in Belfast City Hall to mark our achievement. In those days, that was a great community relations exercise.'

That magnificent Down side won the Ulster championship the following year when they narrowly defeated a gallant Armagh team in the final. The All-Ireland semi-final of that year was a case of 1960 revisited. For the third time in two years, Down and Kerry were to meet in a major contest. In the eyes of some GAA followers, two important questions had been left unanswered in 1960. Was James McCartan's fortuitous goal the real reason why Down beat Kerry, and had Kerry's traditional catch-and-kick style simply been outmanoeuvred by a team which did not play traditional Gaelic football? These questions were emphatically answered on a Sunday in August 1961. In the first minute of the game, Paddy Doherty crossed the ball to Seán O'Neill, who duly planted it in the net. Down dominated the first quarter but Kerry rallied to take control of the second quarter. The half-time scoreline of 1–5 to 0–8 was an accurate reflection of that period. The second half was to see Down at their majestic best. Jarlath Carey and Joe Lennon nullified the aerial power of Mick O'Connell and Séamus Murphy, and their forward line totally mesmerised the Kerry defence with their constant running and pinpoint passing. In the end, Down achieved a 1–12 to 0–9 victory. There were no further doubts or questioning the merits of a truly great footballing side. In that second half, James McCartan gave arguably the greatest display of a star-studded career, and Down, it is said by many, gave their greatest team performance during that last quarter of majestic dominance.

In the final, Down again faced Leinster champions Offaly. This encounter attracted a massive 90,556 spectators, the largest attendance ever at any sporting event in Ireland. The first half of that memorable game was to see Down again carve incisive openings in the Offaly defence, to score three goals. Offaly themselves were not to be outdone, as they graced the occasion with two major scores. Nevertheless, it was the vision, combination and clinical finishing of the Down goals that had a devastating effect on Offaly. Down's first goal was the result of a passing movement between corner-back George Lavery, Jarlath Carey and Paddy Doherty. Doherty then sent the ball high to James McCartan. In one movement, he jumped, caught the ball and turned immediately to send it to the net for an inspirational score. Doherty was again the provider when he crossed the ball for Seán O'Neill to notch goal number two. Corner-forward, the late Brian Morgan, added a third to leave the half-time score 3–2 to 2–3.

Six minutes after the interval, Offaly had strong appeals for a penalty turned down when left half-forward Tommy Greene appeared to be fouled in the square. No free was given and Down went on to record a narrow but deserved victory of 3–6 to 2–8. For the second year in succession, the Mourne men had won the All-Ireland. That day's performance finally clinched the stars of the County Down's entry into the GAA's hall of fame. There was no weakness in the side. Eddie McKay was a safe, competent goalkeeper. Full-back Leo Murphy, a prodigious kicker of the ball, ruled the roost and was flanked by two tigerish markers in George Lavery and the late Pat Rice. Dan McCartan (James's brother) was a commanding figure at centre half-back. In 1960 he had team captain Kevin Mussen and Kevin O'Neill (Seán's brother and James's first cousin) on either side of him, whereas in 1961, Patsy O'Hagan and John Smith were his half-back colleagues. All four were intelligent team players. At midfield, Joe Lennon and Jarlath Carey showed that one did not just have to be a good fielder to control the midfield exchanges. Their innate positional sense and their ability to shadow opponents and box the ball away brought a new dimension to midfield play. The whole Down forward sextet were simply magnificent and must rank as one of the most formidable attacks in the history of the game. The silken skills of Seán O'Neill at right half-forward, the leadership and playmaker qualities of James McCartan on the '40 and the uncanny accuracy of the fleet-footed Doherty completed a magical half-forward trio. Tony Hadden at right corner-forward had a penchant for acting as a third midfielder (another innovation) and for fisting points. In the other corner, Brian Morgan (RIP) was a will o' the wisp player whose darting runs broke the hearts of many defenders. In 1960 the versatile O'Hagan was full-forward, whereas in 1961 P.J. McElroy was an ideal target man.

In 1962 Down again won the National League when they defeated Dublin by a point in the final. They were also rewarded for their All-Ireland successes of the previous two years by being invited on a coast-to-coast tour of the United States in the springtime. When they returned home after their American sojourn, they beat Fermanagh and Tyrone to reach their fifth successive Ulster final. A combination of injuries and tiredness was only partly to blame for Down's heavy defeat by Cavan. The outstanding team play of the Breffni men, capably marshalled by Gabriel Kelly, Tom Maguire, Ray Carolan, Jimmy Stafford and captain Jim McDonnell, ended a glorious era in Down football. Still, they contested the next seven Ulster finals (winning four of them), which in itself was an enormous feat. They also reached the National League finals (home) in both 1963 and 1964. When Down won their third All-Ireland in 1968, James had retired. He knew the edge had gone slightly from his game after the 1966 Ulster final, so he retired gracefully from the scene to concentrate on a newly married life with his wife, Marie.

'King James', as he was affectionately known, had been one of the chief architects of Down's unprecedented success from 1958–1967. He had played in twelve consecutive Ulster championships and nine consecutive Ulster finals, winning six of them. Two All-Ireland senior football titles, two National League titles, four Lagan Cups and three McKenna Cups were testament to his outstanding ability, his undisputed durability and phenomenal work rate. Other Down players, such as the brilliant Seán O'Neill and the marvellous Paddy Doherty, deservedly claimed the plaudits on the scoring stakes. However, in the eyes of thousands of GAA followers, James McCartan was the dynamic force and talisman supreme of that wonderful Down team. The fact that he was the first player to be awarded the Caltex Footballer of the Year Award in successive years, in 1960 and 1961, merely underlined the high esteem in which he was held at national level.

When I met James in his County Down home, he took me on a sightseeing tour of his games room. GAA memorabilia, stretching from a photograph of his father on a Down team of 1929, and incorporating photographs, medals and personal mementoes of Down's glorious days of the 1960s, adorned the room. The football collection was completed with GAA photographs of his five sporting sons, all of whom have achieved sporting success at either county, college or university level. Included in that galaxy of sporting endeavours are pictures of James and his greyhound successes. 'For over twenty years, I owned and raced greyhounds at venues such as Dunmore, Celtic Park, Lifford, Navan, Tralee, Limerick, Harold's Cross and Shelbourne Park. My two greatest dogs were 'Newpark Arkle', which won the Easter Cup in 1973, and

'Gullion Lad', which won the Cesarewitch in 1977. Anto Moriarty, the father of former Armagh footballer Paddy, was my trainer throughout those years. Nowadays, I have no active sporting involvement except to go bowling a few times a week with my wife, Marie,' the semi-retired businessman added.

Looking back on a lifetime of Gaelic games, he has no doubt about who was the greatest footballer he ever saw. 'Seán Purcell of Galway was the best. He was the perfect footballer, who could play equally well in every central position, from full-back to full-forward. What made him extra special was the fact that he was the best in each position he chose to play in. From an Ulster perspective, Jody O'Neill (Tyrone), Jim McKeever (Derry), Tom Maguire (Cavan) and Gabriel Kelly (Cavan) were the best I encountered. At national level my toughest opponent was Paddy Holden (Dublin). He was a very tenacious man-marker. The Kerry team of the 1970s and 1980s had many great players, like Jack O'Shea, Pat Spillane and Mike Sheehy. My old friend Jack Mahon gave the performance of his life when he played for Galway against us in the 1959 All-Ireland semi-final. The player who, to my mind, was the best footballer on that marvellous Kerry team of the recent past was Eoin Liston. He had the intelligence to maximise the potential of those around him. His ability to win a ball and then lay it off was the final piece in the jigsaw which made a fabulous Kerry team great.'

That well-known GAA writer, the late Raymond Smith, writing in *The Football Immortals*, which is universally accepted as the true bible of Gaelic football history, once aptly described McCartan the footballer and McCartan the man in one unique, succinct sentence: 'If there was dynamism and power-packed drive in his play on the field, he pulled no punches either in the viewpoints he expressed.' Three opinions bear out the sharpness, honesty and no-holds-barred approach of McCartan.

1. 'I served as manager of the Down senior team for two periods, 1977–79 and 1982–84. Initially, I took up the position on the understanding that I would appoint my own selectors. Though two selectors had been previously appointed at Annual Convention, I was led to believe that they would step aside. But when I attended my first training session, they were there. So I had to walk out before the original agreement was implemented. On another occasion I was informed at a County Board meeting that the Board's finances were so bad that players would not be given a meal after home games. I resisted this very strongly, especially as most of my players were students in Belfast and would not have any access to

food before they travelled back to college. When the Board meeting was interrupted to provide us with food, I blew my top at the hypocrisy of it all and again walked out. I knew I was a controversial character, but everything I was asking for players back then is now taken for granted.'

2.   'I would open up Croke Park to rugby, basketball, netball, hockey and, when the soccer authorities, north and south, agree to a thirty-two county national side, I would open it for soccer as well, but not until that happens. Speaking of some of the GAA hierarchy who appear to make a lot of these controversial decisions, I think when a President of the GAA retires, he should cease to have any role in the Association. If a farmer today tilled his land like the farmers years ago, with horses and ploughs, he would be living in cloud cuckoo land. There are too many people in positions of authority in the GAA today who are not living in the real world. They are like some of the most conservative politicians we have now. What is wrong with Ireland today is that some extreme unionists are living in 1690 and some extreme nationalists are living in 1916. There are some people in the GAA who always say 'yes' to everything, just to further their own interest. Many important issues are also brushed under the carpet in order to advance their own agendas. To me, this is absolutely wrong. We have to revolutionise the Association and let the young people play a meaningful part. The youth of today are very forward-thinking and fair-minded. They will not let anyone prevent them from expressing an opinion or making necessary changes in the structure of the Association.'

3.   'Another major bone of contention for me is in the whole area of the distribution of tickets for major games. For example, most of those involved in the organisation of the All-Ireland finals are paid, whereas the people at the centre of those great occasions get nothing. I believe, as a small token of appreciation, every player who has played in an All-Ireland senior football or senior hurling final should be given the option of buying two tickets for each year's All-Ireland final. I will give two instances of gross wrongdoing in our Association regarding tickets. A great GAA man, Dan McCartan of Saval, who is Down's Central Council delegate, gave me his two tickets for the VIP section of the Munster hurling final in 2004. We were royally treated, but the only people I saw in the privileged area were GAA officials or ex-officials. The only former player in that section was a current official. This is simply not right. Some years ago, a great GAA man in another county did a

huge financial favour for his County Board. Yet, when his county reached the All-Ireland final, he had to ask me to help him get tickets. That shows a total disregard for people who have done so much, in so many different ways, for the Association.'

In the autumn of 2004, James McCartan's son, James, was held responsible for assault in a Dublin court. The case centred on a challenge match between Dublin and Westmeath in May 2003 in which Westmeath defender Kenny Larkin alleged he was assaulted by McCartan with a 'clenched fist'. McCartan himself, however, had pleaded not guilty to the charge, stating that it was his elbow that had made contact with Larkin and that the first he knew of his marker's plight was when he saw him lying on the ground. In a subsequent court hearing, the judge ordered McCartan to pay €10,000 by way of compensation, to a charity of Larkin's choosing.

'That whole sorry saga was a very traumatic and upsetting time for the whole family, especially as James had such an exemplary disciplinary record, despite the constant abuse he got from so many defenders over the years. There were two issues, in particular, which really angered me. Firstly, I think it was totally wrong for the Gardai to be sitting outside a Croke Park meeting room when James came out after attending a GAA disciplinary meeting regarding the alleged incident. That was a completely intimidating, unfair experience for James. Secondly, from a layman's point of view, I could not understand how the judge arrived at his verdict, when there were so many discrepancies in the prosecution case. To me, that did not make sense. Still, nothing will ever take away from me the many thrills I got from James's brilliant playing career. Those All-Ireland victories of 1991 and 1994 gave me a greater buzz than my own All-Ireland successes. I remember him sitting on my knee in Croke Park as a young child. Even then he had the ability to sum up a game very accurately. He is now the manager of Queen's University Sigerson Cup team, and I have no doubt that James has many more great days ahead of him on a football field,' James the elder concluded.

For his all-time representative sides, James made the following choices:

ULSTER

Thady Turbett
(Tyrone)

Tony Scullion   Gabriel Kelly   Tom O'Hare
(Derry)   (Cavan)   (Down)

Jim McDonnell   Kieran McGeeney   D.J. Kane
(Cavan)   (Armagh)   (Down)

Anthony Tohill   Jim McKeever
(Derry)   (Derry)

Seán O'Neill   Greg Blaney   Paddy Doherty
(Down)   (Down)   (Down)

Frank McGuigan   Peter Canavan   Mickey Linden
(Tyrone)   (Tyrone)   (Down)

IRELAND

Johnny Geraghty
(Galway)

Robbie O'Malley   Noel Tierney   Tony Scullion
(Meath)   (Galway)   (Derry)

Jim McDonnell   Paddy Holden   D.J. Kane
(Cavan)   (Dublin)   (Down)

Jack O'Shea   Frank Eivers
(Kerry)   (Galway)

Greg Blaney   Seán Purcell   Paddy Doherty
(Down)   (Galway)   (Down)

Seán O'Neill   Eoin Liston   Mike Sheehy
(Down)   (Kerry)   (Kerry)

Of all the beautiful memories and wonderful experiences of James McCartan's football life, nothing compares to the enduring friendships that the King of Down football made during the last fifty years. For him, participating in and following the great games of Gaelic football and hurling was one long journey of passion, pride and total fulfilment.

One particular anecdote indelibly reinforces that conclusion.

'Two car loads of us left Down, over twenty years ago, on a Saturday afternoon, to travel to Cork for the following day's Munster final between the home team and Kerry. After we finished being watered and fed in a hotel that night, we discovered that the game was completely sold out. Ticketless at twelve o'clock, I rang a Kerry friend who was a member of the Munster Council and told him my problem. He said, "Be at Gate B at half-one." And at one thirty-five, there were seven Down men with "Maor" written across their chests patrolling the sideline at a Munster final!'

That story epitomises the GAA's great camaraderie for like-minded, kindred spirits and followers of our national games. It also tells us, in no uncertain terms, that one James McCartan will always be 'King' in the hearts and minds of GAA supporters throughout the thirty-two counties.

JAMES MCCARTAN – FACT FILE

Native Place:	Donacloney, Tullylish, Co. Down
Date of Birth:	November 19, 1937
Clubs:	Glenn, Tullylish
Club Honours:	(a) Glenn: Senior Football Championship (3) – 1958, 1962, 1964 Senior League Championship (3) – 1958, 1962, 1964 (b) Tullylish: Junior Football Championship (1) – 1968 Division 4 League Championship (1) – 1968 Division 3 League Championship (1) – 1969 Division 2 League Championship (1) – 1970
County Honours:	All-Ireland Senior Football Championship (2) – 1960, 1961 National Football League (2) – 1960, 1962 Ulster Senior Football Championship (6) – 1959, 1960, 1961, 1963, 1965, 1966 Ulster Junior Football Championship (2) – 1958, 1966 Lagan Cup (4) – 1959, 1961, 1962, 1963 McKenna Cup (3) – 1959, 1961, 1964

Other Honours:	Railway Cup (4) – 1963, 1964, 1965, 1966 (Captain) Ireland v. Combined Universities (2) – 1960, 1961
Managerial Honours:	National Football League, Division One (1) – 1983 National Football League, Division Two – 1982 All-Ireland U-21 Football Championship (1) – 1979 Ulster U-21 Football Championship (3) – 1978, 1979, 1984
Awards:	Caltex Footballer of the Year (2) – 1960, 1961 Irish Independent Sports Star of the Week (3) Down Centenary Team
Occupation:	Director of Tullyraine Quarries
Family:	Married to Marie (née Mulholland) from Glenavy, Co. Antrim
Children:	Brian, James, Delia, Charlie Pat, Maria, Daniel, Eoin

FOUR

The Terrible Twins–Galway

FRANK STOCKWELL AND SEÁN PURCELL TALK TOGETHER

> But I heard about their feats
> How one would get the ball
> Know where the other one would be.
> And we share in all the glory
> Of their legendary wins,
> Seán Purcell, Frank Stockwell: The Terrible Twins
>
> *The Sawdoctors*

Individually two of Ireland's greatest ever Gaelic footballers and collectively the best combination ever to enrich the game, Frank Stockwell and Seán Purcell had as their first coach a lady. Sr Fursey of the local Presentation Primary School in Tuam was the first person to spot the inherent footballing talent of the boys, who were in her infant class. After their primary school days, Frank went to St Patrick's CBS and Seán graduated to St Jarlath's College, already an established GAA nursery. However, it was the local Christian Brothers community who organised all under age GAA activity in the town's GAA club, Tuam Stars. When Tuam Stars won the 1945 Galway county minor championship, they had fourteen CBS students, led by Frank Stockwell, on the team. The only 'outsider' to make the starting fifteen was Seán Purcell.

Having won their first championship together, both Stockwell and Purcell were destined to share in a plethora of outstanding accomplishments during the next fifteen years. Both made their county minor championship debut with the Tribesmen in 1945, with Frank, rather surprisingly, being the goalkeeper. In 1946 they again played on the county minor side and were joined by future Louth All-Ireland medal-winner Stephen White, who was then a student at Mountbellew Agricultural College.

By 1946 St Jarlath's, capably marshalled by Seán Purcell, reached the first All-Ireland Colleges final against St Patrick's College, Armagh. For many Gaelic football aficionados who attended, this was the most marvellously exciting game of football ever played. This was the day that future Tyrone star Iggy Jones gave a display of amazing wizardry and the most supreme skill ever witnessed. He was centre half-forward for St Pat's, and Seán Purcell wore the No. 11 jersey for St Jarlath's. With the Tuam Star masterminding their attack, Jarlath's had the better of the first-half exchanges and went in at the interval leading by 2–3 to 0–6. But they had not quite contained Jones, who had notched four of his side's first-half points.

In the early minutes of the second half, the westerners seemed to have stamped their authority on the game when they stretched their lead to seven points. Then Iggy Jones took over. First he shot a point, before going on a dazzling 50-yard solo run and scoring a spectacular goal. Another Armagh point cut the arrears to two. With the classy Purcell spearheading every move, St Jarlath's attacked constantly without reward. Suddenly, the alert Jones picked up a loose clearance, deep inside his own half, and started for the other end of the field. He dodged and sidestepped opponent after opponent on an incredible solo run. On and on he went, spread-eagling the entire defence, before cracking a searing shot to the back of the Tuam net.

That gifted GAA writer Pádraig Puirséal, in his book *The GAA In Its Time*, recreates the scene for the last ten minutes of that fascinating final: 'At this stage it must have seemed to every spectator present that lightning could not strike a third time but that was exactly what happened. Again Jones went streaking down the field, leaving the defence in tatters as he sped through to complete a hat trick of brilliant goals. This time St Jarlath's, hard though they fought, could not wipe out the arrears and finished a point behind at the end of the most exciting and spectacular Gaelic football match I have ever been lucky enough to watch.

'Though very small in stature, inch for inch and pound for pound, Iggy Jones was the most stylish and brainy forward I have ever seen. On the other hand, that was also the first day that I saw the vast repertoire of skills of Seán Purcell — the most complete Gaelic footballer of all time.'

The following year the Armagh college, now without the irrepressible Jones, met St Jarlath's in a repeat of the 1946 final. This time the maturing Purcell gave an absolute exhibition of Gaelic football at its best, when they defeated the northerners by five points. If Jones had stolen all the national headlines in 1946, then Purcell captivated everyone by his wonderful performance in 1947. Little did they know that both of them would thrill thousands of spectators in Croke Park, playing for their native counties, in a decade thence.

The whole period from 1945 to 1954 was a lean one in Galway footballing terms. Their close neighbours and keen rivals, Mayo, were the dominant Connacht side, winning five provincial and two All-Ireland titles, with Roscommon gaining the remaining Connacht senior honours. Frank Stockwell made his senior championship debut in 1947 at corner-forward, a year ahead of Seán Purcell, who was exam tied. The 1948 championship was to see both of them field for the Tribesmen, together for the first time at senior level. Playing outstanding football, Galway reached the Connacht final against Mayo. Midway through the second half of the final, Mayo appeared to be on their way to victory when young Seán Purcell, playing at centre-field, began to exert his authority. Combined with an exceptional performance by wing half-back Tom Sullivan, Galway gradually reduced the deficit, and Sullivan, appropriately, snatched a deserved equaliser. Left half-forward Jarlath Canavan, who held the unfortunate distinction of being on the losing side in three successive All-Ireland senior finals, in 1940, 1941 and 1942, gave another outstanding display. Frank Stockwell too had an impressive provincial final debut, scoring a very valuable point at a critical stage.

The replay went to extra time before Mayo, inspired by Paddy Prendergast and Pádraic Carney, took control to record a three-point triumph. Though defeated, Galway were rather upbeat. A young team, blended with some experienced performers, had given two sterling displays. What was most encouraging was the fact that Purcell and Stockwell, between them, had contributed 1–4 in the replay.

Meanwhile, however, a job opportunity became available for Frank Stockwell in Dundalk, and he joined the Young Ireland's club there. Here he renewed a friendship with a former minor colleague, Stephen White, who had returned to his native county after a spell in Mountbellew Agricultural College. White had partnered Purcell in that 1946 minor team and with Stockwell in exceptional form in the forward line, they had actually reached the Connacht final, only to be beaten by Mayo. Just as Galway GAA officials had heard of White's football prowess in 1946, so had the Louth officials heard of Stockwell in 1949. As a result, Stockwell was selected on the Louth side that played Meath in the Leinster championship. It took a three-game saga to eventually decide the outcome, with the Royals just shading it in the end by the narrowest of margins. Meath, who had fabulous footballers like Paddy O'Brien, Christo Hand, Mattie McDonnell, Peter McDermott and Captain Brian Smyth, actually reached that year's All-Ireland final against Cavan. The Royals gained their first All-Ireland title when they beat the Breffni men, thus preventing them from recording three-in-a-row successes.

'It was difficult at the time to realise how close I was to winning an All-Ireland medal. Louth were very unfortunate not to win in at least two of these three games against Meath,' Frank told me when I met Seán and himself in their beloved Tuam.

Stephen White, who was an all-time great, won an All-Ireland medal with Louth in 1957 at left half-back. White, who was also a talented left half-forward, recalls with pride and affection Frank Stockwell's playing days with the 'Wee County': 'Only for missing key players, I believe Louth would have beaten Mayo in the 1950 All-Ireland final. We were missing three of the best forwards in the county that year, including a wonderful footballing stylist and Irish sprint champion, Fr Kevin Connolly. All of them were priests and the Irish hierarchy had a rule that forbade priests playing inter-county football. However, the biggest regret in my whole life is that Frank Stockwell also was not available to us for that 1950 campaign. He had left to go to London and had joined the Tara Club there. Even accepting the absence of the three priests, I have no doubt that we would have won the All-Ireland if Frank had been playing. He was a tremendous footballer as well as being a very nice person. He really deserved to win his All-Ireland medal with Galway in 1956. It was funny that Frank and Seán, my ex-minor colleagues, should win a senior All-Ireland in 1956, just the year before I won mine.'

Galway reached their next Connacht final in 1951, only to be completely annihilated by All-Ireland champions Mayo. Things looked rather bleak to say the least for Galway's football future. The first breakthrough really came late in 1952 at Clonakilty, when a young Galway side, captained by Seán Purcell, beat Cork in a National League game. The Galway selectors had given youth its head and they responded in style, with Purcell, Stockwell, Jack Mahon, Tom Dillon and Gerry Kirwan, who had starred in Galway's 1952 All-Ireland minor win over Cavan, all now playing pivotal roles. Though Roscommon subsequently defeated them in the first round of the 1953 Connacht championship, the team was much better organised.

Eagerly they awaited 1954, and their supporters were not let down. In the semi-final, Galway, with Seán Purcell at full-back, defeated Mayo, who were the current National League champions, in a terrific contest. On that day Purcell gave arguably his best ever display in a Galway jersey. In the Connacht final they faced Sligo. At half-time a dominant Galway led by nine points. They then suffered a major blow when Frank Stockwell retired because of injury. Sligo, driven forward relentlessly by a fantastic display from Nace O'Dowd at centre half-back, reduced the deficit to three points. In the dying minutes, Galway goalkeeper Jack Mangan saved a goal-bound shot by Sligo's Mick Gaffney on the line. Gaffney, claiming that the ball was over the line, then grabbed the green flag from an unsuspecting umpire and waved it furiously, signalling a goal for the Yeats County. However, after several minutes of confused chaos, order was restored and a free awarded to Galway. When the full-time whistle sounded, Purcell and Stockwell were now in their first All-Ireland senior semi-final.

It had been nine years since Galway had reached the penultimate stage of the championship. Though beaten in the All-Ireland semi-final by Kerry, the signs for future success were becoming more apparent. After a terrible first half, John 'Tull' Dunne, Galway County Secretary, gave a stern pep talk, saying that 'fifteen Galway men are as good as fifteen Kerry men any day'. That same day Frank Eivers emerged as a future star and Purcell moved back to midfield. A brilliant Galway resurgence meant they were only beaten by three points in the end.

Their optimistic hopes for national glory were again dashed when Roscommon dumped the Galwegians out of the 1955 Connacht championship by a six-point winning margin. The Galway County Board then decided to bring greater organisation and more co-ordinated team management to pursue their All-Ireland dream. Stars of the 1930s John Dunne and Brendan Nestor were put in charge of team affairs. Jack Mangan was also elected captain, and Jack Mahon was vice-captain. Army man and Cork exile as well as player Billy O'Neill was appointed trainer. Fr Paddy Mahon of Dunmore (brother of Jack) became Chairman of the County Board. In the words of Seán Purcell, he brought a great spirit of enthusiasm and confidence in the pursuit of the Holy Grail. All that was required now was for the players to deliver.

After four weeks of hard training, Galway met Mayo in the 1956 Connacht semi-final in Castlebar. Playing fantastic football, the Tribesmen completely overwhelmed Mayo on a scoreline of 5–13 to 2–5. The memories of the 1951 hammering by the same opposition had disappeared into the sands of time. In the Connacht final the roller-coaster campaign continued as the Yeats County succumbed to a 13-point defeat. As Galway reached the All-Ireland semi-final, the two most conspicuous players were the redoubtable Purcell and Stockwell. Seán had now moved to centre half-forward and Frank to full-forward. Between them they were like two conductors guiding the Galway football orchestra. Their central positioning and natural predatory instincts enabled them to have an ever-increasing positive influence on how Galway played.

Their toughest test was yet to come. Tyrone, who were their opponents in the All-Ireland semi-final, had won the Ulster title for the first time. Within their ranks were brothers Eddie and Jim Devlin, who had played in the 1946 Colleges final against Seán Purcell, and of course, there was the mini-maestro himself, Ignatius Jones. Football supporters everywhere could not wait for Purcell and Jones, part two.

In the first half of that game, Galway played very well to lead at half-time by 0–6 to 0–3. The second half really belonged to the O'Neill County as they continually laid siege to the Galway goal, especially in the last quarter. Only brilliant work by goalie Jack Mangan and Seán Purcell, who had switched to midfield to partner the outstanding Frank Eivers, enabled the Tribesmen to gain a narrow 0–8 to 0–6 win. The defining moment of that second half came towards the end. The incomparable Iggy Jones made a typical run, sidestepping his way past man after man. Then he tried to punch the ball to the net, only for the agile Mangan to smother his effort defiantly: 'That was the toughest match we played. Only for that save by Jack we were gone and Tyrone would have won,' added Frank.

Now Galway were in the All-Ireland final against Munster champions Cork. After Mass on the Sunday of the game, they had a short training session on the strand near their hotel. Then they headed to Croke Park for the greatest day in their lives: 'The worst part of that day was the fact that we had to wait so long from the semi-final to the final. The final had been postponed to the first Sunday of October because of an outbreak of polio in Cork,' Seán recalled.

From the throw-in it was obvious that a great game was in prospect. It was a game of Gaelic football at its traditional best, hard but fair. Seán Purcell and Frank Stockwell were obviously brilliant as they constantly tormented the Cork defence with their inter-passing and enterprising play. Seán was the creative playmaker as he gained possession in so many different positions. He was the guiding genius in the lead-up to Galway's two crucial first-half goals. For the first one he sent a pinpoint pass to left half-forward Billy O'Neill, who punched the ball immediately to the alert and elusive Stockwell. Frank expertly dispatched the ball to the net for goal number one. The second major was another gem. Purcell fielded superbly before threading a long, accurate pass behind the Cork defence, where Stockwell was lurking dangerously. In the twinkling of an eye Frank coolly scored goal number two. At the interval the Galwegians were ahead 2–6 to 0–6.

In the second half, Cork switched Paddy O'Driscoll to centre half-back, with the specific instruction to curtail the rampant Purcell. This nullified Purcell's influence for a while and Cork rallied strongly to reduce the deficit considerably. With five minutes to go there was only a point between them. Then Purcell rose majestically to the impending crisis and scored a point from a free after he himself had been fouled.

Frank Stockwell, with a brilliant first touch, obtained possession. He then left several defenders trailing in his wake, before slotting the ball over to ensure victory. The full-time whistle went and, for the first time in eighteen years, Galway were All-Ireland senior football champions.

For Galway it was a magnificent team achievement. For Purcell and Stockwell it was an astonishing personal accomplishment. No outfield player had ever gained as much vital possession as Seán Purcell did that day. No forward in the history of All-Ireland finals ever put on such a scoring spree as Frank Stockwell did. In total he accumulated 2–5, all from play, in a masterful performance during a sixty-minute match. The final score was a convincing 2–13 to 3–7 triumph for the westerners.

When it comes to mentioning their own considerable exploits on the playing field, both Seán and Frank are two of the most unassuming personalities one could ever hope to meet. However, when it comes to speaking about each other, they are fulsome in their praise and generous with their words. No two players have ever had such a unique understanding of what to do to find the other with a defence-splitting pass. Their natural telepathy was instinctive. Purcell's radar-like vision in always being able to find Frank was incredible. Stockwell's consistent execution, in terms of scoring, was phenomenal. 'We never really planned anything. Seán was just the most natural footballer of all time. I only had to move to a proper position and he would give me the perfect pass,' Frank told me, before adding, in a simple sentence, the most profound and accurate summing up of a man popularly acknowledged as the greatest all-round footballer of all time: 'Seán was so good that he could always make his feet do what his head dictated at any time.'

Seán Purcell then generously refers to the scoring sensation that Frank Stockwell undoubtedly was: 'Frank was a very skilful player. He knew when to hold the ball and when to pass it. We just had a natural kind of empathy with each other and it resulted in a lot of scores. Frank's display in the final was marvellous. He practically destroyed the Cork defence on his own. All the rest of us had to do was to get the ball to him. To score 2–5 from play in an All-Ireland senior football final was some achievement.'

After that 1956 final whistle blew, the Galway team returned for a celebratory meal in the Grand Hotel in Malahide. The following morning they read the papers' accounts of their thrilling triumph. One headline in particular Frank Stockwell recalls vividly. It was one penned by the late respected RTÉ broadcaster Mick Dunne, then a journalist with the *Irish Press*: 'The Terrible Twins from Tuam Overwhelm Cork'.

Thus was born the immortal phrase which, since that October day, has always been associated with Frank and Seán. They had become a justifiable part of the GAA's evolving folklore.

On the journey home by car, they will never forget entering the province of Connacht at the bridge of Athlone, before seeing the first bonfire just inside the Galway border on the outskirts of Ballinasloe. A huge crowd of cheering supporters greeted them at Ahascragh, the home of left full-back Tom Dillon. Going towards Tuam, the bonfires increased dramatically both in number and quality. When they reached their hometown, three players in particular were especially proud. All three had lived on the one street — Bishop Street. All three had played leading roles in the previous day's wonderful victory. Jack Mangan, as well as being a superb goalkeeper, had the distinct honour of captaining Galway to their fourth All-Ireland senior football title. No one had done more than Frank Stockwell and Seán Purcell to ensure that their friend and colleague had raised the Sam Maguire Cup on high in Croke Park.

The following spring, Galway again met Tyrone in the National League semi-final. Tyrone and that man again, Iggy Jones, played superbly to lead by two points at half-time. In a spellbinding second half, both teams played excellent football, with the final outcome always in doubt. Then Seán Purcell scored what many real footballing connoisseurs, including Frank Stockwell, maintain was the greatest ever goal. High fetching midfielder Frank Eivers caught magnificently before sending a lovely pass to Seán Purcell. Without breaking stride, the Tuam Star suddenly unleashed a pile driver to the roof of the net from over thirty yards out. 'I remember seeing a photograph in the paper the next day. It showed Tyrone's brilliant goalkeeper Thady Turbett standing, with his hands outstretched, waiting for Seán to shoot. What had actually happened was that Seán's shot was struck with such force that the ball had actually gone into the net, hit a stanchion and bounced out again before poor Thady knew it had gone in. The photographer captured the moment brilliantly.' That Purcell 'special' and another fabulous save by Mangan from Tyrone's Jackie Taggart gave Galway victory by just one point.

In the final, Galway defeated Kerry in a game renowned for Galway's splendid second-half performance. Galway's four-point victory, as well as securing a league title, entitled the Tribesmen to visit New York — a trip that was greatly enjoyed by all: 'When we were over there I had an opportunity to go to a race meeting. At that time, in all our minds, America was much further away than it is now. So imagine my surprise when I immediately recognised one of the stewards at the meeting. It was none other than our old friend, Pat McAndrew from Mayo, who had played at centre half-back against us in the 1948 Connacht final,' Seán added.

For the remainder of their careers, in national terms, lady luck did not shine on Galway and the Terrible Twins. Both of them scored goals against Leitrim in the 1957 Connacht final but they were beaten by Cork in the subsequent All-Ireland semi-final. A fantastic performance by Cork midfielder Eric Ryan and a litany of wides by the Connacht men enabled the southerners to score a one-point victory. They were exceptionally lucky to escape with a two-point victory, again over Leitrim, in the 1958 decider. That match has always been referred to as the Packie McGarty final. This is a celebratory reference to one of Gaelic football's all-time greats. Those at the game maintained that they never witnessed such an exhibition of high fielding, devastating solo runs and incisive passing, as that given by McGarty.

In the All-Ireland semi-final against Dublin, the Tribesmen were again out of luck. Shortly before the end, the brilliant Frank Eivers hit the crossbar with a tremendous shot. Immediately play switched to the other end and Kevin Heffernan was fouled. Ollie Freaney tapped the ball over the bar from the resultant free, thus securing a one-point victory for Dublin. After that defeat, five of the 1956 heroes — Jack Mangan, Tom Dillon, Gerry Daly, Billy O'Neill and Gerry Kirwan — retired. A team that probably should have won three-in-a-row All-Ireland titles was now breaking up, and the signs for future success were not promising. Still, Galway won another Connacht final in 1959, before overwhelming first-timers Down in the All-Ireland semi-final by seven points. In the final they met a Kerry side captained by another GAA icon, Mick O'Connell. Seán Purcell had the honour of leading the Tribesmen. Though they tried hard, Kerry were the much superior team and the Kingdom won rather comfortably by nine points. John Nallen, Mick Greally and Frank Stockwell, who all played that day, were not fully fit and in retrospect probably should not have started. In addition, early in the game, Seán Purcell had collided heavily with Kerry's full-back Niall Sheehy, thus substantially reducing his effectiveness.

'On the night before the game, I had two dogs running in Shelbourne Park and both of them won. I was hoping a Galway win would secure my treble. Anyhow, Kerry deserved to win and their right half-back, Seán Murphy, gave a real Man of the Match performance,' Seán said.

In the 1960 All-Ireland semi-final Galway and Kerry met again, with the westerners losing out by three points. This was the last time the famous duo played together. The superb Purcell scored seven points. The hard-working Stockwell had a glorious goal-effort saved by

Kingdom netminder Johnny Culloty. Five minutes from the end, the intelligent Stockwell found himself all alone in front of the Kerry goal, waiting for the pass that never came. Unfortunately, a colleague did not spot him and instead blazed the ball wide. The last chance of a deserved draw had gone. Having endured a series of injuries, especially in the latter part of his career, Frank Stockwell graciously took his leave from the game that he had adorned so long.

That Galway side reached two further provincial finals in 1961 and 1962 — both against Roscommon. Roscommon won the final of 1961. In the 1962 final Galway were leading by 2–6 to 1–4 at the end of the third quarter when a bizarre incident occurred. In attempting to save a point, Roscommon's goalkeeper Aidan Brady swung off the crossbar. To the consternation of everyone, the crossbar came tumbling down. When it was repaired, Roscommon had revamped their side, sending one of their best ever players, Gerry O'Malley, to midfield. Giving an inspirational performance and using his unique high solo style to devastating effect, the Roscommon forward line responded magnificently. When the long whistle sounded, Roscommon had won by a point. Even though he later played a few league matches, it was effectively Seán Purcell's last big game in the maroon and white. The illustrious career of probably the greatest footballer of all time was over. No Gaelic footballer could fill all central positions, from full-back to full-forward, with such competency, perception and awareness. As the great James McCartan of Down stated: 'No matter what position he played in, he was the best footballer in Ireland in each of them.'

Between 1962 and 1971 Frank Stockwell served as a selector, with many others, of the Galway senior football team. In the midst of his tenure, another great Galway team made an enormous contribution to the annals of Gaelic football, when they annexed three-in-a-row All-Ireland senior football titles (1964–66). That talented team included many brilliant players who became household names — men like goalkeeper par excellence Johnny Geraghty, double-winning captain, the late Enda Colleran, supreme full-back Noel Tierney and boy-wonder midfielder Jimmy Duggan. In an exciting forward line, ace free-taker Cyril Dunne, Séamus Leydon, Liam Sammon and John Keenan gave many hours of pleasure. One man, however, stood out above all others. Charismatic centre half-forward Mattie McDonagh, who sadly passed away in the spring of 2005, was the team's talisman, its undoubted and inspiring leader. He also provided the only playing link with the successful 1956 side, when he was Frank Eivers' very competent 19-year-old midfield partner. Mattie holds the unique record of being the only Connacht man to hold four senior All-Ireland football medals.

During the latter half of his playing career and since his retirement,

Seán Purcell has pursued an enjoyable, relaxing pastime of going to race meetings, both of the canine and equine variety. At one time he owned several greyhounds — the most notable being ' Starbright' and the sprinter 'Star King', which was runner-up in the Irish Oaks in 1959.

Several years ago an ongoing, chronic arthritic condition gradually started to curb Frank Stockwell's ability to move regularly outside his home. Being the practical philosopher that he is, Frank accepts such drawbacks in a spirit of understanding and inevitability. In abundance, he retains his bonhomie, his generosity of spirit and most of all his phenomenal ability to accurately recall the notable deeds of the great footballers that he encountered over the years. Practically every day in the year his old friend makes the short trip across town to visit him. They avidly share their happy reminiscences of the past and speak about former colleagues and opponents who are experiencing the traumas of serious illness or bereavement. These two wonderful human beings have still so much to talk about, to share, to enjoy. The poet Robert Frost accurately portrayed such vision, such innate humanity:

> 'The woods are lovely, dark and deep,
> But I have promises to keep,
> And miles to go before I sleep
> And miles to go before I sleep.'

Seán tends to be the quieter one; Frank the more vocal. As with all of us, the two of them are different, yet the same, in their love of people, of important values, of enduring friendships. When the 'Terrible Twins' arrived on this earth within ten days of each other in 1928, not one, but two 'Terrible beauties were born'. Frank and Seán : 'Go maire sibh an céad.'

FRANK STOCKWELL — FACT FILE

Native Place:	Tuam, Co. Galway
Date of Birth:	December 7, 1928
Club Honours:	(a) Tuam Stars: Minor Football Champions (1) – 1945
	Senior Football Champions (10) – 1947, 1952, 1954, 1955, 1956, 1957, 1958, 1959, 1960, 1962
	Senior Football League (5)
	Connacht Club Senior Football Club (3)

Club Honours— *contd.*	(b) Young Irelands, Dundalk: Senior Football Champions (1) – 1949 Senior Football League (1) – 1949 (c) Tara: English Football Championship (1) – 1950
County Honours:	All-Ireland Senior Football Champions (1) – 1956 Connacht Senior Football Champions (6) – 1954, 1956, 1957, 1958, 1959, 1960 National Football League (1) – 1957 St Brendan's Cup (1) – 1957 Cahill Cup, Irish Press Cup
Other Playing Honours:	Railway Cup (2) – 1957, 1958 Ireland (2) – 1957, 1958
Coaching/Selectorial Honours:	(a) Tuam Stars: Senior Football League (b) All-Ireland Senior Football Champions (3) – 1964, 1965, 1966 (c) Connacht Senior Football Champions (7) – 1963, 1964, 1965, 1966, 1968, 1970, 1971 (d) National Football League (3) – 1965, 1967 (Home), 1981
Other Sports Honours:	Connacht Lightweight Boxing Champion – 1945/46
Awards:	(i) Sports Star of the Week – 1956 All-Ireland (ii) Sports Star of the Week – March, 1957 (awarded for Railway Cup final on Sunday, March 16, and for Ireland v. Combined Universities on the following day) (iii) Galway Hall of Fame – 1978 (iv) Galway Centenary Team (v) City of Tuam – Dedicated Road, i.e. Frank Stockwell Road, June 20, 1999 (vi) Participant in Louis Marcus' Gael Linn GAA Skills film
Occupation:	Retired painting contractor
Family:	Married to the late Pauline
Children:	Fidelis, Marilynn, Francis

SEÁN PURCELL – FACT FILE

Native Place:	Tuam, Co. Galway
Date of Birth:	December 17, 1928
Club:	Tuam Stars
Colleges' Honours:	All-Ireland Colleges 'A' Senior Football Champions – 1947 Connacht Colleges 'A' Senior Football Champions (3) – 1945, 1946, 1947
Third Level:	Sigerson Cup (1) University College Galway, 1950
Club Honours:	Senior Football Champions (10) – 1947, 1952, 1954, 1955, 1956, 1957, 1958, 1959, 1960, 1962 Senior Football League (5) Connacht Club Championships (3) Minor Football Champions (1) – 1945
County Honours:	All-Ireland Senior Football Champions (1) – 1956 Connacht Senior Football Champions (6) – 1954, 1956, 1957, 1958, 1959, 1960 National Football League (1) – 1957 St Brendan's Cup (1) – 1957 Cahill Cup, Irish Press Cup
Other Playing Honours:	Railway Cup (3) – 1951, 1957, 1958 (Captain) Ireland Combined Universities
Awards:	(a) Team of Century – 1984 (b) Millennium Team – 2000 (c) All-time All Star 1991 Various Sport Star of the Week Awards Galway Centenary Team Galway Hall of Fame City of Tuam – Dedicated Road, i.e. Seán Purcell Road, on June 20, 1999 Participant in Louis Marcus' Gael Linn GAA Skills film
Occupation:	Retired primary school teacher
Family:	Married to the late Rita
Children:	John, Robert, Mary, Frances, Louise, and Ruth

FIVE

John O'Keeffe–Kerry

THE PRINCE OF MODERN FULL-BACKS

The pale moon was rising above the green mountains,
The sun was declining beneath the blue sea,
When I strayed with my love to the pure crystal fountain,
That stands in the beautiful vale of Tralee.

William Mulchinock

The town of Tralee and its immediate environs are totally immersed in the great traditions of the GAA. Three of Kerry's most famous clubs — Austin Stack's, John Mitchel's and Kerins -O'Rahilly's — are situated in the county town. There are really no boundaries, no specific catchment areas. Very often brothers in one family have played with different clubs. Each of the three clubs has had its share of footballing stars, of local heroes. The precursor of Austin Stack's was the Rock Street club. The famous Landers brothers, Roundy, Purty and Bill, were born in Rock Street. Other famous Kerry players who came from this street of twenty houses were Miko Doyle, John 'Gal' Slattery, Jimmy 'Gawksie' Gorman and Jackie Ryan. Between them, these seven won a total of 28 All-Ireland football medals. The great Kerry team of the 1970s and 1980s had four Austin Stack members – Ger Power, Mikey Sheehy, Ger O'Keeffe and John O'Keeffe. Future Kerry County GAA secretary Tony O'Keeffe was also another prominent member.

John's father, Frank O'Keeffe, won an All-Ireland medal against Roscommon in 1946 and greatly encouraged his talented young son to pursue his dream of wearing the green and gold of the Kingdom. Frank, who was a very skilful corner-forward, had also played in the famous Polo Grounds final in New York in 1947. The romanticism of that historic trip, as well as his father's other achievements, fuelled the young John's ambition to develop his innate natural Gaelic football ability. Twinned with that inherent family influence were the positive contributions of John's local primary school and the Austin Stack club. Both Micheal Hayes in the school and James Hobbert, who looked after the juveniles in the club, did tremendous work in harnessing the combined talents of all under their control. When John O'Keeffe went to that great nursery of the game, St Brendan's College, Killarney, his GAA education was further enhanced, thanks to the coaching staff there, spearheaded by the renowned Fr James Linnane. In a team that included John's second cousins, the brothers Tony and Ger O'Keeffe, he captained St Brendan's to Hogan Cup success in 1969, when they defeated St Mary's of Galway.

Meanwhile, the talented centre half-back's inspirational displays at both club and college level attracted the attention of the Kerry county minor selectors, and John duly represented his county in three successive Munster finals in 1967, 1968 and 1969. However, defeat was his lot on all three occasions as they came up against exceptionally talented Cork sides that went on to win the All-Ireland in those three years. Kevin Kehilly, Donal Hunt, Denis Long, Jimmy Barrett, Brian Murphy, Martin O'Doherty and Declan Barron were just a sample of future Rebel senior stars that John faced in those encounters.

In 1969 18-year-old John O'Keeffe was drafted into the senior squad for the concluding stages of the All-Ireland senior football championship. Being naturally very strong and exceptionally developed physically for one so young, the Austin Stack minor also appealed to the Kerry selectors because of his superb fetching skills, his versatility and blistering pace. 'That 1969 team had some very experienced and skilful players like goalkeeper Johnny Culloty, Paudie O'Donoghue, Pat Griffin, Tom Prendergast, Séamus Murphy, Mick O'Dwyer, Eamonn O'Donoghue and Mick O'Connell. I was really the baby of the team but I was made very welcome. Mick O'Connell, in particular, was very good to me and always went out of his way to make sure that I felt a part of the whole team. I could not believe my luck. Here was my all-time idol encouraging me and making me feel totally accepted.'

Having narrowly beaten Mayo in the All-Ireland semi-final, Kerry met newcomers Offaly in the All-Ireland final. The pre-match atmosphere was dominated by the possibility that the great Mick O'Connell might not field. When Johnny Culloty led out his team-mates, all heads turned to look at the personnel of the Kerry team. When O'Connell appeared, the whole stadium burst into spontaneous applause for one of the finest players ever to grace a Gaelic football field. However, it was O'Connell's midfield partner, D.J. Crowley, who stole the honours with a super display, enabling the Kingdom to claim their 21st All-Ireland on a score of 0–10 to 0–7. Being named as third sub entitled the 18-year-old John O'Keeffe to claim his first All-Ireland senior medal, even though he had not yet played a senior competitive game.

That all was to change shortly afterwards, when he made his senior debut in the 1969/70 National League. In the 1970 Munster championship, Kerry retained their provincial title when they defeated Cork. The All-Ireland semi-final was against Ulster champions Derry, who totally controlled the first half of this game. When they missed two penalties, their game plan seemed to fall asunder and the Kingdom ran out convincing winners by a 13-point margin. In the final, which incidentally was the first 80-minute decider, Kerry met Meath, who had accounted for a very good Galway team in the semi-final. John O'Keeffe was selected at centre half-back in that year's campaign. He was due to mark Meath's experienced 1967 All-Ireland winner, Mattie Kerrigan. Before the game, some eyebrows were raised about the wisdom of playing a 19-year-old on such a seasoned player. They need not have worried as John played brilliantly, as did his half-back colleagues Tom Prendergast and Mícheál Ó Sé. Donie O'Sullivan, who was one of the longest 'dead' ball kickers in the game and a wonderful exponent of the drop kick, captained that Kingdom side. Even though Donie had to retire injured with a damaged leg muscle, Kerry easily overcame the Royals, 2–19 to 0–18. John O'Keeffe had won his first All-Ireland medal on the field of play and his second in all. 'I was too young to appreciate winning the 1969 All-Ireland fully. Being actively involved in 1970 made me realise the significance of the whole day much more, and consequently I really enjoyed it,' added John when I met him in Tralee.

In 1971, neighbours Cork beat Kerry in the Munster final. Their successful trainer of the previous two years, former star player Jackie Lyne, decided to retire after the 1971 provincial defeat. For the next three years, 1969 captain Johnny Culloty assumed control of the senior team. Under his tutelage the Kingdom regained their provincial title, before comfortably winning against Connacht champions Roscommon in the 1972 All-Ireland semi-final.

The final pairing was to see a repeat of the 1969 opponents. Only this time there was a distinct difference. Kerry were now pitted against an Offaly team that had won their first All-Ireland the previous year when they defeated Galway. They were a really formidable outfit, containing in their ranks players of the calibre of Martin Furlong, Paddy McCormack, Eugene Mulligan, Nicholas Clavin (a really wonderful footballer), Willie Bryan, Kevin Kilmurray and Tony McTague.

It took two games to settle the outcome. The first game was a titanic struggle that eventually concluded in a draw. The replay was to provide Kerry followers with many unhappy memories when they lost heavily by nine points. Though struggling elsewhere, an immaculate first-half performance by midfielder supreme Mick O'Connell ensured that the sides were level at half-time. In the second period Kerry went two points ahead but then an uncharacteristic mix-up in the Kerry defence led to a fortuitous Offaly goal. Thereafter, Kerry basically collapsed and Offaly, inspired by a stupendous display from midfielder Willie Bryan, went on to deservedly record a back-to-back All-Ireland senior success. For John O'Keeffe it was his first All-Ireland final defeat. Being the philosophical and pragmatic man that he was, he accepted such results as part of life. 'One can always point to mistakes and wonder could we have done anything differently, but in the final analysis Offaly were a very good team and deserved their triumph.'

For the following two years Cork defeated Kerry in the Munster final, going on to win the All-Ireland in 1973 — their first senior success since Jack Lynch and company had won the Sam Maguire Cup 28 years earlier in 1945. The unlucky Johnny Culloty then decided to hand in his managerial reins. No one knew it at the time, but the course of GAA football history was to change irrevocably. Long-serving player Mick O'Dwyer, who himself had won four All-Ireland senior medals, was appointed Kerry manager. Only recently retired as a player, he was certainly au fait with all the young talented players in the county. Bravely, he decided on a youth policy. From the first fifteen that featured in the 1972 All-Ireland final, only three players remained: Brendan Lynch, Paudie Lynch and John O'Keeffe.

After two successive Munster final defeats and a similarly disappointing performance in the latter stages of the 1974/75 league, O'Dwyer left no stone unturned as he prepared his side for his first Munster final as manager. The Kerry team trained for an unprecedented 27 consecutive nights before the final. As well as being superbly physically fit, the whole team were naturally imbued with an unquenchable determination. In the Munster final, Cork did not know what hit them as Kerry played with uninhibited passion, combined with blistering pace and exquisite skill. The Kingdom totally dominated the game to run out easy winners by ten points. This was the day, in many pundits' opinions, that the greatest football team in GAA history was conceived. John O'Keeffe, now playing at full-back, was the defensive co-ordinator who put Mick O'Dwyer's theory of 'total' football into practice. Gone were the days when full-backs were simply tall, strong, slow men who could catch a ball. While O'Keeffe was strong and tall, he inaugurated a new dimension to full-back play. True, he had a brilliant fetch, but he also brought his sense of anticipating what forwards were going to do into play. Most of all, he had fantastic pace. In other words, he was a complete footballer in a team of exceptionally gifted and skilful individuals.

In the All-Ireland semi-final, Kerry met surprise packets Sligo, whose most famous player was one of the games' most prolific scorers, Mickey Kearins. Although they missed a penalty in the first half, Sligo trailed by only five points at half-time. With fifteen minutes to go, the Yeats County were still in contention. However, Kerry's relentless pressure began to expose chinks in the Sligo defence, and in a devastating last quarter they scored three goals and two points to emerge comprehensive winners.

The final against Dublin was the first of many such contests during the course of the next ten years. Most people would agree that the intensity of those games, the sheer brilliance and utter determination of so many players from both teams and the phenomenal support that each side engendered were singularly responsible for the enormous popularity that the GAA enjoys today. Be that as it may, one will never forget how the 'young Kerry tigers' performed on that September day. The whole team played brilliantly, their speedy passing movements and spellbinding ball skills literally tearing the Dublin defence apart. Despite losing their captain, Mickey O'Sullivan, through injury after only twelve minutes of play, the Kingdom led at half-time by 1–6 to 0–4. In the second half, Kerry's swift and accurate forwards similarly mesmerised the Dublin defence to win convincingly by 2–12 to 0–11. At the age of 24 and now the undoubted prince of full-backs, John O'Keeffe had won his third All-Ireland medal.

This All-Ireland was also historic for two different reasons. Firstly, it was the first seventy-minute final, and secondly, it was the only time that the Sam Maguire Cup was not presented to the winning captain. Though released the following day, the unfortunate Mickey O'Sullivan had been taken to hospital after his injury. The honour of raising the Sam Maguire Cup on high fell to the ubiquitous Pat Spillane. That was the day, too, that young Spillane, though nominally wearing the No. 15 jersey, appeared all over the field. Wherever the ball was, Pat always seemed to be in close proximity. The greatest ever Gaelic football team had arrived in style, with power, panache, poise and penetration.

Though Kerry won the Munster final the following year and defeated Derry heavily in the All-Ireland semi-final, O'Keeffe and his colleagues were taken by surprise in the All-Ireland final against the metropolitans. Stung by their defeat to O'Dwyer's men in 1975, the Dublin management team totally restructured their half-back line. This new sector of Tommy Drumm, Kevin Moran (future international soccer star) and Pat O'Neill provided the launching pad for a comprehensive 3–8 to 0–10 victory over the Kingdom. Again, in 1977,

Kerry won Munster, only to come up against Dublin in the All-Ireland semi-final. This has been accepted as one of the best games of all time. In hindsight, many commentators have highlighted the superiority of the Dubs on that occasion. True, we saw that wonderful Dublin team at their brilliant best and displaying, at all times, their natural athleticism. In fairness, however, it must be stated that with the definite exception of the last ten minutes, Kerry were as good as, if not better than, Dublin. Anyhow, the record books will show that, in a classic encounter, Dublin won 3–12 to 1–13.

In 1978 Kerry once again beat Cork in the provincial final, and in the All-Ireland semi-final they easily overcame Roscommon before qualifying for another final against the now-familiar opposition, the Dubs. Both sides were meeting for the fourth consecutive championship match. Prior to the 1978 final, manager O'Dwyer, now under pressure from within his own county, intensified the training schedule so much that players actually got physically sick during sessions. Two successive championship defeats to Dublin were hard to take and O'Dwyer was making sure there would be no excuse for a third defeat in a row. In the game itself, Dublin seized the initiative and after twenty minutes led by six points to one, before an opportunist goal by corner-forward John Egan steadied Kerry's nerves. When Mikey Sheehy chipped goalkeeper Paddy Cullen from a free kick for a spectacular goal before the interval, the Kingdom were in the driving seat. In the second half, with Jack O'Shea lording the midfield exchanges, the wonderful Kerry forward line literally tore the Dublin defence apart, with new full-forward Eoin Liston notching three goals in the process. Winning the game by 5–11 to 0–9, no one disputed Kerry's greatness. The addition of O'Shea and Liston provided the two central missing pieces of that marvellous Kerry jigsaw. As a unit, the side was virtually unbeatable. In that 1978 championship season Kerry totted up an impressive 11 goals and 36 points in their last three games; an unbelievable average of 23 points per game.

In 1979 Kerry trounced Clare in the first round of the Munster championship, in a game that subsequently has been referred to as the 'Milltown Malbay massacre'. This was because the final scoreline read: Kerry 9–21, Clare 1–9. Clare were unlucky in that many of the Kerry players were fighting for their places and were anxious to consolidate their selection for the Munster final, in which they narrowly beat Cork. Ulster champions Monaghan were also unfortunate to come up against a side at their imperious best in the All-Ireland semi-final. They, too, suffered a heavy defeat.

For the second year in a row, Dublin were on the receiving end of a rampant Kerry side in the final. When captain Tim Kennelly was presented with the Sam Maguire Cup, Dublin had been beaten by eleven points. John O'Keeffe had the misfortune of suffering concussion in the first half when he hit his head on the ground. At first, he decided to stay on but by the 46th minute he had to retire. Nevertheless, he recovered quickly and was now the proud holder of his fifth All-Ireland medal.

Of all the All-Irelands during that golden Kerry era, the final of 1980 against Roscommon has to be termed as their luckiest. Led by the magnificent Dermot Earley, Roscommon grabbed control from the beginning. Only a tendency to waste good scoring opportunities, in addition to the forward line inexplicably playing too close to each other, prevented the westerners from gaining their first All-Ireland win since the days of Knockcroghery's Jimmy Murray in 1943 and 1944. Ten minutes from the end, when Roscommon's Aidan Dooley burst through the Kerry defence and shot towards an empty goal, a historic victory seemed almost inevitable. As the ball headed in the direction of the goal, Páidí Ó Sé sprang out of nowhere to put the ball over the end line for a 45-metre kick. In that instant, Roscommon's chance was gone and Páidí had assumed the mantle of immortality amongst Kerry followers, as the Kingdom carved out a narrow three-point victory.

After winning another decider when they defeated Offaly by seven points in the 1981 final, the quest for an historic five-in-a-row began in earnest. This magnificent side had now equalled the four-in-a-row record established by Wexford (1915–1918) and Kerry (1929–1932). John O'Keeffe was now perfectly positioned to win a then record-breaking eighth All-Ireland senior medal. In his and Kerry's way stood Offaly, who had made terrific strides in the previous four years, under the astute managership of Longford-born Eugene McGee. Both counties prepared diligently and, true to form, both reached the All-Ireland final again. In the process, Offaly had inflicted the biggest-ever defeat on Dublin in a Leinster final, before somewhat luckily overcoming Galway in the All-Ireland semi-final. Kerry, on the other hand, had defeated Cork in a replayed Munster final and had defeated Armagh, quite comfortably, at the penultimate stage. The stage was now perfectly set for a possible epoch-making success for the Kingdom. All the media hype centred on this. The mental pressure on the Kerry team and their manager was immense.

This suited Offaly perfectly. Having analysed the 1981 final and the Man of the Match performance by Kerry's centre half-back Tim Kennelly, Eugene McGee decided on his match-winning strategy. To ensure that Kennelly would not repeat his 1981 dominance, he decided to play team captain Richie Connor at centre half-forward. This would serve two purposes. Firstly, the enormous strength of Connor would curtail Kennelly, and secondly, his excellent distribution qualities would enable his fellow forwards to open up the Kerry defence.

So, to the game itself. Offaly's midfielders, Padraig Dunne and Tomas O'Connor, controlled the midfield exchanges in the first half. Their half-back line of Pat Fitzgerald, Seán Lowry and Liam Currams kept moving the ball forward at every opportunity. Despite this advantage, the midlanders only led at half-time by 0–10 to 0–9. In the second half, though not playing particularly well, the Kingdom had edged ahead by the minimum of margins when they were awarded a penalty. Martin Furlong, Offaly's 36-year-old netminder, who had won All-Irelands with the Faithful County in 1971 and 1972, brilliantly saved Mikey Sheehy's well-placed shot. This inspired Offaly, and when Matt Connor pointed two frees in the last five minutes, Kerry were holding on to a precarious two-point lead. Ten minutes before the final whistle, Eugene McGee had switched Richie Connor and Gerry Carroll to midfield, to lessen Jack O'Shea's considerable dominance in that sector. This was the move that was to swing the game decidedly in Offaly's favour in those last pulsating minutes.

With two minutes remaining came one of the most dramatic scores ever seen in an All-Ireland football final. Richie Connor and full-back Liam O'Connor exchanged passes before the latter floated a long, high kick into the left corner-forward position. Kerry's Tommy Doyle leapt for the ball. Offaly substitute Séamus Darby, who was only a short while on the field, jumped behind Doyle and appeared to nudge the Kerry man in the back. He grabbed the ball, turned swiftly and crashed a magnificent shot past the despairing cluthches of goalkeeper Charlie Nelligan into the corner of the net. Whatever doubts there may have been about the goal's legality, its execution was worthy of any great occasion. Shortly afterwards, the full-time whistle was blown. Offaly were the new All-Ireland champions, 1–15 to 0–17. Kerry's record-breaking dreams were shattered.

For John O'Keeffe thirteen wonderful years in Croke Park were at an end. He had played in his tenth All-Ireland (including the 1972 replay) and had accumulated an extraordinary total of seven gold medals. 'Of all the dressing rooms I have been in during my career, I never experienced anything like the desolation and dejection felt by all of us after that 1982 final. We tended to be too defensive in the last quarter and when Darby's goal went in, it was as if our whole world collapsed. However, I have to give credit to Offaly. They had been building up towards this for four years and deserved their moment of triumph. It was good that such a great player as Matt Connor won his All-Ireland medal. Eugene McGee also deserves great praise for his tactical know-how. From a personal perspective we could not be too greedy about it. I was extremely fortunate to play with so many fabulous players. Luckily, most of us stayed healthy and none of us suffered too many serious injuries. That is sport. Destiny had decided that Offaly's hour had come and that we would not achieve the five-in-a-row.'

From 1979 onwards, arthritis had developed in John's hip. He played for a further two years after 1982. His last competitive game was in the 1984 Munster championship semi-final. At this stage, he was not even able to train, and consequently was on the sub's bench for the 1984 Munster final. Having consulted his orthopaedic surgeon, he was informed that he must retire, otherwise he was in danger of causing serious permanent damage to himself. On the morning after the Munster final, John relayed this sad news to team manager Mick O'Dwyer. The long and illustrious career of one of the great servants of Kerry football was at an end. Two years later, when regular club full-back Mike Crowley got injured, John played three more games. He helped Austin Stack's in both the semi-final and final of the county championship, which they won. His last appearance was in Austin Stack's unsuccessful game against St Finbarr's of Cork in the Munster club championship.

At club level, John O'Keeffe had the honour of winning All-Ireland club championships both with UCD in 1974 and Austin Stack's in 1977. UCD beat St Vincent's in a tense struggle and eventually won the Dublin county final. It then took a replay to dispose of Wicklow champions Carnew Emmets before easily overcoming Raheens of Kildare to reach the Leinster final against Cooley Kickhams of Louth. After a close game, they emerged victorious by two points and then overwhelmed Knockmore of Mayo in the All-Ireland semi-final. Armagh champions Clan na Gael of Lurgan provided the opposition in the final. In that game, which ended in a draw, the Tralee stalwart was injured, forcing him to retire. However, Stack's performed magnificently in the replay and they beat the Ulstermen by seven points. 'We had a lot of brilliant players on that team, like Garret O'Reilly, Eamonn O'Donoghue, Paddy Kerr, Ollie Leddy, Benny Gaughran, Enda Condron, Kevin Kilmurray, Jackie Walsh and J.P. Kean. It was a great experience travelling around to many venues with so many wonderful players from different counties. Our UCD manager, Eugene McGee, had a major influence on me as a footballer. He was meticulous in his preparation, continually preached the importance of the team ethic and was able to get the best out of his players. He also ensured that no one ever got too big for his boots! With Eugene, the team was always, and correctly so, bigger than any individual.'

Austin Stack's achievement really meant more to John because it was achieved with all the players he knew from boyhood and with whom he grew up. Under trainer Jo Jo Barrett, they defeated Kenmare in the Kerry final. After beating Croom of Limerick, they met St Finbarr's of Cork in the Munster final. The Cork side were the much superior team throughout but were only leading by a point as injury time approached. Dramatically, the Stacks were awarded a penalty. Free-taker Mikey Sheehy did not go for the soft option and tap the ball over the bar for an equaliser. Instead, he banged the ball into the roof of the net, to give the Stacks a shock victory. In the All-Ireland quarter-final they beat Kingdom of London before meeting Portlaoise in O'Moore Park in the All-Ireland semi-final. In front of 10,000 spectators, a marvellous game of fast, exciting football took place. Up to the last ten minutes the outcome was in doubt. However, in those final moments the Stacks, powered by their county stars Ger Power, Ger O'Keeffe, Denis Long (Cork), Mikey Sheehy and captain John O'Keeffe, pulled away to win by five points. In the final they met Ulster champions Ballerin of Derry — home of the late, great Seán O'Connell. Again, it was 'nip and tuck' until the final ten minutes when the Tralee side dug deeper to record a momentous 1–13 to 2–7 victory.

Since his retirement as a player, John has given much back to the game as a coach and manager. Having trained as a primary teacher in St Patrick's Training College in Drumcondra, he then qualified at UCD as a secondary school teacher. He also did a post-graduate course in Loughborough PE College in England. His consequent PE expertise was put to excellent extra-curricular use when he trained both the Limerick and Clare county teams, each for four years. This was quickly followed by a similar stint under Páidí Ó Sé when the Ventry man was Kerry county senior football boss. In addition, he served six years with the International Rules team. Four of those were as physical trainer under managers Colm O'Rourke and Brian McEniff.

In the latter two years, John himself took over the managerial reins. 'I spent many happy days with all of these teams. I enjoyed helping Clare and Limerick, who were perceived as 'weaker' counties. The only negative aspect of my time with them was the huge amount of travelling involved. Helping Kerry to win an All-Ireland in 2000 meant a lot to me. Páidí Ó Sé, the rest of the management team and the players all helped to make it fulfilling. Having given each of those three counties four years was adequate for me. I will never say "never" to another county appointment, but really all I am interested in at present is to continue to look after my school team here in Tralee.

'The whole International Rules experience is a wonderful opportunity for players to represent their country, especially skilful individuals like Eamonn O'Hara, John Quane and Declan Browne, who might not otherwise get an opportunity to display their vast skills. The game has been cleaned up and during my six years I only saw one serious incident, when Declan Browne was "taken out of it" off the ball in a warm-up game. I felt very sorry that he was subjected to such a cynical tackle. This prevented him from taking any further part in the series that he was looking forward to so much. All of us were very impressed with the excellent coaching skills of Mickey Moran, who got the players doing the simple things well,' John concluded.

When John selected his representative sides he made the following choices. He did not consider any Kerry player for his Irish team.

IRELAND (1970–1984)

Billy Morgan
(Cork)

Mick Carthy   Kevin Kehilly   Robbie Kelleher
(Wexford)   (Cork)   (Dublin)

Nicholas Clavin   Kevin Moran   Tommy Drumm
(Offaly)   (Dublin)   (Dublin)

Brian Mullins   Dermot Earley
(Dublin)   (Roscommon)

Peter McGinnity   Declan Barron   Matt Connor
(Fermanagh)   (Cork)   (Offaly)

Tony McManus   Jimmy Keaveney   Frank McGuigan
(Roscommon)   (Dublin)   (Tyrone)

IRELAND'S INTERNATIONAL RULES SELECTION (1998–2004)

Cormac Sullivan
(Meath)

Graham Canty   Darren Fay   Seán M. Lockhart
(Cork)   (Meath)   (Derry)

Tadhg Kennelly   Séamus Moynihan   Anthony Lynch
(Kerry)   (Kerry)   (Cork)

John McDermott   Anthony Tohill
(Meath)   (Derry)

Trevor Giles	Ja Fallon	Michael Donnellan
(Meath)	(Galway)	(Galway)
Stephen McDonnell	Pádraic Joyce	Graham Geraghty
(Armagh)	(Galway)	(Meath)

John O'Keeffe was one of the real stylists of Gaelic football, whose versatility earned him All Star awards both as a midfielder and full-back. When playing centre-field, his motto always was, 'I'll hold the middle and my partner will move forward to attack, should the opportunity present itself.' Former Kerry county chairman Ger McKenna is credited with the decision to switch the classy midfielder to the full-back berth. Initially, the move was born out of necessity. In an U-21 game, Cork's outstanding full-forward Declan Barron was causing chaos in Kerry's defence. The athletic Austin Stack's man immediately remedied that crisis and a new full-back was born. As Gaelic football developed in the mid-1970s, it became increasingly obvious that the role of the traditional high-catching, but static, full-back was changing. John O'Keeffe possessed all the conventional attributes associated with the position. More importantly, however, he was naturally endowed with fantastic pace, exceptional vision and natural perception. Since his halcyon playing days, no one has worn a No. 3 jersey with such success and distinction.

During a Kerry training session in Killarney in the early 1970s the legendary Mick O'Connell, as was his wont, rose majestically to pluck the ball from the clouds. His opponent did likewise, only to rise fractionally higher to catch the ball tightly in his grasp. Mick O'Connell turned to the young pretender and, smilingly, said: 'John, I can retire now!' One was in the autumn of his career, the other in the springtime of his. The master had given John O'Keeffe his imprimatur. That, in itself, was a fantastic tribute to a fabulous footballer.

JOHN O'KEEFFE – FACT FILE

Native Place:	Tralee, Co. Kerry
Date of Birth:	April 15, 1951
Club(s):	Austin Stack's, Tralee University College Dublin
Colleges' Honours:	Hogan Cup with St Brendan's Killarney (Captain) – 1969

Third Level:	Sigerson Cup with UCD (3) – 1973, 1974, 1975
Club Honours:	(a) Austin Stack's – Kerry Senior Football Championship (4) Munster Senior Football Championship (1) All-Ireland Senior Football Championship (1) – 1977 (b) UCD Dublin Senior Football Championship (2) Leinster Senior Football Championship (1) – 1973 All-Ireland Senior Football Championship (1) – 1974
County Honours:	All-Ireland Senior Football Championship (7) – 1969, 1970, 1975, 1978, 1979, 1980, 1981 Munster Senior Football Championship (11) – 1970, 1972, 1975, 1976, 1977, 1978, 1979, 1980, 1981, 1982, 1984 National Football League (6) – 1971, 1972, 1973, 1974, 1977, 1982 U-21 Munster Football Championship (1) – 1972
Other Playing Honours:	(a) Railway Cup with Munster (6) – 1972, 1975, 1977, 1978, 1981, 1982 (b) Railway Cup with Combined Universities (1) – 1973 (c) U-19 All-Ireland Basketball winner with Kerry
Managerial/Coaching Honours:	(1) All-Ireland Senior Football Championship (Kerry) (1) – 2000 (2) Manager of Limerick (3) Manager of Clare (4) Railway Cup Manager (5) International Rules Selector/Physical fitness (1998–2002). Manager (2003 – 2004). (6) Various school teams (2nd level).
Awards:	All Stars (5) – 1973, 1975, 1976, 1978, 1979 Texaco Footballer of the Year – 1975
Occupation:	PE/History teacher
Family:	Married to Liz (née Keane), Tralee
Children:	Sinéad

SIX

Johnny Dooley–Offaly

THE JEWEL IN THE FAITHFUL CROWN

A Rover I will be,
A Rover I will stay,
And to the Faithful County,
I will return some day.

Frank Sweeney

When one researches the reasons for any aspiring young sportsman to take up Gaelic games, three specific factors inevitably come to the fore. The persuasive influence of family and friends, the considerable impact of the local GAA club and the consistent quality performances of the county team are normally the more pertinent components. It was against such a background that Offaly's Johnny Dooley first developed his interest in hurling. His maternal grandfather, Jim Carroll, played in an All-Ireland junior hurling final with the Faithful County in 1915. Jim's brother Joe played on the successful 1923 and 1929 All-Ireland junior sides. In addition, the Carroll brothers won five junior county championships with Coolderry. The next generation of Carrolls — Johnny's uncles — duly won a similar amount of county titles. Johnny's father, who played hurling for Clareen, was an avid follower of the small ball game, supporting his native club through thick and thin. At county level, he continually reminded his five sons — Séamus, Kieran, Billy, Joe and Johnny — of the wonderful exploits of Offaly Railway Cup stars such as Paddy Molloy and Barney Moylan. Incidentally, his father's brother, Tom Dooley, had also been a member of that 1929 Offaly team.

Nothing boosted Johnny's hurling development as much as the meteoric rise in the fortunes of Offaly county hurling in the 1980s. Offaly contested all ten provincial senior hurling titles in that decade, winning six. More importantly, it was the fantastic achievement of winning two senior All-Irelands, in 1981 and 1985, that put Offaly on a par with the traditional strongholds of the ancient game: counties such as Cork, Tipperary, Kilkenny, Wexford and Galway now had a new rival. Coming from such a small hurling base, Offaly must be the success story of modern times in Gaelic games. Added to the fact that the footballers' catchment area in the county is also relatively small, one must conclude that when great GAA counties are discussed, Offaly should be placed at the top of the tree. Offaly, who defeated Galway in both those 1980s triumphs, became a byword for fast, skilful ground hurling.

Johnny Dooley was nine years old when he witnessed Offaly's triumphant return to Birr on the Monday night after that 1981 success. Listening to centre half-back Pat Delaney leading the huge crowd in an emotional rendering of 'The Offaly Rover' made the youngster determined to follow his dream of playing in Croke Park on All-Ireland final day. He vividly recalls some of the stars of those historic years. Wonderful defenders Pat Fleury, Ger Coughlan, Eugene Coughlan, Aidan Fogarty, Pat Delaney and Liam Currams come readily to mind. The courageous exploits of long-serving goalkeeper Damien Martin and magnificent midfielder Joachim Kelly are firmly imprinted on his mind. Pat Carroll, Johnny Flaherty, Pat Cleary and Mark Corrigan were brilliant, incisive forwards. The 1981 captain, Padraig Horan, was not only a great hurler in Johnny's eyes, but also an excellent coach, along with Frank Bergin, who served Birr Community School so well in hurling terms. When Johnny went there as a student, he really entered an oasis of hurling beauty where the game was intricately linked with the culture of the area. It was a Cork man, Brother Denis, many years before, who had nurtured and cultured such a love of hurling in the area.

Regarding Johnny's own secondary school hurling career, it was, unfortunately, a case of always the bridesmaid, never the bride. In all, he played in eight Leinster Colleges finals, losing each of them. 'The nearest we came to winning was in my last year, when I was captain. We drew the first day against St Kieran's of Kilkenny, who had a brilliant team that included D.J. Carey and Pat O'Neill. We had Brian Whelehan, Kevin Kinahan and Adrian Cahill in our team, but we lost the replay and they went on to win the Croke Cup.'

By that stage, the blossoming talent that was Johnny Dooley had already attracted the attention of the Offaly minor selectors. He won an All-Ireland minor hurling medal in 1987. 'I was only 15 years old when I played at right half-back on an Offaly side that had a two-point win over Tipperary in the final. That was the first occasion that I had the pleasure of seeing at first hand the exciting skills of John

Leahy, in the Premier County's half-forward line. I was very nervous going into the game but everything went okay. In 1989 I won another All-Ireland minor title when we beat Clare, rather comfortably. Our captain, Brian Whelehan, had a marvellous game that day. It took us two games before we defeated Kilkenny in that year's provincial decider. In the final, David Fitzgerald was the Clare goalkeeper and the great Jamesie O'Connor came on as a sub for the Banner County.' In that drawn Leinster final, Johnny, playing at right half-forward, had one of his best ever games in an Offaly jersey. Out of their total score of 0–14, he scored 0–10, five points from play and five frees.

Johnny's minor and club exploits had drawn the attention of the Offaly senior selectors. The previous year, 1988, Johnny's club, Seir Kieran of Clareen, had won the Offaly senior title for the first time when they defeated the famed St Rynagh's in the final. Everything went well for Johnny that day, as he scored 0–4 from play. 'It was a fantastic achievement for a parish of only 300 people. I was a 16-year-old wing-forward at the time. In 1990, I made my senior debut against Laois, in Tullamore, in the National League. I was young and carefree and decided to go to Boston to work that summer. When I came back, I decided to take my hurling more seriously. So, from the autumn of 1990, when we commenced the league until I retired twelve years later, I applied myself fully to the cause of Offaly hurling.'

During that 1990/91 league campaign, Johnny established himself as a permanent member of the team, as the midlanders literally cruised to a National League title. They went through the whole campaign undefeated, overcoming Tipperary in the semi-final before accounting for Wexford in the final. Johnny Dooley, having won his first senior national title, was now on top of the world. Offaly had, at that time, an excellent blend of good, experienced championship hurlers plus exciting budding stars like Brian Whelehan and Dooley himself. A promising championship run appeared to be in the offing. Those hopes were unexpectedly dashed when a spirited Dublin team knocked them out of that year's Leinster championship in the first round, by a point. When Dublin, led by two great hurlers in M.J. Ryan and Brian McMahon, were only narrowly defeated in that year's Leinster final against Kilkenny, Offaly were happy enough. The defeat, in their considered view, was just part of a national learning curve. In the 1992 and 1993 championships, Offaly were unfortunate to be pitted against fabulous sides that went on to win back-to-back All-Irelands.

'That whole period between 1989 and 1993 was rather frustrating for me. Even though I won a league medal and an All-Ireland minor title, Kilkenny always seemed to have the proverbial Indian sign over us, at senior level. The 1993 first round defeat to Kilkenny was especially galling. We only lost by two points after playing really well. We were also very unhappy about that result because we felt D.J. Carey had taken far too many steps before being awarded a controversial penalty that they scored. During that period I also played in four U-21 All-Ireland finals, including a replay. In the 1992 drawn encounter with Wexford, we scored 0–16, yet conceded four goals. Luck certainly was not with us that day.'

However, all that was to change in 1994. When Offaly were drawn against Kilkenny in the Leinster championship semi-final, their manager, Eamon Cregan, did not require any extra motivational incentives. The Limerickman, who had starred in his native county's All-Ireland success in 1973, had been appointed Offaly manager in January 1993. Two incidents during that year's defeat to Kilkenny irked him considerably. The controversial nature of Kilkenny's winning goal and the harsh sending off of Offaly's Rory Mannion would be used as a catalyst to spur his side to victory. Bringing in Gerry O'Donovan as trainer to the side while he concentrated on skills and tactical awareness had proved to be a master-stroke both in 1993 and 1994. Offaly and Cregan were now ready for the fray as they diligently approached their moment of destiny in that 1994 provincial semi-final. The fact that Kilkenny were going for three All-Irelands in a row and four successive Leinster titles only added spice to the confrontation.

Helped by a stiff breeze in the first half, Offaly surged ahead to lead by seven points at half-time. In the second half, with Brian Whelehan and Kevin Kinahan superb in defence and Johnny Dooley (aided and abetted by his brothers Joe and Billy) dictating matters throughout the rest of the team, Offaly won by four points. In the Leinster final against Wexford, Offaly showed tremendous grit as well as the usual combination of pace and skill, and defeated Wexford by 1–18 to 0–14. Again, Kinahan starred with excellent support coming from Hubert Rigney, Johnny Pilkington, Daithi Regan and Billy Dooley. Debutante championship goalkeeper David Hughes made a marvellous contribution with two high-class saves. The hotly tipped Slaneysiders had succumbed to a marvellous all-round team performance from the midlanders.

In the All Ireland semi-final, Offaly convincingly defeated Galway in a superlative display of tight marking and the quick release of the ball. It was a much more emphatic victory than the six-point winning margin would suggest. Rigney, John Troy, Whelehan, Kevin Martin and Billy Dooley were outstanding in what was essentially a great team performance. Johnny Dooley, with seven super scores, had now amassed the impressive total of 22 points in that year's championship.

Now, what Offaly manager Eamon Cregan had hoped would never

come to pass was a living reality. The Offaly supremo would be managing the Faithful County against his beloved native county of Limerick in an All-Ireland senior hurling final. The Limerick legend stated when I interviewed him for my previous book, *The Road to Croke Park*, in 1999: 'I had to separate my personal affiliation from my role of planning for an Offaly success. I had marvellous experienced selectors who gave me great advice. Pat McLoughney, Andy Gallagher, Mick Spain and Paudge Mulhaire helped me immensely as we plotted for an Offaly win.'

In the final itself, Limerick totally dominated for the vast portion of the game. Hurling superbly, no one, not even Offaly supporters, would have begrudged them the McCarthy Cup. As the game moved into its last six minutes Limerick were leading, justifiably, by five points. The Treatymen, it would appear, were heading for their first All-Ireland since 1973 (when, ironically, Cregan himself was one of their star performers). Offaly, on the other hand, had not played anywhere near their true potential. It seemed that, once again, imminent defeat was staring them in the face. Then, out of nowhere, came the defining moment of the 1994 All-Ireland senior hurling final. Billy Dooley was fouled about 25 yards from the Limerick goal.

Johnny recalls his thoughts at this point: 'I looked over at the sideline and caught a glimpse of someone telling me to go for a point. The old adage "take your points and the goals will follow" crossed my mind. We were all really disgusted about how poorly we had performed in the final. What made our display so pathetic was the fact that we had won our previous three games so convincingly. We had been chasing the whole game, which now seemed to be fizzling out to its inevitable conclusion — another miserable day in the annals of Offaly hurling. So, I took a chance and went for the goal. It would be easy to say now that I saw a gap and went for it but I did not. The shot managed to squeeze between two defenders and go into the net. I was very relieved, because if it had been saved I would have looked a proper fool.'

With only two points between the sides now, Johnny's goal had kick-started one of the most amazing comebacks in any sport within such a short time-frame. Shortly afterwards, Offaly substitute Pat O'Connor pulled on a ground ball and scored a goal from close range. Unbelievably, Offaly were now a point up and there were still three minutes to go. Playing like men possessed, the pent-up emotions and inhibitions of the previous hour's display were suddenly released. What we now witnessed was a team doing justice to itself, with driving, sweeping moves interspersed with truly magnificent scores from all angles. Offaly, in those dying moments, scored a further five points (three of them by the excellent Billy Dooley) to record a sensational 3–16 to 2–13 victory. Croke Park had just seen one of the most amazing comebacks in the history of hurling.

To complete a wonderful day for the Dooley household, Johnny and his two brothers had scored 2–12 between them. 'It really was a fantastic achievement to be five points down, with six minutes to go and end up winning by six. My favourite memory of that day is meeting my father after the game in the Davenport Hotel. He was grinning from ear to ear and as proud as punch that his three sons had won All-Ireland medals on the same team. The whole experience made me think back to our childhood days when my father was always encouraging us to play and talk hurling. He brought us everywhere to games. When we were young fellows we always had hurls in our hands, pucking stones over walls. Bringing in the cows from school we brought our hurls with us. Even when we went to foot or clamp turf in the bog, the hurleys were constantly by our sides. Dad got great mileage out of that victory.'

The following year, 1995, Offaly again confirmed their superiority over Kilkenny when they defeated the Cats by 11 points in the Leinster final. This display was generally acknowledged as one of the best ever performances by an Offaly side. In the All-Ireland semi-final, however, they gave a very inept performance before disposing of a Down side by eleven points — the same number of minor flags that the ever-accurate Johnny Dooley raised that day.

The All-Ireland final was to see, for the second successive year, another novel pairing. On this occasion Offaly faced Clare, who were now, for the first time since Kilkenny beat them in 1932, in an All-Ireland senior hurling final. Offaly controlled much of the game and appeared set for victory as the game entered its closing stages. Then the decisive moment of the game occurred when Clare were awarded a free, deep inside their own half. Their inspiring captain, Anthony Daly, struck the sliotar hard and sent it high into the Offaly goalmouth. The ball rebounded off the upright. Eamonn Taafe, who had come on as a substitute a short time before, anticipated the deflected ball and sent it crashing to the net. Clare, the no-hopers, were dramatically leading the odds-on favourites by a point. Just before the referee blew the full-time whistle, the imperious Daly sent the ball all the way over the bar from a 65. Victory had been snatched from a gallant Offaly side.

Johnny summarises his feelings about that day: 'That was a great disappointment to us because we had dominated the game for so long. We missed at least five relatively easy scoring chances to put Clare out of sight. Afterwards, and especially when they won the All-Ireland again in 1997, Clare proved themselves to be a fantastic hurling side. In hindsight, that softens, somewhat, the pain of that unexpected defeat.'

Offaly reached their third consecutive Leinster final in 1996 but were overwhelmed by a majestic display by Wexford. In one of the best games ever witnessed in the Leinster championship, the men from the Model County put in a sparkling performance with their half-forward line scoring an incredible 0–15 from play. Lucky to beat Laois in the next year's Leinster quarter-final, the midlanders were very unfortunate to lose in the semi-final against the then current All-Ireland champions, Wexford. Only a point-blank save by goalkeeper Damien Fitzhenry, from Billy Dooley, in the closing stages of that encounter prevented the Offaly men from securing a deserved draw.

When the 1998 campaign opened on May 24, Offaly easily accounted for Meath — a game Johnny missed through injury. Three weeks later, they were decidedly lucky to overcome Wexford in the provincial semi-final, by one point. Still, a win was a win and the manager, Michael 'Babs' Keating, along with his co-selectors, relished the clash with old rivals Kilkenny in the Leinster final. Nevertheless, as the final approached, it became clear that two key members of the Offaly defence, captain Hubert Rigney and full-back Kevin Kinahan, would be missing through injury. For whatever reason, Offaly gave a very lacklustre display before succumbing to a five-point defeat to the Noresiders. Certainly, Offaly would have performed better if their two central defenders had been playing. Then controversy arose amongst players and supporters alike when 'Babs' Keating referred to Offaly's performance as akin to playing 'like sheep in a heap'. Though Keating said this was only a flippant comment, he decided to resign as manager. Galway man Michael Bond replaced him.

Immediately, the Offaly players doubled their efforts to restore their pride and commitment to the Offaly jersey after that rather incompetent exhibition in the Leinster final. Thanks to the new back-door system, which allowed defeated provincial finalists into the All-Ireland quarter-finals, they soon had an ideal opportunity to prove themselves. Bond concentrated his efforts to mould a winning team by emphasising the importance of the players' undoubted skills, while at the same time reinforcing the concept of fast ground hurling. Subsequently, they defeated Antrim in the quarter-final, thus qualifying to meet All-Ireland champions Clare in the All-Ireland semi-final. After a tightly fought contest, that game ended all square.

The replay was a game of high drama, with Offaly playing poorly for most of the match. Midway through the second half, Offaly were ten points in arrears. Suddenly, realising that for most of them this might be their last chance to again savour All-Ireland glory, the whole team collectively upped their performance. With two minutes to go, Offaly had significantly reduced the arrears to three points. With Clare attacking, the referee, Jimmy Cooney of Galway, suddenly blew the full-time whistle. Because of a time-keeping error, Jimmy had prematurely called a halt to proceedings. Chaos reigned before a second replay was ordered by the GAA.

The outcome of this game hung in the balance right through and never more so than in the final ten minutes. With Offaly leading by six points, the Banner men fought valiantly to reduce the deficit. Only brilliant goalkeeping by Offaly netminder Stephen Byrne prevented Clare from obtaining an equalising goal. In the end, the Faithful County emerged deserving winners, 0–16 to 0–13. The contest saw hurling at its majestic best, with Johnny Dooley's elder brother, Joe, notching five wonderful points from all angles and distances. Now the team that had been written off by so many after that disappointing Leinster final were in an All-Ireland final. Ironically, thanks to the vagaries imposed by the back-door system, they were fated once again to meet their Leinster conquerors — the Cats of Kilkenny.

That 1998 All-Ireland senior hurling final was to showcase all that is brilliant in the world's fastest field game. Tenacious tackling and impeccable striking produced drama and tension that permeated the whole stadium from start to finish. A spell-binding save by Byrne and a timely interception by Brian Whelehan stopped Kilkenny from scoring two early goals, as the Noresiders strove to assert their authority. The Offaly selectors then made two vital switches. The flu-stricken Brian Whelehan was moved from his customary defensive position to the forward line, and Michael Duignan, who had started at wing-forward, was switched to Brian's position. Both changes worked a treat. Duignan's presence considerably tightened up Offaly's whole defensive formation, and the versatile Whelehan's pure class shone like the proverbial beacon, especially in the second half. In a Man of the Match performance, the Birr publican notched 1–6. With Hubert Rigney and Kevin Kinahan dictating the central defensive lines, aided by the impressive wing-back Kevin Martin, Offaly severely curtailed the Kilkenny forward line. At midfield the dominant Johnny Pilkington continually supplied his enterprising forward line with quality ball, which they duly converted into match-winning scores. At the final whistle, the midlanders had triumphed, impressively, on a 2–16 to 1–13 scoreline. Thanks to their quiet, thoroughly efficient manager from Galway, Michael Bond, the Offaly team had 'bonded' perfectly to record an historic team victory. The Dooley household celebrated in joyful ecstasy. Johnny and Billy had now secured their second All-Ireland senior medal, whereas big brother Joe had obtained his third (he had won his first in 1985).

Between 1998 and 2002, Johnny Dooley played twelve more games of championship hurling. In 1999, despite a brave fighting performance, eventual All-Ireland champions Cork beat Offaly at the penultimate stage. It was a thoroughly exciting and evenly contested encounter for sixty minutes. Then Cork, inspired by a truly wonderful centre-half display by Brian Corcoran, upped the tempo in the last seven minutes to emerge victorious by three points. The following year was to see Johnny making his farewell appearance in an All-Ireland final, against Kilkenny. 'It was a great moment for me as I was captain. It was a tremendous honour for me to introduce my teammates to the President. Sadly, the game itself ran away from us and we were heavily defeated. We knew in our hearts that the end had come. Too many of us had lost our competitive edge.'

For the following two years Johnny Dooley struggled to reach the required fitness for top-class hurling. The wear and tear of recurring knee problems hastened a premature ending to a great hurling career. Despite many surgical procedures and rehabilitation programmes, he now knew that his hurling career was over. His last appearance in an Offaly jersey was when he made a cameo appearance, as a substitute, in the 2002 All-Ireland quarter-final against Tipperary. Older brother Joe had made his first championship appearance in 1984. It was very difficult for Offaly supporters to grasp the fact that for the first time in eighteen years, the surname Dooley would not appear on an Offaly team sheet.

When I met Johnny at his home in Tullamore, he had just returned from having a coaching session with the Offaly minor team, of which he is manager. Instead of looking back, he tended to look forward, and he aired his views on the following issues.

1. 'I played under eight different managers. In fairness to all of them, I learned something positive during their respective management stints. It would be totally wrong to suggest that Offaly were a difficult county to manage. During my playing years the expectation of success was so immediate that there was a tendency to change managers very quickly. The most important factor in a manager's life is to be lucky enough to be in the right place at the right time. Everyone wants instant success. This is more so in a small county like Offaly, where they never have, on a continuous basis, a large group of quality players to select from.'

2. 'Offaly County Board always looked after their players very well. In terms of playing gear, training facilities, meals provided and travelling expenses I could have no complaints. Everything regarding the welfare of players was always first class.'

3. 'I love all sports. It is great to see so many Irish sports stars like
    Padraig Harrington, Roy Keane and Sonia O'Sullivan perform to
    such a high international level. In hurling, I admire so many
    wonderful exponents of the game from all the traditional
    strongholds. People like Brian Whelehan, Martin Hanamy, Willie
    O'Connor (Kilkenny), Peter Barry (Kilkenny), Seán McMahon
    (Clare), Brian Lohan (Clare), were all superb defenders who
    possessed great leadership qualities. Brian Corcoran's (Cork) ability
    to read a game would earn a special affection for me. Johnny Nevin
    (Carlow), Oliver Collins (Derry), Gerard McGrattan (Down),
    Terence McNaughton (Antrim) and Ciarán Barr (Antrim) from
    the so-called 'weaker' counties could hold their own in any
    company.'

4. 'Looking back on my career, my most fond memories are of
    friendships made, especially on the All Star trips. On one such
    trip to Boston, the All Stars were scheduled to play All-Ireland
    champions Cork. The All Stars were sponsored by Eircom and
    Cork were sponsored by O2. Willie O'Connor (Kilkenny) and
    Tony Browne (Waterford) were two brilliant characters who
    decided to take advantage of the competitiveness between the rival
    sponsors. Before the exhibition game, and in front of the Director
    of Eircom, Willie stood up and, unilaterally, declared that there
    would be free all-night restaurant and bar facilities if the All Stars
    should win the game. Spurred on by this comment, we won the
    game and the Director of Eircom implemented, totally, Willie's
    promise!'

Johnny made the following representative selections.

IRELAND (1985–2005)

Damien Fitzhenry
(Wexford)

Brian Corcoran   Brian Lohan   Martin Hanamy
(Cork)   (Clare)   (Offaly)

Brian Whelehan   Seánie McMahon   Liam Dunne
(Offaly)   (Clare)   (Wexford)

Ciarán Carey   Johnny Pilkington
(Limerick)   (Offaly)

Martin Storey   Gary Kirby   John Leahy
(Wexford)   (Limerick)   (Tipperary)

Pat Fox   D.J.Carey   Henry Shefflin
(Tipperary)   (Kilkenny)   (Kilkenny)

LEINSTER (1985–2005)

Jim Troy
(Offaly)

Willie O'Connor   Kevin Kinahan   Martin Hanamy
(Kilkenny)   (Offaly)   (Offaly)

Brian Whelehan   Liam Dunne   Michael Kavanagh
(Offaly)   (Wexford)   (Kilkenny)

        Adrian Fenlon   Niall Rigney
        (Wexford)   (Laois)

Martin Storey   John Troy   John Power
(Wexford)   (Offaly)   (Kilkenny)

Tom Dempsey   D.J. Carey   Henry Shefflin
(Wexford)   (Kilkenny)   (Kilkenny)

That great Land League personality of the nineteenth century, Michael Davitt, once aptly summed up the indelible impact that the game of hurling had on the national consciousness:

> '... old men have forgotten the miseries of the Famine and had their youth renewed by the sights and sounds that were invoked by the thrilling music of the camán ...'

When Johnny Dooley announced his retirement, in the early spring of 2003, his five-year-old son Jack could not understand why his father was not going hurling anymore. Two years later, it can certainly be stated that both are enthusiastically looking forward to a fourth generation of the Dooleys wielding that musical camán. No doubt it will be done with the purpose and poise of a true hurling craftsman.

JOHNNY DOOLEY – FACT FILE

Native Place:	Clareen, Co. Offaly
Date of Birth:	October 7, 1971
Club:	Seir Kieran, Clareen
Club Honours:	U-14 B Hurling Championship (1) – 1985
	U-16 B Hurling Championship (1) – 1987
	Minor B Hurling Championship (1) – 1988
	Senior Hurling Championship (4) – 1988, 1995, 1996, 1998
	Senior Hurling League (3) – 1988, 1995, 1996
County Honours:	All-Ireland Senior Hurling Championship (2) – 1994, 1998
	Leinster Senior Hurling Championship (2) – 1994, 1995
	Leinster U-21 Hurling Championship (3) – 1989, 1991, 1992
	All-Ireland Minor Hurling Championship (2) – 1987, 1989
	Leinster Minor Hurling Championship (2) – 1987, 1989
	Leinster U-16 Hurling Championship (1) – 1987
Other Playing Honours:	Represented Leinster ten times in the Railway Cup
	Represented Ireland in Shinty/Hurling Internationals twice in 1991, 2001
Awards:	All Star (3) – 1994, 1995, 2000
	Sports Star of the Month — September 1994
	Irish Independent/Jury's Hotel Sports Star of the Week (2)
	Sunday Game Man of the Match awards (5)
	Cavan Crystal Man of the Match awards (6)
	Selected as wing-forward on Offaly Team of the Millennium
Occupation:	Clerk of works with Health Service Executive
Family:	Married to Sinéad (née Boland) from Ferbane
Children:	Jack, Emma, Hannah

SEVEN

Peter Quinn–Fermanagh

A PRESIDENTIAL LEADER OF EXEMPLARY VISION

On the evening of Saturday, August 28, 2004, at Croke Park, Fermanagh's longest GAA fairytale finally ended. They had just lost the All-Ireland semi-final replay to Mayo by two points. From the time when, almost twelve weeks earlier, they had lost the first round of the Ulster championship to All-Ireland holders Tyrone, there had been a continuous, unprecedented mood of total euphoria throughout the Erne County. The reason for this was simple. Not one, but six times more, did the men in green and white play in the championship. Traditionally strong sides like Meath, Cork, Donegal and Armagh, who had all won All-Irelands over the previous 15 years, were swept aside in a constant wave of glorious jubilation as Fermanagh reached their first ever All-Ireland senior football semi-final. Sheer happiness and magnificent entertainment were brilliantly integrated, as the team rose to new heights of footballing excellence, dedicated commitment and unbridled enthusiasm.

Fermanagh now had new GAA icons, like future All Stars Barry Owens and Martin McGrath, to add to the men who kept the spirit of the founding fathers of the GAA alive and well. The county had produced many talented footballers, such as 1960s Railway Cup star P.T. Treacy, the late Mick Brewster and 1982 All Star Peter McGinnity. Apart from all these senior inter-county stars, Fermanagh also gave us one of the really great GAA Presidents in the person of Peter Quinn. Nationally recognised as a man of exceptional ability, it was my pleasure to meet him in Enniskillen. The articulate Teemore man covered a wide variety of topics in his usual unflappable manner.

1. *Where did your life begin?*
   'I was born in the parish of Knockninny in South Fermanagh. There were two main areas in the parish, Derrylin and Teemore. The latter was the more rural of the two, consisting of

approximately one-third in area of the total parish. When I was growing up, there would have been a total of one hundred families, seventy of whom would have been nationalist. My paternal grandfather died when my father was only ten months old. My father never went to school because, from the age of seven years, he helped my grandmother to run the family farm. Consequently, he possessed very few literary or numeracy skills, though he was very good at mental arithmetic. There is a popular assumption that because one cannot read or write, one is unintelligent. This was not the case with my father. Farming was his life and he did not see the need for education. My mother was different. Even though she only received primary school education, she was a very bright, self-educated person. Like so many mothers, she always wanted the best education for her children.'

2. *How did you become interested in the GAA?*
    'Teemore Shamrocks had a long-established tradition in Gaelic football, having won the first two Fermanagh county championships. In 1904 the first ever Inter-Provincial competitions were held, and Teemore had a representative on the Ulster team. In fact Teemore, in the early days, were so prominent that they were the first club in Ulster to win eight successive county championship titles. This record was not beaten until Crossmaglen Rangers recorded their ninth successive Armagh title in 2004. From the time Teemore won their fifteenth county championship in 1935 until the mid-1950s they experienced great difficulties in even fielding a team. I remember being told that the selectors could not pick a team until after second Mass on Sundays. This was because they never knew who had emigrated, either to America or England, since the previous Sunday. When I went to St Michael's College in Enniskillen for my secondary education, my GAA interest increased dramatically. I started to play with Derrylin U-16 team. At the same time, as a 14-year-old, I was drafted into the Teemore senior side. In 1959, I was playing at left half-forward when Teemore won the county junior championship. Having won my first medal, I was delighted with myself.'

3. *How did the rest of your club life pan out?*
    'Centre half-back was my favourite position, but because there was a dearth of forwards in Teemore, I played the most of my club football either in midfield or in the forward line. We had a very good team during my playing career and I was lucky to win four senior county championships and four senior football leagues. In

addition to our junior championship success in 1959, we also won the county minor championship in 1960 and two intermediate football leagues in 1962 and 1964. In 1969 I had the honour of captaining Teemore to a senior championship success for the first time in 34 years. Overall, I have very many happy memories as a club footballer.'

4. *Did you play much football at county level?*
    'When I made my county debut with the Fermanagh minors in 1961, I was excited at the prospect of a promising career. This increased further when I made my initial senior appearance in 1963, as well as representing the U-21 side for three successive years. However, I never played senior championship football for the Erne County. By the mid-1960s, I realised that I was just not good enough for county football. Though I was fairly fast, I was too light to withstand the rigours of football at that level. My brother, Seán, was an excellent footballer. He had a strong physique and was a very intelligent reader of the game. He played for Fermanagh for eight years and was captain for at least two of those years.'

5. *After St Michael's, you went to Queen's University, Belfast. Was that an enjoyable time?*
    'The first time I was in Belfast was the day that I enrolled at Queen's, to do Latin and Mathematics. I did not really like life as an undergraduate. During one Christmas holiday, halfway through my course, I was working with our club goalkeeper. We were up a mountain, putting in drains. I told him that I had been offered a job working in a social club in London where I had worked during the previous summer. When I informed him that I intended to leave Queen's to take up this English position, he stared at me in wonder and said, "Do you want to spend the rest of your life doing physical work like this?" His advice, plus that of family and friends, convinced me to finish my Primary Degree. I will always be grateful for that sound guidance.'

6. *When you finished your Primary Degree, what did you do?*
    'A few weeks before my final university examinations in 1964, a colleague of mine from Derry City suggested that I should do accountancy. In my total innocence I enquired, "What does an accountant do?" "He helps people to fill up tax forms," was the instant reply. Being from South Fermanagh, I realised there would not be many people there who would require such a service.

However, I decided on that lovely May afternoon that anything was better than studying, so I decided to visit the Institute of Chartered Accountants to see if there were any job opportunities. At that stage, accountancy was not an exclusive graduate profession, but eight firms did take graduates. Having picked up an application form, I was about to leave when the lady in the Institute inquired what religion I was. Being somewhat taken aback by this remark, I angrily retorted, "What the blazes does that matter?" "Oh, I thought you might be a Catholic. I am sorry to have upset you, but if you are a Catholic you should return that completed form very quickly." I then apologised for my tetchiness and thanked her. When I met my friend shortly afterwards on the bus home, I told him I was going to study accountancy. He looked at me in utter surprise. "An hour ago you knew nothing about accountancy. What changed your mind?" "Well if these so-and-so's want to confine the whole accountancy business to one side of the community it must be worth their while financially. I just want a chance to make some money, too!"'

7. *What happened next?*
    'Just two graduates, both of us GAA men, were accepted for the course. My fellow graduate, who played in goal for his club in the previous year's Antrim county final, and myself then experienced more assertive bigotry. When we went to our first accountancy lecture, the lecturer, who was a prominent supporter of a well-known sectarian soccer team, literally tore strips off us. Having been extremely courteous to the rest of the class, he started to inform us of the high failure rate of graduates. He also pointed out that graduates always had an inflated opinion of their ability. That sad introduction to the reality of sectarianism was the main motivating factor in choosing my specific career. I went home determined that I definitely would pass my examinations. Anyhow, I eventually qualified as a chartered accountant and that qualification became the basis of my working life.' (What Peter did not tell me was that he came near the top of his class in the subsequent examinations).

8. *You had an unusual Sigerson Cup campaign at Queen's?*
    'Well, I had a very short one anyway! In 1964 I was selected to play at midfield for Queen's in the Sigerson against Trinity College, Dublin. The game had been postponed for a week because of the death of the General Secretary of the GAA, Pádraig Ó Caoimh. I was looking forward to the game, especially as I was scheduled to

mark the great Kevin Coffey, who had won All-Ireland senior medals with Kerry in 1959 and 1962. On the Friday night before the game, I got involved in a card school. I lost a lot of money that I had not got, so I kept on playing to try and recoup my losses. By 5.30 a.m. I had won most of it back before I went to bed. I slept in and missed the bus for the game and Queen's lost. The manager of that team, former Antrim star Paddy O'Hara, was not pleased, to say the least. Even yet, he keeps reminding me that I let him and the team down. It was years later before I really saw the foolishness of playing cards for money, so I resorted to playing for fun.'

9. *Who initially encouraged you to become involved in GAA administration at county level?*

'In 1969 Irvinestown and Teemore played in the county final. With three minutes to go we were a point down and I scored the last two points to win the game. From a playing point of view it was the highlight of my career. We won 0–12 to 1–8 and I was fortunate to score six points. After the game, when I was presented with the Cup, I said a few words in Irish. At that time, I had forgotten that most of the previous winning captains in Fermanagh had not done this. Watching All-Ireland winning captains speaking in Irish made me assume this was the normal thing to do. Two officials of the County Board, Gerry Magee and Malachy Mahon, were duly impressed. Gerry canvassed for me, without my knowledge, at the following December's County Convention, for one of the two Ulster Council delegate positions. The late John Vesey was elected first and I defeated the late Mick Brewster, by one vote, for the other vacancy. Poor Gerry, who is also deceased, has a lot to answer for! His canvassing tactics were my first real insight into GAA politics.'

10. *At this point in time had you any ambition to further your administration career?*

'I never had any interest in any higher form of administration. Being club secretary was the height of my aspirations. Nevertheless, things developed from there. In 1980, I became Ulster Connacht treasurer, its Vice Chairman in 1983 and its President in 1986. Coming home from the 1984 GAA Congress, John Vesey suggested to me that I should run for President in 1987. I laughed it off as I did when Donegal County Board secretary, Bart Whelan, rang me up on the night before the 1987 Donegal County Convention. He told me to stop dithering, as Donegal were going to nominate me the following day. So I relented. The die was now cast and the canvassing began in earnest. John Dowling of Offaly was the clear favourite and rightly so. I was hoping to be second, in order for me to have a realistic chance in 1990. Shortly before the actual vote, the great Tipperary hurler, John Doyle, who also was an experienced Senator, came up to me. "How is the voting going? Will you be second?" "I hope so," I replied. "Well, have you been promised many votes?" I answered in the affirmative. "I have been in politics a long time and I have a tip for you. Take the number of votes you have been promised, divide by two, and subtract seven. That will be your total." And do you know, he was right. John Dowling won easily. Politically, I was learning.'

11. *Nineteen-ninety was a very special year in your life. What was it like to be on the threshold of being head of the greatest sporting organisation in Ireland?*
'There were seven candidates in the field. Jack Boothman of Wicklow was considered the main challenger to me. Former Cavan star footballer Jim McDonnell was the only other Ulster candidate. I thought Jack was going to win, so I wrote down a few lines to say, if that should happen. My wife, Mary, asked me was I not going to write something in case I won. I told her that would be a pointless exercise. However, the gods smiled on me and I was elected President. A future President, Seán McCague, once said it was the greatest honour that could be bestowed on a GAA person. In a spirit of humility, I would have to agree. My acceptance speech was really one from the heart. I outlined what the GAA meant to me and I mentioned the many challenges facing the Association, as I saw them.'

12. *What were the games' highlights of your Presidency?*
'A few years before I was elected President, I stated at an Ulster Convention that the standard of Ulster football was as good, if not better, than in any of the other provinces. All we needed was some county to make the "breakthrough". Afterwards, I often thought, did I really believe what I said? So, when Paddy O'Rourke lifted the Sam Maguire Cup for Down in 1991, that had to be the highlight.'

13. *When Donegal and Derry won their All-Irelands, you must have felt even better?*
'It was great to see these counties win the All-Ireland for the first time. I was not particularly impressed with Donegal's performances against Fermanagh and Mayo in that year's campaign. However,

they certainly performed very well in the Ulster final against Derry and in the All-Ireland against Dublin. Of the three Ulster counties, which won four All-Irelands between 1991 and 1994, Derry had the much better footballers. Their 1993 success should have been followed by at least one more All-Ireland. Unfortunately, inner turmoil amongst the County Board, team management and players contrived to ensure that this did not happen.'

14. *In your time watching Gaelic games, who were your favourite footballers?*

'Tom O'Hare, Enda Colleran and, to a lesser extent, Bosco McDermott were marvellous covering defenders who had allowed their full-backs to attack the ball from the front. Thus, Dan McCartan and Noel Tierney could always go out ahead, knowing that there was always a reliable corner-back to sweep up behind them. Nicholas Clavin and Kevin Moran brought an exciting, attacking dimension to half-back play. Kieran McGeeney and Henry Downey were also good at reading angles and turning defence into attack. Donie O'Sullivan was the best dead ball kicker I ever saw.

'In terms of pure class, Mick O'Connell was the most talented footballer I ever witnessed. He was a fantastic fetcher and a brilliant striker of the ball, either off the ground or out of the hand. However, his class was greater then his contribution over sixty minutes. In fact, Dermot Earley would probably have contributed more during the course of a game. Seán O'Neill, Matt Connor and Mike Sheehy were absolutely fabulous forwards. In terms of pure intelligence, physical strength and undoubted skill, O'Neill and Connor especially were in a class of their own.'

15. *Your hurling favourites?*

'I could go and watch D.J. Carey all day, every day. He is a real hurling artist. Brian Corcoran is a key versatile player who is equally at home in defence or attack. It was great to see him coming back in 2004, and making such an impact in Cork's All-Ireland win. Ger McCarthy and J.B. Murphy were fantastic at 'doubling' on the ball. Nicky English and Eddie Keher were also very impressive forwards. At present, the nearest player to D.J. is his fellow county man Henry Shefflin. He is an all-round hurler. He can tackle, win ball and score from any angle.'

16. *What was the best game that you ever saw?*

'Undoubtedly, the first round of the 1994 Ulster senior football championship between Down and Derry at Celtic Park. It showed all the tremendous attributes of Gaelic football played at its best. There was a very high level of skill. It was very hard but exceptionally clean. Most of all, it was contested at a phenomenal pace throughout. Nobody knew how it was going to end until the final whistle blew.'

17. *There was some controversy during your Presidency in what became known as the RDS Affair. What exactly were the circumstances of this?*
'The Dublin-based Clanna Gael Fontenoy's GAA club decided to stage a Gaelic football/soccer double-header at the RDS in Ballsbridge. The GAA match was to be between Dublin and Down and the soccer game was to involve Shamrock Rovers and Bohemians. The occasion was intended as a fundraising venture for the Fontenoy's, who were celebrating their centenary. After initially sanctioning the idea, the GAA's Management Committee and Central Council decided to withdraw permission for the game. This decision was based on the fact that conditions set out with regard to the fixture by the GAC had not been fulfilled. In other words, there was a lack of clarity about how the disbursement of monies from the RDS game was going to be allocated. Unfortunately, when these decisions were being taken, I was out of the country on pre-arranged business. Though I know the buck stops with the President, I think it was particularly unfair on the part of some journalists who have continued to apportion undue blame to me for something I was not directly involved in.'

18. *What are your views on the GAA's ability to market our games?*
'The games will not sell themselves. Even though our marketing has improved, we still have a long way to go. Both the Bank of Ireland and Guinness have adopted outstanding marketing strategies for the All-Ireland football and hurling championships, respectively. An example of the type of aggressive marketing that we require was the International Rules series between Ireland and Australia three years ago. On the wettest day in ten years, we got 70,000 people in Croke Park for a game that was not even Gaelic football. How did we manage that? The answer is that Coca-Cola did it for us. Had it been left to us, we probably would have had an attendance of 7,000. In order to maximise the full potential of our games, we will have to have an exclusive marketing department within the GAA itself. In addition, we must have a proper

marketing strategy, supported by adequate funding, in order to make it work. Other sporting organisations of a comparable size, such as Australian Rules and American football, have exclusive marketing departments. When I see what they have invested in marketing, our contribution in that area is, quite frankly, pathetic. To do our Association justice we must address this situation urgently.'

19. *You were Chairperson of the Strategic Review Committee, which published its report in January 2002. What are the implications of that report for the Association today?*

'Our brief was to assist the Association in consolidating our place in society and to continue our development and evolution as Ireland's primary sporting and cultural organisation. Even though many of our original recommendations were turned down, I think, in the long term, we will have succeeded in addressing the collective minds of the Association to face the more important challenges that must be undertaken. One of these is to increase our games penetration in urban areas. Over the past twenty years we have not really increased the number of adults playing Gaelic games. When you speak of penetration in some parts of Dublin as being as low as 5 per cent, you realise there is a huge void to be filled. We are not properly utilising our assets and strengths to promote our games. We would not survive if we were a business. We have to respond by catering for the needs of an ever-changing society. If that means more Saturday and Friday night games under floodlights, then so be it. This will require a lot of investment, but if we want to go forward, it simply must be done.'

20. *How would you see club structures in urban areas developing to accommodate a revival of Gaelic games?*

'A community spirit is essential to develop a meaningful club structure. This is much more difficult to organise in an urban setting because, unlike a rural setting, there is no place to identify with. An identifiable urban place is normally too small to foster a community spirit. That's why, in the SRC report, we have argued that we must look at urban areas differently. I would not be averse to having GAA clubs centred around workplaces or schools in such a scenario. For example, we could have a Guinness team in the Dublin championship, because that is the common sense of identity that the workforce in Guinness's have. In the past, O'Connell's schools, using this model, had a very successful club.

We use what is a common bond and then market it accordingly. All of this presents a huge challenge, but, if we are serious, we must invest our money, our time and expertise in this direction.'

21. What overall changes are required to meet all these challenges?
'Basically, there is nothing wrong with the present GAA strategy. It is the current GAA structures that need to be modernised to deliver the needs of these strategies. They must be made more relevant to what present society demands. Successful businesses must have appropriate structures to deliver their strategies. In the SRC report, when we criticised the way in which the Association was being run, by implication we criticised management, Central Council and the Executive staff. It's hardly surprising that we recommended changes in all areas. That's precisely why our report was not welcomed, because we were attacking those who were in the greatest positions of power. This is the greatest challenge. Changes in strategies do not affect people, but changes in structures do. Possibly, the GAA is too democratic. Democracy is normally good in its own right. In some circumstances, benign dictatorships have proven even better. For the fulfilment of its potential, the GAA needs to strike a balance between the two.'

22. Your views on the rules of the game?
'For me, the rules of our games have two basic objectives: (a) to protect players and (b) to be constantly applied within the course of a game. I believe that all players should be protected equally, at all times, by referees. Often, I regret to say, this is not the case. Admittedly, small, light players may need a little more protection, but certainly not at the expense of taller players being continually fouled or unfairly punished. Frequently, some referees seem to think that tall players are fair game to be subjected to persistent fouling. I remember seeing Anthony Tohill being constantly fouled for ten minutes. In total frustration, he drew round his arm. He got a yellow card and the transgressor, who had been consistently fouling him, got off scot-free.

'It is a totally unrealistic expectation to expect every referee in the country to interpret all the rules in the same manner in every game. What is required would be that, during the course of any given game, the referee is consistent. Paddy Collins interpreted the rules practically different from any other referee, yet he was the best referee I ever saw. He had a natural flair, both for consistency and common sense. Micheál Greenan was, technically speaking, an exceptional referee. He also was consistent. I would have no problem with either of them, because they implement the two basic principles of the games' rules. The only addendum I would add to the current rules is the introduction of a suspension penalty for the accumulation of a fixed number of yellow cards.'

23. *Now that you are semi-retired, how do you spend your time?*
'I was an economic consultant for many years. This involved a lot of travelling, both at home and abroad. My brother, Seán, is Executive Chairman and founder of the Quinn Group, which is one of the largest businesses in the country. I am a Director of the Quinn Group and various other companies, which takes up some of my time. For leisure, I love reading, particularly biographies and books of historical interest. Irish history is an especially favourite subject of mine. I suppose the fact that I was not allowed to study it at school motivated me to find out all about my own country, both past and present.'

24. *Finally, Peter, what are your future ambitions?*
'In GAA terms, 2004 was the greatest year of my life. I watched Fermanagh play seven games in the All-Ireland championship. Under the former championship system and given Fermanagh's record, that could have taken seven years to accomplish. As a bonus, four of those games were in Croke Park. It really was a magnificent, roller-coaster year for such a small county. Manager Charlie Mulgrew and all the players deserve all the accolades for this. It was lovely to see people from both sides of the community in Fermanagh supporting us. Many Unionist politicians came to watch our games. That was terrific. A politician once said all politics is local. My two dearest wishes are for Fermanagh to win their first Ulster senior football championship and for Teemore Shamrocks to win another county senior title.'

Peter made the following representative selections:

ULSTER (1960–2004)

Brian McAlinden
(Armagh)

Gabriel Kelly   Tony Scullion   Tom O'Hare
(Cavan)   (Derry)   (Down)

Brian McEniff   Kieran McGeeney   'Nudie' Hughes
(Donegal)   (Armagh)   (Monaghan)

Anthony Tohill   Colm McAlarney
(Derry)   (Down)

Seán O'Neill   Greg Blaney   Paddy Doherty
(Down)   (Down)   (Down)

P.T. Treacy   Frank McGuigan   Peter Canavan
(Fermanagh)   (Tyrone)   (Tyrone)

'I would also have liked to include Finbarr McConnell (Tyrone), Conor Deegan (Down), Henry Downey (Derry), Brian McGilligan (Derry), Peter McGinnity (Fermanagh), Máirtín McHugh (Donegal), Eugene McKenna (Tyrone), Brendan Coulter and Mickey Linden (Down) and Stephen McDonnell (Armagh), but I had only fifteen places.'

IRELAND (1960–2004)

Johnny Geraghty
(Galway)

Enda Colleran   Darren Fay   Tom O'Hare
(Galway)   (Meath)   (Down)

Tommy Drumm   Nicholas Clavin   Mairtin Newell
(Dublin)   (Offaly)   (Galway)

Jack O'Shea   Mick O'Connell
(Kerry)   (Kerry)

Seán O'Neill   Larry Tompkins   Pat Spillane
(Down)   (Cork)   (Kerry)

Mike Sheehy   Matt Connor   Peter Canavan
(Kerry)   (Offaly)   (Tyrone)

'I would have liked to include John O'Keeffe and Donie O'Sullivan (Kerry), Martin O'Connell (Meath), Brian Mullins (Dublin), Anthony Tohill (Derry), Greg Blaney (Down), Eoin 'Bomber' Liston and John Egan (Kerry), Mickey Kearins (Sligo) and Frank McGuigan (Tyrone), but again, like every team manager, I could select only fifteen.'

To complete the jigsaw of Peter Quinn's contribution to the GAA, one must not omit his lifelong ambition of converting Croke Park into a wonderful amphitheatre comparable to any stadium in the world. Many people have been responsible for this magnificent edifice. All the Presidents from 1982, when Paddy Buggy assumed office, right down to the present incumbent, Seán Kelly, have played their part. Ard Stiúrthóir Liam Mulvihill was always a strong advocate of such a development. However, the man primarily credited with making everyone's dream a reality was international economic consultant and former GAA President Peter Quinn. Because of his financial expertise, he was able to convince others to make crucial decisions, thus allowing the embryonic project to reach fruition. Besides, by travelling up and down the country with other officials, he effectively sold the concept of a modern, world-class stadium to the membership at large. As Chairman of the Stadium Project Management Committee, he continued to oversee the almost completed development as it is today.

In his own words, Croke Park is now a place of 'great comfort and complete safety with a touch of elegance'. Showing those inherent characteristics of business acumen, intelligence, determination and vision that he first mooted in the Institute of Chartered Accountants in Belfast in 1964 has paid dividends for the GAA. Peter Quinn has ensured that the coliseum for our national games has arrived in all its spectacular splendour. It is a fitting testimony to a marvellous GAA leader.

Peter Quinn – Fact File

Native Place:	Teemore, Co. Fermanagh
Date of Birth:	November 22, 1943
Club:	Teemore Shamrocks
Club Honours:	Senior Football Championship (4) – 1969 (Captain), 1971, 1974 and 1975 Senior Football League (4) – 1971, 1973, 1975, 1977 Minor Football Championship – 1960 Intermediate Football League (2) – 1962, 1964 Junior Football Championship – 1959
Other Honours:	(Oisín, Lancashire), Senior Football League – 1973
Managerial/Selectorial Career:	(a) Manager, Teemore Shamrocks (b) Ulster Hurling Selector (1984–1986)
Award:	Ulster GAA Personality of the Month, 1991
Administrative Career:	(a) Member of Ulster Council (1970–1990) (b) Treasurer of Ulster Council (1980–1983) (c) Vice-Chairman Ulster Council (1983–1986) (d) President of Ulster Council (1986–1989) (e) President of GAA (1991–1994) (f) Chairperson of Strategic Review Committee (2000–2002) (g) Chairperson of Stadium Project
Occupation:	Economic Consultant Director of Quinn Group and various other companies
Family:	Married to Mary (née Clarke) from Roosky, Co. Tyrone
Children:	Oisín, Miriam, Peter, Claire, Niamh

EIGHT

Paul Curran–Dublin

Looking Forward to Going 'Back to the Hill'

When GAA historians recall the great games of the past, there is absolutely no doubt that a special section will be devoted to the marvellous four-game marathon between Dublin and Meath in the first round of the 1991 Leinster senior football championship. Initially, in three of the games, Dublin dominated only to be pulled back by the sheer determination and unyielding spirit of the Royal County. In the first game, Meath's P.J. Gillic literally obtained a lucky bounce of the ball to equalise in the dying moments. Though Meath led by three points at half-time in the second encounter, they had had the advantage of the strong wind. In the second period, Dublin drew level, took control, but did not turn their outfield superiority into scores. Nevertheless, only a tremendous save by Meath goalkeeper Michael McQuillan prevented the metropolitans from winning at the end of normal time. With the heat now intense and the pace of the game considerably slower, both sides again finished level after extra time.

In the third meeting, Dublin were leading by five points with ten minutes to go. A brilliant goal by the elusive Bernard Flynn and two converted frees, courtesy of the impeccable accuracy of Brian Stafford, again brought the sides level. During extra time the sides, incredibly, scored 1–4 apiece to send the apparent never-ending series to another meeting. Both teams had by now displayed a fantastic inner resolve and mental capacity to keep going, regardless of the circumstances or the unbelievable tension amongst both players and spectators. This characteristic was typified by the vision and courage, whilst under tremendous pressure, of 22-year-old Paul Curran, who scored Dublin's fine equalising point as the game neared its end. Curran, who had played in the first two games, was dropped for the third meeting before coming on to score that dramatic equaliser. For the fourth game he regained his position, this time at centre half-forward.

What a reception awaited the two teams as they ran on to the field for what eventually proved to be the decisive game in the saga. Seldom, if ever, has there been such a cauldron of noise, tension and expectation in a packed stadium, as thirty of the world's greatest amateur athletes prepared for the throw-in. 'I will never in all my life forget such a great sense of occasion when I ran onto the field, as 62,000 people forced Croke Park to literally explode in a welter of excitement,' Paul recalled.

A full stadium, an estimated live television audience of one million and thousands more listening on radio, set the final scene for the most exciting saga in Irish sport. Though Meath took the lead at the beginning of the contest, it was again Dublin who dictated the pace and, with two minutes remaining, they were leading by three points. At last, or so it appeared, Dublin were about to progress to the next round.

As the ground stewards circled the field preparing for the game's end, Meath defender Kevin Foley, realising that time was nearly up, threw caution to the wind and decided to join the attack. There was nothing to lose and plenty to gain. Within seconds of Foley's forward move, the most famous passing movement in GAA history unfolded before the eyes of those privileged to witness it. Involving seven players, two of them (Colm O'Rourke and Foley) twice, the ball eventually reached Foley in an advanced position on the edge of the square. Promptly, he dispatched it to the net for one of the greatest goals of all time. With fleetness of foot and dexterity of hand, this brilliantly conceived goal was scored in the most dramatic of circumstances. The teams were now level and the momentum was decidedly in favour of the Royal County. An important fetch by the impressive Meath midfielder, Liam Hayes, merely compounded this view. Quickly, the rangy Skryne man passed the ball to P.J. Gillic, who transferred it immediately to the alert, pacey David Beggy. In a flash, the Navan player had scored the lead point. When shortly afterwards, another hero of the series, referee Tommy Howard of Kildare, blew the full-time whistle, 340 minutes of Gaelic football at its very best had finally ended. Meath were both relieved and elated. Understandably, Paul Curran and the whole Dublin team were dumbfounded and totally devastated. Since that magical championship series ended, all GAA aficionados everywhere are unanimous in their view that both Dublin and Meath equally deserved all the accolades from such a magnificent football marathon.

Paul Curran is now quite philosophical about the result. 'The games were incredible, the atmosphere superb and the whole hype was a huge marketing promotion tool for Gaelic football. It was amazing how honest both sides were in their endeavours and commitment. It was a pity that Meath did not go on and win that year's All-Ireland, after all their phenomenal displays throughout that campaign. However, they came up against a very good Down team, with brilliant incisive forwards like Mickey Linden and James McCartan. They also had in centre half-forward Greg Blaney a very creative playmaker. Often, I look back on those games and think of what might have been; then, inevitably, a humorous anecdote comes to mind. I had been dropped for the third game but came on in the second half and actually scored the equalising point. On the following Tuesday night our manager, Paddy Cullen, had a team meeting with the players. He had a video of the game and there was a thorough analysis of every aspect of our performance. Paddy complained bitterly that in the first half our forwards were playing too deep and constantly kept coming back too far into our defence. Addressing our forward line, he asked what were they doing in the first half, then addressed me, sitting at the back, and said: "Paul, where were you in the first half?" "Sitting beside you, as a substitute on the bench, Paddy!" Suffice to say that ended our detailed analysis, but Paddy, nevertheless, being the sportsman that he is, saw the humour of it all.'

To begin the story of Paul Curran, All-Ireland winner, Footballer of the Year and thrice All Star, one must go back to the 1967 All-Ireland senior football final between Meath and Cork, when one of the outstanding performers in the winning Royal team was top-scoring forward Noel Curran. Noel, who played for his native Dunshaughlin club in County Meath until he was 35 years old, subsequently transferred to the Dublin side Thomas Davis of Tallaght. In the interim Noel married, became domiciled in the metropolis and had a son called Paul.

'Dad brought me to matches every Sunday when I was young and I became totally infatuated with football. He played club football until he was fifty years old. I had the great pleasure of playing with him in the Thomas Davis Intermediate side. You could say he was on his way down and I was on my way up.'

Paul first came to the attention of the county minor selectors when he consistently put in sterling displays for his club at under age level. When he was selected on the county minor team in successive years in 1986 and 1987, he had natural aspirations to make it at senior level. Straight after minor level, Paul emigrated to London when an attractive work opportunity presented itself. However, that did not work out and Dublin manager Gerry McCaul drafted him into the senior squad shortly after his return, prior to the 1989 championship season. In his debut championship game, against Kildare in Newbridge, Paul dislocated a finger in the first half and, while in hospital, found out that Dublin had won the game.

His quick powers of recovery ensured that Paul was ready for the Leinster semi-final against Wicklow. When they defeated the Garden County, Dublin had now qualified to meet their old adversaries, Meath, for their fourth successive Leinster final. Playing superb, controlled football, the men in blue ran out convincing winners by five points. This was a huge psychological achievement for Dublin as they had at last broken Meath's dominance of the previous three years in Leinster. In addition, the Royals had won back-to-back All-Irelands in 1987 and 1988. Paul Curran, at the age of twenty, was thrilled and delighted in this, his 'rookie' year. 'I could not believe it. Beating All-Ireland champions Meath made it all the more important. I found it hard to believe that my Dad would be cheering against his native county, but I suppose blood is thicker than water. Whenever Dublin were knocked out of the championship, he returned to his roots and became a fervent Royal man again.

'After that provincial success, we seemed to lose our coolness under pressure in the All-Ireland semi-final against Cork. This was particularly disturbing as we began superbly and were up 1–4 to 0–0 in the first quarter. Then, we conceded two penalties and had our star player, Keith Barr, sent off. So, from being in a totally dominant position, we actually went in at half-time a point behind and a man less. After that, we seemed to lose our confidence and the Munster men ran out easy winners before going on to win the All-Ireland final against Mayo. The following season, Meath got their revenge when they overcame Dublin by three points in the 1990 Leinster final.'

As Dublin approached that eventful 1991 championship game against Meath, they were quietly confident, particularly as they had defeated a very good Kildare side in the National Football League final, at the beginning of May. Though initially traumatised by the circumstances of their defeat in the fourth game, Curran and his teammates soon realised that the potential for success was there. Those positive aspirations were further enhanced when they reached the 1992 All-Ireland final in impressive fashion. First of all, they overcame Kildare by six points in the Leinster final, before easily overcoming surprise Munster champions Clare in the All-Ireland semi-final.

In the All-Ireland final, Dublin were the hottest of hot favourites when they faced Ulster champions Donegal, who were making their debut in a senior decider. After early supremacy and missed chances, including a penalty miss by Charlie Redmond, Donegal asserted total authority and were excellent value for their thoroughly deserved 0–18 to 0–14 victory. Curran was shocked, but very wise in hindsight. 'We were completely blasé going into the final. We went as a team to see the All-Ireland semi-final between Mayo and Donegal. It was really a very poor quality game and even though we were very much aware of the pitfalls of being favourites, I think deep down, psychologically, we felt we were a much better side than Donegal. Of course, Donegal proved us totally wrong. Lots of other mistakes were made prior to the final. For example, players were giving interviews up to and including the Friday before the game. The focus was not there and we paid the price. In the game itself, our full-forward, Vinny Murphy, won a lot of possession, which was not translated into scores. We simply missed too many chances. 1992 was really a terrible year for me as my club also lost to Dr Crokes of Killarney, by just a point, in the All-Ireland club final.

'In 1993, we exacted revenge on the now All-Ireland champions Donegal when we beat them in the National League final, after a replay. In the first game we had Keith Barr and Charlie Redmond sent off, and in the second game, Tommy Carr got an early shower. Despite these setbacks and the consequent repositioning of our team, we went on to record a very satisfactory victory.'

With even more renewed confidence than in previous years, the Dublin manager, former All-Ireland medallist of the 1970s Dr Pat O'Neill, assiduously prepared his team for the championship campaign of 1993. Everything appeared to be going according to plan when Dublin accounted for Kildare by four points in the Leinster final. They now faced new Ulster champions Derry in the All-Ireland semi-final. Playing fast, enterprising football, Dublin dominated the first half against the Oak Leaf County and led at half-time by five points. But Derry had forgotten either to read or obey the script. Exceptional displays by attacking half-backs Johnny McGurk and Henry Downey enabled the irrepressible Joe Brolly and Derry to wreak havoc in the Dublin defence. Johnny McGurk, who had the proverbial 'blinder' all through, scored the winning point for the Ulstermen. Dublin had lost a major championship game in Croke Park for the fourth year in a row.

So, it was back again for Pat O'Neill and his ageing troops for the 1994 championship season. Again, everything seemed to be going as planned when Meath were accounted for in the Leinster decider and new Connacht champions Leitrim were easily overcome in the All-Ireland semi-final. Down beckoned in the All-Ireland final, but the gods appeared again to destabilise the Leinster men. Paul Curran had been injured for the Leitrim game and had been replaced by Paul Clarke. As Clarke had performed well, he was retained in the same position for the final, and a fit-again Curran was placed in the left corner of the defence, instead of regular defender Ciarán Walsh, who had been injured in a club game. The versatile Curran was always recognised as a superb player in any position, but the consensus amongst true Dublin supporters was that he was at his most effective as a wing-back.

Be that as it may, a magnificent performance by Down's attacking ace, Mickey Linden, allowed the northerners to lead by four points at half-time. With twenty minutes to go in the second half, Down led by six points. Incredibly, they were not to score for the remainder of the game. Paul Bealin and Jack Sheedy were now exerting total control at centre-field and Dublin's share of the possession stakes increased accordingly. However, the glaring inadequacies of the Dublin forwards were exemplified by the fact that they only scored four points in twenty minutes of almost non-stop pressure. Dublin's ill-luck was reinforced when the unfortunate Charlie Redmond missed another penalty in a major game. To be fair to Redmond, it must be said that Down goalkeeper Neil Collins made a fantastic save. It must also be added that the Down defence performed heroics far beyond the call of normal defensive play, on their way to their fifth All-Ireland title. Those conclusions were of little consolation as Dublin experienced their fifth major successive loss, in what many perceived as their lucky hunting ground.

The following year, 1995, was definitely make or break year for a Dublin side whose mental and physical capacity to keep going, in spite of so many setbacks, was highly commendable. They had a terrific Leinster campaign, easily casting aside both Louth and Laois, as they progressed to another final with Meath. In a brilliant team performance, aided and abetted by fine individual performances from Dessie Farrell, Paul Clarke, the new kid on the block Jason Sherlock, and Charlie Redmond, Dublin literally tore the Meath defence apart. In the end, the Dubs emerged victorious by an impressive ten-point margin and the press were unanimous in their total admiration for the magnificence of Paul Curran's performance.

In the All-Ireland semi-final, Dublin defeated Cork by three points. With Brian Stynes being truly outstanding in centre-field, the Dublin forward line were guaranteed a good ball supply. When Sherlock pounced for a very good first-half goal, both 'Jason mania' and Dublin were on their way to an All-Ireland final meeting with Ulster champions Tyrone.

In the final, however, Dublin never reached the heights that they had achieved throughout the rest of the championship, particularly the Leinster final against Meath. It was apparent that the unprecedented pressure to succeed was having an adverse effect. The style and panache normally associated with Dublin performances was sadly absent. The absence of full-back Dermot Deasy because of injury was another contributing factor to Dublin's apparent inertia.

In the opening part of the game, Tyrone's Fergal Logan and Peter Canavan were the dominant figures as Tyrone raced into an early three-point lead. It was just the tonic they required and it added to the tremendous psychological pressure on their opponents. However, a magnificent 65m free kick from Keith Barr after seven minutes had a settling effect on his colleagues. When Charlie Redmond expertly reduced the deficit to the minimum, two minutes later, Dublin began to assert control. When Paul Clarke then levelled with another magnificent free kick, after ten minutes, the pendulum had swung in favour of the metropolitans. Soon afterwards, the majestic Barr, whose influence on proceedings was progressing rapidly, spotted the unmarked Dessie Farrell. The Na Fianna club man duly dispatched the ball over the bar for the lead point. Canavan and Farrell then exchanged pointed frees, to leave the men in blue still a point ahead. It was at this stage that Dublin midfielder Paul Bealin and right half-back Paul Curran seemed to own the ball as they caught or intercepted it before driving it effortlessly and frequently downfield. On one such occasion, Bealin sent a long, probing kick to the left of the Tyrone goalmouth. Unlucky for Tyrone and lucky for Dublin, the ball hit off Tyrone full-back Chris Lawn and broke to the feet of Jason Sherlock. The speedy 19-year-old hit it to the totally unmarked Charlie Redmond, who had the simplest of chances to put the ball in the net and leave the score reading Dublin 1–5, Tyrone 0–4. Shortly afterwards, the stylish, overlapping Paul Curran soloed upfield and slotted the ball over the bar. Canavan and Dublin right half-forward Jim Gavin had points apiece before referee Paddy Russell blew the half-time whistle. Dublin 1–7, Tyrone 0–5 was the scoreline as a rejuvenated and reinvigorated Dublin side went into their dressing rooms. The Hill was now alive with the continuous chorus of happy Dubliners, as they anticipated a comparatively easy victory.

Tyrone, who had to field without their influential and talented forward Adrian Cush, who was injured, looked deflated and disconsolate when they trooped off at half-time. However, on the restart, they took control and the deadly accurate Peter Canavan had, after seven minutes, reduced the deficit to two points when he scored three frees. Now, it appeared that a fantastic contest lay ahead. Nobody could legislate for what happened next. A mixture of recklessness and cruel fate took a hand when Charlie Redmond seemed to be sent off for an over-robust tackle on Tyrone midfielder Fergal Logan. There was chaos all around when Redmond was still on the field after play resumed. Normality returned when, after consulting with a linesman, the referee clearly sent Redmond off and Charlie duly obliged. Though Dessie Farrell restored Dublin's three-point advantage shortly afterwards, Dublin seemed to lose their way in terms of moving the ball forward.

Being a man down, it was really a damage limitation display as Dublin defended heroically at times, but in sheer desperation at others. Still, with three minutes of normal time left, that three-point lead was intact.

After this, Tyrone captain Ciarán Corr was fouled and Peter the Great pointed, to leave just two points in the difference. Then, very importantly, Paul Clarke scored a crucial 55m free to restore the three-point advantage. Canavan kicked two more frees (the latter his eleventh of the game) to leave the minimum between the teams. As Dublin supporters loudly whistled, begging the referee to blow for full-time, the classy Canavan intercepted a clearance from Dublin goalkeeper and team captain John O'Leary. The Errigal Ciarán man slipped to the ground but managed to flick the ball away to the inrushing half-back, Seán McLoughlin, who sent the ball over the bar for an apparent equaliser. The referee disallowed the score as he ruled the Tyrone man had touched the ball on the ground. Shortly afterwards, the full-time whistle sounded. Dublin were totally overjoyed. The long wait for success was over. All the disappointments of the previous four years were forgotten when the long-serving John O'Leary raised aloft the Sam Maguire Cup.

Dublin had many great performers during that 1995 championship. Goalkeeper John O'Leary, half-backs Paul Curran and Keith Barr, midfielder Brian Stynes and forwards Dessie Farrell and Charlie Redmond stood out, and it was fitting that all six should receive All Star awards. All at the game agreed that Paul Curran was a class apart, as he had been throughout the year. One cameo of his greatness still lingers in the mind. His 'robbing' of Tyrone forward Ciarán Loughran in the 24th minute was absolutely brilliant and his subsequent pass to Jim Gavin equally adept, especially as Gavin passed to Farrell, who notched an exquisite point. No one was a more worthy recipient of the Texaco Footballer of the Year award than Paul Curran when he received this honour in late 1995.

From that 1995 All-Ireland success until he retired in 2002, there were very few highlights in Paul's playing career. 'In that period I won another All Star award in 1996 and two Railway Cup medals in 1996 and 1997. When Tommy Lyons was appointed manager of the Dublin side in November 2001, he stated that he would put the swagger back into Dublin football. It would have to be said that he delivered on that promise, as we beat both Meath and Kildare en route to winning our first Leinster final in seven years, in 2002. In the All-Ireland quarter-final we beat Donegal after a replay. Both games were fabulous and thrilling occasions. But I now knew that my days as an inter-county player were numbered. Because of work commitments abroad, it was necessary to train a lot on my own, in foreign lands, in the last four years of my career. I loved training but eventually it took its toll and I knew instinctively that 2002 would be my last season. My last county appearance was when I came on, as a sub, in the replay against Donegal. I have no regrets, just happy memories.'

When I met Paul, in the Spa Hotel in Lucan, he recalled the memories of those halcyon years of Dublin being at or near the top of Gaelic games. 'We played three All-Ireland finals in four years. We really should have lost that game against Tyrone and won at least one of the other two deciders. Peter Canavan was decidedly unlucky to have been pulled up for flicking the ball along the ground. Nine out of ten referees would have allowed Seán McLoughlin's point, thus ensuring a draw. Everyone would then have been happy. I am convinced that Tyrone would have won if it had gone to a replay, because the momentum was with them. Over the course of those few years, our performances definitely merited an All-Ireland title.'

Paul is particularly proud of his All Star awards, especially the 1995 and 1996 ones because his peers selected him. He has tremendous respect for all the players he either played with or against in a senior career that stretched from 1989 to 2002. 'Maurice Fitzgerald, Peter Canavan and Mickey Linden simply oozed pure class in everything they did. Stephen O'Brien of Cork was a brilliant player, at a very young age, whereas both Colm O'Rourke of Meath and Larry Tompkins of Cork gave long and distinguished service to the game. When I was in Australia in 1990, with the International Rules team, I was delighted to see how brilliant players from the so-called 'weak' counties really were. Pat O'Byrne (Wicklow), Noel Roche (Clare), the Grimley twins (Armagh) and Dessie Barry (Longford) were all very talented athletes. Barry, in particular, was an especially strong and pacey player. Kevin O'Brien (Wicklow) was one of the best footballers that I ever saw anywhere. It was a pity that he did not get an opportunity to parade his vast array of skills to a bigger audience.'

Paul, who writes a weekly GAA column for the *Evening Herald*, has interesting thoughts and even radical opinions on a host of GAA topics. Three areas of the game predominate his thinking: competitions, rules of the game and players' welfare.

1. 'First of all, unfortunately, I believe the Railway Cup should be scrapped because its attractiveness has been squeezed out and overtaken by both the All-Ireland Club Championship and the International Rules series. Secondly, I am not happy with the present championship format. The old system directly honoured the provincial process and when you were eliminated that was it. The current system is neither one thing nor the other. It gives the

stronger counties a realistic second chance and the weaker counties a second game, in which they are likely to suffer two successive and humiliating defeats. If the GAA wants to change our championship system, they should do it properly by changing to a champions league format. This would allow all teams to have a realistic chance of progressing, at their own level, in a meaningful competition.'

2. 'In my opinion, our playing rules are very satisfactory and should not require alteration. What is needed is a comprehensive education programme on the rules themselves. Administrators, players, officials and team managements, as well as referees, should be regularly informed of the implications of all the playing rules. In order that the rules are applied fairly and that those who transgress the rules are sufficiently punished, I would introduce a two-referee system, allowing two points for any free scored as a result of a personal foul. I have seen this system employed, in the annual Evening Herald floodlit league, here in Dublin. It has been an outstanding success. Pulling and dragging is severely curtailed, the game is much faster, more enjoyable, and is a very spectator-friendly spectacle as a result. I have no doubt that if this system were adopted at national level, Gaelic football would reach its full potential. This would be because players would concentrate more on playing rather than on fouling.'

3. 'I think the GAA is a great organisation. It has first-class facilities in every county and club in Ireland. Totally dedicated officials and other voluntary helpers do terrific work in promoting and developing Gaelic games in every unit of the Association. The GPA has performed a great service for all of us in highlighting the need for improvement in players' welfare. The hurling and football championships, as well as all teams in the organisation, are sponsored, yet the welfare of the players, who provide the entertainment, has only marginally improved. If footballers or hurlers did not play, there would be no supporters and therefore no revenue. Players should not be out of pocket owing to missing work either for training or matches. Once a player is selected on each county's senior championship squad, I believe he should automatically qualify for some kind of benefit or tax break. I would not be averse to financially rewarding players in such situations. Gone are the days when players are satisfied with an end of year holiday.'

Paul made the following choices for his representative team.

LEINSTER (1983–2003)

John O'Leary
(Dublin)

Bobby O'Malley   Paddy Christie   Mick Kennedy
(Meath)   (Dublin)   (Dublin)

Finbar Cullen   Glen Ryan   Eamonn Heery
(Offaly)   (Kildare)   (Dublin)

Séamus O'Hanlon   Brian Mullins
(Louth)   (Dublin)

David Beggy   Dessie Farrell   Vinnie Claffey
(Meath)   (Dublin)   (Offaly)

Colm O' Rourke   Kevin O'Brien   Charlie Redmond
(Meath)   (Wicklow)   (Dublin)

IRELAND (1983–2003)

John O'Leary
(Dublin)

Bobby O'Malley   Niall Cahalane   Tony Scullion
(Meath)   (Cork)   (Derry)

Páidí Ó Sé   Stephen O'Brien   Séamus Moynihan
(Kerry)   (Cork)   (Kerry)

Brian Mullins   Jack O'Shea
(Dublin)   (Kerry)

Michael Donnellan   Dessie Farrell   Maurice Fitzgerald
(Galway)   (Dublin)   (Kerry)

Colm O'Rourke   Peter Canavan   Mike Sheehy
(Meath)   (Tyrone)   (Kerry)

When the Dublin players triumphantly returned to their dressing rooms after their 1995 All-Ireland success, one man, Dublin selector and three times All-Ireland medal-winner Bobby Doyle, excitedly reached for the coveted trophy and gently bounced it off the ground in sheer joy. In that symbolic gesture, he reminded his players of the significance

and importance of that wonderful moment in their lives. Leaving Paul
Curran's charming company, I was left with the distinct impression
that he would like to follow in the hallowed footsteps of so many great
Dublin players who honoured the return of Sam Maguire – in their
second coming – either as manager or coach. Paul's current enthusiastic
under age coaching involvement with his beloved Thomas Davis club
undoubtedly heralds his first tentative steps on the road to walking the
line on senior All-Ireland final day. One can justifiably predict that
both time and talent are on his side to achieve that ultimate goal.

PAUL CURRAN – FACT FILE

Native Place:	Dublin
Date of Birth:	April 9, 1969
Club:	Thomas Davis, Tallaght

Club Honours:	Dublin League (3) – 1999, 2001, 2002
	Dublin Senior Football Championship (3) –
	    1989, 1990, 1991
	Leinster Senior Football Championship (2) –
	    1990/91, 1991/92
	Vincent de Paul Medal (2) – 1996, 1999

County Honours:	All-Ireland Senior Football Championship (1) –
	    1995
	Leinster Senior Football Championship (6) –
	    1989, 1992, 1993, 1994, 1995, 2002
	National Football League (2) – 1991, 1993

Other Playing Honours:	Railway Cup with Leinster (2) – 1996 (Captain), 1997 International Rules team member – 1990
Awards:	All Star (3) – 1992, 1995, 1996 Texaco Footballer of the Year – 1995 Dublin Player of the Year – 1989, 1995 Numerous weekly/monthly awards.
Occupation:	Travel agent
Family:	Parents – Noel and Teresa Married to Fidelma (from Palmerstown)
Children:	Luke

NINE

Mickey Moran–Derry

SUPREME COUNTY AND INTERNATIONAL COACH

The half-time whistle had just sounded in the 1993 All-Ireland senior football semi-final between Ulster champions Derry, and Leinster champions Dublin. Derry manager Eamon Coleman, with selectors Harry Gribben and Denis McKeever, made their way hurriedly to the dressing room. Fellow selector and team coach Mickey Moran, like his colleagues, was totally bewildered at Derry's inept first-half performance. A team that had promised so much in previous games was now five points behind. The omens were not looking good. Two distinctive strands of incredulity and acute disappointment occupied Moran's mind. In the minute that it took the disconsolate coach to walk from the sideline to the beleaguered dressing room, a multitude of unhappy memories, unfortunate occurrences and 24 years of a chequered football career flashed across his subconscious. During those years, Derry and Moran had experienced in Croke Park, on countless occasions, the agonising traumas of defeat as well as seeing hugely talented fellow athletes being lost to Gaelic football forever.

One of the most talented under age players ever produced by Derry was Martin O'Neill. In 1969 and 1970 he had won Ulster minor championship medals along with his friend and minor club colleague, Mickey Moran. They had played together in the 1969 All-Ireland minor final as well as the 1970 All-Ireland minor semi-final. On both occasions, despite playing relatively well, the Oak Leafers never reached their true heights of attainment and lost narrowly. In addition, O'Neill, who was equally talented at soccer, left Derry to pursue a very successful soccer career in England. All Star Gerry McElhinney, who had played with Mickey on the Derry senior team of the mid-1970s, had also gone to England to ply his soccer skills. Mickey's greatest football friend, Colm P. Mullan, had been paralysed in a bad car crash in 1973. Thus, another promising GAA career had prematurely ended. Individually, all three were supremely gifted players. Together, along with players like Seán O'Connell, Mickey Niblock, Adrian McGuckin, Tom McGuinness, Gerry O'Loughlin and Moran himself, they would surely have brought a first senior All-Ireland to the Oak Leaf County.

In 1975 and 1976, Derry won successive Ulster senior championships. They arrived in Croke Park for the subsequent All-Ireland semi-finals with very impressive credentials, only to flop to Dublin and Kerry respectively. One of the best games that Derry team ever played was the 1976 National Football League final against a Dublin side who were then at the peak of their powers. Derry played absolutely spellbinding football, only to be totally deflated by two Dublin goals, both of which were of the controversial variety. In the end, Derry narrowly lost on a 2–10 to 0–15 scoreline. From a Derry perspective, there were two significant highlights. A virtuoso display by centre half-forward Mickey Lynch, who scored 0–6 from play, earned him an Irish Independent Sports Star of the Week award. While Lynch deservedly earned the accolades in the scoring stakes, it was, however, Mickey Moran's finest hour in a Derry jersey. Playing at left half-back, the 1976 All Star replacement was simply superb as he continually intercepted promising Dublin attacks, before setting up his own colleagues with pinpoint passes. Still, until he joined the Derry senior management team of Eamon Coleman, Harry Gribben and Denis McKeever in early 1991, that was to be the unassuming Glen man's only real positive highlight.

When Derry drew with Down in that year's Ulster semi-final, having been seven points adrift, Moran knew for the first time that this team had definite All-Ireland potential. They had a coterie of well-established, skilful players, in goalkeeper Damien McCusker, defenders Tony Scullion and Kieran McKeever and towering influential midfielder, Brian McGilligan. Damian Barton, Damian Cassidy and Enda Gormley all added class, intelligence and scoring accuracy to a competent forward line. There were three other powerful arguments to sustain Moran's analysis. After suffering a broken leg four years previously in a first-round U-21 championship match, Lavey's Henry Downey was now back to his brilliant best. Anthony Tohill, a minor prodigy in 1989, had returned from Australia after an eighteen-month experiment with Australian Rules, and exciting corner-forward Joe Brolly was beginning to wreak havoc on opposing defences. Even though Derry lost that replay to the Down men, Moran and his colleagues were happy with a 'work in progress'.

When Derry resumed training in September 1991, it was decided to make a concerted effort to win the National Football League. This would, hopefully, serve the dual purpose of laying to rest the Croke Park 'bogey', while at the same time building up team spirit and a pattern of consistent play that would stand them in good stead come championship time. Beating Meath in the semi-final and then Tyrone in the league final itself ensured that target number one was achieved. During the latter game, even though Derry were losing at the time, Mickey Moran and Johnny McGurk, who was a substitute, turned to each other and mutually proclaimed 'regardless of today's result, this team are now going places'. Their gut instinct was rewarded two minutes from the end of that contest. It took a quirk of luck to change Derry from gallant losers to champion winners. They were three points behind their archrivals when Anthony Tohill landed a 45 in the Tyrone goalmouth. Two Tyrone men, unbelievably, left the ball to each other. Neither of them grabbed it and instead it drifted into the back of the net. Then, suddenly released from the enveloping chains of negative history, Derry played like men possessed. In the remaining time the inspirational Tohill and the impressive Dermot Heaney added further points. Thus, they won the National League for the first time since they had their inaugural win in 1947. When Derry followed this up with a magnificent championship victory over the same opposition two weeks later, the shackles of fear, hoodoos and disappointments had been removed ... or had they? From Mickey Moran's perspective, Derry should now have reached their true potential in terms of achievement. Hopefully, they would be totally uninhibited by any negative influences.

Down's winning of the 1991 All-Ireland had given Derry further impetus towards their own success in 1992. Everything was going according to plan. When Derry gave a fantastic display in overcoming Down in that year's Ulster semi-final, Mickey and his management team were exceedingly happy. However, the surprise loss against a 14-man Donegal side in the Ulster final almost dealt a fatal blow to Derry's future championship hopes. Derry began tentatively and eased in front, but then Donegal had a man sent off just before half-time. With nothing to lose, Donegal played the game of their lives in the second half and won, deservedly, by two points. Team management and supporters were now completely despondent that over-confidence or some other mysterious jinx had returned to haunt Derry just as they stood on the threshold of greatness. Only time, patience and more diligent pre-paration would indelibly remove such a 'hoodoo' mentality.

In August of that year, four weeks after the Ulster final dis-appointment, the management and players came together again. After a thorough analysis of their previous physical and mental preparation, all pledged to play their part in ensuring that no stone would be left unturned for a winning assault on the 1993 championship. When Donegal went on to win the 1992 All-Ireland, Moran definitely knew that it was up to him and his management colleagues to mould a winning team. From a player's point of view, Donegal's success really impressed on them how close they were to All-Ireland glory.

That historic campaign began the following year, in The Marshes in Newry, when Derry faced old adversaries, Down. The first half's torrential downpour proved no impediment to a magnificent Derry display. Spearheaded by the best midfield pairing in the land, Anthony Tohill and Brian McGilligan, the Oak Leaf County led by 1–6 to 0–5. In the second half, Derry gave a scintillating performance, before coasting to a 3–11 to 0–9 victory. That display was a perfect blend of skill and physical and mental toughness, as well as an unyielding spirit. Derry, it was hoped by all their supporters, were now on their way.

For three-quarters of the Ulster semi-final clash with Monaghan, the Farney men more than held their own. Then Derry re-arranged their defence, introducing substitute Joe Brolly, who had missed a lot of training owing to barrister examinations, and the whole team totally upped the tempo, playing fantastic football in the process. A marvellous display by Enda Gormley in the forward line was the icing on the cake as Derry, in the end, won comfortably by 0–19 to 0–11. Derry were now looking forward to their second successive Ulster final. The fact that the opposition was again provided by Donegal — their conquerors in the previous year as well as in the quarter final of the 1992/93 league — was an added incentive. Also, playing the current All-Ireland champions would test the true mettle of this current Derry team.

Played in atrocious underfoot and overhead conditions, the first half required tremendous physical courage and unrelenting mental resolve from both sides as they tried to cope with the terrible conditions. In a tense, determined struggle, Donegal went in at half-time leading by 0–5 to 0–4. During the interval, Derry players and management did not need to speak many words. The talking would be done on the field of play during the second half.

Within 60 seconds of the restart, Anthony Tohill landed a colossal 60-metre free to draw the sides level. Playing brilliant football despite the utter misery of the elements, Damian Barton, Damian Cassidy and Enda Gormley all scored quality points to send Derry into a 0–8 to 0–5 lead. For the remaining 28 minutes of a hard-fought contest, Derry did not score again and Donegal only managed a point. The tension was intense as both sides tried to assert their superiority in the closing quarter. Only a marvellous catch and interception by maestro midfielder Brian McGilligan in the closing minutes prevented Donegal from notching a match-winning goal. When the whistle blew, Derry were both relieved and overjoyed. A sporting Donegal manager, Brian McEniff, prophetically stated in the immediate aftermath of his side's loss that he himself would be in Maghera on the last Monday night in September. He expected to be welcoming home Henry Downey and his heroes with the Sam Maguire Cup. For Mickey Moran, it was more important to concentrate on the task in hand: 'We prepared meticulously for the All-Ireland semi-final against Dublin. Some of our team, such as Damien McCusker, Tony Scullion, Brian McGilligan, Damian Barton, Damian Cassidy, Johnny McGurk and Enda Gormley, had been there six years earlier. Derry had won their last Ulster title in 1987, but had been beaten subsequently by eventual All-Ireland champions Meath in the All-Ireland semi-final. So we brought them to Dublin and Croke Park in advance, in order to familiarise themselves with the stadium.'

Derry were now in their fifth All-Ireland semi-final since 1958, having lost at the penultimate stage in 1970, 1975, 1976 and 1987. Besides, they were also facing Dublin, the team which had thwarted their All-Ireland ambitions back in 1958, when Derry had made their one and only final appearance.

In the actual game itself, after a poor beginning, Derry gradually found their feet but still went in at half-time five points down. In normal conditions, Derry half-time talks usually consisted of manager Eamon Coleman using the heavy-handed approach if required and then Mickey Moran quietly adding some tactical advice. This, in Moran's opinion, was no ordinary occasion and he waited rather impatiently as Coleman and some players spoke in reasoned tones. Suddenly, to the complete consternation of the players and the rest of the management team, the quiet, unflappable Glen man spoke as never before. First of all, he outlined, in precise detail, the litany of unforced errors that each Derry player had committed in the first half. Secondly, and most importantly, he appealed to their collective judgement. Were they just going to be remembered as another great Derry side that had come down to Croke Park with so much promise and then completely flopped when the difficult questions were asked? Then, mindful of the importance of the next 35 minutes, he urged them to prove how really good they were and to lead Derry into an All-Ireland final. The ghosts of past failures deserved to be exorcised. The players reacted immediately and silently. If Mickey Moran felt like this, they were the only ones who could do something about it. With renewed vigour and commitment, they left the hushed dressing room behind them.

In a tremendous second-half display, Derry gradually wore Dublin down, and two minutes from time, substitute Dermot McNicholl secured possession and sent the ball ahead to overlapping half-back Johnny McGurk on the right side of the pitch. The Lavey man turned and with his left foot sent a high, curling kick over the bar for the lead point. For all Derry fans and many neutrals, that kick deserved to be included in RTÉ's top twenty GAA moments. That was the kick that sent Derry into their first All-Ireland final for 35 years. The Derry fans were in raptures when referee Tommy Sugrue signalled the end of a magnificent contest. In the words of Anne and Francie Brolly, the husband and wife songsters duo from Dungiven:

> 'And now we face the final test
> With heart both proud and free;
> And we will show the boys from
> Rebel Cork, what Derry men can do.'

The All-Ireland final against Cork was the day for which Mickey Moran and his management team had waited 14 months. Even though Derry conceded an early goal, they soon began to play to their usual high standard. Thoughts of history repeating itself momentarily crossed Derry minds when Cork had Tony Davis rather harshly sent off just before half-time. However, Coleman, Moran and company were able during the interval to instruct the team how to use the extra player. Johnny McGurk was given the role and was so successful in maximising Derry possession that he was voted Man of the Match. An early second-half goal by Cork was a worry. That John O'Driscoll goal put the Leesiders 2–8 to 1–10 ahead, but that would be their last score of the game. Eight minutes later, Gormley equalised. Then Tohill, McGurk and Gormley again each scored, to record a momentous victory. At 4.57 p.m., with the score Derry 1–14, Cork 2–8, referee Tommy Howard blew the full-time whistle. Every Derry man, woman and child jumped and cheered. Derry had won their first All-Ireland senior football title! When Derry captain Henry Downey raised the Sam Maguire Cup aloft, thousands of Derry fans who had encroached on the famous hallowed turf were in their seventh heaven. The whole team were heroes. Goalkeeper Damien McCusker fronted a magnificent defence of Kieran McKeever, Tony Scullion, Gary Coleman, John McGurk, Henry Downey and Fergal McCusker. Anthony Tohill and Brian McGilligan were simply awesome in the middle of the field. Their opportunist goal-scorer Séamus Downey, at full-forward, was capably assisted by Dermot Heaney, Damian Barton, Damian Cassidy, Joe Brolly and Enda Gormley. Substitutes Dermot McNicholl and Eamon Burns also played their part in this red-letter day in the annals of Derry football.

That night's celebratory reception for the Derry team and the lunch for all the teams on the following day were more perfunctory than enjoyable. As Anthony Tohill so aptly stated, there was 'an impatient urgency to go home and celebrate among our own people'. On the longest road journey home for a winning team in modern times, Mickey Moran will never forget the crowds that came to greet them. Newry, Armagh and the Moy were crowded with thousands of well-wishers from other counties. The Moy is situated at the entrance to Tyrone — Derry's greatest rivals. He treasures the sporting tribute that the people of Tyrone paid to them. The fantastic reception by Tyrone fans continued as the triumphant Derry team passed through Dungannon and Cookstown. The Cookstown welcome was particularly pleasing, as it was on the Derry border and covered a hinterland where the rivalry between the two counties was at its most intense.

But it was the journey into his native Derry that made the greatest impact of all. The all-consuming happiness on so many faces as the victorious team passed on their way through Moneymore and Magherafelt to journey's end — Maghera — will live long in the memory. This was what players, management and supporters longed for most — to arrive back in Maghera as All-Ireland champions. Traditionally, Maghera is perceived as the centre of all GAA activity within the county. The euphoria and the sense of celebration in Maghera on that Monday night, in front of 25,000 excited supporters, surpassed everyone's greatest expectations. For Mickey Moran it was extra special. 'As our bus turned the corner of Bank Square and I saw the whole town jammed with cheering, flag-waving fans, it was the culmination of all I had ever dreamed of. It was a wonderful privilege to see Derry's greatest celebration in my home town of Maghera.' Eamon, Denis, Harry and Mickey were on 'top of the world looking down on their creation'.

Like so many others, Mickey Moran inherited a love of Gaelic games from his late father, Charlie. Charlie Moran played for Derry, in goals, for fourteen years during the 1940s and early 1950s. He was the county's custodian when the Oak Leaf team won their first national title by defeating Clare in the 1947 league final. The all-Magherafelt half-forward line of captain Pat Keenan, Frankie Niblock and Larry Higgins were among the stars in an epoch-making side. Mickey's only memory of his father playing was standing behind the goals at Ballinascreen in a junior championship final. 'I was very young and I remember the crossbar breaking and nearly injuring my father.' In the mid-1960s a new secondary school, St Patrick's College, Maghera, opened its doors for the first time. Since then, it has become one of the leading Gaelic nurseries in the country. Former Derry stars Adrian McGuckin and latterly Dermot McNicholl have been the main architects of this phenomenal development, which has yielded twelve Mac Rory Cup triumphs as well as four Hogan Cup titles. The college first participated, under the guidance of Seán Murphy in 1969, in the Ulster Colleges 'B' championship. That year they won their first provincial title — the McLarnon Cup — when they comfortably overcame St Michael's College, Enniskillen, led by future Fermanagh All Star Peter McGinnity. The St Pat's winning team included Mickey Moran and eventual senior county colleagues Eugene Laverty and Fintan McCloskey. After his secondary student days, Mickey went to De La Salle College in Manchester to train as a PE teacher.

'When I first went there, Gaelic football was in its infancy, so I played wing-forward on the rugby team. Fellow students and Derry county players Adrian McGuckin and Laurence Diamond were so good at rugby that our coach predicted that, if they continued to play the game, they would become Irish International rugby players.'

When regular Derry senior goalkeepers John Somers and Jimmy Hasson got injured during the 1970/71 league campaign, 18-year-old Mickey Moran was drafted into the side as an emergency goalkeeper. Later, in 1971, he made his first senior championship debut in the Ulster semi-final against Armagh as a midfielder. From then until 1984, Moran played in every position for the county team, winning successive Ulster championships in 1975 and 1976. His outstanding performances in the half-back line were to see him being selected as a replacement All Star in 1978 and gaining two Railway Cup medals in 1979 and 1980. During the last four years of his career, Mickey Moran was Derry's player-manager. This dual role curtailed his actual playing involvement. His last game was against Roscommon, when he came on as a substitute in the National League in 1984. Having represented the county for 16 years, Mickey bowed out, both as a player and manager, in the GAA's centenary year.

Being part of Derry's All-Ireland success in 1993 once again propelled Moran into the limelight, this time as one of the country's most prominent coaches. However, circumstances in 1994 were to see the profile of Derry football become a source of controversy, which would eventually lead to a different role for the likeable Glen man. In the first round of that year's Ulster championship, Derry lost both their provincial and national titles to Down in a classic encounter at Celtic Park. Just two points was the difference in the end. To compound the supremacy of Ulster football at that time, the Mourne men went on to defeat Dublin in the All-Ireland final and thus bring four successive All-Irelands to the province. However, one immediate result of Derry's defeat was the decision of the County Board not to re-appoint Eamon Coleman as manager. This precipitated controversy amongst players and spectators alike. Eventually, Moran was appointed manager, with Denis McKeever and Harry Gribben continuing as selectors. Some players refused to play in the opening rounds of the National League. Finally, all came on board and Derry returned to their winning ways when they annexed the league title the following year by defeating Donegal. Nevertheless, when Tyrone knocked Derry out of that year's championship, Mickey decided to relinquish his position. Former Dublin star Brian Mullins was then appointed to replace a tired Mickey, who had just given six years' total commitment to his native county.

Initially intending to take a complete break from football, the Maghera man was soon persuaded to become Sligo manager, a position he held from 1996–2000. During that period, he steered the Yeats County from Division Three to Division One of the league. Travelling a round trip of 260 miles twice weekly to Tubbercurry, as well as at weekends, took its toll, so he ended his fruitful stint with the westerners. Shortly afterwards, neighbouring Donegal enticed him to take over their senior side, a position he held for two years. The highlight of that period was a magnificent performance in the 2002 All-Ireland quarter-final against Dublin, when it took two games for the metropolitans to dispose of the resilient northerners.

When Eamon Coleman stepped down after his second managerial term with the Oak Leaf County in 2002, the call again came for Moran to take control of Derry — a position he insists is his last senior managership. In 2004, he guided them to an unsuccessful All-Ireland semi-final meeting with Kerry, who went on to convincingly beat Mayo in the final. In 2005, he steered them back to Division One of the league. This present Derry side have a nucleus of talented and experienced players in Barry Gillis, Seán Martin Lockhart, Niall McCusker, Paul McFlynn, Fergal Doherty, Enda Muldoon, Johnny McBride, Kevin McGuckin and Paddy Bradley. Derry can also call upon many other stars from the magnificent All-Ireland winning minor side of 2002. Gerard O'Kane, Patsy Bradley and Mark Lynch from that team have already made the transition in style. All Derry supporters are hoping that these players will give them another momentous September night very soon. Moran would certainly love to see that happen.

When I met Mickey in his Maghera home, he enthusiastically recalled all the players, events and coaches who positively impacted on his long years of service to Gaelic football.

1. 'Anton O'Toole, John Tobin, Jimmy Duggan, Liam Sammon and Pat Spillane were all fantastic players and friends. Eamonn O'Hara, Dessie Sloyan and Paul Taylor were very gifted Sligo players, who received great support from their colleagues during my spell there. I never came across so many truly skilful exponents of the game as

I did when I was in charge of Donegal. They could all play equally well either with or against the wind. During my time as a player, my own clubman, Frankie Kearney, was an outstanding manager. He bonded the county team into one unit. Before his time, there was a tendency for players from north and south of the county to stay in their own cliques. Since he joined our management team as a coach, Armagh man John Morrison has brought our coaching and tactical awareness skills to a new level. One other person deserves praise for Derry's 1993 All-Ireland victory. We introduced a sports psychologist, Craig Mahoney, to our management set-up that year. After Donegal beat us in that year's National League quarter-final, we had a four-hour team meeting in Ballymaguigan, at our next training session. I have no doubt that meeting, under Craig's guidance, was totally responsible for all of us making a concerted, united effort in ensuring that the Sam Maguire Cup came to Derry.'

2. 'I was reluctant, at first, to become involved in the International Rules management team in 1998. However, when I saw the high all-round standard of athleticism and commitment of the Irish players, my view changed. John O'Keeffe was a brilliant trainer, while Colm O'Rourke excelled with the wide range of his man-management attributes. I really enjoyed doing all the skills drills with such a talented group of athletes. The fabulous atmosphere during the matches, especially in the MCG in Melbourne and in Adelaide, will live with me forever.'

3. 'Since we played for Derry in 1969, Martin O'Neill and myself have kept up regular contact. Only last year, the Derry players went over to see Celtic and Martin in Glasgow. We were treated royally. In his office, three framed photographs take centre stage. One is of the St Malachy's College team from Belfast, of which Martin was a prominent member, which reached the Hogan Cup final in 1970. The others are of the Kilrea minor championship winning side and the Derry Ulster minor winning team, also of 1970. He is still a totally committed Derry GAA fan. Considering all that he has achieved in soccer, it is wonderful to see him retaining such an interest in his Gaelic roots.'

4. 'Regarding the rules of Gaelic football, I think there should be regular and structural meetings between management teams, players, referees and GAA administrators. These meetings should take place well in advance of the championship season. Once the championship season begins, any follow-up meetings would

concentrate on any difficulties, real or imagined, which would arise. At present, there is not enough communication between the people who really matter; i.e. management, players and referees. The whole process should be overseen, in a structured manner, by Croke Park.'

5. 'The current U-21 and U-18 championships should be scrapped and replaced by a new U-19 championship. All third-level competitions should be confined to the first term before Christmas. If these proposals of mine were introduced, they would alleviate the recurring problem of so many young players being answerable to so many different managers at the same time. More importantly, they would help considerably to reduce the stress or "burn out" factor that is the greatest single problem facing our young players today.'

Mickey made the following representative selections:

ULSTER (1970–2005)

Brian McAlinden
(Armagh)

Seán M. Lockhart   Gerry McCarville   Tony Scullion
(Derry)   (Monaghan)   (Derry)

Eugene Hughes   Henry Downey   Jim Reilly
(Monaghan)   (Derry)   (Cavan)

Anthony Tohill   Colm McAlarney
(Derry)   (Down)

Eugene McKenna   Frank McGuigan   Peter McGinnity
(Tyrone)   (Tyrone)   (Fermanagh)

Seán O'Connell   Seán O'Neill   Peter Canavan
(Derry)   (Down)   (Tyrone)

IRELAND (1970–2005)

John O'Leary
(Dublin)

| Seán M.Lockhart | Darren Fay | Tony Scullion |
| (Derry) | (Meath) | (Derry) |

| Séamus Moynihan | Henry Downey | Ger Power |
| (Kerry) | (Derry) | (Kerry) |

John McDermott   Anthony Tohill
(Meath)   (Derry)

| Pádraic Joyce | Frank McGuigan | Pat Spillane |
| (Galway) | (Tyrone) | (Kerry) |

| Jimmy Barry Murphy | Seán O'Neill | Peter Canavan |
| (Cork) | (Down) | (Tyrone) |

On the Saturday before Derry's 1993 All-Ireland final win, one man who dearly wished to be in Croke Park the following day knew he could not be there. His soccer duties with English club Wycombe Wanderers meant that he could not make the trip. He telephoned his two brothers in Ireland, Leo and Gerry, both former Derry players, to inform them that he would be videotaping the game and did not want to know the result in advance. To ensure this, all phones and answering machines were switched off on the Sunday. He wanted to experience the game 'live', soak up the atmosphere and see the players and the people of his native county. Just after nine o'clock on the Monday morning, he sat down to view the video. Alone in his sitting room, he enjoyed and suffered the full gambit of emotions that dedicated sports people do on such occasions. After the match ended, the Derry exile danced around the room in sheer joy, just as he had done as a six-year-old in Kilrea, when Derry beat Dublin in the 1958 All-Ireland semi-final. Then he rang his brothers and his old teammate to rejoice in Derry's finest hour.

Martin O'Neill, despite all the wonderful days that he had witnessed in the spacious soccer stadia of England and Europe, had returned to his first love. Mickey Moran hopes that Martin, some time soon, will be similarly rejoicing. Then, perhaps, the two of them will celebrate 'live' together in Croke Park. Derry fans certainly hope so.

MICKEY MORAN – FACT FILE

Native Place:	Maghera, Co. Derry
Date of Birth:	April 26, 1952
Club:	Watty Graham's, Glen

Colleges' Honours:	(a) St Patrick's College, Maghera
	    McLarnon Cup Winners, 1969
	(b) De La Salle, Manchester
	    British Club Senior Football Championship
	       (1973–74)

Club Honours:	(a) Glen Intermediate Football Championship
	    – 1981, 1984
	(b) Kilrea (amalgamation with Glen) Minor
	    Football Championship – 1970
	(c) Dungiven Hurling Club Minor Hurling
	    Championship (goalie)

County Honours:	Ulster Minor Football Championship – 1969, 1970 Ulster Senior Football Club – 1975, 1976 McKenna Cup 1974
Other Playing Honours:	Railway Cup – 1979, 1980 Rest of Ireland All Star Replacement, 1977
Awards:	Derry Player of the Year, 1976 Nominated for Derry Millennium Team Phillips Manager of the Month

Managerial and Coaching Honours: *(1) Club*	(a) Club, Omagh, St Enda's, Senior Football Championship Senior League
	(b) Carrrickmore Senior Football Championship (2) League (1)
	(c) Bellaghy Senior Football Championship Ulster Senior Football Championship
	(d) Faughanvale Junior Football Championship Intermediate Football Championship
	(e) Limavady Junior Football Championship Intermediate Football Championship
	(f) Clonakilty, Cork Senior Football Championship (Assistant)
	(g) Dunloy Ulster Senior Hurling Championship (Assistant)
(2) Schools	St Mary's, Limavady U-16 (5 county titles) Ulster champions – 1984
(3) County	Ulster Senior Football Championship – 1993 All-Ireland Senior Football Championship – 1993 National League – 1992, 1995 Ulster U-21 Football Championship – 1993
(4) Other	Coached Ireland International Rules Team to victory against Australia 1998, 1999
Occupation:	PE teacher
Family:	Married to Rita (née McAteer) from Creggan, Co. Antrim
Children:	Antoin, Conleth, Caoimhe

TEN

John Doyle–Tipperary

A GOLDEN HURLING LEGEND

Alone, all alone, by the wave washed strand,
And alone in the crowded hall;
The hall it is gay, and the waves they are grand,
But my heart is not there at all!
It flies far away, by night and by day,
To the times and the joys that are gone!
And I never can forget the sweet maiden I met,
In the valley near Slievenamon.

Charles Kickham

Well-known Tipperary GAA historian Bob Stakelum, in his excellent history of *Gaelic Games in Holycross-Ballycahill*, referred to the practical difficulties in ensuring that all relevant personalities and significant events were properly recorded: 'There is a good story about a publication based on the activities of a flying column during the War of Independence. A self-designated freedom fighter was annoyed because his name was not mentioned in connection with a particular engagement. He stormed into his local, some nights after the publication came on sale, and proceeded to annoy the customers with his complaints. "My name should be in the book," was the phrase he kept repeating. The publican noted signs of unease amongst his customers and, as there was a rival establishment nearby, decided to take action. He called the offender over to the counter, pulled out his ledger and in a voice that all could hear, said, "Your name may not be in the book but it is here in my book for £50 for the last three years! What are you going to do about it?" Peace descended on the establishment.'

Wherever and whenever the story of hurling all-time greats is told, the name of Holycross legend John Doyle will never be omitted. There is, however, one complicated dilemma. His feats were so many and so great that it is virtually impossible to do justice to his career within the constraints of a single chapter. With that caveat in mind, let us begin at the beginning. John Doyle was born in February 1930. Just a few days after his birth his mother died, leaving his father to raise their only child single-handedly. The local national school and the CBS secondary school in Thurles were to provide John with his formal hurling experiences. Being strong of stature and resolute of mind, he rapidly developed into a highly competent exponent of Ireland's national game. Timmy Hammersley, of Clonoulty, once recalled the burgeoning talent. 'It was an U-15 game between Holycross-Ballycahill and a neighbouring parish. Doyle lined out at centre half-back and dominated the game to such an extent that the opposition decided to "soften the cough" by introducing a player who looked as if he would never see twenty years of age again. Not to be outdone, Doyle played better than ever and the substitute was a sore and sorry man by the end of the game.'

In 1946, at the age of 16, John made his first appearance in a Tipperary jersey, going on to win a Munster minor championship medal by beating Cork in the final. Though defeated by Dublin in that year's All-Ireland minor final, Doyle and Tipperary went one better the following year when they won the All-Ireland minor title for the first time since 1934. Doyle was back again as a minor in 1948, only to be beaten by a brilliant Waterford side, which later claimed their second national crown at this level. The maturing Doyle was totally immersed in hurling at this early stage. Mick Mackey and, incredibly, future opponent Christy Ring were role models. It was, however, the silken skills of fellow Tipperary men Johnny Ryan, John Maher and the inimitable Tommy Doyle that he really wanted to emulate.

Two other factors dictated his hurling future. Holycross, being relatively close to where the GAA was founded in Thurles in 1884, was a proverbial hotbed of hurling activity. Outside of family, religion and politics, nothing else really mattered. Wherever you went in the parish, at the crossroads, at the forge, at funerals and at Mass, hurling was the predominant topic of conversation. Being reared on a farm, Doyle was familiar with prolonged hurling discussions at the threshing of the corn and the saving of the hay. In addition, he possessed an unyielding spirit of determination. 'I remember cycling down to the hurling field in Holycross and passing a young fellow who was a better hurler than I was. He asked me where I was going and when I told him, he said, "What are you going down there for, killing yourself?" I nearly turned back but, thankfully, I did not. Otherwise, I could have given up hurling altogether.'

In 1947, at the age of 17, John Doyle was selected for a National

Brian Corcoran,
the man who came
back, celebrates
another match-
winning score for
the Rebel County.

Trevor Giles, the
visionary royal leader,
receiving his Footballer
of the Year award in
1999.

Eugene McGee, former
All-Ireland-winning
Offaly football manager
and eminent journalist,
who wrote the
Foreword to this book.

Author, Séamus McRory.

James McCartan
(left) being greeted
by the late Séamus
Fitzpatrick just
after the full-time
whistle sounded at
the end of Down's
first All-Ireland
football final victory
in 1960.

Erected in honour of Frank Stockwell.
(*Courtesy of Francis Stockwell, Tuam*)

Erected in honour of Seán Purcell. (*Courtesy of Francis Stockwell, Tuam*)

The King of a Mourne dynasty – James McCartan (senior) with his grandson James the third (son of 'wee James').

Seán Purcell and Frank Stockwell talk together with GAA President Seán Kelly (centre) in Tuam. (*Courtesy of Francis Stockwell, Tuam*)

Johnny Dooley – the jewel in the faithful crown, an All-Ireland senior hurling medal winner in 1994 and 1998.

John O'Keeffe, prince of modern full-backs, who has won seven All-Ireland senior football medals with Kerry.

Mary Robinson, former President of Ireland, with Peter Quinn, a GAA President of exemplary vision, about to present the Liam McCarthy Cup to Kilkenny's 1993 All-Ireland winning captain, Eddie O'Connor.

Mickey Moran (second from right) pictured with the Derry team that won the
Oak Leaf County's first All-Ireland senior football title in 1993.
(*Courtesy of Danny O'Kane, Dungiven*)

A happy GAA President – Peter Quinn presenting the Sam Maguire Cup
to 1993 winning Derry captain Henry Downey (former Taoiseach, Albert
Reynolds, is in the background).

Paul Curran, Dublin's former Footballer of the Year, who is now looking forward to 'going back to the hill'! (*Courtesy of Hogan Stand*)

The Millennium Men (left to right) — Tony Reddan (Tipperary), Jimmy Doyle (Tipperary), Brian Whelehan (Offaly), Eddie Keher (Kilkenny), John Doyle (Tipperary), Ray Cummins (Cork). (*Courtesy of Hogan Stand*)

John Doyle (left), the winner of eight All-Ireland senior hurling medals, with long-serving Tipperary GAA official, Tommy Barrett.

Dickie Murphy with his wife Jacqui, and John Bannon with his wife Paula at the 1998 All Stars Banquet.

Dickie Murphy (centre) with captains Johnny Pilkington – Offaly (left) and Anthony Daly – Clare (right) prior to the 1995 All-Ireland senior hurling final.

John Bannon – the much-respected Longford official was Football Referee of the Year both in 1998 and 2002.

League game against Kilkenny. However, he did not appear again for the Premier County until October of the following year when he came on as a substitute in the 1948 league final against Cork. Having lost that final, Doyle experienced better luck when they got their revenge on the Leesiders by annexing the following year's league. John Doyle had just won the first of many senior National League titles that would come his way during the next two decades.

For both Tipperary and Doyle, 1949 was to be a wonderful year. Defeating Limerick in the Munster final was a major stepping-stone to All-Ireland glory. Tipp's team captain was another legendary Holycross man, Pat Stakelum. Doyle recalls that first significant victory: 'I will never forget the excitement of winning our first Munster senior title. We all came home from Thurles on our bicycles with the boots, togs and socks strung over the handlebars. Pat Stakelum tied the Cup to the bicycle as well. Nobody, now, would believe that. Of all the All-Irelands that I won, the first one, in 1949, stands out. All the others were memorable in their own way, but 1949 was extra special. We were playing Laois, who were captained by a fellow called Ruschitzko, who was of Polish extraction. We went to Dublin on the train and then got a bus out to Blackrock College where we were staying. We went to bed at 11 p.m. I remember us going to Mass the following morning and watching the steamers, out in the sea, going to England. When we came back into Dublin, on the bus, we saw all the colours of both teams. There was now no hiding place. The moment of truth was at hand. I was too young to be really nervous. Still, when a Croke Park official came in and told us we had ten minutes to be on the pitch, the importance of the whole occasion suddenly hit me. In the match, Laois did not do themselves justice and we won, rather easily, on a score of 3–11 to 0–3. From my own point of view, I was exceedingly happy my dream had come true and I had won an All-Ireland senior medal at 19 years of age. When we arrived home, the whole county seemed to be there to greet us. Thurles was jammed with people and bicycles.'

That was the first of three-in-a-row titles for the Premier County. In the 1950 final they beat Kilkenny by a point, and in the following year's decider they overwhelmed Wexford by 7–7 to 3–9. This was a magnificent achievement by a side that had a marvellous blend of physically strong as well as exceptionally gifted hurlers. John Doyle, who played at left half-back during those halcyon years, was just one star amongst many. Goalkeeper Tony Reddan, Pat Stakelum, Tommy Doyle, Seán Kenny (1950 captain), Mickey Byrne and Jimmy Finn (1951 captain) were the most accomplished players of that successful era.

During John Doyle's hurling career it was normal practice for the

National League winners to play a 'home' final in Ireland and the victors would play New York in the League final proper, in America. As John was a member of eleven Tipperary winning league sides, it meant that he was a regular transatlantic traveller. It was the first such trip, in 1950, which remains etched in his memory as a wonderful adventure into the unknown. 'In the 1950s very few of us would ever have got the opportunity of travelling, particularly on a plane, were it not for winning the National League. On our first journey, we boarded the plane at Shannon and flew for about an hour and a half. Then we heard a voice over the public address system. The plane had developed engine trouble. We were totally petrified. Thankfully, the plane was able to return safely to Shannon. The repairs were quickly attended to and, eventually, we landed in New York. There were over 2,000 people there to greet us and they really gave us a rapturous welcome. As emigration was rife at the time, the GAA were very strong in New York. All the Irish people would meet for a social get-together, every Sunday, in Gaelic Park. If you ever went to New York and you wanted to meet someone, Gaelic Park was the normal meeting venue.

'The final itself was an extremely hard-fought encounter and we were very lucky to win it by two points. There were 30,000 at the game. New York had a lot of excellent players such as Phil Grimes of Waterford and Terry Leahy of Kilkenny. Terry had won several All-Ireland medals with the Marble County and Phil would win his All-Ireland medal in 1959. It was almost a month before we returned home in mid-October. Coming back by ship to Cobh added to the tremendous enjoyment of the whole experience. I really enjoyed all those trips. They made us like one big happy family.'

When Tipperary did not win even a Munster title for the next six years, John Doyle began seriously to think about retiring. Even though Tipp had won four National Leagues during that period, the cut and thrust necessary for a good championship team was missing. By 1957 he had won three senior All-Irelands, six National Leagues and four Railway Cups. Besides, he was an only son with a huge responsibility in the running of a very large dairy and tillage farm. It was both a time-consuming and demanding type of work on its own, without the added complication of training several nights a week and being absent at weekends. John discussed his impending retirement with his long-term mentor and chairman of the hurling selection committee, the renowned hurling impresario Paddy Leahy. Paddy reminded John that he was only 27 years old and that he might later regret such a decision, and with this in mind John relented. With rare abandon, he prepared himself for the 1958 Munster senior hurling championship campaign.

In a totally devastating performance, Tipperary reclaimed the title when they literally annihilated Waterford in the provincial final. This was all the more impressive as the Decies were decidedly unlucky to have been beaten by only a point in the previous year's All-Ireland final against Kilkenny. Tipperary scored a highly impressive 4–9 to 2–5 win against Galway in that year's All-Ireland final. Doyle felt vindicated in his decision to remain at the epicentre of the Tipperary defence. Moreover, he had rediscovered his insatiable appetite for the game, which would see him appear in six out of the following nine senior finals. John Doyle, along with corner-back Mickey Byrne, had now won four All-Irelands, whereas Jimmy Finn had won three. Tipperary had also unearthed a galaxy of talented hurlers who would become household names in the following years. Defenders Michael Maher, Kieran Carey and Tony Wall especially were all tenacious tackling defenders who could always be relied on to hurl themselves out of trouble. Theo English, Jimmy Doyle, Donie Nealon and Liam Devaney were all approaching the zenith of their careers. However, it would be a few years before all that blossoming talent would have matured properly.

In 1960 they reached the All-Ireland final only to be beaten by a terrific Wexford side, led by full-back Nick O'Donnell. The Slaneysiders, for whom Tom Neville, Willie Rackard, Ned Wheeler and Padge Kehoe excelled, were simply too good for the Premier County. Undaunted, Tipperary returned to the championship in 1961 with renewed fervour and optimism. For the second successive year they defeated Cork in the Munster final, only this time the winning margin was an impressive eight points as compared to the previous year's two. In the final, new Leinster champions Dublin were in their first All-Ireland senior final since 1952. In a terrific game of fast and furious hurling, Tipperary just managed to edge out the gallant Dubliners by 0–16 to 1–12. John Doyle remembers vividly that tremendous Dublin side. 'That Dublin team deserved to win an All-Ireland. Jimmy Grey was a brilliant goalkeeper. Their captain, the late Noel Drumgoole, was a very commanding figure at full-back. Two very strong hurlers, Des Ferguson and the late Lar Foley, flanked him. His brother Des was one of the best midfielders I ever saw. The two Boothman brothers, in the forward line, nearly broke our hearts. I was playing left half-back and both of them were playing in the right side for the Dublin forward line. I never really knew which of them I was supposed to be marking. I still think it would be great for the game of hurling if Dublin would win an All-Ireland soon.'

Including that 1961 success, the Premier County won four All-Irelands in the 1960s, thus giving John Doyle four more Celtic Crosses, to make a grand total of eight gold medals. They followed up the 1961 success with outstanding triumphs in 1962, 1964 and 1965 over Wexford, Kilkenny and Wexford again. They also appeared in two further finals, in 1967 and 1968, when Kilkenny and Wexford beat them. This decade was an exciting one for hurling. On the one hand, Tipperary had established themselves as one of the greatest ever teams in the history of hurling. A terrific young Kilkenny side were emerging and about to seriously threaten their number one position. On the other hand, Cork were, as ever, dangerous but were not as dominant as they had been in the heyday of Christy Ring, who bowed out of competitive hurling in 1963. Though they won All-Irelands in 1960 and 1968, Wexford did not pose as great a threat as they did when the Rackard brothers, Wheeler, and English were in their prime in 1955 and 1956. To most neutrals and all Tipp fans, that Premier side of the 1960s was the team of the decade. The full-back line of John Doyle, Michael Maher and Kieran Carey, collectively known as 'Hell's Kitchen', were all strong, physical players who did not know the meaning of the word defeat. Mick Burns, Tony Wall and Len Gaynor were true hurling stylists. Theo English, Jimmy Doyle, Babs Keating and Donie Nealon would, in a decade hence, have been automatic nominations for the All Star awards. Centre half-forward or left wing-forward Liam Devaney was a highly intelligent player who led the attack with considerable aplomb and dash. The icing on the cake of that remarkable side was midfielder Mick Roche. Equally at home at centre half-back, Roche was one of hurling's greatest ever players. His striking, fetching and all-round athleticism made him a joy to watch.

In 1967, Tipperary again reached the All-Ireland final. This was hyped as a fascinating contest between the tried and trusted titans of Tipperary against the young pretenders — the Cats of Kilkenny. This journalistic scenario prompted John Doyle to remark: 'Do they think we will all be playing on crutches!' This was in reference to the fact that eight of the Tipperary side were over thirty years of age. However, come match day the big question on everyone's lips was, would John Doyle win his ninth All-Ireland senior medal and thus go ahead of Christy Ring in the medal stakes? Despite Doyle's best efforts, Kilkenny played superbly to emerge convincing and deserving winners. After the game, John Doyle announced his immediate retirement from inter-county hurling. One of the really great hurlers of all time had said goodbye to a world that had given him eight All-Ireland senior medals and eleven National Hurling League medals to add to his six Oireachtas medals, eight Railway Cup medals and 10 Munster championship medals. During those years he had also shown his unique versatility. He won his first three All-Irelands as a left corner-back, his next two as a left half-back and his remaining three as a right corner-back.

Sport is really a reflection of life. One man's disappointment is nearly always another person's opportunity. Kilkenny had prevented the Holycross hero from securing his record-breaking medal haul while they, at the same time, beat Tipperary for the first time in the All-Ireland championship since 1922. Doyle himself is totally philosophical and pragmatic about the significance of 1967: 'Listen, it would have been lovely to win the ninth medal but let me be honest. Hurling was good to me and I won more than enough. I often think of all the fabulous hurlers who either won very little or, in some cases, no medals at all. One of the best hurling artists I ever met was Jimmy Smyth of Clare. He never even won a Munster championship medal, never mind an All-Ireland medal. I was also 37 years of age. It was time to give up hurling as I had been training regularly at least twice a week for 18 years. I needed to concentrate more on my home and farming life.

'For about a year, I found it hard to adjust to the fact that I would be at home every weekend and that the trips to New York and England were but a distant memory. I also knew that I could not take it for granted anymore that I would keep my place on the team. I had played in three different eras with three separate sides. They were all great hurlers with their own individual styles and skills. During the sixties the competition for places was so intense that the Tipperary substitutes were nearly the second best team in Ireland! One of my only regrets is that I possibly let hurling dominate my life too much, to the detriment of not looking after things properly at home. Overall, however, hurling was fantastic to me. The GAA was not just a game to me. It was an institution, a way of life. I will always be thankful to the GAA for giving me such a marvellous time.'

During the course of John Doyle's illustrious career, he and his county were not just pre-occupied with All-Ireland success but also with the many tenacious battles in the Munster championship. Having played in fourteen Munster finals, the Holycross stalwart acquired ten provincial winners' medals. Their most intriguing encounters were with their nearest neighbours and deadly rivals, Cork. Anyone who witnessed the five successive finals (1950–1954) between these combatants will never forget the sheer intensity and relentless play of two of hurling's most superlative teams. It was not unusual for over 60,000 fans to attend these gladiatorial displays. In the early 1950s the country's greatest defender, John Doyle, and hurling's most brilliant marksman, Christy Ring, were at the peak of their careers. In John Doyle's view, however, it was the 1960 Munster hurling final between those traditional rivals that was the greatest game of all. So energy-sapping was it that many Tipperary supporters believed that the fierceness of that game meant that Tipp had nothing left in reserve for the subsequent

All-Ireland final against Wexford, which they lost rather easily. In the course of that Munster final an altercation took place between Doyle and his marker, Paddy Barry. John himself takes up the story. 'We had a row in the middle of the game. Then we did the honourable thing. We put the hurleys down, fought each other, finished the fight and then picked up the hurleys again. There was not a word about it afterwards but the crowd really loved it. If that happened now the red cards would be flashing ... and rightly so.'

At club level Doyle made his senior championship debut in a first round tie against Moycarkey at right half-back. During the 1947 mid-Tipperary final, against Thurles Sarsfields, he was switched to left half-back to mark Tommy Ryan, who was giving a lot of trouble to the Holycross defence. The 17-year-old gave a brilliant performance against one of the most stylish and accurate forwards ever to play for Tipperary. In October 1948 Holycross-Ballycahill, with John Doyle starting in the right half-back position, won their first ever senior county championship title when they defeated Lorrha. It was a particularly proud day for the club that was originally founded 63 years earlier, in 1885. John Doyle won two further senior championships in 1951 and 1954 as well as four mid-Tipperary championships. Two years after he retired from county hurling, in 1969, the Holycross man finally gave up club hurling as well. It is extremely doubtful that anyone will give such long service to the game of hurling, at such a high level, ever again.

John Doyle was renowned for his fearlessness and dedication on the field of play. His job, as he saw it, was to obtain possession and clear the ball downfield. He did not like forwards who tried fancy tricks or flashy play. He went for the ball, got it and cleared it, regardless of the many tackles and blows that came his way. All aficionados of hurling agree that John Doyle was, first and foremost, a good hurler who used his enormous strength and physique to clear his lines. Those privileged to see the duels between Pat Stakelum and John at Holycross training sessions are unanimous in their view that no one could see a better display of hurling craftsmanship anywhere. John himself is quite honest, as ever, about his hurling qualities. 'This whole business about our full-back line being like 'Hell's Kitchen' is really a myth. We were all big, strong players but we had to be if we were to get the better of such strong, skilful players as Nicky Rackard and Ned Wheeler. Furthermore, if we were not good, competent hurlers in the first place, we had no business trying to curb the likes of Christy Ring, Phil Grimes, Jimmy Smyth or Eddie Keher.'

When I met John in the Abbey Tavern in Holycross, which is owned by his daughter Sandra and her husband, he recalled with instant fervour and enthusiasm his great playing days and the wonderful players he met. 'Christy Ring was by far the best hurler I ever saw. He had uncanny skill and could do anything with a ball. He thought or dreamed about nothing except hurling. I remember beating Cork in a Munster final in Thurles. About an hour after the game I was walking past Hayes' Hotel when I saw the maestro himself. There he was talking to another Cork player and telling him what they would have to do to beat Tipperary in the following year's championship. How do you keep down anyone with a mind like that?

'Ring was also a very tough hurler. I remember there was a mighty tussle between Christy and another Tipperary player in a match in Cork. Though I was not involved in the dispute, I happened to be lying on the ground close to it and I got a fierce belt of a hurl as both men drew on the ball together. The result was that I got four stitches on my chin, and the scar is still there. Unlike most other players, the older Christy became, the better he seemed to perform. He was always trying to perfect and practise his skills.

'Christy was also a very kind, helpful person. When I went to stand for the Senate in the late sixties, I went down to Cork to do some canvassing. I went into Johnny Quirke's pub. Who was sitting in the corner, drinking a mineral, but the bould Christy? After he asked me what I was doing in Cork, I explained the complicated electoral procedures of going for the Senate. Immediately, he volunteered to go canvassing with me and we went round all his friends, who not only promised to vote for me but actually did. I could not believe how generous he was with his time.

'Frank Murphy of Cork was the best hurling referee I ever saw. He never went out on a field with any preconceived ideas about how he was going to handle certain players. No one knew the rules better than he did. He used the greatest skill of all — common sense. He just called it as he saw it. I am not happy about the way the GAA handles the whole rules issue. Hurling and football are different games and should be treated as such. Granted, you must have common disciplinary procedures, but hurling should not have to pay for the sins of football. In hurling you must have the two hands on the hurl to propel the ball. Thus, there is not as much pulling and dragging in it. Unfortunately, there are more football counties in Ireland than hurling counties. The end result of this is that football dictates what is done in hurling. It is totally unfair that a lot of hurling skills are being legislated out of the game. I know how the system works because I was on the Central Council for eleven years.

'The whole managerial system in football and hurling should be scrapped. We tend to copy what is done in soccer; people seem to forget that soccer managers are well-paid, full-time professionals. It is completely wrong to expect every manager in the country to steer his county to immediate success. We over-praise our managers when they win and we disown them when their team loses. The manager is always blamed for all of the ills of his team. I think the GAA should return to our original system where a selection committee, under a chairman, would make all the decisions regarding team management. In that way there would be collective responsibility and no one person would be isolated. Some of the personal criticisms that managers have received are just not acceptable.'

When selecting his representative teams, John Doyle did not consider any Tipperary player.

Munster (1948–1975)

Mick Cashman
(Cork)

Jimmy Brohan   Pat Hartigan   Tony O'Shaughnessy
(Cork)   (Limerick)   (Cork)

Mattie Fuohy   Paddy O'Donovan   Seán Herbert
(Cork)   (Cork)   (Limerick)

Séamus Power   John Kiely
(Waterford)   (Waterford)

Willie John Daly   Josie Hartnett   Christy Ring
(Cork)   (Cork)   (Cork)

Jimmy Smyth   Joe McKenna   Phil Grimes
(Clare)   (Limerick)   (Waterford)

Ireland (1948–1975)

Ollie Walsh
(Kilkenny)

Pat Henderson   Nick O'Donnell   Mark Marnell
(Kilkenny)   (Wexford)   (Kilkenny)

Jimmy Duggan   Billy Rackard   Johnny McGovern
(Galway)   (Wexford)   (Kilkenny)

Des Foley   John Connolly
(Dublin)   (Galway)

Seán Clohessey	Ned Wheeler	Eddie Keher
(Kilkenny)	(Wexford)	(Kilkenny)
Jimmy Smyth	Nicky Rackard	Christy Ring
(Clare)	(Wexford)	(Cork)

John Doyle's two sons, Michael and Johnny, also had success on hurling's playing fields. Michael won an All-Ireland minor medal in 1976 and was team captain when the Premier County secured their third All-Ireland U-21 title in 1979. Both Michael and Johnny won Munster U-21 championship medals in 1978. It was Michael, however, who was to play a central role in the revival of Tipp's senior hurling fortunes in 1987.

The years 1972 to 1986 are known as the barren years in senior hurling in Tipperary. For those 15 years a Tipp team did not win a single senior Munster championship title. When John Doyle's former colleagues Babs Keating, Donie Nealon and Theo English were ushered in as the new senior hurling management team in 1986, a spirit of renewed optimism permeated the county. Under the guidance of team manager Keating, Tipperary defeated Kerry in the first round of the 1987 Munster championship. The Premier County then went on to defeat Clare, at the second attempt, quite comfortably in the Munster semi-final. In a pulsating encounter, Tipperary and Cork drew in the Munster final. The replay, in Killarney, has been labelled as one of the greatest games of all time. Cork led by a five-point margin at the interval. Thanks to the individual brilliance of ace forward Nicholas English, a resurgent Tipperary pegged back the deficit. When the final whistle sounded, the sides were level. A standing ovation then acknowledged the magnificence of the spectacle that a packed Fitzgerald Stadium had just witnessed. In extra time, substitute Michael Doyle scored two wonderful goals to seal victory for the Premier County, on a scoreline of 4–22 to 1–22. When Tipperary captain Richard Stakelum began singing 'Slievenamon' on receiving the Munster Cup, all Tipperary supporters were ecstatic in their excitement. A 15-year famine of Munster titles had ended. Just as in 1949, the surnames Stakelum and Doyle had been central to a monumental triumph.

On All-Ireland hurling Sunday in 1987, three wonderful ambassadors of Tipperary hurling — Tommy Doyle, Jimmy Doyle and John Doyle — were selected as the Premier County's representatives to commemorate, in Croke Park, 100 years of championship hurling. When their names were read out, the whole stadium spontaneously arose to acclaim their never-to-be-forgotten heroes. John Doyle had taken his final bow in the theatre of his most memorable performances.

No one brought more honour to the blue and gold of Tipperary than the man from Holycross.

JOHN DOYLE – FACT FILE

Native Place:	Holycross, Co. Tipperary
Date of Birth:	February 12, 1930
Club:	Holycross-Ballycahill
Club Honours:	Senior Hurling Championship (3) – 1948, 1951, 1954
	Mid. Senior Hurling Championship (5) – 1947, 1948, 1951, 1954, 1966
County Honours:	All-Ireland Minor Hurling Championship (1) – 1947
	Munster Minor Hurling Championship (2) – 1946, 1947
	All-Ireland Senior Hurling Championship (8) – 1949, 1950, 1951, 1958, 1961, 1962, 1964, 1965
	Munster Senior Hurling Championship (10) – 1949, 1950, 1951, 1958, 1960, 1961, 1962, 1964, 1965, 1967
	National Hurling League (11) – 1949, 1950, 1952, 1954, 1955 (Captain), 1957, 1959, 1960, 1961, 1964, 1965
Other Honours:	Railway Cup (6) – 1951, 1952, 1953, 1955, 1960, 1963
	Oireachtas (6) – 1949, 1960, 1961, 1963, 1964, 1965
Awards:	Texaco Player of the Year 1964
	Hall of Fame 1992
Administration:	Central Council Representative – 1975/76, 1978/79, 1983–1990
Occupation:	Retired dairy farmer
Family:	Married to Ann (née Reidy)
	John, Michael, Margaret, Elizabeth, Ann-Marie, Colette, Sandra

ELEVEN

John Bannon/Dickie Murphy–
Longford/Wexford

BLOWING THE WHISTLE FOR FAIR PLAY

'The majority of referees are of doubtful parentage, blind in both eyes, geriatric, stupid, always prejudiced in favour of the other team — or must be, if you were to believe the perpetual cribbers in the game. Although the conduct of most officials, players and spectators is exemplary, there are always those who must dispute practically every decision, those who feel that the referee is a personal enemy of their team.' These comments are an excerpt from a very incisive and thought-provoking article on the role — perceived and real — of the referee in Gaelic games. Prominent Derry GAA official Séamus Mullan from Dungiven wrote those words, in his county's GAA yearbook, in 1978. Unfortunately, those observations and the general tone of the article are as relevant today as when Séamus, a former inter-county referee, made them over a quarter of a century ago.

It is interesting to note that when there is trouble during a game, very often the performance of the referee comes under the microscope at an early stage. Too often a referee is held responsible for outbreaks of violence on the field of play. Too often he is made the scapegoat for the thuggery of players and the abject lack of courage by team officials. It must be repeated, ad infinitum, that the primary responsibility for ensuring good conduct and sportsmanship on the field rests, not with the referee, but with the officials of the club or county. The task of the referee is to decide between right and wrong according to a set of rules, implicitly accepted by those who play the game. If club and county officials actively and openly assisted the referee during a game, insisting that players accept decisions without question and substituting players who are involved in dangerous play, then the task of the referee would be much easier, and the game would benefit immensely.

Since the foundation of the GAA, the Association has been blessed with thousands of eminent officials who have ensured the smooth and efficient administration of Gaelic games on the field of play at club, county and provincial levels. Two such outstanding exponents are Wexford's leading hurling referee, Dickie Murphy, and his football counterpart, from Longford, John Bannon. It was my privilege to meet these two present-day knights of the whistle, in the Heritage Hotel in Portlaoise, where we covered a variety of topical refereeing issues. Being the fair-minded individuals they undoubtedly are, they insisted that their job was made considerably easier by the commitment and vigilance of their long-serving umpires. For the record, Dickie's are John Tyrell, Paddy Shiggins, Paddy Buckley, Matt Flynn, Jim Doyle and Morgan Murphy. Mick Doherty, Tommy McCormack, Johnny Marlowe and Peter O'Reilly are John's trusted assistants.

1. *What were your early GAA experiences?*

   D.M. 'My parents were very interested in Gaelic games and when I was growing up, in the late sixties and early seventies, Wexford had a great hurling team. My heroes would have been Tony Doran and especially the Quigleys, Dan, John, Martin and Pat. Our club, in my hometown of Enniscorthy, the Rapparees, also had a tremendous influence on me. Even though Wexford did not win any more All-Irelands during my formative years, I still followed them religiously because we looked upon them as the second best team in Ireland. They were just unfortunate to come up against a brilliant Kilkenny side so often. From my own point of view, I played for Wexford at minor, U-21 and senior levels. I won a Leinster U-21 medal in 1979, when we beat Kilkenny by a point. At senior level, even though I won Oireachtas and Walsh Cup medals playing as a forward, I was never considered good enough for senior championship hurling.'

   J.B. 'We had a pub at home, in Carrickboy in County Longford. During the seventies we were the first to get a colour television in the parish and people from all around used to come in on Sunday afternoons to watch the big games. Kerry and Dublin were the dominant teams at the time. For an All-Ireland semi-final or final there would be at least 120 people in to watch the game. The locals were split equally in their loyalties to the Dubs and the Kingdom. Our pub, on those occasions, had the atmosphere of a minor Croke Park, such was the partisanship of both sets of supporters. I know some Kerry people might not believe it, but I was a very enthusiastic fan of Kerry. Players like John O'Keeffe, Jack O'Shea, Mikey Sheehy, Pat Spillane and Eoin Liston were my heroes. My father and uncles were all great GAA followers. At St Mel's College my interest increased dramatically. I played on the 'B' team and scored six points in a Fr McGee Cup final. The score in that game was very unusual. We were beaten by 5 goals to 1–11. Later I won two junior championships and a senior 'B' championship with my club, Legan Sarsfields.'

2. *How did you become interested in refereeing?*
    D.M. 'As a 17-year-old, I had become a district secretary of Bord Na nÓg in Wexford. The county was divided into four such areas. One of my tasks was to get referees for each of the eight finals. Through a mixture of unavailability of referees and my laziness, I ended up refereeing seven and a 'half' finals. The 'half' occurred because my own team was involved, so a representative of our opponents refereed the first half and I refereed the second half. The whole refereeing 'bug' took off from there. My first inter-county game was a Division Three National League contest in 1985. That was the same year that I refereed my first county final, between Buffer's Alley and Faythe Harriers. Terence Murray of Limerick and John Denton of Wexford were my favourite referees. My first really major game was the 1989 Leinster minor hurling final between Kilkenny and Offaly, which ended in a draw.'

    J.B. 'Growing up, I was always conscious of how difficult it was to get All-Ireland tickets. Even though I was a club delegate to the County Board, this problem seemed to be always there. I made a conscious decision to take up refereeing in order to qualify for an All-Ireland ticket and then I did a GAA referees' course. At the same time I was a student in Maynooth, so I went and did a soccer referees' course. However, I never actually took charge of a soccer game. My initial interest in the Maynooth course was because referees got paid and third-level students always needed money. To my mind when one speaks of great referees, and there have been many, Paddy Collins and Tommy Moran were the best. My first senior inter-county match was a National League game in Carlow, between the home side and London in front of about twenty people. Just before that, I was in charge of a Leinster junior championship game between Kilkenny and Westmeath in Castletowngeoghegan. In my first senior championship game, between Kildare and Laois, I had to send off three players.'

3. *What was the highlight of your refereeing career?*
    D.M. 'I was lucky to referee four senior All-Ireland finals in 1992,

1995, 1997 and 1998. The first one was rather special because it
was my first. Earlier in 1992, I was honoured to be selected to
officiate at the All-Ireland club final between Kiltormer of Galway
and Birr of Offaly. There was a great feeling getting ready for that
1992 All-Ireland between Kilkenny and Cork. My umpires and
myself went up on the Saturday. We went to the annual seven-a-
side competitions that were, as always, splendidly organised by
Kilmacud Crokes. We stayed in the Clarence Hotel that night and
met up with Terence Murray, who was in charge of the following
day's minor final. Terence was a great help to me because he had
refereed a senior final a few years before that. Just before the actual
game began was the worst time. I remember meeting my father
after the game. As he watched me waiting for the game to start,
the words of the song 'Alone, All Alone in a Crowded Hall' came
into his mind. I could not think of a better way to sum up the
thoughts of a referee before a major game.'

J.B. 'Like Dickie, my first All-Ireland, in 1998, was my favourite
occasion. The secretary of the GAC rang me on a Wednesday
morning, a few weeks before the All-Ireland, to officially confirm
my appointment. I could not believe it. It was always my dream to
be in charge of an All-Ireland senior football final. Unfortunately,
my late mother was diagnosed with cancer on the Friday before
the game and she had to undergo a surgical procedure in the
General Hospital in Portlaoise. My wife, Paula, and myself called
to see her on Sunday and she was feeling fine. Being very relieved,
we drove to Dublin only to discover one of my umpires, Johnny
Marlowe, had awoken with a pain in his back. Anyhow, Johnny
passed a 'late fitness test', so we celebrated all our good news by
having an assortment of expensive sandwiches in the Shelbourne
Hotel for £70! I was very lucky with my two All-Ireland finals as
both of them were very sporting contests. Like playing, luck plays
a huge part in a referee's career. The only time that negative doubts
can enter your mind is during the pre-match parade. During that
time I have thought of the implications if I did something wrong.
But when the ball is thrown in, I might as well be refereeing an
ordinary club game.'

4.   *What was your worst refereeing experience?*
     D.M. 'Back in 2001, Clare and Tipperary were playing in a very
     tense, action-packed Munster championship game in Páirc Uí
     Chaoimh. There was no quarter asked or given. In the end,
     Tipperary won by a point and I came in for an awful lot of criticism.

Both sides had already met in the League final the previous spring and Clare apparently had missed a lot of scores. Unfortunately for Clare, in the championship game, they also were very wasteful in front of goal. I felt the criticism was unwarranted because I always called every decision as I saw it. When I blew the full-time whistle that day, I was happy with my performance and I am still happy with it.'

J.B. 'My worst experience was the drawn All-Ireland semi-final between Kerry and Armagh in 2000. Armagh were leading when Maurice Fitzgerald, deep into the last quarter, scored a brilliant goal to leave Kerry only a point behind. Just before I blew the final whistle, Fitzgerald scored an excellent free to draw the match. It was the only time after a match I ever came off the field to so many 'boos'. Kerry supporters were annoyed that Armagh got four times as many frees as Kerry, and Armagh were crestfallen because they felt that I played too much injury time. What happens in this situation is that people forget the total picture. Kerry had dwelt on the frees given against them in the second half, without thinking of the first half. Armagh, on the other hand, forgot that I had to allow extra time for a Kerry player being injured.'

5. *Do you recall any unusual incidents during the course of your career?*
    D.M. 'I was refereeing a league semi-final between Laois and Tipperary in 1998. A dog came onto the pitch and, after much running around, I eventually caught him and took him off the field. A few years later, a player in Leitrim fell over a dog during a game and injured himself. He then took the County Board to court and I was asked to appear as a witness, because of my 'dog control' experience. I had to make two court appearances, one in Dundalk and one in Dublin. However, the case was settled out of court but I was happy. I got my expenses, accommodation and meal allowances, thanks to two matches and a dog!

J.B. 'I remember refereeing a Leinster club game some years ago. I thought I did well. The following week I met a mentor of one of the participants. Not recognising me in my 'civvies', he told me, in front of former GAA President, the late John Dowling, that he had witnessed the worst ever display of refereeing at the above-mentioned game. 'What was his name?' Dowling ventured. 'All I know he was some stupid referee from Longford,' came the reply. John immediately recognised the man's faux pas. That club official has been exceptionally nice to me ever since!'

6. *What was your reaction after you made a major error in an important game?*

    D.M. 'As far as I know I did not make any big mistake in any game that I officiated. People might believe otherwise! I have been very fortunate in that regard. When games produce a close result, referees' performances are under closer scrutiny. The referee who does not make mistakes has not yet been born. The real difference between a good referee and a better referee is that the latter makes fewer mistakes.'

    J.B. 'When I went home and watched the highlights of that Armagh/Kerry All-Ireland semi-final of 2000, I realised I made a very bad decision. After two minutes in that game, an Armagh defender fouled Dara Ó Cinnéide about a metre outside the large rectangle, but Dara fell inside it. I am not making excuses but Croke Park was being developed at the time and I misread Dara's actual position where he was fouled. It was rather ironic that afterwards, many Kerry supporters criticised my overall performance but did not mention the penalty incident.'

7. *Do you believe there should be more formal communication between managers, players and referees?*

    D.M. and J.B. 'We believe there should be three well-structured meetings each year. At the start of the year there should be a 'get-together' of managers, players, administrators and referees. All issues pertaining to the implication of the rules should be òn the agenda. Then a proper report on decisions taken should be circulated to all parties. About four weeks before the beginning of the All-Ireland hurling and football championships, a further meeting should take place between the managers, administrators and referees. All problems, real or imaginary, should be sorted out. The National Leagues, both in hurling and football, would probably have thrown up some contentious areas. It is important that these meetings be made compulsory for all the interested parties. In the past, arrangements have been haphazard. To be fair to managers, they need plenty of advance notice for such meetings so that they can plan their county training sessions accordingly.

    'When the provincial championships are over, it is vitally important that the referees, the administrators and the managers meet to review the situation. We believe it would help the communications lines, for all concerned, if the referees who would be involved in the concluding stages of the championships were at this meeting. However, that would mean that they would have to be selected sooner than at present. We believe that if the system were as structured as we suggest, it would lead to less confusion and a more harmonious relationship between all parties.'

8. *In rugby, managers sit in the stand. Do you believe this should happen in Gaelic games?*
    D.M. 'Having been a Wexford selector for a few years made me see both sides of this argument. One of the most common complaints against us as selectors was that we were sitting in our seats and doing nothing to help the team. I know players definitely want to see their manager active on the sideline. It makes them feel that someone really cares about what is happening on the field.'

    J.B. 'This is a problem which starts at under age level and is particularly prevalent in the club scene. At club level, the manager is really like a 16th player. This is wrong and leads to a lot of hassle. I think Eamon Coleman got it right. When asked, after being temporarily banished from the sideline, did he feel it unfair to have to direct operations from a seat in the stand, he said, "It took this punishment to make me realise how much more a manager can see from the stand." Walking along the sideline, a manager cannot see a proper overview of the game. Yes, it is better for all concerned that the manager should be in a designated area in the stand.'

9. *Should all umpires at major games be experienced referees?*
    D.M. and J.B. 'Not at all. Umpiring is a very specialist art in itself. About three or four times a year, we hold regular briefing sessions with our own umpires. If one of our umpires receives a negative comment, in our assessment we naturally refer to it and try to rectify the problem. At those briefing sessions we reinforce our checklist of "do's" and "don'ts". If there are changes in the games' rules we study them in detail, as we do with all existing rules. Before every match we repeat our time-worn mantra: "Watch everything. Don't get involved in enjoying the game. You can watch that when you go home tonight."'

10. *What are your views on the current referee recruitment system?*
    D.M. 'The greatest problem here is the negative attitude adopted by many parents in the U-12 and U-14 age categories. Regarding the number of new recruits becoming referees, we in Wexford are lucky. Many soccer referees officiate at GAA matches and vice versa. However, the main stumbling block to the recruitment

system are the parents, who give shocking verbal abuse to referees. We have to try to change the mindset of those parents who only see their own children on the field of play.'

J.B. 'At national level our recruitment system is okay but, despite the valiant efforts of many, at county level the whole process leaves a lot to be desired. What is required is a specialist refereeing department at Croke Park. Those involved at present are doing the best they can but they have responsibility in other areas such as administration, coaching and games development. We should move everything forward on a more expert footing, with special emphasis on fitness, assessment and video analysis. The GAA has paid too much lip service to the importance of referees. It is time for the referees to be treated on a par with all other units of the association, especially as regards availability of match tickets and achievement awards. If this were seen to be done and a high-profile marketing strategy adopted, then referee recruitment would be much easier.'

11. *What are your views on other often-asked questions such as having two referees and a faster implementation of the referees' reports?*
    D.M. and J.B. 'There is no apparent need for two referees. There are seven officials at any game. If they are doing their jobs properly, as most of them do, then there is no need for a second referee. With so much modern technology at our disposal, there is no excuse for not having referees' reports dealt with on the Monday night, following each inter-county league and championship game. With a new separate disciplinary committee now in place, this should lead to a much speedier resolution of all referees' reports.'

12. *Should time-keeping be in the hands of a fourth official or hooter?*
    D.M. 'The present regulation does not present a problem for me and neither would I have any qualms if a new procedure was introduced. Regardless of which system is in place, it must always be remembered that the referee has to announce the proposed additional time to whoever is in charge.'

J.B. 'In last year's All-Ireland semi-final between Mayo and Fermanagh, some Mayo supporters booed me coming off the field when I blew the half-time whistle. The reason for this was that I stopped the game when Mayo were attacking. My job was to blow the whistle exactly when the two additional minutes were up. This I did. Even though the present time board has brought more credibility to the referees' honesty, I would be totally in favour of introducing the hooter system, as in ladies' football.'

13. *Do you think the assessment process needs revamping?*
D.M. 'The purpose of the assessment routine is to help the referee improve his overall capability as a referee. Whatever about the age profile of the assessors, I would be happy with the present assessment system.'

J.B. 'I have two serious problems regarding assessment. The present assessors are a fine group of dedicated men, but most of them were assessing when I joined the inter-county referees' panel over fifteen years ago. Secondly, I read recently one startling statistic. Out of a sample group of seventy assessments, 25 were rated as good, 45 were evaluated as very good and none received a fair or poor mark. Now, no referee wants to receive a bad report but it beggars belief to really think that there were no bad performances. It is my opinion that this is symbolic of a GAA mentality which implies that you never criticise your own.'

14. *What are your views on the rules of football and hurling?*
D.M. 'I don't believe hurling rules should be changed just to accommodate problems in football. Of course, we must have common disciplinary procedures. Many referees in the stronger, dual counties, such as Tipperary and Cork, referee both hurling and football games. If the disciplinary rules were changed, this would lead to much confusion amongst referees, particularly in the above counties. A suspension system, though, should be introduced for those who accumulate a certain number of yellow cards. If this were done, it would put manners on the persistent offender and thus considerably clean up the game.'

J.B. 'I was disappointed with the experimental rules introduced at the beginning of 2005. They were too rushed and much too confined. The most serious problem in Gaelic football is the hand pass. In its execution it has really become a throw and makes football look like rugby league. Some commentators complain about the massed defensive system currently in vogue. As a referee I have no problem with it. It is open to team managements to use strategies to defeat this ploy. To me, the hand pass needs to be re-addressed urgently. Its overuse and abuse is severely curtailing the basic skill of kicking.'

15. *Finally Dickie and John, what are your overall impressions of your refereeing careers and how do you see the future panning out?*

D.M. and J.B. 'Well, first of all, we will probably referee for another few years, both at club and inter-county levels. Despite our reservations in some areas of procedure, the whole refereeing experience has been one of tremendous pleasure and enjoyment. It has also been a huge privilege to be part of so many fabulous GAA occasions. We would like to express our thanks to the GAA for selecting us to officiate in such faraway places as America, Australia, Scotland and Hong Kong. Only for them, we probably would never have had an opportunity to see so much of the world.'

Dickie and John made the following representative selections. Dickie did not consider any Wexford players for either of his teams.

DICKIE'S LEINSTER HURLING XV (1985–2005)

Michael Walsh
(Kilkenny)

Pat O'Dwyer   Kevin Kinahan   Willie O'Connor
(Kilkenny)   (Offaly)   (Kilkenny)

Brian Whelelan   Joe Dollard   Pat O'Neill
(Offaly)   (Laois)   (Kilkenny)

Johnny Pilkington   Niall Rigney
(Offaly)   (Laois)

John Troy   John Power   Joe Dooley
(Offaly)   (Kilkenny)   (Offaly)

Johnny Dooley   D.J. Carey   Charlie Carter
(Offaly)   (Kilkenny)   Kilkenny

DICKIE'S IRELAND HURLING XV (1985–2005)

Brendan Cummins
(Tipperary)

Conor Hayes   Brian Lohan   Willie O'Connor
(Galway)   (Clare)   (Kilkenny)

Brian Whelehan   Brian Corcoran   Seán Óg Ó hAilpín
(Offaly)   (Cork)   (Cork)

Ken McGrath
(Waterford)

Ciarán Carey
(Limerick)

John Leahy
(Tipperary)

Joe Cooney
(Galway)

Jamesie O'Connor
(Clare)

Joe Dooley
(Offaly)

D.J. Carey
(Kilkenny)

Joe Deane
(Cork)

JOHN'S LEINSTER FOOTBALL XV (1975–2005)

John O'Leary
(Dublin)

Robbie O'Malley
(Meath)

Mick Lyons
(Meath)

Robbie Kelleher
(Dublin)

Paul Curran
(Dublin)

Kevin Moran
(Dublin)

Michael 'Spike' Fagan
(Westmeath)

Brian Mullins
(Dublin)

John McDermott
(Meath)

Matt Connor
(Offaly)

Colm O'Rourke
(Meath)

Trevor Giles
(Meath)

Dessie Barry
(Longford)

Kevin O'Brien
(Wicklow)

Dessie Dolan
(Westmeath)

JOHN'S IRELAND FOOTBALL XV (1975–2005)

John O'Leary
(Dublin)

Robbie O'Malley
(Meath)

Mick Lyons
(Meath)

Robbie Kelleher
(Dublin)

Páidí Ó Sé
(Kerry)

Kieran McGeeney
(Armagh)

Séamus Moynihan
(Kerry)

Jack O'Shea
(Kerry)

Brian Mullins
(Dublin)

Matt Connor
(Offaly)

Peter Canavan
(Tyrone)

Maurice Fitzgerald
(Kerry)

Colm O'Rourke
(Meath)

Eoin Liston
(Kerry)

John Egan
(Kerry)

In 1942 former GAA President Paddy McFlynn played for his club, Magherafelt O'Donovan Rossa's, in the Derry county final against Glenullin. The referee appointed for the game was County Chairman Paddy Larkin — a fellow teacher and friend of McFlynn's. To add novelty to the occasion, McFlynn was also County Secretary. Both being natives of South Derry and transport being scarce in wartime, they naturally travelled together to the game in Dungiven. Though the Rossa's were winning a lot of possession, their small forwards could not cope with the tall, strong Glenullin defenders. To counteract this forward fragility, the commanding figure of centre half-back McFlynn was switched to full-forward. Nearing the end of the game, McFlynn gave a full-blooded shoulder charge to the Glenullin full-back, putting him not only over the end line but also into the railing surrounding the pitch. Referee Larkin immediately took McFlynn's name and sent him off. In a totally dispassionate manner, the County Chairman had dismissed the County Secretary!

After the game, the two friends 'togged in', gathered their belongings and drove home together. There was no bitterness, no rancour, just two GAA aficionados recalling the merits of the Rossa's victory and the demerits of Glenullin's performance. Both acted completely oblivious to anything remotely untoward having occurred on the field of play. Each one, instinctively, knew that the rules of the game were greater than personal prejudices or camaraderie. Those parameters were confined to an hour on the football field. Their friendship endured for over 50 years, until Paddy Larkin died in the latter half of the 1990s.

Today, what the GAA urgently requires is a return to those values of honesty, courage and equality with regards to how we treat our referees. If this were done, then the Dickie Murphys and John Bannons of the refereeing world would gain the iconic status of playing superstars. After all, they are the men in the middle who continually and expertly conduct the games of the Gael. All of them deserve our deepest gratitude and constant appreciation.

Dickie Murphy – Fact File

Native Place:	Enniscorthy, Co. Wexford
Date of Birth:	September 18, 1961
Club:	(a) Rapparees, Enniscorthy; Starlights, Enniscorthy

Club Honours:	(a) Rapparees
	    U-12, U-14, U-16, U-18 Junior Hurling
	        Championship
	(b) Starlights
	    U-21 Football Championship
	    U-21 Hurling Championship

County Honours:	Leinster U-21 Hurling Championship – 1979
	Walsh Cup Senior Hurling Championship –
	   1987
	Oireachtas Senior Hurling Championship –
	   1987

Selectorial Honours:	Leinster Minor Hurling Championship – 1985 Leinster U-21 Hurling Championship – 1997 Leinster Senior Hurling Championship – 2004

Refereeing Honours:	All-Ireland Senior Hurling Final (4) – 1992,
	   1995, 1997, 1998
	All-Ireland U-21 Hurling Final (2) – 1998, 2001
	All-Ireland Club Hurling Final (1) – 1992
	National Hurling League Final (1) – 1992
	Leinster Senior Hurling Final (3) – 1991, 1995,
	   1998
	Leinster U-21 Final (2) – 1998, 2001
	Leinster Minor Hurling Final (2) – 1989, 1997
	Leinster Club Hurling Final (4)
	Munster Senior Hurling Final (1) – 1999
	Ulster Senior Hurling Final (2) – 1992, 1993
	Fitzgibbon Cup Hurling Final (4)
	Wexford Senior Hurling Final (8)
	Shinty Internationals (2)
	Australasia Hurling Final (1) – 2003
	Australasia Football Final (1) – 2003
	North American Hurling Final (1) – 1998

Awards:	National Irish Bank Referee of the Year (2) – 1992, 1997 Eircell Referee of the Year (1) – 1998
Occupation:	An Post Employee
Family:	Married to Jacqui (née Doyle) from Enniscorthy)
Children:	Cathal, Brian, Ruairí

JOHN BANNON – FACT FILE

Native Place:	Carrickboy, Co. Longford
Date of Birth:	November 1, 1963
Club:	Legan Sarsfields
Club Honours:	Senior 'B' Championship (1) – 1995
	Intermediate Championship (1) – 1981
	Junior Championships (2) – 1990, 1994
	Former Longford Minor Board Chairman
Refereeing Honours:	All-Ireland Senior Football Final (2) – 1998, 2002
	All-Ireland Senior Football Club Final (2) – 1998, 2000
	All-Ireland Minor Football Final (1) – 1997
	Leinster Senior Football Final (1) 1998
	Munster Senior Football Final (1) – 2000
	Longford Senior Football Final (3) – 1994, 1997, 2001
	All-Ireland Colleges Senior 'A' Final 2003
	All-Ireland Colleges Senior 'B' Final 2000
	All-Ireland Colleges Senior 'C' Final 2004
	Leinster Club Senior Football Final (2) – 1997, 2001
	Sigerson Cup Final (2) – 1999, 2003
	Leinster Minor Football Final (1) – 1986 (plus replay)
	Wicklow Senior Football Final (1) – 2002
	Longford Minor Football Final (2) 1990, 1993
	All-Ireland Masters Senior Football Final (1) – 1996
	North American Senior Football Final (1) – 1999
	Asian Senior Football Championship Final (1) – 2003
Award:	Football Referee of the Year (2) – 1998, 2002
Occupation:	Sales Executive
Family:	Married to Paula (née McElligott)
Children:	Mark

Twelve

Jimmy Murray—Roscommon

KNOCKCROGHERY'S MOST REVERED SON

When Roscommon took the field for the first time in an All-Ireland senior football final, on September 26, 1943, their captain, Jimmy Murray, took a deep breath as he surveyed the lush green sward of Croke Park. Never had he seen such a carpet of exquisite green as it stretched quietly amidst the cauldron of deafening noise and unadulterated excitement that comprised the stands and terraces of the famous arena. In that moment of entry, a thousand thoughts and a multiplicity of experiences flashed through his mind: 'I thought of how fate had prepared me for this great day. Felix Walls had left his Magherafelt home in County Derry over forty years previously to take up a teaching post in Athleague National School in the heart of County Roscommon. Subsequently, his younger sister Susan, who was over twenty years his junior, joined him to act both as his housekeeper and to complete her secondary school education in Roscommon town. She too, eventually qualified as a teacher in the same school, met my father John, married him and settled down to rear a family of ten children in my native Knockcroghery. I was the eldest of eight boys and two girls, and as a young fellow I had often imagined myself leading the parade around Croke Park on All-Ireland final day. I could not now believe that those parades of fantasy around our back garden or in my bed at night were to be replaced by reality. I always looked at the newspapers on a Monday morning after a final, and stared in wonder at the photograph of the teams marching behind the band. Now here I was, not only in the parade but also as captain of my beloved Roscommon, about to lead it. In addition, my brother Phelim was in that parade as he was a member of the team. When the actual parade began, I momentarily became very afraid and wished that I was away from the pitch and sitting up in the stands. I then looked up at Mícheál Ó Hehir in the commentary box. I imagined he was probably saying "... and here comes Roscommon, led by the fair-haired Jimmy Murray from Knockcroghery ..." My spine started to tremble and I immediately thought of my home village as I tried to envisage what my father and mother were doing. My mother was a deeply religious woman and I knew she would be up in the room and praying the Rosary. There she would remain until the game was over, periodically checking with my father down in the kitchen to find out the score and to hear how her two sons were playing. I knew my father and all our neighbours would be huddled together, listening intently to the radio and constantly staring at it in the corner of the kitchen. All these thoughts inculcated in me a great sense of bursting pride. I was intensely happy, totally focused and determined to do or die for the sake of Knockcroghery and Roscommon. As we reached the middle of Croke Park, I was suddenly awoken from my trance. The referee called me over and I met the Cavan captain, Big Tom O'Reilly. He had a huge, friendly smile and appeared totally relaxed. However, when the ball was thrown in, personal friendships had to be cast aside. I had to turn my All-Ireland dream into actual fact.'

Cavan, the Ulster champions, started the game more impressively and raced into an early lead. In the second quarter Roscommon, though still playing poorly, recovered somewhat. An inspirational point by young Roscommon midfielder Liam Gilmartin, followed by a brace of minor scores from Jimmy's brother Phelim, reduced the deficit and by half-time the men from the west were only four points adrift.

Shortly into the second half, Jimmy Murray scored the most important goal of his career. Right half-back Brendan Lynch sent a very long, high kick deep into the Cavan defence. Realising that the ball would probably break away from the clutching hands of both backs and forwards, Jimmy astutely positioned himself where he felt the ball might drop. 'It fell right in front of me as I faced the Cavan goalmouth. I caught it and in the one moment, instinctively, kicked it straight to the net. I could not believe it, and when, soon afterwards, I scored the equalising point, I definitely knew my mother's prayers were being answered.'

Ace free-taker Donal Keenan, a future GAA President, appeared to have the game won for Roscommon when he converted a late free. However, Cavan were not to be outdone, and that wonderful left half-back John Joe O'Reilly restored parity on the call of time. Despite Roscommon's great fight back, the Ulstermen had survived to fight another day. The consequent replay was anti-climactic. The game was close, tough and uncompromising, with Cavan having a player sent off. Nevertheless, Roscommon had considerably improved from the drawn encounter. They retained their composure and recorded a momentous victory on a 2–7 to 2–2 scoreline. Opportunist goals by

Jack McQuillan and Frankie Kinlough ensured a famous triumph for Jimmy Murray and his record-breaking colleagues.

Jimmy will never forget the next forty-eight hours. 'There was a great reception for us when the final whistle went, and later a celebratory meal, hosted by the Roscommon Association in Dublin. One of my most treasured possessions is the telegram of congratulations from my mother and my father as we sat down for that meal. On Monday evening, Roscommon people living in Dublin came in their hundreds to the train station to applaud us on our way home. The train, bedecked with the Roscommon colours, was greeted by supporters at every station that we passed through. At Athlone, where we crossed the River Shannon into our home province of Connacht, the platform and surrounding areas were packed with well-wishers and I got out and said a few words. All along the train route from Athlone to Roscommon town, a continuous line of bonfires blazed brightly on that lovely, mild and happy October evening. Along that route and six miles from Roscommon town lies Knockcroghery. There, in my home village, a massive bonfire blazed at the railway gate as children and adults in their hundreds marched in a torchlight procession. That was a very special moment for me. It was made even more special when Phelim and I saw our parents for the first time since Roscommon and Knockcroghery had become the centre of attention in the whole of Ireland. After we arrived in the county town, the County Council hosted an official reception in the Harrison Hall. The dancing and the celebrations lasted until daylight the following morning. Jimmy Murray's life had changed irreversibly, and beautifully so, forever.'

Jimmy Murray was born on May 5, 1917. From an early age, he was totally infatuated with Gaelic football. When a senior pupil in the local national school collected donations from his fellow pupils to purchase a football for 5/11 in Smarts' shop in Dublin, Jimmy's first official induction into the world of Gaelic football commenced. That pupil, Frank Owens, who sadly died early in life, was the most influential person in Jimmy's fledgling Gaelic football career. His first letter to Santa Claus epitomised his love affair with football. 'I got my first football from Santa. My brothers, our neighbours and myself kicked the ball for hours on Christmas Day, on the fairgreen. On St Stephen's Day, we played again for countless hours. That evening, I greased the ball with Neat's foot oil, which was normally used by farmers to soften leather boots. When I had it greased, I left it, in my innocence, in front of a big open fire to dry. Of course, after a few minutes there was a loud explosion and the ball was in bits. However, Santa Claus came again, rather mysteriously, two nights later with a new and better football. It was only afterwards that I realised the sacrifices my parents made. They allowed me to go training five nights a week, or for three or four months at a stretch, when we were doing collective training with Roscommon during the 1940s. My family ran a country business — bar, grocery, hardware and drapery. Most of our customers were farmers and the majority of the business was done in the evening or at night. Even though I felt guilty about not helping them, my parents forced me to go to the training sessions because they knew I just loved Gaelic football.'

Eventually, the young Murray progressed so well that he was selected on the Roscommon minor team in two successive years, 1934 and 1935. Incredibly, Roscommon did not have a senior team when they reached the All-Ireland junior semi-final against Limerick in 1939. That Limerick side, which included the famous Mackey hurling brothers Mick and John, went down to the westerners by five points. However, that Roscommon team, which included Jimmy Murray amongst its ranks, was defeated by Dublin in the home final. That same year, Roscommon won their first All-Ireland minor title when they defeated Monaghan. Future senior star Liam Gilmartin was their winning captain. The following season, 1940, Roscommon won their first All-Ireland junior football title when they defeated Westmeath by ten points. Jimmy Murray, Donal Keenan, Owensie Hoare and captain Hugh Gibbons played starring roles, and Jimmy's brother Phelim came on as a substitute. When Roscommon won another All-Ireland minor title in 1941, their supporters knew that with proper management the county that was now regarded as a senior side could make further significant progress. The new, emerging senior side had, after all, suffered narrow one-point defeats to Galway in both the 1941 and 1942 Connacht senior finals. A major breakthrough was now awaited by all and sundry.

In the Connacht final at St Coman's Park in Roscommon in 1943, that vital senior success duly arrived when the home side dethroned a Galway team that had appeared in the previous three All-Ireland finals. 'This, up to then, was our greatest victory. Galway had terrific footballers in Dinny and Tom Sullivan, Charlie Connolly and Jarlath Canavan. Frankie Kinlough notched a brilliant goal for us but he got injured and had to retire. Young Liam Gilmartin came on at midfield and played a blinder.' When Roscommon's scorer supreme, Donal Keenan, raised another major flag in the second half, they were on their way to their first Connacht title in 29 years. 'Once the final whistle blew, the scenes of euphoria were absolutely mind-boggling. We had an all Pioneer Piper's band in Knockcroghery at the time, and they always led the team around the field before our games. After this game, they lined up again and they marched through the town playing stirring music, with most of the Roscommon supporters following them, cheering and shouting, "Come on, Roscommon".'

In the All-Ireland semi-final, Roscommon met Louth. It was a brilliant game of fast, flowing, competitive football. That prince of full-backs, Eddie Boyle, and his brother Seán were outstanding in the Louth defence, with All-Ireland sprint champion Kevin Connolly and the incisive Peter Corr equally impressive in the forward line. Nevertheless, it was Roscommon who were the overall superior side. Again, the peerless Frankie Kinlough scored a decisive goal when he punched a cross into the Louth net, thus ensuring an eventual four-point victory for the westerners. So the stage was set for that first All-Ireland senior final for Jimmy Murray and his team.

To win one All-Ireland takes great players, magnificent effort and a total communal focus to the immediate task in hand. When Roscommon returned to win the title the following year, they and their back-to-back captain proved themselves to be something special. What made the occasion and the achievement even more significant was the fact that they defeated Kerry, the renowned kingpins of Gaelic football.

In the 1944 campaign, Roscommon defeated Sligo (after a replay), Mayo and Cavan again on their way to the final. That game attracted a then record crowd of over 79,000. There was a contrasting clash of styles — the traditional catch and kick of the Kingdom as against the combined, passing movement of Roscommon. Even though World War II was ongoing and both public and private transport facilities were limited, Roscommon fans literally left by all modes of transport, traditional and unconventional. Overloaded trains, jammed with Roscommon supporters, in dark and dismal carriages, creaked and hissed their way to the metropolis.

That great GAA author, the late Raymond Smith, in his book *The Football Immortals*, sets the scene so well, in his own inimitable style: 'Youngsters thumbed lifts on lorries bringing turf to the city; others walked the ninety miles to Dublin, setting out days beforehand; one man left Roscommon on his bicycle at midnight on the eve of the match and cycled all through the night. The gates had to be closed before the beginning of the game. Fifteen minutes from the end of this wonderfully exciting match, as the crowds, caught by the excitement of the struggle, bent like corn in the wind on the embankments, Kerry stood two point in front.'

It was then that this Roscommon side rose heroically to the phenomenal task with an exceptional display of ball-winning, radar-like passing and deadly opportunism. Time and time again their superb half-back line of Brendan Lynch, Bill Carlos and the versatile Phelim

Murray intercepted fine Kerry moves and relentlessly drove the ball forward. Eamon Boland and Liam Gilmartin reasserted their midfield superiority, and the forward line, led by the swerving, side-stepping Jimmy Murray, did the rest. The Kerry defence, particularly Joe Keohane and Tadhg Healy, were fine, almost unstoppable, high fielders but the clever Murray decided to keep the ball low and away from them. He played like a third midfielder, waiting for Boland and Gilmartin to break the ball down to him before he would send sweeping passes out to his roving wing-forwards Donal Keenan and Frankie Kinlough. When the aforesaid Keenan pointed two frees to bring the sides level, the Roscommon supporters were in full voice. With ten minutes to go, Murray increased the volume as he constantly cajoled his teammates with his renowned and repetitive mantra of 'Come on Roscommon'. How fitting it was that Murray would win the next vital ball and then thread a lovely precision pass to the unmarked Kinlough. To a crescendo of ear-splitting cheering, Frankie put the ball over the bar for the lead point. With time almost up, the deadly accurate Donal Keenan, from a free, added another minor to leave Roscommon ahead at the final whistle by two points. Roscommon had now passed the ultimate football litmus test of beating Kerry in an All-Ireland final. As in the previous year, bonfires blazed all along the final leg of the homeward journey from Athlone to Roscommon. What a transformation in the fortunes of Roscommon football! Within six years they had progressed from a junior side to back-to-back All-Ireland senior winners, and Jimmy Murray was at the fulcrum of it all.

In 1945, Roscommon lost their Connacht title to a Mayo team whose star player was Henry Kenny, the father of the present Fine Gael political party leader. Thanks to a last-minute goal by Jimmy Murray in the following year's Connacht final, Roscommon edged Mayo out by the minimum of margins. However, the legality of this score was disputed and a replay was ordered. Jimmy is still very defiant on this issue. 'The dispute arose because I was allegedly in the square when I gained possession. I was well outside it when I sent the ball to the net. The umpires appeared hesitant as to what to do, so I ran in and raised the flag myself. Funnily enough, I had watched my own boyhood idol, Brendan Nestor of Galway, doing the same thing in a Connacht final. Still, justice was done when we won the replay by seven points.' In the All-Ireland semi-final Roscommon overcame Leinster champions Laois by two points to secure another final meeting with Kerry in the 1946 final.

In the first half of that game Roscommon were absolutely fantastic as they cantered to a half-time interval lead of seven points. With time running out, six points still separated the teams but their captain fantastic was now lying on the sideline with a broken nose. Then, incredibly, Roscommon conceded two late goals to allow Kerry to equalise. A bloodied Murray returned to the fray and almost scored a winning point. When the full-time whistle sounded, the sides were level and another replay loomed. 'That was our greatest ever display, as a team, yet I do not know how we managed to lose such a commanding lead. It will also always rate as my greatest disappointment.'

When the replay date came around, Roscommon had lost their competitive edge and their insatiable appetite for the game. A combination of circumstances was responsible for this: 'We did two weeks collective training before the Connacht semi-final, another two weeks prior to our replay against Mayo, as well as further training before the Laois match and the two All-Ireland finals. In addition, the replay was postponed to the end of October, because of the bad harvest. Nonetheless, to all Kerry supporters and many neutrals, the replayed game was a classic. But when we lost by four points we instinctively knew we had really said goodbye to the big time, even though we were to win the following year's Connacht final. It would now be up to another Roscommon team to play on All-Ireland senior final day. Little did we think that it would be sixteen years later before the great Gerry O'Malley would have that singular honour of leading Roscommon in 1962.'

When I met Jimmy Murray shortly before his 88th birthday in May 2005, he was like a young child with a newfound toy as he pleasantly recalled a host of wonderful memories on the Gaelic fields of Ireland in the 1930s and 1940s. The beautifully appointed lounge and modern supermarket, where he was proprietor for so long, is now run by John, his eldest son. A fabulous array of GAA memorabilia adorns the walls of the lounge, and a large scrapbook depicting the career and times of Gaelic footballer extraordinaire, Jimmy Murray, takes pride of place in the corner. More than anything else, Jimmy's most precious artefact is the All-Ireland winning ball of 1943, which has been suspended from the bar ceiling since then. The man himself is reserved, a great storyteller who loves to reminisce about times past. His gentleness and humility belie the strength of character that manifested itself so assuredly on the playing fields of Ireland so long ago.

'I have seen some wonderful footballers in my time. I would not like to dwell too much on my former teammates, but I would single out Brendan Lynch for his consistency, my own brother Phelim for his versatility (he has won Connacht colleges inter-provincial medals in both hurling and football and was regarded by the famous Limerick hurler Dick Stokes as a naturally gifted wielder of the camán), Frankie

Kinlough for his scoring proficiency, Donal Keenan for his free-taking ability. Bill Carlos and Eamon Boland were great leaders on the field of play. Henry Kenny of Mayo was the longest kicker of a ball and the cleanest player I ever encountered. Gerry O'Malley and Dermot Earley were Roscommon's most outstanding footballers. Seán Purcell was the best footballer I ever saw. Jim McKeever (Derry), Mick O'Connell (Kerry) and Tommy Murphy (Laois) were my favourite midfielders.'

When it came to picking his Connacht and Ireland teams, Jimmy made the following choices:

CONNACHT (1940–1960)

Aidan Brady
(Roscommon)

Willie Casey	Mick Connaire	Dinny Sullivan
(Mayo)	(Galway)	(Galway)

Tom Regan	Bill Carlos	Frank Fox
(Mayo)	(Roscommon)	(Galway)

Gerry O'Malley   Eamon Boland
(Roscommon)   (Roscommon)

Donal Keenan	Seán Purcell	Nace O'Dowd
(Roscommon)	(Galway)	(Sligo)

Frankie Stockwell	Tom Langan	Packie McGarty
(Galway)	(Mayo)	(Leitrim)

IRELAND (1940–1990)

Aidan Brady
(Roscommon)

Willie Casey	Joe Keohane	Dinny Sullivan
(Mayo)	(Kerry)	(Galway)

Tom Regan	Tommy Murphy	John Joe O'Reilly
(Mayo)	(Laois)	(Cavan)

Jim McKeever   Mick O'Connell
(Derry)   (Kerry)

Iggy Jones	Seán Purcell	Pat Spillane
(Tyrone)	(Galway)	(Kerry)
Matt Connor	Tom Langan	Mike Sheehy
(Offaly)	(Mayo)	(Kerry)

As well as joining that unique band of captains who have led their county to two successive All-Ireland senior football titles, Jimmy is the only man to have led his team on five occasions on All-Ireland final day. This occurred twice in 1943, once in 1944 and twice again in 1946. When I asked Jimmy what did he really attribute Roscommon's unparalleled success in the 1940s to, his reply was succinct and definite: 'Our County Chairman, Dan O'Rourke (another future President), and our county secretary, John Joe Fahy, left no stone unturned to secure our success. When we started collective training at first, we stayed in Dan's house in Tarmon, near Castlerea, and his own family fed us for weeks on end. His garage was converted into an emergency dormitory. John Joe Fahy's belief in us was total. Before the first round of the Connacht championship, against Leitrim in 1943, John Joe handed me our team sheet in the dressing rooms and added, quite seriously, "I hope I'll be doing the same thing on the last Sunday in September!" Both Dan and John Joe were very religious men. On the night before the 1943 All-Ireland, just as we were about to go to bed, they led us in a recitation of the Rosary. I could not imagine that happening now.

'The contribution of Galway man Tom Molloy, who trained Roscommon in 1943, and Billy Keogh's enormous training assistance in 1944 earn a particular niche of affection in Jimmy's memory. Billy was ahead of his time when he used different psychological tactics to motivate his players. Before the Kerry game he put a notice over each player's bed: 'Keep the ball low.' 'It was in the dining hall, in the corridors. In fact, the same maxim was everywhere. We just could not miss it, but, most importantly, we kept it,' concluded Jimmy.

Jimmy loves all kinds of music, especially the music of the famous tenors such as Mario Lanza and John McCormack. He himself is no mean performer and in 2003 he recorded his first CD, entitled 'The West's Awake'. Not bad for a man of eighty-five!

When I left Jimmy's hospitable company, I was armed with a plethora of wonderful stories and joyful experiences, recalled in the twilight of a great life. Two final memories highlight the greatness, loyalty, determination and pure love of Gaelic football that Jimmy Murray possessed in such abundance. In January 1990, over 46 years after his initial All-Ireland triumph, a huge fire enveloped his licensed premises and grocery business in Knockcroghery. Neighbours and the local fire brigade fought bravely to quench the raging flames, which quickly engulfed the whole business complex. Suddenly, in the midst of all the pandemonium, someone screamed, 'Where's Jimmy?' As several men rushed towards the building, fearing the worst, a sprightly, grey-haired figure suddenly emerged from amidst the smoke, swerving and sidestepping his way, as he had done so often in his football heydays. For one last precious time, he had clutched that magical pigskin — this time from the imminent danger of being destroyed forever as it lay amongst the charred ruins of his smoke-filled bar room. Though slightly blackened today, that ball, with all the signatures of Roscommon's first senior All-Ireland team, remains Jimmy's most precious possession and a lasting testament to that first historic day in the annals of Roscommon football.

Finally, Knockcroghery's most famous son meditates for a short while before explaining in clear, simple terms what he values in life and what he aspires to in the future: 'Every morning, now, I say my prayers and think about the welfare of all my family. Then, I look at that old ball of leather, which brought so much joy to so many Roscommon people all those years ago. My fondest and most abiding memory of that year is when Phelim and I returned home with the ball and the Cup, after all the public celebrations had ended on the Tuesday morning. We walked into the kitchen, where our parents literally welcomed us with open arms. There were just the four of us in the whole wide world and as we hugged each other, we kept staring at the Sam Maguire Cup and the ball in an intimate moment of complete privacy.

'Somewhere between Castlerea and Tarmonbarry, or Boyle and Kiltoom, there is a boy playing in his back garden or sleeping in his bed, and dreaming my ancient dream. I hope that boy's dream comes true before I leave Knockcroghery. Roscommon people deserve another All-Ireland soon.'

JIMMY MURRAY – FACT FILE

Native Place:	Knockcroghery, Co. Roscommon
Date of Birth:	May 5, 1917
Clubs:	(a) St Patrick's, Knockcroghery (b) Roscommon Gaels
Club Honours:	(a) St Patrick's Senior Football Championships (6) – 1942, 1943, 1945, 1946, 1948, 1949 Junior Football Championships (2) – 1936, 1938 Junior Hurling Championship (1) – 1945 (b) Roscommon Gaels Senior Hurling Championship (1) – 1938
County Honours:	All-Ireland Senior Football Championship (2) – 1943, 1944 All-Ireland Junior Football Championship (1) – 1940 Connacht Senior Football Championship (4) – 1943, 1944, 1946, 1947 Connacht Junior Football Championship (2) – 1939, 1940
Other Honours:	Oireachtas Medal in 1943 Hall of Fame 1993
Family:	Married to the late Ann Costello from Headford in Galway
Children:	John, Michael (aide de camp to An Taoiseach Bertie Ahern), Jimmy, Mary, Susan

THIRTEEN

Mick Higgins–Cavan

FROM NEW YORK AND BACK AGAIN

He led Cavan to victory on that
Memorable day,
In the final against Kerry in New York
Far away.
The next year in Croke Park, when our
Boys beat Mayo,
Once again, they were led by the gallant
John Joe.
In each corner of Breifne, there's sorrow
And pain.
Such a true-hearted sportsman we'll
Ne'er see again.
New players may come and old players
May go.
But we'll ne'er have another like the
Gallant John Joe.

Tommy Gilronan

Between 1933 and 1952 Cavan won five senior All-Ireland football titles and were beaten finalists on four other occasions. In this, the zenith of Cavan football, sixteen Ulster titles were also secured. During this era, the Breffni County produced a plethora of outstanding footballers. Those All-Ireland winning captains — Jim Smith, Hugh O'Reilly, John Joe O'Reilly (twice) and Mick Higgins — fall into this category. Cavan supporters of that time will enthusiastically proclaim that Higgins was the best centre half-forward of all. Former Kerry half-back Jackie Lyne, who played against Higgins in the 1947 All-Ireland final in New York's Polo Grounds, had no doubts about the veracity of this. Mick was 'the greatest centre half-forward I ever faced bar none'.

On the Monday morning after the 1952 All-Ireland final when Higgins led Cavan to their fifth national senior championship title by beating Meath, the *Irish Independent* was fulsome in its praise of the Cavan captain: 'It is not often that an All-Ireland turns out to be such a triumph for an individual but without him, and the apparent indifference with which he ambled up to every free, the result could have been different.' On the following Friday, the same paper nominated him as Sports Star of the Week. Later, in December of that year, he was awarded Sportsman of the Year. Higgins, who was born in America, lived in Mayo and played minor football with Kildare, was now a true blue Cavan hero.

Shortly after his birth in New York in 1922, Mick Higgins came to his mother's home place in Kilnaleck in County Cavan. Then he changed abode, for three years, to his father's native Kiltimagh, in County Mayo, before returning to Kilnaleck to complete his primary education. Future Cavan star forward Peter Donoghue was a fellow primary school pupil. Tony Tighe from Ballyjamesduff joined them when he started playing football in the U-14 county league with Mountnugent. It is no coincidence that in later years, when the Cavan senior football team became famous for their radar-like passing movements, the names of Higgins, Donoghue and Tighe were all part of their magnificent forward line.

When his primary days were over, Mick went to St Mary's Marist Brothers' Secondary School as a boarder, in Dundalk. Here he came under the tutelage of Derry-born Fr MacOscar, who was a real GAA enthusiast. Mick's footballing career blossomed rapidly and he played at right half-forward on the school's Ulster Colleges' Mac Rory Cup winning team of 1938. With the Louth side, which then played in Ulster Colleges' competitions, the 15-year-old had won his first major trophy. Paddy Meegan, who would later win All-Ireland medals with Meath in 1949 and 1954 and who played against Mick on numerous occasions, was also on that Mac Rory Cup winning team.

After completing his secondary education, Mick went to live with his uncle-in-law, in Celbridge in County Kildare. His prowess on the football field soon came to the attention of the Kildare minor selectors. In 1940, with Mick at centre-field, Kildare reached the Leinster minor final, only to be defeated by Louth. The 'Wee County' then went on to win that year's All-Ireland minor title and thus became the first holders of the Tom Markham Cup. Despite being relatively happy in the Short Grass County, there was a longing in the young barman to return to his Cavan roots. His boyhood heroes, like big Tom O'Reilly, Paddy Smith and Jackie Smallhorn, had all played for Cavan in the 1937 All-Ireland final against Kerry, which they had only lost after a replay. His number one icon from that 1937 team was Cornafean's greatest ever player — the redoubtable John Joe O'Reilly. Mick thought to himself, rather modestly, that maybe some day he, too, would play alongside the gallant John Joe.

In 1942, Mick played his first match for the Cavan junior team, and he made his senior championship debut in the following year's Ulster championship. When they beat Monaghan in the Ulster final, Cavan were destined to face Cork in the All-Ireland semi-final. A one-point win over Cork meant that Mick, at the age of 21, was in his first senior All-Ireland final. However, luck was not with the Ulstermen as they lost, after a replay, to first-time All-Ireland senior winners Roscommon. 'That 1943 season was a great experience. We played well in the first half of the game, but Roscommon came back brilliantly to take the lead. We had to depend on a fantastic last-minute point from John Joe O'Reilly to save the match. In the replay, we played poorly and had a man sent off. Roscommon deserved to win. They had a magnificent midfield pairing in Eamon Boland and Liam Gilmartin. Jimmy Murray was a wonderful footballer and an inspiring captain on the field,' added the lithe and very fit-looking 82-year-old when I met him at his home, outside Virginia.

In 1944 Cavan again reached the All-Ireland semi-final, only to be heavily defeated again by that exceptional Roscommon side, who went on to repeat their All-Ireland success of the previous year. The following year, 1945, was to see Cavan meet Wexford at the penultimate stage. In spite of sterling performances from Wexford's centre half-back Bill Goodison and full-forward Nick Rackard, the Breffni men scraped through to the final against Cork. Again luck was not with them as the Munster men won convincingly. 'I was beginning to think there was a jinx on us. This was further emphasised when Antrim, in the following year's Ulster final, beat us. No one really expected this to happen. We were somewhat consoled when Antrim played very well in the All-Ireland semi-final against Kerry. They lost only by three points in a game that is best remembered for the toughness of its physical exchanges. At that time, Antrim were really the only other Ulster side which provided real, consistent opposition. They had a lot of great footballers like Harry O'Neill, George Watterson, Seán Gallagher, Kevin Armstrong, Seán Gibson and Paddy O'Hara.'

One man did not let the awful spring of 1947 deflect him from his ambition of having the All-Ireland football final of that year played in New York. For the three previous years, Canon Hamilton of Clare had unsuccessfully made the same plea that the All-Ireland be played in New York to commemorate how the American people had opened their arms to the emigrant Irish a hundred years before. 'Black 47', as

1847 was known, was the year that the potato blight had driven Irish people in their thousands to America. Canon Hamilton argued that playing the All-Ireland in America would be a huge psychological boost for generations of Irish Americans who might never see the 'auld country' again.

At the 1947 Annual GAA Congress, it appeared that the Canon's motion was doomed to failure. During an adjournment in the debate, he again canvassed the delegates for their support. This time he showed them a heart-rending letter from an exiled priest, stating how privileged he would be if the All-Ireland would take place in the US. When Congress resumed, the motion was passed. Though it subsequently turned out that the letter was a hoax, no one complained and all the arrangements were made for the historic trip.

Meanwhile, both the Cavan and Kerry teams were returning by boat from a tournament game in England when the word came through that Congress had passed the momentous motion. Renowned Kerry full-back Joe Keohane turned to Mick Higgins and uttered the prophetic words, 'The next time we will meet will be in the All-Ireland final in New York. I have no doubt about that.' Because of the prospect of a transatlantic journey, no provincial or All-Ireland semi-finals were ever as keenly contested as those of 1947. One incident from that year — the Munster final between Kerry and Cork — highlights this. Simon Deignan, a Cavan player, who was to feature as a left half-back in that year's decider, was the referee. Raymond Smith, in his book *Football Immortals*, recounts a controversial incident described to him by Kerry's legendary Joe Keohane: "'Simon Deignan awarded a penalty to Cork. Kerry protested, claiming it was an unfair decision. At the same time there was a break in play, owing to an injured player receiving attention. I had my foot on the ball, on the penalty spot. As I argued with the referee, I kept pressing the heavy ball deep down into the muddy ground. Jim Aherne, the penalty taker, then naturally missed the kick, which trickled along the ground into the safe arms of our goalkeeper, Danno O'Keeffe.'" After the game, with tongue in cheek, Keohane told Cork trainer Jim Barry, "It was awful, Jim, to see 15,000 Corkmen being fooled, at 3 o'clock on a Sunday afternoon in a big field!" Afterwards Keohane admitted to Cork's stalwart midfielder, Eamonn Young: "It was not very sporting, I admit, but Eamonn, I could see the Manhattan skyline."'

As events panned out, defending All-Ireland champions Kerry easily accounted for Meath in the semi-final. Cavan, who had gained their revenge over Antrim in the Ulster final, beat the unsuccessful 1946 All-Ireland finalists Roscommon in the All-Ireland semi-final by 2–4 to 0–6. Mick Higgins was destined to play his third All-Ireland final in the land of his birth, 3,000 miles away from home and amongst three generations of the Irish Diaspora.

In their preparations for the final, Cavan trained much longer than their Kerry opponents. This was because the Kingdom made the journey by sea, whereas the vast majority of the Cavan side went by air. Almost 35,000 spectators turned up on a blistering hot afternoon to see the historic All-Ireland. The venue was the Polo Grounds, the home of the New York Giants' baseball team. The mayor of New York, Bill O'Dwyer, a native of Bohola in Mayo, threw the ball in on the bone-hard pitch. Simultaneously, every household in Ireland with a wireless set was crowded as they listened intently to the words of Mícheál Ó Hehir's commentary on a game so far away. Radio Eireann had done marvellous work in securing a cable for the broadcast.

The Kerry team, which had taken the precaution of wearing white peaked caps as a protection against the blazing sun, totally dominated the early stages of the game. After fifteen minutes, they were ahead by eight points. During the opening quarter they had scored two goals and had two others controversially disallowed, much to the annoyance of their supporters. As a result, the referee, Wexford man Martin O'Neill, who was also Leinster Secretary, did not endear himself to the Kingdom's supporters. At this stage their wing-forward, Batt Garvey, was getting a plentiful supply of the ball from his midfield colleagues. His dazzling runs were primarily responsible for the Munster man's two goals. Necessity demanded that Cavan revamp their side, and this they did, with an almost immediate and positive effect. With midfielder P.J. Duke now back in defence, a totally focused Cavan took the game to their opponents.

As Cavan started to attack constantly, a sudden sea change occurred in the attitude of the majority of the spectators, who at the outset were partisan Kerry supporters. Cavan right half-forward Tony Tighe sped towards the Kerry defence. He avoided one Kerry defender but collided heavily with Kerry star Jackie Lyne, who had anticipated the sidestep. The spectators, not being familiar with the rules of Gaelic football, unfairly branded Kerry as a dirty team and loudly booed the incident. Thereafter, they were very vociferous in their support of the Breffni men.

It was now that Cavan centre half-forward, Mick Higgins, was seen at his majestic best, when he dashed through the Kerry defence to score a fantastic goal. With their style of continually hand-passing the ball at speed, Higgins, Tighe, Peter Donoghue and Joe Stafford were causing all kinds of pandemonium for increasingly nervous Kerry defenders. Only a brilliant save by Kerry netminder Danno O'Keeffe prevented another Cavan goal. Still, thanks to a host of frees, scored with consummate ease by full-forward Donoghue, the Breffni men retired at the interval leading 2–5 to 2–4.

Just before half-time, Kerry had suffered a cruel blow when ace midfielder Eddie Dowling was forced to retire injured, after falling heavily on the hard ground. The previous year's captain, the great Paddy Kennedy, who had lined out at corner-forward with a heavily strapped ankle, also had to retire in the second half. 'Even when we were eight points down after fifteen minutes, I was pretty hopeful because we had scored our two points fairly handily. I realised that if the Kerry midfield could be curbed, we had the forwards to cause trouble in their defence. Eddie Dowling's injury was a definite loss to Kerry. So, at half-time we were reasonably optimistic of a successful outcome,' Mick honestly admitted.

The second half proved to be a much more dogged affair, with very little open play and defences generally on top. The sweltering heat, the unfamiliar humidity and the rock-hard surface all combined to slow down the pace of the game and reduce the quality of the football. With five minutes left, each side had only added three points, leaving the score 2–8 to 2–7. Suddenly, Cavan's apparently superior fitness and youth seemed to allow them to attack at will. The game's three concluding scores all came from the Breffni men. First, the unerring boot of Peter Donoghue gave Cavan a two-point advantage, before the magnificent Higgins notched two further excellent scores, after sweeping downfield movements. When the final whistle went, shortly afterwards, Cavan had made history by being the first (and probably only) team to win the All-Ireland outside of Ireland. The final score was 2–11 to 2–7. They had also completed the second leg of the double, having won their National League title when they defeated Cork in the springtime.

The 1947 final was a unique occasion, but it will be remembered for Mícheál Ó Hehir's pleading with the radio authorities for five more minutes of air time as the game reached its concluding stages. The commentary, which was carried over the transatlantic cable, had been scheduled to end five minutes before the match actually finished (apparently official speeches prior to the game had delayed its proper starting time). Luckily, Ó Hehir's pleas were heeded and listeners all over Ireland heard the game in its totality.

Mick Higgins and his fellow players were overwhelmed with joy at having won an All-Ireland at last. 'It really was a fantastic achievement. We were lucky to have so many fine players. P.J. Duke and our captain, John Joe O'Reilly, were absolutely outstanding. Phil Brady was a very strong midfielder. We had really top-class forwards in Tony Tighe, Columba McDyer, Joe Stafford, T.P. O'Reilly and Peter Donoghue.

Donoghue gave a magical exhibition of free-taking. The highest honour that could be paid to him was to be called the 'Babe Ruth of Gaelic Football' by two leading American sportswriters, Arthur Daley of the *New York Times* and Don Parker of the *Mirror*. The result was the culmination of a never-to-be-forgotten trip abroad. It had been a 27-hour journey, by plane, with a stop for refuelling at Gander and travelling via the Azores. Owing to a faulty engine, we had to stay at Gander for four hours while repairs were carried out. We were really happy to eventually arrive in New York. We then decided it would be safer to return home by boat. On our homeward journey, it was when we reached Southampton that we realised the significance of our achievement. We had come home on the *Queen Mary*, then travelled by train to London, and eventually arrived at Dun Laoghaire by boat, where we were given a civic reception. A cavalcade of cars and bicycles met us outside Virginia on the Cavan/Meath border. There were hundreds of people there and it took us four hours to reach Cavan town, because of all the celebrations and crowds of people along the way. The thousands of happy cheering people in Cavan had to be seen to be believed. It was there that we really appreciated the enormity of our success.'

The following year, Cavan retained their Ulster title before going on to defeat Louth in the All-Ireland semi-final. In the final they faced Connacht champions Mayo, who had many fine footballers such as Paddy Prendergast, Seán Flanagan, Eamon Mongey, Pádraic Carney, Tom Langan and Peter Solon in their ranks. This also was a close, tense match with the issue very much in doubt until the very last minute. Cavan were holding on to a one-point lead when Mayo were awarded a scoreable free in the last minute. Higgins, at first, stood on the goal line. Then, realising the likely trajectory of the kick, he raced out to block Pádraic Carney's poorly struck effort. Rather than kicking the ball aimlessly downfield, the crafty Cavan man retained possession by soloing his way out the field with the ball, thus wasting precious time and not conceding possession. When the whistle blew, Cavan had won successive senior All-Ireland titles, on a scoreline of 4–5 to 4–4. Back-to-back Mayo All-Ireland winning captain of 1950 and 1951, Seán Flanagan, who played that day, once stated: 'The secret of that great Cavan side was the effectiveness of their forward line. Ultimately, they depended on the genius of two brilliant forwards, Mick Higgins and Tony Tighe, who always knew where each other was. Higgins had the ability to objectively view a game and then apply his wonderful tactical brain.'

Mick Higgins won two further Ulster medals in 1949 and 1952, reaching All-Ireland finals in both years. In the former year, Meath, who were winning their first senior All-Ireland, halted Cavan's bid for three-in-a-row All-Irelands. Captained by attack leader Brian Smyth, the Royal County had a well-balanced team. They had a powerful full-back line in Mick O'Brien, Paddy O'Brien and Kevin McConnell. Christo Hand was a tenacious wing half-back. Frankie Byrne, Mattie McDonnell, Paddy Meegan (Mick Higgins's old school pal) and the 'man with the cap', Peter Mc Dermott, were all enterprising and elusive forwards. This combination, deservedly, beat Cavan by four points.

The same two counties met again in the 1952 All-Ireland final. This game will always be remembered for the unique contribution of three Cavan-born brothers, Liam, Des and Brendan Maguire. Liam and Des played for Cavan while Brendan played for Meath. Before the game started, the three Cornafean brothers met at the centre of the pitch and shook hands. This symbolic gesture was a recognition of the historic fact that, in the history of the GAA, they were the only brothers to play against each other on All-Ireland final day.

Cavan were very determined to win that 1952 All-Ireland, though they were somewhat lucky to be there. In the All-Ireland semi-final they had defeated an excellent Cork side in one of the greatest comebacks of all time. They scored five points in the last seven minutes to record a narrow one-point victory. This was a very special year for Mick Higgins as he had, as Cavan's longest-serving player, been selected as team captain. From the Monday to the Thursday prior to the game, he had been in bed with the flu, but he recovered sufficiently to lead his team out in front of over 62,000 spectators. Played in atrocious weather conditions, it was level pegging at half-time. For the remainder of this poor-quality game it was 'nip and tuck' all the way. Cavan had to rely on a controversial Edwin Carolan point to put the sides level, just before the final whistle, and thus send the game to a replay. The second game, though played in similar conditions, was much superior in quality. The whole Cavan side played superbly to record a comfortable 0–9 to 0–5 win. Particularly outstanding for the Breffni men were Phil Brady, Liam Maguire, Séamus Hetherton and Tony Tighe. Goalkeeper Séamus Morris had a fine game. The superb fielding and lengthy deliveries of midfielder Victor Sherlock paved the way for Cavan's victory. However, without doubt it was the immaculate playmaking and scoring skills of captain Mick Higgins that won the hearts of those who attended. The day was really a personal triumph for Mick as he scored 0–7 (six frees) out of Cavan's total. Rarely has a winning captain been greeted by so many well-wishers as he was chaired around the whole field, again and again, in triumph, even before he was presented with the Cup. Mick Higgins had now won his third and last All-Ireland senior medal. Few GAA commentators at that time would have predicted that in the fifty plus years after Higgins led Cavan to their fifth All-Ireland senior title, they would not even appear in another senior All-Ireland final.

Higgins played with Cavan the following year when they were beaten in the National League final and in the Ulster final against Armagh, which they also lost. When the 1953/54 National League commenced in October, Cavan were scheduled to play Mayo in the first game on a very wet day in Ballina. 'I told the selectors I did not want to play football for a while. I was never asked back, so I really drifted out of the game. Anyhow, I was 31 years of age, had won a lot and I was now a married man.' Thus the exciting, illustrious career of one of the greatest players ever to grace Gaelic football came to a rather premature end.

Though his playing career had finished, Higgins then made significant contributions to the GAA both as a brilliant trainer and as a highly competent referee at inter-county level. He trained the Cavan senior team from 1962 to 1969, leading them to Anglo-Celt Cup success in 1962, 1964, 1967 and 1969. During the mid-1960s, well-known Longford GAA officials Fr Phil McGee and Jimmy Flynn persuaded him to train Longford for the 1965/66 league campaign. 'On a Friday night I brought two greyhounds to race at Longford track, left them in charge of a friend and then went to Pearse Park to take my first training session. When I went to the park there were more officials than players and just one football. I then told Jimmy that if there were not a full team out on the following Friday night, I would not return. Seven days later I brought my two dogs back for the racing. More importantly, there was a full squad at training as well as six footballs! Incidentally, both dogs won their races on both nights. There was one complication, however. I was also training Cavan at the same time. Everything went well until Cavan and Longford qualified to meet each other in the semi-final of the league. I had always made it clear that Cavan would be my first choice if such an eventuality arose. So, two Longford players, Brendan Barden and Seán Murray, took charge of the Longford team against Cavan. When Longford beat Cavan, I resumed control of the O'Farrell County, who went on to win the league title — their first national senior success. I continued to train Longford, on an ad hoc basis, and was with them when they won their first Leinster senior title, by beating Laois, in 1968. All the Longford players were a great bunch of people to work with. Brendan Barden was a fantastic all-round footballer and Jackie Devine was a beautiful, skilful player. Larry Gillen, John Donlon, the late Seán Murray, Seán Donnelly, Jimmy Hanniffy, Mick Hopkins and Bobby Burns all made great contributions to Longford's successes.'

In 1972 Mick was asked by his 1947 All-Ireland winning colleague, Columba McDyer, and manager Brian McEniff to train the Donegal senior team. Again Higgins, the trainer extraordinaire, experienced more provincial success when he guided them to their first Ulster title. Thus, Higgins has the fantastic record of training three different counties to provincial titles. Not to be outdone by his inter-county success, Higgins also played a pivotal role in managing Ulster to six Railway Cup successes in the 1960s and 1970s.

The treble All-Ireland winner took charge of his first inter-county match as a referee in a National League contest between Mayo and Galway in 1955 and concluded his refereeing career, 13 years later, after the 1968 Connacht final between the same two sides. 'I never really liked refereeing because I was always thinking about the negative consequences if I made a major mistake during a game. Also, it appeared to me that if a referee was a defender in his playing days there was a tendency to referee from a back's viewpoint. Similarly, if a referee had been a forward as a player, there was the inclination to always give the advantage to the attacker. Overall, refereeing was a no-win situation.' Mick joined the Garda Síochána in October 1944 and served in George's Cross, in Co. Meath, Drogheda and Bailieborough. During the remaining 29 years of his working life he was Garda Sergeant in Tullyvin in County Cavan. For the last 60 years Mick has trained many outstanding greyhounds which have won many trophies at various dog tracks throughout the country. His most famous dog was 'Snub Nose', which won the McAlinden Cup in Belfast's Celtic Park in the late 1950s. Later, that same dog almost won the English Derby, only to be beaten by a short head by 'Milebush Pride'.

Before I left Mick's most amiable company, he recalled two examples of how the GAA has changed from his playing days. 'For most of my playing days Hughie Reilly of Cootehill was our trainer. He was very thorough in his preparation. In 1947 collective training started for the first time. This meant training full-time for two weeks before big games. We stayed in a variety of hotels and big houses in places like Bingfield, Ballyhaise and Ballyjamesduff. The County Board paid for our accommodation and food, which were always excellent. Those of us who were working took our annual leave, if possible, during the collective training. If this were not possible, players were given up to a maximum of £4 per week for loss of earnings. Students, both lay and clerical, were given a £2 per week allowance. However, the whole collective training practice ceased in the early fifties because the GAA authorities felt that the players were becoming professional.

'The pace of life was generally slower and people were more laid back, I feel. This laissez-faire attitude sometimes applied to football also. When I was manager of Cavan I once saw a frustrating side of this. We were playing Armagh in an Ulster championship match on a very wet day. We had been well ahead until Armagh started to dominate midfield. Our lead was gradually being whittled away. One of our subs was a big strong fellow who could field a ball well, so I decided to bring him on. Just after he went on to the pitch, he suddenly turned around and walked slowly back to the dug-out, taking from me the official piece of paper bearing his name for the referee. On his way back to the pitch he again stopped and came back, wanting gloves. Then I saw him, still dithering along the sideline, and I roared at him, 'For God's sake, would you take your place?' With Armagh at the time bombarding the Cavan goalmouth I did not need any more distractions, but I got one. Our sub was not finished yet. "Mick, would you ever look after my false teeth?" My reply is unprintable!'

Mick's representative selections are as follows:

ULSTER (1944–1953)

John O'Hare
(Down)

Jim McCullagh   George Watterson   John McKnight
(Armagh)   (Antrim)   (Armagh)

P.J. Duke   John Joe O'Reilly   Eddie Devlin
(Cavan)   (Cavan)   (Tyrone)

Jim McKeever   Columba McDyer
(Derry)   (Donegal/Cavan)

Tony Tighe   Kevin Armstrong   Seán Gallagher
(Cavan)   (Antrim)   (Antrim)

Seán Gibson   Peter Donoghue   Victor Sherlock
(Antrim)   (Cavan)   (Cavan)

IRELAND (1944–1953)

Danno O'Keeffe
(Kerry)

Paddy Prendergast   Paddy O'Brien   Jim McCullagh
(Mayo)   (Meath)   (Armagh)

Seán Boyle   John Joe O'Reilly   Stephen White
(Louth)   (Cavan)   (Louth)

Jim McKeever   Paddy Kennedy
(Derry)   (Kerry)

Tony Tighe   Jimmy Murray   Pádraic Carney
(Cavan)   (Roscommon)   (Mayo)

Victor Sherlock   Tom Langan   Peter Donoghue
(Cavan)   (Mayo)   (Cavan)

No Cavan football story would be complete without paying homage to two of its most famous sons, who sadly departed this life in the prime of manhood. The names of P.J. Duke and John Joe O'Reilly will, forever, be carved in the hearts and minds of all Cavan Gaels. Both of them were key figures in the Polo Grounds victory. Duke was the versatile attacker cum defender who snuffed out the Kingdom's attacking threat. O'Reilly was the extraordinary, charismatic leader who, by personal example, led his men to so many notable triumphs. His subsequent selection on both the GAA's centenary and millennium sides is proof positive of his immense stature in the game.

On May 1, 1950, UCD student and 25-year-old treble Sigerson Cup winner P.J. Duke died suddenly from pleurisy in St Vincent's Hospital, Dublin. The Capital's O'Connell Street came to a standstill as his funeral cortège began the long journey home for his burial in his native Stradone.

'New stars may rise in the years before us,
But none like him will they then dethrone,
The boy from Breifne, the pride of Ulster,
God rest you, P.J. in sweet Stradone.

Pádraig Puirséal

Two and a half years later, on November 21, 1952, 34-year-old Commandant John Joe O'Reilly also passed to his eternal reward. After bring diagnosed with a kidney complaint, he died, unexpectedly, in the Curragh Military Hospital. The gun carriage bearing his remains was brought to Killeshandra, where he was buried with full military honours, close to his beloved Cornafean.

'It was very difficult for all of us to believe that those two great servants of Cavan football, who had played with us in our All-Ireland successes of 1947 and 1948, were both dead just four years later. In fact, John Joe attended many of our training sessions as well as the 1952 All-Ireland. Both men were outstanding examples of all that is great about Gaelic games,' Mick Higgins concluded.

Another man that must also assume that mantle of greatness is the young American-born boy who brought so much honour and football glory to the Breffni County. When Mick Higgins won both the Bank of Ireland and the Texaco Hall of Fame awards in 1988 and 1989 respectively, all Gaeldom concurred. It could not have happened to a more worthy recipient.

MICK HIGGINS – FACT FILE

Native Place:	New York, USA
Date of Birth:	August 19, 1922
Clubs:	St Mary's College, Dundalk, Co. Louth; Celbridge, Co. Kildare
	Junior: Kill, Co. Cavan.
	Senior: Mountnugent, Co. Cavan; St Magdalene's, Drogheda, Co. Louth; Bailieborough, Co. Cavan
College Honours:	Mac Rory Cup, 1938
Club Honours:	(a) Mountnugent Senior Football Championship (2) Senior Football League (2) Junior Football Championship (1)
	(b) Bailieborough Senior Football League (1)

County Honours:	All-Ireland Senior Football Championship (3) – 1947, 1948, 1952
	Ulster Senior Football Championship (7) – 1943, 1944, 1945, 1947, 1948, 1949, 1952
	National Football League (2) – 1948 and 1950 (won the home final in 1950, but beaten by New York in final)
	Railway Cup (2) – 1947, 1950
	McKenna Cup (3) – 1943, 1951, 1953
	Ireland v. Combined Universities (3) – 1950, 1951, 1952
Managerial/Coaching: **(Honours)**	(a) Cavan Ulster Senior Football Championship (4) – 1962, 1964, 1967, 1969

	(b) Longford
	    National Football League (1) – 1966
	    Leinster Senior Football Championship (1) – 1968

	(c) Donegal Ulster Senior Football Championship (1) – 1972
	(d) Ulster Railway Cup (6) – 1964, 1965, 1966, 1968, 1970, 1971
	(e) Ulster Colleges' D'Alton Cup (1) St Norbert's College, Kilnacrott, Co. Cavan
Awards:	Bank of Ireland Hall of Fame – 1988
	Texaco Hall of Fame – 1989
	Anglo-Celt Hall of Fame – 1988
	Coiste Siamsa – Garda Síochána – Sports Star, 2001
	Greatest Football Team – Garda – 2005
Occupation:	Retired Garda Sergeant
Family:	Married to Margaret (née O'Connell) from Carlanstown, Co. Meath
Children:	John, Jean, Terry, Brenda

FOURTEEN

Pat Henderson–Kilkenny

THREE DECADES OF TREMENDOUS SERVICE

Flow on lovely river, flow gently along
By your waters so clear, sounds the lark's merry song,
On your green banks I'll wander, where first I did join
With your lovely Molly, the Rose of Mooncoin.

Watt Murphy

Pat Henderson sat quietly in the train carriage contemplating all the possibilities that the day ahead might present. For over twelve years he had waited for this occasion. Kilkenny, he reckoned, had at last a golden opportunity to defeat Tipperary in a senior All-Ireland hurling final. When he attended Thurles CBS as a secondary school student in the late 1950s and early 1960s, he became acquainted, at first hand, with what hurling meant to the people of Tipperary. He was also constantly being reminded of the great iconic deeds of the Premier County's hurlers.

Despite having the utmost respect for Tipperary and their giants of the ash, one thing above all others rankled with the budding Kilkenny star. During those student days, he was continually being accosted with one oft-repeated mantra of condescension: 'Despite your county's many All-Ireland successes, you have never beaten Tipperary in a championship game since 1922' (the game actually took place in 1923). As the Johnstown club man anxiously awaited that 1967 showpiece, he instinctively knew Kilkenny's hour had come. Kilkenny had always possessed master hurling craftsmen, but their detractors had often accused them of lacking the necessary cutting edge for hard-fought encounters. This Kilkenny side, he reasoned, was different. They possessed hurling artistry in abundance and, more importantly, they had added a greater physical dimension to their performance. The Noresiders had proven this when they defeated Tipperary for the first time in a major competitive game, eighteen months previously, in the

1966 National Hurling League decider. Furthermore, they had confirmed this newfound superiority over the Premier County in the 1967 league final in May.

Three years earlier, Henderson had made his All-Ireland senior debut against Tipperary in the 1964 final. Playing at right half-back, Pat and his colleagues were totally decimated as Tipperary strolled to an emphatic 5–13 to 2–8 victory. The Cats had been out-hurled and out-played by a truly wonderful display of hurling from a side that had won four All-Irelands in the previous six years. As the train rumbled on its way to the metropolis, Pat became, progressively, more intense in his determination. The time had definitely arrived for the wearers of the black and amber to exact sweet, sporting revenge. Then, suddenly, he was awoken from his meditative slumber.

The crashing sound of splintering glass echoed throughout the carriage, as players and mentors alike dived for cover. To pass those hours of anxious waiting, some of the Kilkenny players had decided to play pitch and toss on the corridor of the carriage. Ace Kilkenny goalkeeper Ollie Walsh, who had already won All-Ireland medals in 1957 and 1963, elected to play a prank upon himself. When he lost a 'toss', he drove his fist through a carriage window, in a pique of simulated temper. His colleagues wrapped a towel tightly around Ollie's wrist, which was bleeding profusely. After arriving in Dublin, Walsh was shielded from hundreds of Kilkenny supporters before being secretly whisked away to the Mater Hospital for emergency treatment. Much to the relief of everyone, Ollie was subsequently passed fit to play. The whole episode proved a blessing in disguise, as the normally unflappable goalkeeper, despite his obvious discomfort, proceeded to play the game of his life. In the game itself, Tipperary, despite playing with a strong wind, soon found themselves four points in arrears. Showing their traditional fighting spirit and considerable hurling élan, they recovered quickly to lead by 2–6 to 1–3 at the interval. That lead would have been much greater if Walsh had not been in such inspiring form.

In the second half, Kilkenny played spellbinding hurling before recording a historic 3–8 to 2–7 victory. The Tipperary hoodoo had at last been lifted. From a Tipperary perspective, it had been a huge disappointment. Their long-serving defender, John Doyle, was going for a record ninth All-Ireland medal, one more than Christy Ring. All the publicity prior to the game had centred on this unique opportunity. Sadly for him, it was not to be. Kilkenny, on the other hand, were totally ecstatic. Ollie Walsh had simply been outstanding. On six occasions he miraculously stopped goalbound shots. Near the end of the game, 'Babs' Keating unleashed a piledriver which seemed destined for the net. Then, apparently out of nowhere, Walsh stuck out his hurley, stopping the ball dead. Sidestepping his way past incoming forwards, he sent a long, relieving clearance downfield. Pat Henderson and his fellow defenders, especially the full-back line of Ted Carroll, 'Pa' Dillon and Jim Treacy, were simply tremendous. This was the day that Henderson really became one of hurling's peerless centre half-backs. Kilkenny's winning margin would undoubtedly have been greater only for injuries to Eddie Keher and Tom Walsh that forced them to leave the field. Walsh was particularly unfortunate, as he received an accidental eye injury that forced him to retire prematurely from the game. For Henderson and many of his colleagues it was a memorable victory. Most of them had experienced the devastation of final defeat in both 1964 and 1966. The defeat to the Rebel County in 1966 had been totally unexpected. As a result of their 1966 home league victory over Tipperary, the Cats had entered that year's All-Ireland final as red-hot favourites. Defeat, however, was their lot when Cork, with the three unrelated McCarthys — Justin, Charlie and captain Gerald — to the fore, notched up a convincing 3–9 to 1–10 victory. All those disappointments were quickly forgotten as a joyful Henderson savoured that glorious moment when the McCarthy Cup was raised by their captain, Jim Treacy.

Life for Pat Henderson began in the small parish of Johnstown, in north Kilkenny, close to the borders with Laois and Tipperary. His first induction into hurling was the local schools' league, which catered for the Rathdowney and Durrow areas of Laois, as well as his native north Kilkenny. He then attended Thurles CBS, where he won Dean Ryan and Croke Cup under age medals in the Munster Colleges championship. In his final year he played midfield for his school in their unsuccessful Harty Cup campaign. Then, the call that he always wished for came.

'I always wanted to wear the black and amber and I was delighted when I was selected for the Kilkenny minor team in 1961. We beat Wexford and Dublin before being drawn against Tipperary in the All-Ireland minor final. In that game, I was in direct opposition to Babs Keating. I knew a lot of their players because they had been colleagues of mine in Thurles. Joe Dunphy was our captain. Midfielder Tom Barry, who is now deceased, had a fabulous game that day. I was delighted we won that minor final. That initial success only whetted my appetite for more glorious days in the Kilkenny jersey.'

In 1964 Henderson played for Kilkenny in the inaugural U-21 championship, but Wexford defeated them. During the autumn of 1963, Henderson had made his senior debut when the Cats played Wexford in a tournament game. Incidentally, the Slaneysiders' Tony Doran also made his initial senior appearance that day. For good measure, the debutantes were marking each other. Henderson's second senior county appearance was in March 1964, when the Rest of Ireland provided the opposition. On that occasion, the Johnstown 'rookie' was marking the legendary Jimmy Smyth of Clare fame. All of the foregoing, as well as three tough championship seasons prior to 1967, had moulded Henderson into a strong, resilient defender. By now, he had found his natural position, from which he could literally play a central role in dictating his team's fortunes.

There was an extra-special significance to that 1967 All-Ireland success. Pat was the first Johnstown person since John Holohan, the full-back on the 1922 team, to win a senior medal. There was, however, a difference. Holohan had played his hurling with the neighbouring Tullaroan team, whereas Henderson had always played with his parish team, the Fenians.

Two years later, in 1969, under the captaincy of Eddie Keher, Kilkenny defeated a fancied Cork side by six points, to enable them to claim three All-Ireland titles in the 1960s. Henderson, again a colossus in the half-back line, had now won two senior All-Ireland medals. In 1971 Tipperary avenged their 1967 defeat to the Marble County when they just edged out Kilkenny in a very high-scoring game, 5–17 to 5–14. That day is remembered for an inspirational display by Tipp's Babs Keating, who played the whole second half in his bare feet. Just after half-time, a nail had protruded up into his boot and he was left with no option but to go barefooted. The outstanding feature of the game was the superlative scoring performance of Eddie Keher. In an impeccable display of marksmanship, Keher scored the colossal total of 2–11 and still ended up on the losing side.

It is often said that this particular Kilkenny side reached its peak in the 1972 decider against Cork. Ranked as one of the best All-Irelands within the previous 50 years, it will always stand out as a snapshot of all that is great in hurling. Tremendous artistry, total commitment and terrific scores were the norm as both Kilkenny and Cork fought to achieve the ultimate prize. The last quarter display by Kilkenny has, justifiably, entered the folklore of Gaelic games. As the game entered its final twenty minutes, Cork, galvanised by the magnificence of Seánie O'Leary and Ray Cummins, seemed to have an unassailable lead of eight points. Then, that swerving sidestepping of Eddie Keher, ably abetted by Kieran Purcell at full-forward and Pat Delaney at centre half-forward, changed everything. Surging into continual action, the Noresiders scored 2–9 without reply to complete one of the most amazing comebacks in hurling history. Though Keher was the hero up front, it was the dominant commanding presence of Pat Henderson who really copper-fastened the Cats' territorial advantage. Time and time again he repulsed imminent danger. Broadening his wide shoulders, he drove forward, sending the sliotar repeatedly into enemy territory. Thus, the Fenian's man won his third gold medal prize.

In 1973, after giving one of their best ever performances, in scoring 4–22 in a ten-point defeat of Wexford in the Leinster final, disaster struck Kilkenny before the All-Ireland final. Eamon Morrissey had emigrated to Australia and Jim Treacy and Eddie Keher were missing through injury. Kieran Purcell, though he came on for the second half of the final against Limerick, had had an appendix operation a few weeks previously. However, Henderson gives credit to the talented Limerick side: 'Despite these setbacks, we still pushed them to the limit. Still, one could not begrudge them their long-awaited success. They were a very good team with marvellous performers in Pat Hartigan, Phil Bennis, Eamon Cregan, Seán Foley, Eamon Grimes, Bernie Hartigan and Joe McKenna.'

In the following year's decider, with the injured duo back in harness, Kilkenny romped to an easy twelve-point victory against the Treaty men. Kilkenny were now acknowledged as one of the greatest teams ever to play the game. For Pat Henderson, it was a particularly satisfying season, as he was not only selected as an All Star but also as Texaco Hurler of the Year. The gentleman with the soft-spoken voice and the swashbuckling style was now at the height of his hurling prowess.

The year 1975 effectively marked the end of that great Kilkenny side. This was the year that the 70-minute final was introduced, and Kilkenny took full advantage of it when they comprehensively accounted for Galway, 2–22, 2–10. For Henderson, it marked his last full game in an All-Ireland, albeit with a fifth winners' medal. Three years later, in 1978, he made a brief appearance as a substitute against Cork, who achieved their magical three-in-a-row All-Ireland titles. Pat Henderson had now played his last championship game. He continued to play National League hurling but, realising he was not sure of his place any longer, he retired just before Christmas 1978. After fifteen such campaigns, he could retire gracefully, in the knowledge that he had made a massive contribution to Kilkenny hurling. He had played in ten All-Irelands, winning five of them, as well as accumulating a host of other wonderful achievements. Ten Leinster senior championships, two National Leagues and six Railway Cups merely represent a microcosm of the totality of his considerable accomplishments.

That great GAA writer, Pádraig Puirséal, himself a Kilkenny native, reckoned that the Kilkenny team between 1971 and 1975 was the best Noresiders team of all time. Legendary manager Fr Tommy Maher and physical trainer Mick Lanigan played a central role in those halcyon years. Five consecutive Leinster titles were won and five successive All-Ireland finals were reached. Writing in the 1976 'Our Games' Annual, he stated that, in the final analysis, it was the number of great players they possessed at the one time which was chiefly responsible for so many spectacular victories. Noel Skehan, Fan Larkin, Jim Treacy, Frank Cummins, Pat Delaney, Liam O'Brien, Eddie Keher, Kieran Purcell and Pat Henderson were all highly talented individuals who, collectively, made Kilkenny such a team of awesome beauty and clinical achievers. 'The uncanny saves by Skehan, the amazing dashes by Larkin, the scintillating runs of Chunky O'Brien and the menacing bursts of Purcell were a delight to watch. The superlative skill of Keher completely embellished the tremendous attributes of the forward line, whereas, in the defence, Pat Henderson was consistently standing across the field like the Berlin Wall.'

When Henderson retired in 1978, little did he think that, within twelve months, he would be back with Kilkenny in another capacity. Fr Tommy Maher, who had been Kilkenny supremo since 1957, retired after the 1978 final defeat. Ballyhale Shamrocks had won the Kilkenny senior hurling championship that year and were thus entitled to nominate the county hurling selectors. Club representative Kevin Fennelly (father of future winning captains Ger and Liam) asked Henderson to manage Kilkenny for the 1979 season, along with Eddie Keher. 'It was a great challenge for me,' he recalled. 'Informally, I had been de facto manager of my club side since 1968, so I had a fair idea of what was involved, in terms of man management, organisational ability and team tactics. So, with the exception of one year, 1981, when we were effectively sacked, I was in charge of Kilkenny from 1979 to 1987.'

Henderson, the manager, became just as successful as Henderson, the player. During his managership, the Cats won three senior All-Irelands — in 1979, 1982 and 1983 — and three National Leagues — in 1982, 1983 and 1986. Five Leinster championships were also won within that timeframe. In his first year in charge, the Henderson/Keher combination saw the Noresiders score a convincing victory over a Joe McDonagh-led Galway side. Under the captaincy of Brian Cody, Kilkenny defeated the then All-Ireland champions, Offaly, by two points in the 1982 Leinster final. An impressive display in recording a ten-point winning margin against Galway in the All-Ireland semi-final now meant that the Cats would face the men of Cork in the All-Ireland final. On a day that Cork were firm favourites, Cody led his side to one of the biggest victories over the Rebel County, beating them by an 11-point margin. For Pat Henderson, it was an especially proud occasion as his two brothers, Ger and John, were both key figures in that surprise result. Ger, who had also played on the 1979 winning team, had now inherited Pat's old No. 6 jersey, while John was a tight, tigerish right corner-back. Incidentally, Nicky Brennan, who was selected as President elect of the GAA at their annual congress in April 2005, was a very competent wing half-back on both those sides.

The following year Cork and Kilkenny again met in the final, in a windswept Croke Park. Again Cork, captained for the second successive year by that wonderful maestro of the camán, Jimmy Barry Murphy, were favourites. Possessing players of the calibre of goalkeeper Ger Cunningham, ace defenders Brian Murphy (a Garda then based in Kilkenny), Dermot McCurtin, John Crowley and Tom Cashman, midfielder supreme John Fenton and classy forwards such as Barry Murphy, Tony O'Sullivan and Seánie O'Leary, entitled them to the favourites tag. Kilkenny, however, had other ideas. The Henderson brothers, Ger and John, ably assisted by Joe Hennessy, Dick O'Hara and Paddy Prendergast, patrolled their defensive lines with typical defiant efficiency. Cork-based Frank Cummins performed trojan deeds at midfield, while the Fennelly brothers, 1979 captain Ger and that year's captain Liam, along with Billy Fitzpatrick and Christy Heffernan, were the more conspicuous in a very impressive forward sextet. Goals by Liam Fennelly and Richie Power had the Cats in a commanding position shortly after half-time. However, goals by Tomas Mulcahy and Seánie O'Leary ignited a fantastic Cork rally. In the end, Kilkenny were both happy and relieved to hold out for a two-point victory, 2–14 to 2–12. In historic terms, 1983 was an exceptional year for Kilkenny hurling, even by their own high standards. Within 24 months, they had achieved the double double, having won both the league and championship in 1982 and 1983. During that magnificent run, they were beaten in just one match — when Clare defeated them, in Ennis, by a single point in the league.

One record, nevertheless, stood out above all others. That 1983 triumph was a personal record-breaking milestone in the career of 39-year-old goalkeeper Noel Skehan. He had now won his ninth All-Ireland senior medal, three of them as a substitute to his famous cousin, Ollie Walsh. Noel, whose uncle Dan Kennedy captained Kilkenny to their 1947 senior triumph, also over Cork, had now won more All-Ireland senior medals than anyone else. Both Christy Ring and John Doyle, however, won all their eight senior medals on the field of play. Since he became a member of the Kilkenny senior panel in 1963, Noel had waited nine years before he became a permanent fixture on the side, in 1972. He had the honour of being winning captain that year. Now 11 years later and 20 years since he first became a senior 'Cat', he was the Cat of all Cats! Patience and durability had rightly rewarded the

Bennettsbridge hero, who also had amassed an impressive seven All Star awards.

Meanwhile, for the remaining four years of Pat Henderson's managerial tenure, Kilkenny successes were at a decided premium. A further National League title was secured in 1986, when the Marble County defeated Galway by four points.

Additional Leinster championships were also attained, in both 1986 and 1987. Galway were their conquerors in the 1986 All-Ireland semi-final and 1987 final. Sylvie Linnane, Conor Hayes, Peter Finnerty, Tony Keady, Ger McInerney, Steven Mahon, Michael McGrath and Joe Cooney were the western stars on a day that the Marble County were outclassed, on a scoreline of 1–12 to 0–9.

Except for 1981, when Fan Larkin acted as manager, Pat Henderson had given the incredible total of 25 years of unbroken service for the cause of Kilkenny hurling. After that 1987 defeat, Pat the manager quietly bowed out, just as inconspicuously as he had done as a player.

In the spring of 2005, I met Pat at his home in Talbot Inch, just a few miles outside Kilkenny city. Apart from his hectic hurling schedule for so many years, Pat also had a very fulfilled working life. For 20 years, he worked with Kilkenny Design, being its CEO for five years, before he became Managing Director of a printing company in Waterford. However, a health scare some years ago prompted Pat to retire. Retirement for Pat means acting as schools' GAA development officer for South Leinster and looking after the substantial financial accounts of the Kilkenny County Board. He is also Chairman of the Kilkenny GAA yearbook committee, which publish annually a very comprehensive 200-page review of Gaelic games activities in the Marble County. In a very friendly atmosphere of recall and nostalgia, Pat enthusiastically presented his views on the past and his hopes for the future of the GAA, in a very reasoned, calm, self-assured manner. The following points took centre stage:

1. 'As well as the wonderful Limerick hurlers whom I have already referred to, I have seen an enormous amount of talented hurlers, especially in all the Munster counties. Tipperary's much-vaunted full-back line of John Doyle, Michael Maher and Kieran Carey were not just strong physical players. They were, primarily, good hurlers. Liam Devaney was a highly intelligent centre half-forward. Len Gaynor, Tony Wall, Jimmy Doyle, Babs Keating and Francis Loughnane were all formidable opponents. Wexford had great men in the Quigley brothers, Tom Neville, Phil Wilson and Mick Jacob. Des Foley (Dublin), Paddy Molloy and Barney Moylan, both of Offaly, were all very good too. Cork always had a vast array of

talented individuals. Players like Con Roche, all the McCarthys, Denis Coughlan and Ray Cummins were All Stars in their own right. Tipperary's Mick Roche was probably one of the best players I ever saw.'

2. 'Like most Kilkenny hurling fans, I have been a great admirer of Gaelic football over the years, especially the magnificent Down, Dublin and Kerry teams of the past. I thought the Tyrone team of 2003 were a very skilful side. To my mind, Peter Canavan was one of the best ever forwards. I have no doubt that if he had been introduced to hurling at a very young age, he would have become equally good with the camán. Unfortunately, I do not see any great future for football in Kilkenny. It is really too small a county to accommodate both codes. Every young person in Kilkenny wants to hurl because the glamour and tradition associated with winning is with the small ball game. Offaly, though also small in area, is different because essentially it is mainly divided into separate areas — one for hurling and one for football. In the past, we have had some good dual players, notably Frank Cummins. However, I believe current logistics don't allow for this to be replicated in Kilkenny at present.'

3. 'Regarding the future development of hurling, I think the GAA will have to concentrate, in the first instance, in ensuring the survival of hurling in the traditional strong counties such as Cork, Kilkenny and Tipperary. Then their financial, personnel and ancillary services should be focused on the current second tier of hurling counties such as Waterford, Clare, Limerick, Galway, Offaly, Wexford, Laois and Dublin. Thirdly, there should be a concerted effort to revitalise hurling where, historically, there have been pockets of the game. Places like the Glens of Antrim, Ards Peninsula, Central Roscommon, parts of Carlow, Wicklow, Derry, Meath and Kerry, as well as other places, would fall into this category. Without sounding defeatist, there is no point in literally throwing resources at the problem and, in places, where there is not at least a small vibrant club on the ground. My brother John, along with some hurling friends from other parts of the country, are making great strides building up a core of hurling support in Bray, in Wicklow. Without sounding too egotistical, perhaps there is scope for other small hurling communities to imitate the Bray model.'

4. 'One of the greatest characters I ever met, in all of my years associated with hurling, was Phil 'Fan' Larkin. One accurate

anecdote encapsulates the complexities of the man's dedication, loyalty and humour. Just before the 1979 All-Ireland, I met Fan as he was about to enter our dressing room. He had three hurleys in one bag and his accompanying wife had three hurleys in another bag. I said to her, "What are all the hurleys for?" She replied, "The poor man is like a bag of cats because he cannot make up his mind which hurl to use. What's really annoying him more is the fact that he has not been to Mass yet!" Fan, who was a great favourite with the supporters, subsequently made his high-octane contribution to a Kilkenny victory. The excitement immediately afterwards in our dressing room was mighty as all the players rejoiced. One man, Fan, had other things on his mind, as he hurriedly dressed and bolted out the door. With mud-splattered face and rumpled clothes, he was eventually stopped in his tracks by an RTÉ reporter, the late Mick Dunne. "Sorry Mick, I have no time to talk to you because I am on my way to Mass!" came the quick riposte. What made the whole scenario so riveting was the fact that it was broadcast live on RTÉ television! That whole episode personified the greatness of Fan!'

Pat Henderson, who played club hurling until he was 42, made the following representative selections:

LEINSTER (1964–1978)

Ollie Walsh
(Kilkenny)

Tom Neville   Pa Dillon   Fan Larkin
(Wexford)   (Kilkenny)   (Kilkenny)

Mick Jacob   Dan Quigley   Séamus Cleere
(Wexford)   (Wexford)   (Kilkenny)

Chunky O'Brien   Des Foley
(Kilkenny)   (Dublin)

Mick Crotty   Pat Delaney   Martin Quigley
(Kilkenny)   (Kilkenny)   (Wexford)

Mick Bermingham   Tony Doran   Eddie Keher
(Dublin)   (Wexford)   (Kilkenny)

IRELAND (1964–1978)

Ollie Walsh
(Kilkenny)

Tom Neville   Pat Hartigan   Fan Larkin
(Wexford)   (Limerick)   (Kilkenny)

Séamus Cleere   Dan Quigley   Con Roche
(Kilkenny)   (Wexford)   (Cork)

        John Connolly   Mick Roche
        (Galway)   (Tipperary)

Jimmy Doyle   Pat Delaney   Babs Keating
(Tipperary)   (Kilkenny)   (Tipperary)

Eamon Cregan   Tony Doran   Eddie Keher
(Limerick)   (Wexford)   (Kilkenny)

Since its foundation, the GAA has been an integral part of Irish society. Nowhere is this relationship more apparent than in the predominance of so many families, in every county, who have voluntarily given their time and talents to the GAA. The Hendersons of Johnstown and Kilkenny fame have been such a family. From 1964 to 1991 the name Henderson was an ever-present one on every Kilkenny senior hurling team sheet. In that 27-year period, brothers Pat, Ger and John, between them, accumulated the phenomenal total of 11 senior All-Ireland hurling medals and 8 All-Ireland medals at under age level. Countless other playing honours and All Star awards also came their way.

On the suggestion of the former County Secretary of the Kilkenny County Board, the late Paddy Grace, it was decided many years ago to adopt 'The Rose of Mooncoin' as the county's official GAA anthem. For everyone associated with Gaelic games, that beautiful, haunting ballad reflects both the inherent ethos and the local affinity of Kilkenny hurling. When Pat Henderson got that desired call to don the black and amber back in 1961, he, too, initiated a family dynasty that has equally become synonymous with all that is good and much that is great in our national game. He has done his club and county proud.

PAT HENDERSON – FACT FILE

Native Place:	Johnstown, Co. Kilkenny
Date of Birth:	January 30, 1943
Club:	Fenians, Johnstown
Club Honours:	Senior Hurling Championship (5) – 1970, 1972, 1973, 1974, 1978
	Junior Hurling Championship – 1968
	Junior Football Championship – 1971
	Leinster Senior Hurling Championship – 1974/75
County Honours:	All-Ireland Senior Hurling Championship (5) – 1967, 1969, 1972, 1974, 1975
	Leinster Senior Hurling Championship (10) – 1964, 1966, 1967, 1969, 1971, 1972, 1973, 1974, 1975, 1978
	National Hurling League (2) – 1966, 1976
	Oireachtas Medal (3) – 1966, 1967, 1969
	Walsh Cup (3) – 1970, 1973, 1974
	Leinster Minor (1) – 1961
	Various tournaments
Other Honours:	Railway Cup (6) – 1967, 1971, 1973, 1974 (Captain), 1975, 1977
Managerial Honours:	(a) Club Dicksboro
	Intermediate Hurling Championship – 1991
	Senior Hurling Championship – 1993
	(b) County
	All-Ireland Senior Hurling Championship (3) – 1979, 1982, 1983
	Leinster Senior Hurling Championship (5) – 1979, 1982, 1983, 1986, 1987
	National Hurling League (3) – 1982, 1983, 1986
Others:	Railway Cup 1985
	All Star, 1983
Awards:	Gaelic Weekly All Star (3) – 1964, 1966, 1967
	All Star – 1973, 1974
	Texaco Hurler of the Year 1974
	Sports Star of the Week (1)
	RTÉ Man of the Match (1)
	Manager of the Month (3) – 1982/83
	Manager of the Year (1) – 1982

Occupation:	Retired businessman. Currently GAA Development Officer with South Leinster
Family:	Married to Mary (née Gibbs) from Kilkenny city
Children:	Ger, Tom, Patrick, Elizabeth

Fifteen

Marty Morrissey–Clare/RTÉ

The Banner's Glorious Nineties Revisited

At 10.30 p.m. on Saturday, October 27, 1984, what appeared to be a routine visitor arrived at the home of a young science teacher, Marty Morrissey, in the picturesque village of Mullagh in County Clare. The village was part of the parish of Kilmurry-Ibrickane. Marty had four burning ambitions in life. All of these dreams were Gaelic games-oriented. He wanted to see Clare's hurling and football county teams achieve their true potential. In addition, he was very keen to become a GAA commentator as well as hoping for his club team to win county and provincial football honours. He avidly longed for the day when Clare county hurling would take its rightful place amongst the elite of Ireland's national game. Clare had always had great hurlers and many fine teams, but none of them had succeeded in making a major championship breakthrough since 1932. No one epitomised those years of disappointment more than the talented Jimmy Smyth, who had played for the Banner County in the 1950s and early 1960s. He was one of the greatest scoring forwards of any era. Against Limerick in the 1954 championship, the Ruan hurling artist scored an impressive 6–4. Two years later, he totalled 13 goals for the 1956 season — a feat he himself bettered in 1963, when he amassed a phenomenal 17 green flags. Yet this man, who won 6 Railway Cup medals, never won any honour with the Banner County. An air of hopelessness and disappointment had prevailed in Clare over the years. In the 1978 *Our Games Annual*, Jimmy had penned the following sentiments: 'We admire your courage, we appreciate your worth, your loyalties are unquestionable, but where are your victories?'

This scenario was something that young Marty wanted rectified. Being a native of West Clare — the footballing heartland of the county — he had also become exceedingly disillusioned with both the standard and organisation of football at club and county level. So desperate was he to modernise strategies that he decided to sacrifice his own promising playing career in order to enter team management. Simultaneously, the Spanish Point-based teacher was at a crossroads in his personal working life. He liked teaching, but there was a deep-seated inner force telling him that his true working vocation lay in the world of radio and television. He wanted to be at the centre of 'breaking' news, particularly GAA events, which for him were an integral part of what he was and what he wanted to be. In essence, he wanted to be a TV commentator who could observe and report on events, and impart his own personal views to a wider audience of GAA followers. Though too modest to say so, he knew he had a special inherent quality for transmitting events in a charismatic, consumer-friendly fashion.

On that October evening when local post office official Patrick Galvin stood at Marty's door, the first tentative steps towards Marty's TV career were taken. Patrick wanted him to do the video commentary on the following day's Clare U-21 final between Marty's home club of Kilmurry-Ibrickane and Milltown Malbay, which ironically enveloped Spanish Point in its catchment area. Very reluctantly, Marty agreed to do the commentary, with good friend Paschal Brooks being his very able cameraman. So successful were they that they were asked to link up again to video the Munster club hurling final, in Semple Stadium, between Patrickswell of Limerick and Sixmilebridge of Clare. All who watched both videos knew that a budding TV commentator had arrived, and many friends encouraged Marty to apply to RTÉ for a GAA commentating audition. At first, Marty himself was undecided. Two further events helped to make his mind up for him.

Every year the GAA presents national awards to those who have made outstanding contributions in the area of communications. Those awards, known as the McNamee Awards and named after a former President of the GAA, Pádraig McNamee, are acknowledged as the most prestigious honour that can be bestowed on any media person. In 1986 and 1987 the Clare duo were recipients of the annual video prize for their presentation of the Clare County final and a documentary on the Ennistymon GAA club, respectively. When one of the adjudicators, Mícheál Ó Muircheartaigh, commented very favourably on Marty's achievement, the die was surely cast for an exciting TV career.

Shortly before his birth, Marty's parents returned from America to his mother's native place in Mallow, Co. Cork. Soon afterwards, the only child went to New York with his parents. Thus, for the first 11 years of his life Marty was reared in the 'Big Apple'. Gaelic Park, every Sunday, was his first induction into the world of Gaelic games. His father, being involved in the travel agency business, was very familiar with the comings and goings of the Irish Diaspora, and Gaelic Park

Jimmy Murray, Knockcroghery's most revered son (just left of centre),
waiting for the breaking ball.
(*Courtesy of John Murray, Knockcroghery*)

Jimmy Murray (fourth from right in front row) in Croke Park with
his 1940s Roscommon All-Ireland-winning teammates.
(*Courtesy of John Murray, Knockcroghery*)

The four Doran bothers – Tony, Joe, Billy and Colm – who have helped enormously in making Buffer's Alley a national household name.

Pat Henderson, the manager, issuing typical sideline instructions, and below, Pat, the Kilkenny player, clearing his lines against Galway.

Treble All-Ireland senior football winner Mick Higgins, who played in the historic Polo Grounds final as well as captaining the Breffni men to glory in 1952.
(*Courtesy of* Hogan Stand)

Ace RTÉ Gaelic games' commentator Marty Morrissey (right) in the company of Tom McGuinness (of the Longford Pipe Band), who is the author of 'Do Chormac' on page 292.

Anthony Molloy (left) bringing Sam back to the hills after Donegal's 1992 All-Ireland football success.

Colm Browne, the man who has played a significant role in leading the men of Laois to the threshold of the Holy Grail.
(*Courtesy of Hogan Stand*)

Martin Carney – two counties, two provinces, one ambition – in pensive mood as a Mayo football manager.
(*Courtesy of Hogan Stand*)

Anthony Rainbow, one of the Lilywhites' most loyal sons,
prepares to initiate another Kildare attack.
(*Courtesy of Hogan Stand*)

Frank McGuigan – no one
will ever forget his 11 points
from play for Tyrone in the
1984 Ulster final. (*Courtesy of
Hogan Stand*)

Joe McKenna – just recently
appointed for another two
years in charge of Limerick's
senior hurling team. (*Courtesy
of Hogan Stand*)

Jarlath Burns, a man for all seasons, introducing President Mary McAleese to his Armagh teammates before the 1999 Ulster final against Down.

Cormac McAnallen (RIP) – the late Cormac 'enveloped a people so desperate for real icons of transparent humanity'.
(*Courtesy of the Hogan Stand*)

A historic picture of Ulster's four-in-a-row All-Ireland winning captains of the 1990s. (Left to right) D.J. Kane (Down), Henry Downey (Derry), Anthony Molloy (Donegal) and Paddy O'Rourke (Down).
(*Courtesy of Danny O'Kane, Dungiven*)

Armagh's Jarlath Burns bursts forward in determined fashion.

Tony Doran, Wexford's legendary folk hero, receiving one of his many national awards.

Anthony Molloy in a minor managerial role – a portent of more important things to come?

The Faithful Trio – the three All-Ireland-winning brothers, Joe, Billy and Johnny Dooley, who have contributed so much to the success of Offaly hurling.

was the perpetual fulcrum of Irish cultural and social meetings. Down All-Ireland winning goalkeeper of 1968, Danny Kelly, became both a hero and friend to the young GAA aspirant.

Marty's father then came back to Ireland and his native Clare, where he bought a pub, shop and a dance hall. Marty's GAA education was further enhanced when he enrolled at the famous St Flannan's College in Ennis for his secondary education. Immersed in Clare's renowned Irish dancing and traditional music scene, Marty became a totally 'rounded' Irishman in all facets of sporting and cultural activity. He developed a great passion and no little skill as he pursued a dual Gaelic games career, playing corner-forward in the college's hurling sides and goalkeeper on the football team. After his secondary education, he briefly decided on a career in medicine, before finally concluding that a science degree in University College, Cork, was more appropriate to his aptitude. His prominent displays at club level duly attracted the attention of both the county football and hurling selectors. He played in goals for the minor and U-21 football sides, while he had one outing against Galway in a senior hurling challenge. It was at this stage, at the age of 20, that he took over the management of his club's U-16 football side. Having played Sigerson Cup football with UCC alongside such football luminaries as Seánie Walsh and Johnny Mulvihill from Kerry, and Cork's Martin O'Doherty, he convinced his club to change from the traditional 'catch and kick' style to that of possession football. This, he believed, created a situation where all the individual talents of the players were collectively harnessed into a more cohesive and formidable unit. As coach at St Joseph's, Spanish Point, he guided his side to a Munster Colleges 'B' title in 1983. Marty, the player, had prematurely retired, but Marty, the manager, had begun a process which would ultimately lead to a fantastic football renaissance, both at club and colleges level.

Having begun a teaching career and spurred on by his growing reputation as an exceptionally gifted video commentator, the Mullagh man kept beseeching RTÉ to fulfil his ambition of being a GAA presenter. During the course of the following ten years, Marty's media profile gradually increased. He took a leave of absence from teaching in May 1988 to become a presenter with Cork Multi-Channel TV. Later he became News Editor of new local radio station, Clare FM. However, it was the phone call from RTÉ to ask him to commentate on the concluding stages of the 1988/89 National Football and Hurling Leagues which first propelled him into the national limelight. Marty was ever hopeful that a full-time job was in the offing. That did not occur until over four years later, when he was appointed a permanent member of the RTÉ sports department in May 1994. In 1990 Marty had become a full-time news presenter with RTÉ Cork. Scarcely in the history of broadcasting has any sports commentator served in such a wide variety of roles, carrying out each of them with equal aplomb. For good measure, in the summer of 1989 he had also fulfilled a three-month contract with 'Lifestyle' Cable Company, which was a subsidiary of Sky TV. This involved doing a series of documentaries on Irish personalities such as Daniel O'Donnell and Olivia Tracey. This multiplicity of experiences, in a host of many broadcasting disciplines, has contributed enormously to making Marty Morrissey such a highly respected commentator of Gaelic games.

The years 1992, 1995 and 2004 were to see Marty achieving his dearest wishes for Clare hurling and football, both at county and club levels. Not having any other managerial ambition, Mayo's John Maughan was dumbfounded when the Clare County Board asked him to manage their county team in October 1990. With his army training and national organisational skills, Maughan set about the task of reviving the Banner County's footballing fortunes. His first taste of success with them, albeit a small one, was when they won the All-Ireland 'B' championship in 1991. After extra time, Clare defeated Longford in Ballinasloe to gain their first football success since they won the Munster senior championship in 1917.

Earlier in 1991, in John Maughan's first championship campaign, Clare had stayed with Kerry until 15 minutes from the end. Even though they had trained hard for the previous six months, the required fitness level could only be achieved over a longer period of time. Therefore, Maughan was optimistic about the 1991/92 National Football League. This optimism was justified when the Banner County qualified for the league quarter-final. In that game and with only 14 men, they put up a gallant performance against Meath, losing narrowly by two points.

After Clare defeated Tipperary in the semi-final of the 1992 Munster championship, they were in the Munster final for the first time since 1949. Even though they were due to face the mighty Kerry in the final, Clare management and players were in buoyant mood. Since taking over, Maughan had set four attainable targets. In sequence, three of these had been achieved — the 'B' championship, league promotion and the McGrath Cup. Only a long-awaited and much-coveted Munster senior football title remained. The supposedly perpetual 'no hopers' had gained the aura of winners.

The 1992 Munster final took place in Limerick's Gaelic grounds. Five minutes into the game, Clare's long-serving Noel Roche was brought down in the square. The resultant penalty, by Gerry Killeen, was parried to safety by Kerry goalkeeper Peter O'Leary. For the next ten minutes, thoughts of previous ignominious defeats surfaced as Clare failed to score. Nevertheless, the firm belief that victory was possible brought the Clare side back into the game. Consequently, at the interval, Clare had edged into a 0–7 to 0–6 lead. In one of the great GAA managerial speeches of our time, John Maughan addressed, at half-time, his eager and expectant team. Noting his players' ability and the passion that they displayed in the first half, Maughan knew that this Clare team were on the verge of a historic achievement. He asked each of his players to respond positively to the rhetorical question he posed to them, before they left the dressing room: 'How badly do you want to win it, lads?'

In the second half, Clare continued to play as they had done in the first, with Tom Morrissey and Aidan Moloney increasingly dominating the centre of the field. Two significant scores were to signal Clare's growing maturity. Firstly, in the 13th minute, their captain, Francis McInerney, gained possession and passed the ball to Colm Clancy, who hammered it to the net. It was the second score and the events surrounding it bore the hallmark of Clare's newfound confidence. A Kerry defender got the ball in the 24th minute near his own end line. The inrushing Gerry Killeen hit him so hard with a fair shoulder that he sent the Kerry man over the line. From the subsequent 45, the ball was broken down, and substitute Martin Daly fisted the ball to the net. This left Clare leading by 2–8 to 0–9, but Kerry were not finished yet. Pa Laide sent a great shot towards the Clare net but goalie James Hanrahan knocked it to safety. Kerry's Timmy Fleming and Connie Murphy reduced the deficit to three points with two well-taken scores. However, a further two points from the brilliant Killeen and a consolation one for the Kingdom concluded the scoring. Clare, the complete underdogs, were Munster champions for the first time since 1917. At long last, a 75-year gap had been successfully bridged.

When people recall that game, one famous comment by TV commentator Marty Morrissey is remembered. Looking down on the field and watching so many happy Clare supporters, he stated: 'There is one thing for sure, there won't be a cow milked in County Clare for at least a week.'

Marty relived the moment when I met him in Ennis. 'It was one of the happiest moments of my life and I was especially privileged to be commentating on the game. I knew, when Clare were able to curtail Kerry's danger men, that we were in with a good chance of success. What made the whole occasion especially memorable for me was the fact that I had been a young fellow sitting on a wall back in 1979 when Kerry trounced us. That game, known as the "Milltown Malbay Massacre", was a total disaster for Clare. Kerry beat us 9–21 to 1–9!

How could anyone forget that?'

West Clare is the home of Clare football and it was here that Clare's Munster final victory was celebrated in style. Along the banks of the River Shannon, bonfires raged against the night sky and Clare people came from all over Ireland to join in the festivities. Traditional music, song and dance could be heard in every nook and cranny in the western peninsula. The parishes and towns of the football hinterland became household words. Cooraclare, Kilrush, Kilkee, Doonbeg, Corofin, Lisdoonvarna and Milltown Malbay were some of the poetic and lyrical names on everyone's lips.

It was a tradition in Clare that, when an occasion of momentous jubilation took place in the county, a famous chant called the 'Clare Shout' would rend the air. The last time the 'Shout' was heard was over 30 years previously when the late President de Valera was touring his old Dáil constituency for the last time. It had been heard when De Valera became TD for Clare for the first time in 1917. Now the time had come again and, instinctively, the people rendered that famous chant throughout the county for three nights following the game. After two days of further travelling and celebration, some normality was restored, allowing the team to concentrate on their preparation for the All-Ireland semi-final against Dublin.

In that match, two dubious refereeing decisions made life difficult for the Banner County. First, corner-forward Pádraig Clancy had what many felt was a legitimate goal disallowed in the 17th minute. Then, in the second half, Dublin scored a controversial goal. In the opinion of many neutral observers, a free out should have been awarded instead. Still, Clare fought bravely and they only went down by a five-point margin in the end. Marty recalled the atmosphere at the game that day. 'Of all the sights, sounds and jubilation that I have witnessed over the years, nothing, I feel, will ever compare to the "support" the Clare team received that day. That was the day that the "Clare Shout" arrived outside of Clare for the first time. It was unbelievable that thousands of Clare people could perform it so impressively and in unison.'

If 1992 belonged to John Maughan and his footballers, then Ger Loughnane and his hurlers surely staked, in 1995, their claim for sporting immortality. In the autumn of 1994, Clare hurling manager Len Gaynor stepped down. A new management team, comprising trainer Michael McNamara and selector Tony Considine, under the tutelage of then current selector and former All Star Ger Loughnane, took up duty. Enthusiastic and totally committed, Loughnane upped the training schedule to previously unheard-of heights. With Clare leading Division One of the league at Christmas, his infectious belief in the men under his control was rewarded. In the last game before the recess,

Clare beat Limerick. This victory proved to be a psychological watershed for the Banner County, as practically the same Limerick personnel had trounced Clare just four months earlier in the Munster final.

Clare's good form continued when they defeated Tipperary and then Waterford in the league semi-final. In the decider, however, they were defeated by Kilkenny 2–12 to 0–9. As Clare supporters walked away disconsolately from this latest debacle, the players hung their heads in the dressing rooms. However, one man had no doubts about what his team were capable of achieving if they applied themselves. With all players seated and all doors shut, heads gradually started to lift and to listen to the messianic voice of Ger Loughnane. 'I guarantee you, lads, one thing. We're going to win this year's Munster championship. We might or might not win the All-Ireland. The work, is only starting now. You may think that we have done a lot of work but we haven't done anything yet.' All the players thought that Loughnane was being over-optimistic. Nevertheless, as the weeks passed, all knew that Ger's words were beginning to permeate.

The championship began with a Munster semi-final clash with Cork in June. Clare played superbly and appeared to be on their way to their third consecutive Munster final when Cork staged a dramatic comeback. Half a minute from the end, the Rebel County edged in front when Cork forward Kevin Murray sent the sliotar to the Clare net. Then, into the breach stepped the indomitable Seán McMahon, Clare's commanding half-back. Fifteen minutes earlier, Seán had sustained a broken collarbone but he could not be replaced because the Banner men had already used their quota of three substitutes. Now playing at corner-forward and in obvious pain, McMahon somehow managed to win a sideline ball not far from the corner flag. Fergus Tuohy accurately crossed the resultant sideline cut into substitute Ollie Baker, who connected with the ball to send it to the net for a sensational winning goal.

Displaying fantastic character and resilience, Clare's Munster final performance against Limerick was a magnificent team effort. Their speed and support play pulverised the Treaty men, who had unluckily lost the previous year's All-Ireland final against Offaly. In the end, for the first time in 63 years, Clare had won the Munster senior hurling championship, 1–17 to 0–11. Ironically, Clare supporters in their thousands had stayed away from this game. They simply could not believe it as they listened to the final moments of the radio commentary on the game. This result banished negativity and inferiority complexes from the county. A huge psychological barrier was now gone. Ger Loughnane had been the catalyst for its removal. 'Winning the Munster hurling title was a phenomenal achievement. The belief that Ger

Loughnane had instilled in his team was incredible. The players had responded magnificently to fulfil Ger's prophetic words after the league final defeat,' Marty recalled.

The All-Ireland semi-final against Galway was to see Clare translate that newfound confidence onto a bigger stage. Clare, for the first time in years, showed their power, skill and determination in the greatest GAA stadium of all, as they convincingly defeated the westerners by 3–12 to 1–13. The now fully recovered Seán McMahon was simply tremendous. His exhibition was emblematic of a brilliant cohesive performance. Clare were now, for the first time since Kilkenny beat them in 1932, in an All-Ireland senior hurling final.

Loughnane and his management team planned the preparation for the final against Offaly down to the minutest detail. Every hour in the lead-up to the game would see the players usefully occupied. On the morning of the game the players assembled in Ennis, took a coach to Shannon Airport and flew to Dublin, where they had breakfast in a hotel convenient to the airport. They then slept for two hours, had a light training session and a snack before watching the first half of the minor game. They were extremely relaxed and confident as Ger Loughnane addressed them with his deliberately repetitive mantra, before they left their Croke Park dressing room: 'Lads,' he said, 'we are going to do it.'

Though Offaly seemed to control much of the game, the Clare players did not panic as they might have done in the past. They kept totally focused on the task in hand, remembering at all times the belief that their extraordinary manager had placed in them. As the game entered its closing stages, Offaly were leading by two points when Clare were awarded a free deep inside their own half. Seán McMahon, who had scored many long-range frees during the year, moved across to take the free. Oozing confidence, his captain Anthony Daly waved his colleague aside and took the free himself. He struck the sliotar hard and sent it high into the goalmouth. The ball rebounded off an upright. Éamonn Taafe, who had just come on as a substitute, anticipated the deflected ball and sent it crashing to the net. Spurred on by this glorious goal, Clare were now in the ascendant. Two minutes from the end they were awarded a 65 and Daly, again leading by example, sent the ball all the way over the bar, to put his side two points ahead. Shortly afterwards, referee Dickie Murphy blew the full-time whistle. Thousands of overjoyed Clare supporters rushed onto the pitch to laud their team's wondrous achievement. Victory had been snatched from a gallant Offaly side, thanks to a herculean effort from a team obsessed with the idea of obliterating years of constant failure.

In one of the most inspiring speeches ever given by an All-Ireland winning captain, Anthony Daly captured the minds and hearts of a nation by repeatedly referring to what the occasion and the result meant to a county starved of success for so long and bedevilled by the ravages of emigration. The following evening, 15,000 flag-waving fans greeted the team when they arrived back at Shannon Airport. The plane journey from Dublin had only taken 25 minutes but the coach trip from Shannon to Ennis took four hours of sheer bedlam and joy. As Ger Loughnane stood to address the vast throng in Ennis, silence descended. Adopting one of the slogans of the sponsors, 'Hell for leather', as his theme, Loughnane reflected: 'Our endless hell began just a year ago when we began training in the hills near Shannon and in the muck at Crusheen … and the leather began in April following our league final defeat. After having gone through the torture and pain of a ferocious winter training programme, no one was going to put us down,' he concluded, to thunderous applause.

For Marty Morrissey it was now a case of three down, just one to go, as he savoured another lifetime's ambition. 'I will never forget Ennis on the Tuesday morning following the homecoming. The music, the craic and the unadulterated happiness will live with me forever. To see all the pubs open at 5 a.m. in Ennis, with the Gardaí strolling up the street, was really surreal. The victory brought a great sense of confidence to the whole business community. One memory above all others remains imprinted on my mind. At half-time, in the final itself, I asked Ger Loughnane how the second half was going to pan out. He stared at the camera and defiantly stated, "We are going to do it."'

That year and the following two years were really roller-coaster years for Clare hurling. In 1996 Clare lost to Limerick in the Munster championship, in a brilliant game of top-class hurling. With the sides deadlocked, Limerick centre half-back Ciarán Carey sent over a tremendous long-range point, in the dying moments, to dethrone the Banner men in quite dramatic circumstances. So 1997 was to present, in the words of Loughnane, a new challenge to Clare. His message was simple: 'Good teams win one All-Ireland, great teams win two. Now prove yourselves great.'

'This was the year that Clare confirmed to all and sundry that they were not a flash in the pan. For the first time they beat Tipperary in a Munster final. Jamesie O'Connor, with nine points, gave a real virtuoso display, as did Seán McMahon, in the heart of defence, when they subsequently overwhelmed Kilkenny in the All-Ireland semi-final. Owing to the introduction of the back-door system in hurling, Tipperary had beaten Down and Wexford to qualify to meet Clare in the final. So, the All-Ireland was really a replay of the Munster final. This was a fantastic game with the issue in doubt up to the end. A majestic point by Ollie Baker brought the sides level. Just when everyone had settled for a draw, Jamesie O'Connor secured possession to loft over the winning point. All Clare people, players, management, officials and supporters can now justifiably say "That was a great Clare team",' Marty added.

For Marty, 2004 was a very special year as his home club Kilmurry-Ibrickane not only won the Clare senior football championship, but annexed the Munster club title as well. Marty himself deserves some of the reflected glory. In 1979, when he was manager of their U-16 team, he had introduced a system of possession football, best suited to smallish, skilful players. Club officials like Patrick Murrihy and Michael Talty and many others had developed this style over the years. By 2004, their manager, Patrick O'Dwyer, had maximised the individual potential of all his players into an impressive, winning combination. In the process, he had instilled in his players a spirit of confidence and an unyielding 'never say die' attitude. These twin characteristics stood them in good stead as they journeyed on that magnificent odyssey of success.

'A lot of people, over the years, played their part in this wonderful achievement. Family names like the Murrihys, O'Dwyers, Taltys, McCarthys and Hickeys made significant contributions. Kilmurry-Ibrickane is what football is all about, because it epitomises the roles of local people serving the local community to the best of their ability. Three of the manager's sons — Odhran, who has played International Rules for Ireland, Peter, who is now playing for Clare, and young forward Michael — are especially talented players, as are many others. Luck also played a part in their campaign. Only a terrific comeback prevented them being beaten by Cooraclare in the Clare quarter-final. It also took two games to overcome Eire Óg of Ennis in the county final. Initially in the provincial championship, Drumcollogher/Broadford of Limerick provided stern resistance before they defeated Milltown-Castlemaine of Kerry in the Munster semi-final. Stradbally of Waterford really put it up to us in the final. They were a lovely, sporting team. We did not play well against Ballina in the All-Ireland semi-final, yet only lost by two points. Still, we got some satisfaction when the Mayo side deservedly went on to win the All-Ireland club final. Overall, it was a fabulous achievement for our club to win a provincial title. To see your neighbours and your friends that you have known from childhood achieve such success makes life worthwhile. Watching a clip of your own club's historic Munster club final triumph on RTÉ's six o'clock news was really great for the people of Kilmurry-Ibrickane. I think I might be forgiven for my part in that!' concluded Marty Morrissey.

Marty made the following selections for his representative teams.

IRELAND – FOOTBALL (1975–2005)

Billy Morgan
(Cork)

Robbie O'Malley
(Meath)

John O'Keeffe
(Kerry)

Tony Scullion
(Derry)

Declan Meehan
(Galway)

Kieran McGeeney
(Armagh)

Martin O'Connell
(Meath)

Jack O'Shea
(Kerry)

Brian Mullins
(Dublin)

Maurice Fitzgerald
(Kerry)

Peter Canavan
(Tyrone)

Pat Spillane
(Kerry)

Jimmy Barry-Murphy
(Cork)

Declan Browne
(Tipperary)

Matt Connor
(Offaly)

IRELAND – HURLING (1975–2005)

David Fitzgerald
(Clare)

Fan Larkin
(Kilkenny)

Brian Lohan
(Clare)

Martin Hanamy
(Offaly)

Brian Whelehan
(Offaly)

Seán McMahon
(Clare)

J.J. Delaney
(Kilkenny)

John Fenton
(Cork)

Ciarán Carey
(Limerick)

Jamesie O'Connor
(Clare)

Ken McGrath
(Waterford)

Henry Shefflin
(Kilkenny)

Joe Deane
(Cork)

D.J. Carey
(Kilkenny)

Nicholas English
(Tipperary)

After Clare hurlers won the Liam McCarthy Cup in 1995, a gala presentation evening was arranged for the official presentation of the All-Ireland medals in the West County Hotel in Ennis. Just as Ger Loughnane and his management team had been meticulous in their team preparation, so had the organising committee for this wonderful evening in Clare hurling history. A large circular opening was cut in the ceiling of the hotel's spacious ballroom. Aer Lingus kindly provided one of their stairways, which was strategically placed from the opening to the floor. All the players stood in the room above, awaiting the moment of their dramatic entry. The building was packed with Clare supporters. To simulated coloured smoke, each player's name was announced and, individually, they walked down the stairway to the presentation area. As each Banner star accepted his Celtic Cross medal, the invited guests burst into spontaneous applause. The master of ceremonies captivated both the audience and the historic event with his natural intuitive 'feel' for such a wondrous night. This 'helicopter effect' brilliantly choreographed the significant sense of occasion.

For Marty Morrissey, apprentice choreographer, ace commentator and now M.C., it was a particularly proud moment. He had now joined the pantheon of outstanding GAA presenters who can instinctively summarise the magic of the moment of a Gaelic games-loving people, with considerable aplomb and distinctive dignity. His original icon — the golden-voiced Mícheál Ó Hehir, who was a son of a Clare man — would certainly have approved.

Marty Morrissey – Fact File

Place of Birth:	Mallow, Co. Cork
Home Place:	Mullagh, Co. Clare (he also lived in New York for ten years)
Clubs:	Kilmurry-Ibrickane; University College, Cork
Playing Honours:	(a) Played hurling/football at all levels with club and with St Flannan's College, Ennis
	(b) Represented Clare at minor and U-21 levels (football)
	(c) Member of UCC Sigerson Cup team
Managing Career:	(a) Managed Kilmurry-Ibrickane at all levels
	(b) Guided St Joseph's, Spanish Point, to Munster Colleges 'B' title
Original Occupation:	Science teacher in St Joseph's Secondary School, Spanish Point, Co. Clare
Media Career:	(a) Cork Multi-Channel TV (presenter)
	(b) Clare FM (News Editor)
	(c) Lifestyle Cable Company (Subsidiary of Sky TV) (presenter)
	(d) RTÉ Cork (Presenter 1990–94)
	(e) RTÉ Radio and TV part-time commentator (1989–1994)
	(f) RTÉ sports commentator — permanent staff member (1994 to present)
	(g) Columnist with *Clare People*
Awards:	GAA McNamee Communications Awards (2) – 1986, 1987 (in association with Paschal Brooks)
	Masters in Education (National University of Ireland, Galway – 2005)

SIXTEEN

Anthony Molloy–Donegal

BRINGING SAM BACK TO THE HILLS AGAIN

In Jack Mahon's wonderful book, *History of Gaelic Football*, he stresses the pivotal psychological role played by the *Donegal Democrat's* weekly GAA columnist, Cormac McGill, in Tír Conaill's 1992 All-Ireland senior football triumph: 'After the All-Ireland U-21 success in 1987 its sports editor, Gerry McDermott, prevailed on the then *Longford Leader* columnist Cormac McGill, a staunch Donegal supporter, to write a column under the pen-name "The Follower". It became a clarion call, a rousing weekly diet of hope, an optimistic appraisal of the scene and a popular and readable column linking supporter, team member and management in the huge "desire to bring Sam to the Hills for the first time".'

It was against such a background of optimism and ever-growing expectation that team captain Anthony Molloy led Donegal into the first round of the 1992 Ulster senior football championship. Playing Cavan in Breffni Park was no easy task at any time, and once again the boys in blue proved their worth when they raced into a six-point lead. With Cavan midfielder Stephen King in superb form, the omens did not look good. However, that all changed when Molloy upped the tempo and his colleagues responded in a similar fashion to haul back the deficit to draw level. Then Martin McHugh, from a magnificent 50-yard free kick, put the northerners a point ahead as the game entered its final stages. Just before the final whistle, Cavan's Damien O'Reilly let fly with a spectacular left-footed volley for the equalising score. In the replay, at Ballybofey, Donegal showed their superior fitness in winning easily by 0–20 to 1–6.

In the semi-final against Fermanagh at Omagh, the Ernesiders had a man sent off and Donegal strolled to a 2–17 to 0–7 victory. When I met Anthony in his hometown of Ardara, he emphasised the importance of that win: 'There is no doubt that the Fermanagh game was the defining moment in most of our team's football careers. After the game, Martin McHugh and myself asked our trainer, Anthony Harkin, and manager, Brian McEniff, to dramatically increase our training schedule. I had just played 100 competitive games for Donegal and I knew, like many others, that our careers were coming to an end. If we were serious about winning an All-Ireland, we had to radically change out attitude to training. In preparation for the Ulster final we decided to train three nights a week — two of those were pure physical; some ball work was allowed in the third. Horses would not have been asked to do such stamina work, but we needed it badly if we were to compete on a level with our rivals.'

Donegal's Ulster final opponents were the current National Football League champions and near neighbours, Derry. They came into the final with impressive credentials, having accounted for Tyrone and All-Ireland champions Down during their provincial campaign. The decider was a tremendous contest. Despite having the wind in their favour, Donegal failed to dominate the opening exchanges and when new star full-forward Tony Boyle was injured, the signs looked rather bleak. Proceedings seemed to go from bad to worse with the sending off of corner-back John Cunningham before half-time. At the break, the Tír Conaill men went in level with the Oak Leafers on a score of 0–5 each. During the interval the Donegal management and players decided that the team would have to play the games of their lives to get a result: 'We changed our game plan and used the short ball to great effect. The fact that John Cunningham had rather harshly been sent off was also an inspiration to us. That decision really forced us to do what we were best at, possession football.'

When the history of Donegal football is fully documented, their second-half display against Derry will rank as one of their finest achievements. They adapted to their strategy of possession football with ease, superbly building up from the full-back line, with half-backs Donal Reid, Martin Gavigan and Martin Shovlin stamping their authority on the game. The now fully fit Anthony Molloy exerted an ever-increasing influence at midfield, along with his centre-field partner, Brian Murray. Invariably, with accurate passes they found centre-forward Martin McHugh, who frequently prised open the Derry defence. In the end, Donegal won by 0–14 to 1–9. It was a much more comfortable victory than the narrow two-point winning margin suggests.

For Anthony Molloy it was an especially joyful experience. He could not believe how the tide of fortune had turned in his favour. The previous year he had retired from the game and now here he was holding the Anglo-Celt Cup in his hands: 'During 1991 I had a serious knee problem and found it extremely difficult to regain full fitness. My back was also giving trouble. After not being selected for the 1991 Ulster final, I decided to retire. In October I went to America, started to play again, and actually won a local championship medal there. After Christmas, Brian McEniff asked me not only to rejoin the team but also to captain it. I was totally elated and willing to put in one final effort to capture Sam.'

Now Donegal were in the All-Ireland semi-final against Mayo. Manager McEniff, being very conscious of Donegal's four previous All-Ireland semi-final failures in 1972, 1974, 1983 and 1990, worked hard to remove the mental block. In the first half, Tír Conaill had plenty of possession but squandered a host of scoring chances. At half-time, McEniff told his players to keep playing as they were and everything would work out. 'It was a fear of winning, not of losing, that possessed us at that stage,' the friendly hotelier once famously stated. As the game developed in the second half, Donegal continued to dominate while still spurning scoring opportunities. It was only when McEniff made two inspired substitutions that his side found some composure. Manus Boyle, a good free-taker who had not started a game since the first match against Cavan, came on seven minutes into the second half and Barry Cunningham joined the fray at centre-field seventeen minutes later. Cunningham's fetching, power and pace wreaked havoc. This direct running modified Donegal's over-indulgence in the short passing game while creating more pressure at the heart of the Mayo defence. Thanks to three pointed frees from Manus and an overall improvement in the Donegal attack, they turned a 0–8 to 0–6 deficit into a 0–12 to 0–9 advantage as the game entered injury time. Then, after another magnificent catch and searing run, Cunningham was stopped illegally in the parallelogram. It was a penalty. Sensing that the hoodoo was at last to be broken, McEniff signalled to Martin McHugh to tap the penalty over the bar. McHugh duly obliged and the final whistle followed. That insurance point had left the score 0–13 to 0–9 in Donegal's favour. More pertinently, after years of heartbreak, they were in their first All-Ireland senior football final. 'It was a huge relief because we had been the bookies' favourites to succeed against Mayo, after our fantastic display against Derry. Our biggest problem had been to overcome the mental barrier of flopping yet again in Croke Park.'

Immediately after the game, the whole county went absolutely hysterical. Banners and bunting were erected in every town, village and crossroads as the whole northwestern county became alive with a sense of anticipation. All minds were now focused on the All-Ireland final against Dublin: 'This whole attitude made us all the more determined to win for the pride of Donegal. Dublin were out-and-out favourites but, deep down, we knew we could win. In the quarter final of the league, the previous spring, Donegal were leading the Dubs by four points with only four minutes to go. Unbelievably, within the next 90 seconds we lost our composure and conceded two soft goals to the now rampant Dublin team. We had lost a game we should have won by two points. The time had come for meaningful revenge and what better time to obtain it than in our first All-Ireland senior final.'

On the day before the 1992 All-Ireland, Molloy walked into a betting shop in Killybegs and placed a small bet on a horse that galloped home at ten to one. Maybe, he thought, this was a sign of greater things to come. Just after one o'clock the whole team and management left Donegal town by coach. The streets were lined with people as they cheered them on their way: 'We knew the people were craving for Sam Maguire and we had to deliver him. Brian McEniff and his mentors had planned everything so meticulously that they even had a man dressed in disguise at all of Dublin's training sessions! When we arrived in Dublin, we went to Shelbourne Park for a greyhound meeting. Then we played cards before retiring for the night and kept wondering what the next day would bring for us.'

McEniff and his management team had done their homework well. Discussing the mental pressures of All-Ireland final day, he consulted with many managers and players who had first-hand experiences of such an occasion. Tactically, McEniff had decided that the Dublin half-back line of Paul Curran, Keith Barr and Eamon Heery were central to Dublin's success. Not only were they good defenders but they also had the ability to come forward in numbers, thus exerting pressure on opposing backs. Barr in particular had a penchant for attacking. To counteract this, McEniff realised that his own playmaker, Martin McHugh, would have to play the game of his life. Thus, Donegal's match-winning strategy was hatched. Playing the possession game, midfielder Molloy would give short passes to McHugh who would run at the Dublin defence.

Before the game, two selection problems worried McEniff. He had to decide between free-taker Manus Boyle, who had impressed in the semi-final, and Tommy Ryan, who had done so well in the Ulster championship. Settling for the place-kicker and holding super sub Barry Cunningham in reserve, McEniff had another agonising decision to make when half-back Martin Shovlin failed a late fitness test. To the obvious disappointment of another couple of players, John Joe Doherty was called in to deputise for the unfortunate Shovlin. However, a rallying cry led by the inspirational Molloy that they would all play for Shovlin ensured that McEniff's men were united in a common purpose — to bring Sam to the hills of Donegal.

Starting nervously, Donegal looked ill at ease as Dublin went into a 0–2 to 0–1 lead. Soon Molloy looked at his long-suffering colleague-in-arms, Martin McHugh, and uttered one defiant sentence: 'We are not going to let this opportunity pass without doing ourselves justice.' When Dublin were awarded a penalty, past ghosts began to haunt everyone from Donegal. When the unlucky Charlie Redmond missed the spot kick, the siege was lifted. Even though Vinny Murphy notched a point for the metropolitans, Donegal were noticeably improving. With self-belief rising within him, each Donegal player started to take the initiative and play to the pre-ordained plan. Dublin only scored four more points in the first half as Martin McHugh (2), Manus Boyle (3), Declan Bonner (2), James McHugh and Tony Boyle tacked on points with almost monotonous regularity. Added to McHugh's opening point in the seventh minute, this spell of brilliant play in the second quarter had put Donegal 0–10 to 0–7 in front as the referee blew for half-time.

At the interval Brian McEniff praised his team for their first-half efforts and reminded them of the 40,000 Donegal people in Croke Park at that moment and the reception they would receive in Donegal if they kept playing the same way. In the third quarter Tír Conaill were really on top of their game and added four points to Dublin's two as the game entered the last quarter, to leave the score 0–14 to 0–9 in their favour. 'At this stage of the game I noticed that the Dublin players were starting to panic and to get annoyed with each other. I kept telling my colleagues to keep their composure because I realised that if we did so, the game was ours. At the same time, Brian McEniff ran onto the field to tell us to keep the pressure on for the last fifteen minutes and to keep watching the clock to see how much time was left. That was something he had instilled in each player before the game.'

In that last pulsating quarter, the Donegal half-forward line kept running at the Dublin defence. The aerial threat of Dublin's only really dangerous forward, Vinny Murphy, was curtailed by the close marking of Donegal full-back Matt Gallagher. Dublin were becoming increasingly frustrated as the clock ticked against them. Then Manus Boyle scored another point to leave the scoreline 0–15 to 0–9. However, apparent tragedy seemed to strike Donegal as Anthony Molloy aggravated his old knee injury and Brian Murray had to retire with a similar problem. This enabled a rejuvenated Dublin side to assume midfield supremacy. With eight minutes to go, Dublin had scored three unanswered points to leave just three minors in the difference. During the next six minutes, both sides exchanged two points apiece as Dublin pressed forward looking for a goal. The Donegal defence rose magnificently to the challenge, with goalkeeper Gary Walshe and his fellow defenders keeping Dublin at bay. The brilliance of substitute Barry Cunningham, who had come on for Murray, proved vital as time and time again he drove forward from midfield. This ploy, as well as the constant interchanging of the Donegal forward line, leaving the impressive Tony Boyle with plenty of space up front, confused the Dublin defence. With one minute to go, James McHugh gained possession and passed the ball to Declan Bonner. The red-haired Rosses man curled the ball over the bar with his preferred left foot. When referee Tommy Sugrue of Kerry blew the full-time whistle shortly afterwards, the score read Donegal 0–18, Dublin 0–14.

Going up the steps of the Hogan Stand to receive the coveted trophy, Anthony Molloy realised that he had left his speech back at home. However, he improvised brilliantly, concluding that it was time to take Sam to the hills of Donegal for the first time. The scene was now set for a week of the most enjoyable celebrations ever witnessed for an All-Ireland winning team. 'I will never forget the feeling when the full-time whistle went. Immediately John Leonard and other stewards, who guided me towards the presentation area, surrounded me. I was particularly happy that twelve members of my own family were present, including my mother and father. My father had always wanted to go to Croke Park and this was his first visit, at the age of seventy-five. I was very happy for him.'

When Anthony Molloy held the Sam Maguire Cup high in the September sky, Brian McEniff had just heard some discomforting news. It was rumoured that star-forward Joyce McMullen's brother, who was suffering from leukaemia, had died. Brian, accompanied by the Bishop of Raphoe, Dr Séamus Hegarty, quietly broke the news as the victorious team filled the dressing room. Silence fell. Then Joyce's sister came in and shouted, 'He's not dead.' Brian phoned the McMullen household in Donegal to find it had been a cruel rumour. Having gone through a variety of emotions, the now jubilant team left for a night of celebration at the Grand Hotel in Malahide. The Donegal class of 92, led by Anthony Molloy and the Man of the Match, Manus Boyle, who had contributed nine points in all, had written themselves into history. Not since Offaly, in 1971, had a team won the All-Ireland for the first time.

The journey home on the Monday was one of the longest and most emotional homecomings for any victor in any Irish sport. As the winners' train left Connolly Station on its way to Sligo, the doors were locked as Sam began his long journey. Huge numbers of well-wishers gathered to pay homage to the new heroes, as the train snaked through the towns of Kildare, Meath, Westmeath, and Longford. In Dromod, in County Leitrim, there was a brief stop as 3,000 people shouted,

'We want Gary.' This was a reference to goalkeeper Gary Walshe, who had worked in the village. Nine thousand supporters greeted them in Sligo when they reached the train terminus there. They were then transferred to a coach and, accompanied by an ever-growing cavalcade of cars; they made their way to the land of O'Donnell. When the team coach approached the Drowes River, on the Donegal/Leitrim border, captain Anthony Molloy and manager Brian McEniff left the coach and symbolically carried the Sam Maguire Cup into their native county. Arriving in Bundoran, the victory parade stopped at the Holyrood Hotel, where Brian McEniff had plotted and planned, often into the early hours, so that his great hour would come. In the Diamond, in Donegal town, 25,000 happy people waved and cheered as the champions arrived. When the song 'Simply the Best' was played, everyone was overcome with emotion.

During the course of the next few days the bonfires continued to blaze and the music never ceased, as a whole county and its far-flung Diaspora celebrated. Every part of Donegal was to have its own special moment of glory as the Sam Maguire Cup was proudly paraded around one of Ireland's most beautiful counties. For Anthony Molloy the next few weeks were hectic, as he was in demand everywhere and by everyone. At the game in Croke Park a large banner with Anthony's home address emblazoned on it was draped proudly amongst the crowd. As a result, Anthony received almost a thousand letters and congratulatory cards from each of Ireland's 32 counties, Great Britain and America. Today those greetings are a permanent reminder of the glories of 1992.

Before Christmas, Anthony and Martin McHugh travelled to America and one of the high points was when they took the Cup to the Sam Maguire Pub in New York, which is jointly owned by Anthony's brother and his uncle, James McGonigle. The year of '92 ended on a high note for Ardara's most famous son when he was one of seven Donegal men selected to receive a prestigious All Star award.

In 1993 Donegal lost their Ulster and All-Ireland titles when they were defeated by Derry in the Ulster final. 'Played under atrocious conditions in Clones, it was a match that really should have been postponed. Nevertheless, Derry deserved to win and I was absolutely thrilled when they also went on to win their first All-Ireland. One of my greatest memories of Derry's success was shaking the hand of Brian McGilligan as he and his victorious teammates ascended the steps of the Hogan Stand. Brian and I had many hard-fought tussles, but we have great admiration for each other. When I saw the big wide smile on his face I knew what Derry's victory meant to him.'

Anthony Molloy was born in 1962, one of 12 children had by Lanty and Nora Molloy, in the townland of Leamagowra, in the parish of Ardara. His brother Connie was the first member of Anthony's family to don the Ardara jersey, and naturally Anthony and his brothers, Lanty and Frank, went along to encourage him. Thus Anthony's insatiable appetite for Gaelic football was born. This started with ten-a-sides played in the back garden and continued up to the deafening crescendo that was the hallowed sod of Croke Park on All-Ireland final day in 1992.

His first ever game was at U-14 level, at centre half-back, against Rosses Rovers, who had future legendary soccer goalkeeper Packie Bonner at midfield. Soon afterwards, Anthony won his first medal and coveted Man of the Match award (an honour he was to be the recipient of on six further occasions) when Ardara won the 1976 Donegal U-14 championship. At Glenties Comprehensive School he scooped County Vocational mementoes at U-15, U-16, U-17 and U-19 levels. Moreover, during that time he was a member of the Donegal Vocational County team for three successive years. In 1979 and 1980, he represented Donegal minors while he played for the U-21's for four consecutive years between 1979 and 1982.

The latter year was to prove unusual, yet critical, in Anthony's football development: 'Because I had a reputation of being fond of partying and not being dedicated to training, I was not in the Donegal U-21 panel at the commencement of the 1982 campaign. Then something unusual happened. As a spectator, I met U-21 manager Tom Conaghan after the Ulster U-21 drawn semi-final between Down and Donegal. He asked me to rejoin the squad. This I did, returned to training on the Tuesday night and was picked at midfield for the replay on the following Sunday in Newry. Tom really straightened me and my attitude out. For that, I will always be deeply grateful to him. We then beat Down and subsequently went on to record a narrow victory over Derry in the Ulster final.'

In the All-Ireland semi-final, Dún na nGall overcame Laois to reach the All-Ireland final against Roscommon. In the final, the northerners defeated the westerners by 0–8 to 0–5. The 'mighty midget maestro', Martin McHugh, scored five points. There were four others, along with McHugh, who were to star on All-Ireland senior final day, ten years later. They were Donal Reid, Matt Gallagher, Joyce McMullen and the comeback kid himself, Anthony Molloy.

The following ten years were to provide a mixture of happiness, disappointment and despair. True, Molloy and others won Ulster senior championship medals in 1983 and 1990. Another U-21 All-Ireland was also annexed in 1987. This time players like John Joe Doherty, John Cunningham, Barry McGowan, Manus Boyle, Tommy Ryan and Barry Cunningham — all men who would feature prominently in

1992 — were on the winner's podium. In the final analysis, however, it was Donegal's inability to perform on the bigger stage in Croke Park on All-Ireland semi-final days that preoccupied the collective minds of the masses. Both in 1983 and 1990 Donegal had failed miserably when the big questions were asked.

Molloy made his senior competitive debut for Donegal against Wexford, in the 1982/83 National League and was at midfield when they beat Cavan in the Ulster final, only to lose to Galway in the All-Ireland semi-final. Again, in 1990, a promising performance against Armagh in the Ulster final gave them a semi-final spot with Meath at the penultimate stage of the championship. An eight-point defeat did not do justice to the display of the magnificent Molloy, who was voted Man of the Match. Donegal reached their third successive Ulster final in 1991, only to lose to eventual All-Ireland champions Down. When Molloy disappeared from the Donegal scene for the next six months, it appeared that the end had come. But the hand of fate and the astuteness of Brian McEniff were to irrevocably change the fortunes of Donegal, within fourteen months. It all began when the sometimes errant midfielder once again answered the call to arms as Brian McEniff pleaded for one more year's all-out effort. Just as with Tom Conaghan in 1982, Molloy's recall was the dynamic catalyst that drove Donegal to that historic victory of 1992.

Molloy's last competitive match for Donegal was the 1994 Ulster semi-final against Tyrone: 'I got the proverbial roasting from Ciarán Corr, and when I was replaced I knew it was all over. The arthritis had returned with a vengeance but, more importantly, my appetite for the game and that necessary competitive edge were both gone. It was a wonderful privilege to have played for Donegal for twelve years and most of all to have had the honour of being Donegal's first All-Ireland senior winning captain.'

Though not now actively involved in Gaelic football, Molloy loves recalling the great moments and the talented players that he encountered, as well as his hopes for the future.

1. 'My first senior game for Ardara was in the 1979 Shield final against Glen, and I scored the winning goal from the corner-forward position. The last club game I played in was the semi-final of the 1994 Senior Football Championship against Naomh Columba. My greatest regrets were the All-Ireland semi-final defeats against Galway and Meath. Altogether I played 123 competitive games for Donegal. People say that my best performances were when we played Meath in that semi-final and in a National League game with Galway in the 1988/89 series. I got a Man of the Match

award in that Royal encounter. In the week after the Galway game the *Tuam Herald* ran the banner headline "Molloy owned Tuam".'

2. 'Without a doubt the greatest footballer I ever saw was Matt Connor of Offaly. He had everything: power, pace, vision and accuracy. It was a tragedy that his career was so suddenly cut short. All the Kerry and Dublin players of the seventies and the eighties were heroes of mine because they brought the game to new heights of skill and work-rate. I came up against a whole lot of tremendous fielders. People like Stephen King, Peter McGinnity, Gerry McCarville, Plunket Donaghy, Pádraic Dunne and Larry Tompkins were all fantastic players. I would have to single out Brian McGilligan as my greatest opponent. For footballing intelligence there was no one to beat the wee man from Kilcar, Martin McHugh. More than anyone else he brought Sam to the hills.'

3. 'I was in charge of the county minors on two separate occasions: (a) 1995/96 and (b) 1999/2000. In 1996, we won an Ulster title only to come up against a brilliant Laois side in the All-Ireland semi-final. They then went on to win the All-Ireland. They had a lot of talented individuals, like Colm Parkinson, Martin Delaney, Chris Conway, Brian McDonald and Kevin Fitzpatrick. The nucleus of the present Donegal senior side is made up of players from those minor teams I was in charge of. Like most other counties, football politics is rife in Donegal. A lot of very capable people have been overlooked either as county managers or as members of management teams. I would welcome an opportunity to play a part as a minor manager or as part of a senior set-up.'

As a young teenager growing up in the mid to late seventies, Anthony Molloy had two heroes — Kerry all-time great midfielder Jack O'Shea and the equally talented, strapping Brian Mullins of Dublin. At that stage of his life there was no TV in his or the neighbouring townlands. A few miles away, on the day of All-Ireland final or semi-final, crowds of men and boys would descend upon the only house that had a TV in the area. Anthony and his friends often stared in wonder at the magic box in the corner, which relayed the spectacular achievements of those Kerry and Dublin sides. Though a Kerry supporter, the Ardara man wanted one day to emulate the All-Ireland winning achievements of either O'Shea or Mullins. When the game was over, thirty young men would put on their boots and go to the nearest field and play until darkness interrupted their mini All-Ireland final, three or four hours later. They dreamed the dream that one day some of them would climb the Hogan Stand and claim Gaeldom's greatest prize for Donegal.

'I was lucky to achieve my dream. However, there is not a day passes when I wonder what is happening in a Donegal senior football dressing room. I know I have the passion and the commitment to do a job. Nothing would satisfy me more than to help bring Sam back to the hills for a second time.'

Only time will tell whether Ardara's pride and joy will achieve his most desired wish.

ANTHONY MOLLOY – FACT FILE

Native place:	Ardara, Co. Donegal
Date of Birth:	May 28, 1962
Clubs:	Ardara; New York
Club Honours:	(a) Ardara: Senior Football Championship (1) – 1981 U-21 Football Championship (2) – 1980, 1982 U-16 Football Championship (1) – 1977 U-14 Football Championship (1) – 1976 Senior League Football Championship (1) – 1989 Senior Shield Football Championship (2) (b) New York: Senior Football Championship (3)
County Honours:	Vocational Schools U-15 Football Championship (1) – 1977 Vocational Schools U-16 Football Championship (1) – 1978 Vocational Schools U-17 Football Championship (1) – 1979 Vocational Schools U-19 Football Championship (1) – 1980 All-Ireland Senior Football Championship (1) – 1992 Ulster Senior Football Championship (3) – 1983, 1990, 1992 All-Ireland U-21 Football Championship (1) – 1982 Ulster U-21 Football Championship (1) – 1982 McKenna Cup (2) – 1985, 1991
Other Honours:	Railway Cup 1989

Awards:	All Star 1992
	Man of the Match, All-Ireland Semi-Final 1990
	Donegal Player of the Year 1998, 1999
	BBC Player of the Championship 1992
	Sports Star of the Week
	Player of the Month, April 1993
	New York Player of the Year 1986
Managerial Honours:	Ulster Minor Football Championship (1) – 1996
Occupation:	Financial services consultant and publican

SEVENTEEN

Anthony Rainbow–Kildare

ONE OF THE LILYWHITES' MOST LOYAL SONS

> Here's to Merriman, Conlon and Cribben,
> Two Murrays, Fitzgeralds and Scott,
> To the Kennedys, Kehoe and young Kelly,
> And to Losty the best of the lot,
> To Rafferty, Conlon and Bracken,
> To Gorman, a star anywhere,
> For they brought home the crown of All Ireland,
> Those stalwarts from Gallant Kildare.

From The Football Immortals by Raymond Smith

It was the Monday morning after the 1998 All-Ireland football final. In a game of exceptional skill, outstanding sportsmanship and huge entertainment, Galway had edged out hot favourites Kildare by 1–14 to 1–10. The whole world, however, seemed totally oblivious to one man's feeling of isolation as he sat, disconsolately, in the corner of the foyer of the losers' team hotel. Having spent a sleepless night pondering on what might have been, classy Kildare wing half-back Anthony Rainbow stared pensively into the distance. Tall buildings of impersonal, imposing concrete and never-ending glass crowded in on him as he tried to come to terms with the disappointments of the past 24 hours. All the unprecedented publicity, the hype, the excitement and glorious expectation of the previous few weeks seemed so meaningless now. Those terrible demons of Kildare's traditional misfortunes on the football field had returned with a vengeance.

Anthony Rainbow tried to understand how Galway, who had performed so moderately against mediocre teams in that year's championship campaign, had suddenly improved so dramatically. Gradually, the futility of looking back and self-analysis dawned on the Suncroft club man. It was time to put his life and reasoning into proper perspective. 'The sun rose that morning. I saw hundreds of people going to work. Most of them, probably, did not even realise that the All-Ireland final was on the previous day. That same scenario was being replicated in every village, town and city in Ireland. Many people throughout the whole country had either mental or physical disabilities. Hundreds more were dying from terminal illness and here was I, worrying about a wrong result of a football match. Then, a further reality struck me. In our sports psyche, we had been inculcated with the age-old maxim: "To the victor the spoils; to the vanquished, only the ignominy of defeat." The aura of that All-Ireland victory would be bestowed on Galway alone. That was not fair, I now concluded. Kildare, by their preparation and performance, had equally contributed to a magnificent occasion. My colleagues and I should enjoy with celebratory enthusiasm all that we achieved, I told myself.'

That 1998 All-Ireland senior football final was the culmination of a GAA life which began for Anthony when he won the Primary Schools U-12 championship with Curragh National School in 1982. Then he won the All-Ireland Colleges 'B' championship with the Patrician Brothers Secondary School in Newbridge in 1989. At club level, he won an Intermediate county championship with his club, Suncroft, also in 1989. At this time the versatile Anthony was starring on the rugby scene, representing both Leinster and Ireland at U-18 level. A talented full-back, he was hotly tipped as a future star in the oval ball code. His six provincial caps and one Irish cap merely added to his growing reputation as an outstanding rugby prospect. When 1990 came around, he was in a quandary as to where his future sporting allegiance would lie. One man, however, was soon to make up his mind for him.

After an absence of 50 years, the town of Naas was back in the county GAA senior championship final. A huge crowd turned up for that decider with Clane. On that September day in 1990, the legendary Kerry GAA football manager, Mick O'Dwyer, attended his first ever Kildare county final. The renowned Kingdom footballer and manager had just been appointed as the Short Grass County manager. It was felt that he was the one person who could revive Kildare's flagging football fortunes. Morale was at an all-time low in the county, especially since, earlier that year, Wicklow had recorded their first-ever championship victory over the Lilywhites. When Michael Osborne and his Kildare supporters' club members entered the ground just before the game, quickly followed by the Kerry maestro, the massive attendance burst into a spontaneous round of applause. The die was now cast for the future of Kildare football. O'Dwyer, in the ensuing months, ignited the sleeping giant that was Kildare. Supporters, long starved of success and any realistic expectation, flocked to Kildare games in the 1990/91 league in their thousands. Vast amounts of money poured into the supporters' club's coffers and, more importantly, the team began to win.

Anthony Rainbow was one of the new players called up to the senior panel. 'I made my first appearance against Tyrone. The professionalism and widespread, infectious enthusiasm amongst officials, management, players and supporters alike had to be seen to be believed. The most impressive characteristic of Micko was his considerable man-management skills. Individually, he made every player feel that if they played to their full potential, they could be the best player in Ireland in their respective position. Collectively, he made the whole team aware that if they performed to their strengths and eliminated their weaknesses, Kildare could be the best team in the country. We won our way to the quarter-final of the league where, ironically, we faced Kerry. Beating them by a point was a massive morale booster. When we followed this with another one-point win, against Donegal in the semi-final, we simply could not believe it. Thanks to Mick O'Dwyer's tactics, training methods and his positive attitude, he had totally transformed Kildare football within a short space of seven months. However, a freak goal by Vinny Murphy and two fantastic saves by Dublin goalkeeper John O'Leary contributed largely to our two-point defeat against Dublin in the league final.'

Six weeks later, Kildare's newfound optimism was suddenly shattered when Louth defeated them, by the minimum of margins, in the first round of the Leinster championship. A virtuoso display by Louth's brilliant forward, Stefan White, who scored 2–4, effectively put paid to Kildare's chances.

In 1992 Kildare defeated Wicklow and Westmeath to reach their first Leinster final since losing to Dublin in 1978. Once again they faced Dublin. Kildare were playing reasonably well until a skirmish broke out. This seemed to affect the Lilywhites' concentration and they surrendered, rather tamely, in the last quarter, to lose by six points. For Anthony, now the side's established left half-back, there was some consolation as he had been a member of Kildare's successful U-21 team, which had beaten Dublin earlier in the year, in the provincial final.

Wicklow again provided the opposition for the first round of the 1993 Leinster championship. The Garden County led at the interval by nine points before a tremendous Kildare comeback, inspired by Martin Lynch, yielded a narrow two-point victory, courtesy of late points by Dermot Doyle and Paul McLoughlin. When Kildare trounced Offaly by eleven points in the semi-final, they were once again scheduled to meet Dublin in the provincial final. Almost 60,000 attended headquarters to see Kildare again lose to Dublin on a big match day. Despite negative rumblings against the security of O'Dwyer's managerial tenure, the Waterville hotelier prepared for another season. An ensuing disappointing league campaign did not augur well for the championship, particularly as Kildare were drawn against Dublin in the first round. Playing with the wind, Kildare went in at the interval five points up but Dublin recovered to snatch a draw. In the replay, Kildare performed poorly and were beaten by five points. Having been four years in charge with no silverware to show for his trouble, Mick O'Dwyer resigned. Most pundits forecast that was the end for Kildare.

Former Roscommon All Star and Newbridge resident Dermot Earley was then appointed manager. Narrow defeats in 1995 and 1996 in the Leinster championship, to Louth and Laois respectively, made him decide to relinquish his position. Anthony explained the circumstances that went against Earley: 'Dermot was a very unlucky manager. He had tremendous organisational ability. Nobody could put in a greater effort than he did. There were a lot of key players injured for important matches as well as 50/50 decisions going against us on the field of play.'

After Earley's retirement, a loud clarion call from the County Board again went out to Mick O'Dwyer. They still believed that if he did not bring them to the Promised Land, they would, with his help, come within sight of it. In the autumn of 1996 O'Dwyer returned to the helm of Kildare football. The 1997 Leinster championship provided some inspiration and hope for the future, when it took Meath three games to dispose of Kildare. Their 1997 performances convinced O'Dwyer that Kildare had now developed a necessary cutting edge to their style of play. The Kerryman meticulously prepared his team with greater eagerness than ever before. The additional reason for this newfound optimism was the fact that two players of real quality had joined the panel. Former Tipperary star Brian Lacey was available for selection in the Kildare defence and Mick's own son, Karl, had also transferred to the Lilywhites. Having obtained a teaching position in Rathangan, he would add both mobility and accuracy to the forward line.

During the next twelve months, O'Dwyer and Kildare blended perfectly together to create a winning combination. They simply had a fantastic 1998 Leinster senior championship campaign. Playing a fast, crisp brand of exciting, intelligent football they strode the playing fields with a new confidence. They beat Dublin by a point in a replay after they had drawn in the first game. Thus their long-standing 'hoodoo' team had been eliminated. For the first time since 1972, a Kildare team had beaten Dublin in the championship. They were on their way. This fact was further emphasised when Kildare overwhelmed Laois by 2–13 to 0–8 in the Leinster semi-final.

The Leinster final matched Kildare with their old rivals and neighbours, Meath. In a superb game the two sides served up a thrilling 70 minutes of entertainment. With right full-back Brian Lacey outstanding and forwards Dermot Earley and Martin Lynch equally impressive, they led by three points as the game entered the last quarter. Then Meath, as always, dug deep and clinically responded with three unanswered points. There were seven minutes left. It was now that Kildare showed their true mettle. Following a kick-out by goalkeeper Christy Byrne, young Dermot Earley, son of the former manager, rose high to fetch the ball and sent it down the left wing. An ever-alert Martin Lynch secured possession and accurately crossed the ball to substitute Brian Murphy. With poise and confidence, Cork-born Murphy slammed the ball to the net for a wonderful goal. Now totally dominant, Kildare added further points by midfielder Willie McCreery and right half-forward Eddie McCormack. When the full-time whistle blew, Kildare had won their first provincial title since 1956, by 1–12 to 0–10. Though Meath had been reduced to 14 men when Brendan Reilly was sent off, no one disputed the merits of Kildare's victory. An ecstatic captain, Glen Ryan, held aloft the Leinster trophy. Anthony Rainbow, who had given an exceptional display in the Lilywhites' half-back line, will never forget that moment of glory: 'It was just an incredible feeling after all the heartbreaks of our previous Leinster final defeats. As well as a fabulous all-round performance by all my colleagues, especially our outstanding captain Glen Ryan, I must give credit to Mick O'Dwyer. By his total commitment to our cause, he had shown his total belief in our ability. We, in turn, had responded to his challenge.'

That night, and for the following week, the whole county celebrated. Having been prisoners of their past glory and slaves to years of failure, the Kildare supporters now had something to cheer about. Glen Ryan, Anthony Rainbow and all the others were real and accessible heroes with whom they could identify. The subsequent All-Ireland semi-final against Kerry was an exceptionally colourful and tension-laden occasion as Kildare supporters packed the stands and terraces of Croke Park in their thousands. For Mick O'Dwyer it was a time of personal conflict. Here he was managing Kildare against his native Kerry, with whom he had played in six All-Ireland finals, as well as successfully leading them to eight All-Ireland titles as a manager. This man, who had served his county for an incredible span of 36 years (1954–1990), was now plotting its downfall.

Immediately prior to the game, Kildare's majestic midfielder, Niall Buckley, failed a fitness test. His withdrawal resulted in left half-forward Dermot Earley being switched to midfield and Ken Doyle being drafted in to Earley's position. During the game itself, they played exceptionally well. With Brian Lacey, Glen Ryan, Eddie McCormack, Dermot Earley, Martin Lynch and, especially, roving full-forward Karl O'Dwyer being particularly outstanding, the Lilywhites won 0–13 to 1–9. The final scoreline did not really reflect Kildare's dominance but O'Dwyer was not worried, as he prepared for the first time since 1986 to return as manager to Croke Park on All-Ireland final day.

Before the All-Ireland final against Galway began, regular full-back Ronan Quinn had to withdraw because of injury, and normal right half-back John Finn was switched to full-back. Veteran corner back Sos Dowling was dovetailed to fill Finn's position. Meanwhile, another unfortunate development had occurred. Team captain Glen Ryan got intensive physiotherapy treatment for a freak thigh injury that he had received while walking with a few friends on his local golf course, just 48 hours before the game. Even though he was passed fit just before the game, he was decidedly ill at ease during most of the contest. All of this would upset the normal fluidity and composure of the Kildare defence.

When the game began, Galway seized the initiative and scored three points without reply. Playing fast, direct football, it appeared at first that they were going to demolish Kildare. However, the resilient Ryan, ably assisted by the talented Rainbow and wonderful midfielder Willie McCreery, reasserted Kildare's authority. As a result, they scored an unanswered 1–2. The goal by Earley seemed to ignite the whole team out of their apparent lethargy. Using their short passing game effectively, the Lilywhites seemed to own the ball as half-time approached. At the interval, the score read 1–5 to 0–4.

When the second half commenced, Galway played like a team totally transformed. During the first half, Glen Ryan's opponent Jarlath Fallon had been largely anonymous. Now he appeared a completely different player, very focused on the task at hand. When he cleverly turned inside Ryan to score a tremendous long-distance point, both his and Galway's confidence were considerably boosted. Ryan himself stated, quite candidly: 'I believe that was the turning point of the game. It is impossible to legislate for such a wonderful score.'

For the remainder of the game Galway took control. Being more assured on the ball and hitting long, defence-splitting kick passes, they upped their performances. With speed star Michael Donnellan nominally positioned at right half-forward but picking up the ball in the half-back line and making deep surging runs into the heart of the

Kildare defence, Galway had an alternative attacking option. The whole Galway team had come alive, and with Fallon and Donnellan especially prominent, the Tribesmen went on to deservedly win their first senior All-Ireland title since 1968. The final scoreline of 1–14 to 1–10 was a fair reflection of their second-half superiority. In fairness to Kildare, it must be said that they made an enormous contribution to what was, in essence, a display of Gaelic football at its very best. If those late injuries had not upset the solidity of the Lilywhites' defence, there is no doubt that the final outcome would not have been as decisive. Still, that is sport and no one could detract from Galway's success. As the final whistle blew, the gallant Kildare players fell to their knees in total dejection. A marvellous championship journey, which, for so long, had promised so much, had now ended in failure. But that conclusion, as Anthony Rainbow had so accurately portrayed in his post-match introspective analysis, was totally untrue and decidedly unfair. Beating the three most recent All-Ireland winners, Dublin, Meath and Kerry, in the one season was no mean feat by any standards.

Since that 1998 Leinster success, Kildare have appeared in three more Leinster deciders, in 2000, 2002 and 2003. They began the 2000 campaign rather tentatively as they faced their bogey side, Louth, who had just won Division Two of the National Football League. In addition, three seasoned campaigners, Niall Buckley, Declan Kerrigan and Sos Dowling, had now gone from the inter-county scene. That was offset by promising new players like Ronan Sweeney, John Doyle, Tadhg Fennin and Pádraig Brennan joining the ranks of experienced players such as Lacey, O'Dwyer, Lynch, McCreery, Earley, Ryan and Rainbow. Anyhow, a controversial late penalty awarded to Kildare late in the game, and scored by Pádraig Gravin, enabled the Lilywhites to escape with a three-point victory. It then took two games to dispose of Offaly at the penultimate stage of the Leinster championship. In the first game Offaly were lucky to snatch a draw, but in the first half of the replay they played superbly and scored two goals in the opening twenty minutes. The second half, however, belonged to Kildare. Playing fast, attacking football, they dominated proceedings to score an impressive three-point victory. Furthermore, the ring rustiness and inertia of the Louth match were replaced with boundless energy, laced with a definite incisiveness about their forward play.

Again, it took two games to separate winners and losers in the Leinster final between Dublin and Kildare. The first outing was undoubtedly the game of the year. It was full of flowing football, non-stop running and brilliant scores. A draw of 0–14 apiece was a fair result. The replay was, essentially, a game of two halves. Dublin were absolutely fantastic in the first half. When they led at half-time by 0–

11 to 0–5, a facile win for the metropolitans appeared the more likely outcome. Kildare, nevertheless, had not read the script because Dermot Earley and Tadhg Fennin both scored goals within a minute of the restart. In a dramatic turnaround, Kildare scored 2–6 in the second half, restricting the dumbfounded Dublin to a single point. For the second time in three years, Glen Ryan lifted the Leinster trophy.

'It was a really spirited and spectacular performance, especially in the second half. That season, particularly in the replays, we showed a greater mental resolve and a better capacity to dig deep,' stated Anthony, when I met him in the Red Cow Moran's Hotel, on the Naas Road outside Dublin.

In the subsequent All-Ireland semi-final, the Tribesmen of Galway shattered Kildare hopes yet again. When Brian Murphy scored an opportunist goal for the Lilywhites, on 45 minutes, to put them three points ahead, Kildare supporters started to dream of another visit to Croke Park on All-Ireland final day. John Finn's controversial dismissal eleven minutes later was a huge blow to Kildare's hopes of success. With only three minutes left, they were still narrowly ahead. Finally, despite the heroics of Anthony Rainbow and his fellow defenders, the resistance crumbled. Galway finished them off, with four successive minors, to record a somewhat lucky victory. Kildare's wonderful championship odyssey had ended in a very unsatisfactory manner.

The 2002 Leinster final, again between Kildare and Dublin, was a high-quality contest. Played in front of 78,000 spectators, the biggest provincial final attendance since 1963, the Dubs just edged out the Lilywhites by two points. When Kerry convincingly beat Kildare in the qualifier, Mick O'Dwyer decided, for the second time, to relinquish his Kildare managerial reins. His job was done. With a great GAA county now on firm footing, he rode quietly off into the sunset.

The following year, 2003, was to see Kildare in the fourth Leinster final in six years. Now under the guidance of Kildare native Pádraig Nolan, they put up stern resistance before losing to Laois, who were winning their first provincial title in 57 years. Ironically, Laois, now managed by the mercurial and much-travelled O'Dwyer, were the nation's new romantic GAA icons, as they eked out a narrow victory. Whereas the victory itself was popular, the fact that Kildare had two men sent off, as against Laois's one, had to have a negative influence on the Lilywhites' performance and consequential outcome.

As Anthony Rainbow continues to give his full commitment on the playing fields with Kildare, he often ponders how the GAA, both structurally and socially, could be improved at national level.

1. 'I believe the National Football League should be restructured into

four separate divisions of eight teams. Using a two-up, two-down promotion/relegation system between each division would make the league more balanced and more competitive. Also, I think the league should revert to its former start-up date in October. There are really very few county players involved in the latter stages of the provincial club championships. An autumn beginning to the league would also allow for Friday or Saturday night floodlit games. That would be a great bonus for all concerned. With a fortnight between games after Christmas, there would be less pressure on players, especially those involved in Sigerson or U-21 competitions. This, in turn, would help alleviate "burn out" and allow for a longer recovery period for players, as well as improving the quality of preparation for the U-21's.'

2. 'When Karl O'Dwyer, Brian Lacey and Brian Murphy came from their native counties of Kerry, Tipperary and Cork respectively, they gave a huge commitment to Kildare football. We always looked upon ourselves as one big happy family, all doing our utmost for the success of Kildare. Their arrival increased the competition for places and, as a result, the overall standard of our team improved considerably. The fact that Karl and Brian became All Stars when playing for Kildare is ample proof of their total dedication to the Lilywhite cause.'

3. 'I enjoyed my experiences with the International Rules Series, in terms of camaraderie, travel opportunities and as a reward for top players from all counties. I still have some reservations on the game, at times, being too physical. Nevertheless, the speed of the game, the fast thinking required and the "mark" are very positive characteristics. The introduction of the "mark" would be great for Gaelic football.'

4. 'The whole drink culture in Irish society presents a big problem. This means that many people, either in private business or in public positions, do not develop their full potential. Likewise, in sport there is too much emphasis on meeting in pubs after matches. If we are to mature properly, in sport or in life, this mindset has to change. This pub mentality has to be taken from the centre of our socialising habits. The GAA must play its part in helping others achieve this. If the GAA did this, they would be giving a great example to the whole of Ireland.'

When choosing his representative sides Anthony Rainbow made the following selections.

Leinster (1995–2005)

Christy Byrne
(Kildare)

Brian Lacey
(Kildare)

Darren Fay
(Meath)

Paddy Christie
(Dublin)

Finbar Cullen
(Offaly)

Glen Ryan
(Kildare)

John Finn
(Kildare)

Ciarán Whelan
(Dublin)

John McDermott
(Meath)

Dermot Earley
(Kildare)

Trevor Giles
(Meath)

Paul Barden
(Longford)

Johnny Doyle
(Kildare)

Graham Geraghty
(Meath)

Mattie Ford
(Wexford)

Ireland (1995–2005)

Christy Byrne
(Kildare)

Anthony Lynch
(Cork)

Séamus Moynihan
(Kerry)

Seán Lockhart
(Derry)

Kieran McGeeney
(Armagh)

Glen Ryan
(Kildare)

Seán Óg De Paor
(Galway)

Anthony Tohill
(Derry)

John McDermott
(Meath)

Éamonn O'Hara
(Sligo)

Trevor Giles
(Meath)

Michael Donnellan
(Galway)

Maurice Fitzgerald
(Kerry)

Peter Canavan
(Tyrone)

Brendan Devenney
(Donegal)

Kildare were the first glamour team of the GAA. In the early years of the twentieth century, county selections wore the colours of the champion club. In the 1903 final, inspired by Joe Rafferty of Clane, the team wore Clane's all-white jerseys and the players painted their boots white to match. The public loved the all-white strip so much that the county decided to adopt it as their official colour. Thus, the Lilywhites were born. It took three games to separate Kerry and Kildare in that 1903 final, before the Kingdom won. That marathon struggle was seminal in two significant areas. It was the first time that those now-familiar GAA shouts of 'Up Kerry', 'Up Kildare' were heard. Kildare, who also introduced the passing game to Gaelic football, had a fantastic following of supporters, singers and musicians. In retrospect, those early Kerry/Kildare clashes were primarily responsible for popularising Gaelic football beyond all expectations.

Having won senior All-Irelands in 1905, 1919, 1927 and 1928, Kildare set themselves high standards for others to emulate. They have given us many magnificent players. Larry Stanley, who captained the 1919 side, was a 1924 Olympian. Paul Doyle played in Kildare's six successive provincial winning teams (1926–1931). Mick Buckley, Bill Gannon and Jack Higgins were inspiring captains in 1927, 1928 and 1929 respectively. Since then, the Lilywhites have given the GAA many top-class players and administrators. No one epitomised versatility in Gaelic games more than Pat Dunny of Prosperous. The long-serving Central Council representative holds the proud distinction of winning Railway Cup medals in both hurling and football, on successive days, in 1974.

Anthony Rainbow is following a glorious, time-honoured legacy of longevity of service, total loyalty and dedicated labour to Kildare's footballing fortunes. At the outset of this chapter, a congratulatory verse eulogising the tremendous exploits of Kildare's first great team was quoted. Before he hangs up his boots for the last time, Anthony would love to be remembered in celebratory verse for his part in Kildare's next great team. Only time will determine whether or not he obtains his most fervent wish.

ANTHONY RAINBOW – FACT FILE

Native place:	Curragh, Co. Kildare
Date of Birth:	October 5, 1971
Club:	Suncroft
Schools/Colleges Honours:	(a) Primary: Curragh National School U-12 Schools Championship (b) Secondary: Patrician Brothers, Newbridge, Leinster Schools B Championship – 1989 (c) All-Ireland Schools 'B' Championship – 1989 (d) Third level: Athlone R.T.C. Schools League – 1992, 1993
Club Honours:	Suncroft Intermediate Football Championship – 1989 Intermediate Football Championship (runners up) – 2003 Manager 2003
County Honours:	Leinster U-21 Football Championship – 1992 Leinster Senior Football Championship – 1998, 2000 All-Ireland Senior Football Championship (runners up) – 1998 O'Byrne Cup 2003
Other Playing Honours:	Railway Cup (2) Compromise Rules Winners – 2001
Other Codes:	Rugby: 6 Leinster Caps, U-18 Rugby Cup – 1988/89 1 Ireland (U-18) – 1989
Awards:	(a) County: All Star 2000 Player of the Month 1999 Footballer of the year 2000 (b) Club: Footballer of the Year – 1990, 1998 (c) Schools: Most improved Player 1989
Occupation:	Technical Sales Representative with Tegral Building Products
Family:	Parents – Christopher and Elizabeth Married to Niamh (née Moran) from Naas

EIGHTEEN

Martin Carney–Mayo/RTÉ

TWO COUNTIES, TWO PROVINCES, ONE AMBITION

Local 'derbies' are by their nature thoroughly exciting but extremely tense occasions of contrasting emotions. When two neighbouring sides in such a scenario have fabulous teams at the same time and over a protracted period, that rivalry intensifies considerably. That was the case in Connacht in the 1930s, when Galway and Mayo produced so many fine teams and a host of exceptionally gifted players. From 1933 to 1940, Galway and Mayo contested every Connacht final, each of them winning four. The Tribesmen also claimed two All-Ireland senior football successes in 1934 and 1938, whilst Mayo annexed the national honour for the first time when they easily disposed of Laois in the 1936 final. It was only after a replay that eventual All-Ireland champions Kerry defeated Mayo at the penultimate stage in 1939. This era, too, saw a fantastic Mayo side win an unprecedented six National Football League titles, five of them in a row from 1933 to 1938 inclusively. Henry Kenny, Séamus O'Malley, Paddy Moclair, Patsy Flannelly, Josie Munnelly, Gerald Courell and Jackie Carney are just a mere handful of the more talented Mayo men who inscribed their names indelibly in that golden period of Mayo football.

When young Martin Carney, who was born in Bundoran, Co. Donegal, and grew up in Ballyshannon, listened to his father, a Mayo man, expound on those brilliant Mayo achievements, something magical clicked in his mind. He wanted not only to know more about the great game of Gaelic football, he also wanted to become part of it. Martin's father Owen, who was Jackie Carney's brother, was well placed to impart the inherent characteristics of Gaelic football — its skills, its traditions, its almost mysterious aura as a source of beauty, fun and entertainment.

Martin went to the De La Salle Brothers' Primary School in Ballyshannon. His instinctive, searching GAA curiosity was immediately rewarded. Br Abban, Br Raphael and Br Kieran were three dedicated and enthusiastic GAA coaches, who ensured that young Carney's blossoming love of Gaelic football was developed and enhanced. By the time he went as a boarder to St Eunan's College in Letterkenny, Martin was showing distinct signs of future stardom. For three years he played on the college's Mac Rory Cup team, also winning an Ulster Colleges 'B' McLarnon Cup medal while only a third-year student. He then represented Donegal at both minor and U-21 levels, without experiencing any luck.

Donegal had always had a fair quota of stylish footballers and good teams, but it was 1963 before they had a sufficiently balanced and competent unit to compete seriously for senior provincial honours. Then, despite having super players of the calibre of Séamus Hoare, Bernard Brady, Seán O'Donnell, John Hannigan, Frankie McFeely and captain Seán Ferriter, they failed to perform and were easily beaten by the Mourne men. 'I remember that day well. It was a sweltering hot afternoon. My father had to carry me on his shoulders after the game because I felt so tired and miserable. It was also the first time I saw a goalkeeper swinging like a monkey off the crossbar, every time the ball went over for a point. Donegal were also in the minor final that day and our netminder, Willie McNeilis, was the man who provided the high jinks in the goal mouth,' Martin told me when I met him in Castlebar.

In 1966 all the aforementioned were still playing as Donegal reached their second provincial final, only to lose again to Down. However, there was a vast improvement performance-wise and they only lost by two points. They had also unearthed new talent — like their diminutive but highly skilled captain Mickey McLoone, Pauric McShea and Declan O'Carroll. Moreover, a certain Brian McEniff returned to the fold when he came on as a substitute.

While still only a teenager Martin made his senior inter-county debut in a Dr Lagan Cup game against Tyrone at Dungannon in November 1970, when he came on as a substitute. Shortly afterwards, he was selected for his first 'start' when he lined out against Armagh at Ballyshannon in another Lagan Cup game. (At that time the National League was divided into geographical regions. The winners of the Northern section, as well as qualifying for the latter stages of the league, were also awarded the then prestigious Lagan Cup.) Unfortunately, in that Armagh encounter, Martin broke his collarbone so he was unable to return to the playing fields until the late spring of 1971. A few months later, Martin made his senior championship debut when Donegal were beaten by Down in Newry.

Before qualifying as a secondary school teacher, Martin attended University College, Galway. On the football field there also, lady luck did not shine on him. He was a star player on a UCG team that reached three Sigerson Cup finals during his time. However, the westerners lost all three deciders. 'I really enjoyed my football and life generally at UCG. Having been in the confined environment of a boarding school for five years, I could not believe the sense of freedom that prevailed at university. It was brilliant to meet and play with so many exceptional footballers from different parts of the country. Kerry future All-Ireland winners Paudie O'Mahoney and Ger O'Keefe were there in my time. Tony Regan of Roscommon was just ahead of me. There was a wonderful spirit of friendship amongst all students but especially amongst the Sigerson Cup squads. At that time each college's Sigerson team was at least as good as most senior inter-county teams. UCC had Séamus Looney, Paudie and Brendan Lynch and future rugby star Moss Keane. UCD had a fantastic number of exceptionally gifted footballers like John O'Keeffe, Oliver Leddy, Ogie Moran, J.P. Kean, Kevin Kimurray and Paddy Kerr.

'In 1973 the combined universities won the Railway Cup when we defeated Connacht after a replay, in Athlone. I was left half-forward when we won the replay. It really was a team of stars. Pat O'Neill of Dublin, John O'Keeffe of Kerry, Kevin Kilmurray of Offaly, Brendan Lynch of Kerry, Anthony McGurk of Derry and Paddy Moriarty of Armagh were on that team. All of these, with the exception of Lynch, became All Stars.

'UCG was also to provide me with an opportunity of meeting, at first hand, Kerry's great Mick O'Connell. Mick was doing a sea skippers' course in Galway. Former Galway All-Ireland winning star of 1956 and well-known GAA author, Jack Mahon, organised a football training session for Mick in Pearse Stadium. Tony Regan, a few others and myself gratefully accepted the offer to train with O'Connell. That was really an enthralling experience.'

For both Martin and Donegal, 1972 proved to be a historic year. Playing brilliantly, the Tír Conaill men surprisingly overcame a star-studded Down 15 at Ballybofey, in the first round of the Ulster championship. That Mourne outfit contained many of the side that had defeated Kerry only four years previously in the All-Ireland final. The great Seán O'Neill and the powerful Dan McCartan were holders of three All-Ireland medals. In the centre of the field was Colm McAlarney — a majestic midfielder then in the prime of a superb career.

Donegal defeated Cavan after a replay in the semi-final to reach a rare Ulster final against Tyrone. Neutrals remember that day for its incessant rain and terrible underfoot conditions — not unlike the infamous weather during the 1993 Ulster final between Donegal and

Derry. Donegal players and supporters, however, savour it as the momentous moment when the Anglo-Celt Cup came to Dun na nGall for the first time.

In the muck and rain of mud-splattered St Tiernach's Park, Donegal played fantastically well to defeat Tyrone by 2–13 to 1–11. With Donal Monaghan, Pauric McShea and Brian McEniff keeping the quicksilver Tyrone forward line in check, midfielder Séamus Bonner and Frankie McFeely gave the forward line a plentiful supply of the ball. Tricky corner-forward Séamus Granaghan and the very accurate Joe Winston did the most damage.

Though most spectators were impressed with the skill and pace of the new right half-forward, Martin Carney himself was somewhat self-deprecatory. 'I was only average. My marker, a small little dynamic player, Mickey Hughes, really was vastly superior to me. Brian McEniff was the real hero of the hour. He was not only the game's outstanding player but our manager as well. Like many other university students at the time, I spent the summer holidays working on building sites in New York, hoping to earn enough money to ease the financial burden on my family while at UCG. I was flown home for all the games, with the exception of the Cavan replay, before which I did not return to America. Being away from all the hype, I was able to be very relaxed about it all. It was only when Joe Winston scored a fantastic equalising point in the drawn match against Cavan that I ever thought of the possibility of getting to an Ulster final. I was also too young to appreciate fully what that Ulster success meant to so many long-suffering Donegal supporters. Anyhow, I had to return to America on the following day.'

On the Thursday before the 1972 All-Ireland semi-final against Offaly, the transatlantic commuter came home again. Overawed by the occasion, Donegal did not repeat their provincial form and were beaten by four points. The talented midlanders then went on to retain their All-Ireland title, which they had won for the first time the previous year. 'Two of our best players, Neilly Gallagher and Mickey McLoone, were missing because of long-term injuries for much of that season. I firmly believe that if they had been available, our chances would have increased immeasurably. Mickey, who was my boyhood hero growing up in Ballyshannon, was a terrible loss. At this stage the Donegal team whom I was playing with in New York were very strong and extremely dedicated to training. So I was both physically and mentally in good shape. Nevertheless, I could not see any current team management tolerating that type of preparation,' Martin told me when I met him in Castlebar.

In 1973 Tyrone dethroned Donegal in the first round of the Ulster championship in Ballybofey. It was a tempestuous game, as tempers flared on several occasions with an air of unpalatable tension never far away. 'We togged out in Jackson's Hotel before the game. Because of all the bad feeling around, we waited until the crowd had dissipated after the game before we walked, by a circuitous route, back to the hotel to tog in.'

When the draw for the 1974 Ulster championship took place, the unbelievable happened. For the third year in a row Tyrone and Donegal were fated to meet again — this time in the first round at Omagh. With the 'series' at one each, this was to be the GAA equivalent of a 'rubber'. 'For that crunch tie I had been selected originally at right half-forward. After we boarded the team bus at Strabane, Brian McEniff, who had become our player-manager, told me that I was to play midfield against Tyrone's rising young star, Frank McGuigan. McEniff reckoned that if McGuigan could be curtailed, then we had a very realistic chance of being successful against the O'Neill County. It was an 80-minute game then. As I could run forever, Brian probably thought I could counteract the dominance of McGuigan. As it turned out, everything went well for me and I scored three points from midfield. It was my best performance in a county jersey. The fact that Donegal won the third leg of the 'rubber' 1–9 to 0–8, given the keen rivalry at that particular time between the two counties, made that game extra special.

'In all those games against Tyrone I never got an opportunity to say a word to Frank McGuigan. He had appeared such a quiet, though exceptionally gifted footballer, as was another Tyrone player from that period, Séamus Donaghy. Some years later I was working in New York for the summer. One day I got on a wrong train. As I was cursing my luck, who did I spot sitting in front of me but Frank McGuigan? For the next hour or so we happily chatted about football, the Derby matches in the early seventies and a host of other GAA topics. He was just a nice, totally relaxed individual and completely unaffected by his icon-like status back in Ireland. It really was worthwhile getting lost to get to know a footballer 3,000 miles away from the madding crowds of Clones, Ballybofey and Omagh.'

After Donegal's impressive performance against Tyrone, they comfortably defeated Antrim in the semi-final before renewing acquaintance with Down in the Ulster final. It took two games to separate two excellent sides, before Donegal deservedly won the replay to claim their second provincial trophy in three years. When team captain Pauric McShea accepted the Anglo-Celt Cup, Martin Carney was much more aware of what an Ulster final success meant to so many people. Furthermore, thanks to the vision of Brian McEniff, Carney had become one of a select group of players who played the running game from a midfield position. Prior to the 1970s there was a tendency to select midfielders who were first and foremost tall and strong fielders of the ball. Carney and others, like Colm McAlarney and later Jack O'Shea and Bernard Brogan, brought a new dimension to midfield play. The one type of player that any defender does not like is a man running at him, especially from deep positions. Of present-day players, Tyrone's Seán Cavanagh and Kerry's Eoin Brosnan are particularly adept at creating panic in opposing defences. Carney's role, doing just that, played a pivotal part in Donegal's 1974 Ulster success.

In the 1974 All-Ireland semi-final, Galway won quite comfortably in the end against a Donegal side who once more under-performed, before going down on a 3–13 to 1–14 scoreline. For Martin Carney, the future omens for Donegal were not good. 'We had a much better team, I feel, in 1972. Though I played for Donegal for four more championship seasons, up to and including 1978, we never won another championship game — always falling at the first hurdle. It really ended for me with a humiliating defeat to Derry at Ballinascreen in 1978. Gerry McElhinney and Mickey Lynch were the architects of that Derry triumph. I played with Donegal for the first part of the 1978/79 National Football League, bowing out against Longford in Pearse Park just before Christmas.'

In 1975, Martin Carney returned to his father's native county of Mayo to take up a teaching position. When many of his Donegal friends and colleagues either retired or were retired from the county team, Martin began to make the more practical decision of playing where he lived. At this time Donegal were going through a lean period; there was also much disharmony around. Donegal's messiah-in-waiting, Brian McEniff, was effectively sacked from his managerial position in 1976. With more stability in mind, Martin transferred his club-playing allegiance initially to Islandeady and then subsequently to Castlebar Mitchels, with whom he is still primarily associated.

It was not long until the Mayo senior selectors came knocking and Martin was duly drafted into the Mayo squad for the 1979 championship. They reached the final but were beaten by Roscommon. Two years later Martin was selected as team captain and he led them to provincial success for the first time in twelve years when they overcame Sligo. 'It is hard to believe that Mayo went for so long without a Connacht senior title. They had experienced much under age success during that period, securing a minor All-Ireland in 1971 as well as reaching the 1973 All-Ireland U-21 final. They also had performed magnificently in the National League, reaching four finals and winning the league outright in 1970. So, it was a very enjoyable and celebratory occasion when we won the Nestor Cup in 1981.'

During the 1980s Martin Carney won three more Connacht

medals, in 1985, 1988 and 1989. About 1983 Martin realised he did not have the same turn of speed as of old, and he seriously considered retiring from the game. One man, however, decided otherwise. Realising Martin's inner determination, in addition to his handling ability, Mayo manager and former Galway All Star Liam O'Neill asked Martin to transfer from his customary forward berth to right corner-back.

'In my university days I mostly played in the half-back line or at midfield. Consequently, I found it quite easy to adjust to a defensive role. What I liked about being a back was that you did not have to rely on someone else to give you the ball. It was a more specific challenge and it was up to you to make the most of it. Having been a forward also helped you to be more creative in your general play. It is much more difficult to switch from being a defender and take up a forward position. I am very grateful to Liam for extending my career and giving me three superb defensive years from 1985 to 1987.'

Ironically, when John O'Mahony became manager in 1987, he asked Martin to become a forward again. This he did for the following two years and was a valued member of the Mayo senior squad that reached the All-Ireland final of 1989.

The 1989 final between Mayo and Cork was a spectacle of all that is best in Gaelic football — free-flowing movements, no rancour and most of all some magnificent high fielding by both Teddy McCarthy of Cork and Mayo's own cult figure and hero, Willie Joe Padden. At half-time Cork led Mayo on a scoreline of 0–10 to 0–8. Just three and a half minutes into the second half, Mayo's Liam McHale and Noel Durkin combined to send substitute Anthony Finnerty in for a great goal. Mayo were in front, but Cork fought back and soon regained the lead. Then Mayo had a golden chance when Finnerty gained possession close to goal. However, he blasted the ball wide. Cork then took control to finish strongly. The final score was 0–17 to 1–11 in the Rebels' favour. Mayo, though beaten, had restored pride not only to themselves but also to Connacht football. It is extremely hard to believe it now, but prior to this game Ulster and Connacht football were seen as inferior to that of the other provinces.

When the final whistle blew in that 1989 final, Martin Carney knew that a fantastic football career in terms of service, dedication and ability was almost at an end. A gold Celtic Cross medal may have been missing from his trophy cabinet but there were two Ulster medals and four Connacht medals — a unique record by any standards. When he won the 1981, 1985 and 1988 Connacht medals, Mayo subsequently disappointed just as Donegal had done in 1972 and 1974. When Martin Carney came on as a substitute in a National League play-off match in Croke Park against Meath, he scored two points. Being comprehensively beaten by the Royals, Martin finally decided to bow out of inter-county football. It was March 1990. For almost twenty years he had worn the green and gold of Donegal and the green and red of Mayo with equal distinction.

At club level, Martin Carney was initially involved with the Aodh Ruadh club in Ballyshannon. Subsequently, Ballyshannon and the neighbouring Bundoran club amalgamated and played under the name St Joseph's. Martin won six senior championships with them as well as an Ulster club medal in 1975. In 1968 the young teenager also won an unofficial All-Ireland club medal when St Joseph's beat the Galway champions — the famed Dunmore MacHales — in a two-legged final. With Castlebar Mitchell's, he added a further two county championship medals to his collection.

At provincial level, Martin, at different times, played for three different teams in the Railway Cup competitions. As well as the universities selection, he represented Ulster and Connacht. His memory of the 1975 game with Ulster stands out for contrasting reasons. 'Firstly, it was the last game that Seán O'Neill, who had won eight Railway Cup medals, played for Ulster. Secondly, Jimmy Barry Murphy got the ball five times and he scored four goals and a point. What made his achievement all the more noteworthy was the fact that he had played in the All-Ireland club hurling final the day before, when his team, St Finbarr's, defeated the Fenians of Johnstown in the final. In a brilliant second-half performance, Jimmy, who scored a wonder goal, was by popular acclaim the Man of the Match. The same accolade was given to him in the Railway Cup football final. That must constitute some kind of record, to put two match winning performances back-to-back in two different codes.'

Shortly after Martin retired from playing, he became Mayo's minor team manager in 1991, bringing them to the All-Ireland final, only to lose to Cork. Then he took over the U-21 team, also bringing them to the All-Ireland finals in 1994 and 1995, only to lose to Cork and Kerry (after a replay) respectively. 'That 1995 team were a particularly good one. If Kieran McDonald had been available for the replay, perhaps we could have won. Having been involved in management for five years without any national success, I decided it was time to move on and take a back seat.'

In a comprehensive overview of the game, from both his own experiences and as an RTÉ Sunday game analyst, Martin made the following points to me:

1. 'RTÉ's Bill Lalor, who is the producer of *The Sunday Game*, asked me in 1996 to become an analyst for their GAA commentaries.

Even though I thoroughly enjoy the programme, I would not feel entirely comfortable or blasé about doing it. To me, it is always a learning process. In order to do justice to the programme and to myself, one must always prepare well for it. Overall, however, it is a pleasant opportunity to see, at close hand, the great players and wonderful teams which make Gaelic football such compelling viewing.

'The programme is not without its lighter moments. I remember, one time, sitting high up in the old Nally Stand, in our studio, during a game. Suddenly, the studio door burst open and a man ran in, hotly pursued by a security guard. Apparently, the man had been sitting on the roof of the stand, fell through it and landed on a girder, outside the studio. Only by the grace of God had he fallen onto the girder. Otherwise, he would probably have fallen to his certain death, fifty feet below on the concrete floor of the stand. Luckily, also, it happened during an advertisement break. It would have been dramatic television viewing if it occurred while we were on air.'

2. 'Some years ago I was part of a committee selected to present a set of proposals to restructure GAA football competitions. Though most of our proposals were thrown out, I feel they helped to change the fixed mindset of many people in the GAA. In essence they created the opportunity to introduce the All-Ireland qualifiers for those teams knocked out either in the first or subsequent rounds of the provincial championships. Though not perfect, I believe, with a little alteration, the current system can be improved whilst still retaining the provincial system that has served the association so well.'

3. 'The National Football League should be altered to allow three separate divisions. At present there is too big a gap in class between the top and bottom teams in Division Two. When you look at some of the scoring differences in that division in the 2005 league, they do nothing either for the victor or the vanquished. Ten games in a three-tier league would, inevitably, produce a more meaningful and competitive series.'

4. 'At club level there is a very serious issue facing the GAA at the present time. In most counties there is significant disruption to all club activity when the county team is playing. If a county is doing really well, very often there are little or no club games played for up to two months. In Down there is a compulsory system where clubs must play a certain amount of games without their county

players. This format must be introduced on a structured basis at national level. If this is not addressed urgently, the very life-blood of our association will be irrevocably altered.'

5. 'The two basic skills of Gaelic football are catching and kicking. The hand pass has been used and abused to the detriment of kicking the ball. The hand pass should only be used as a secondary support system, not as the primary vehicle for propelling the ball. What is strangling the game at present is the mentality which maintains that possession should not be given away at any cost. As a result, players are so afraid of surrendering possession that they keep laying the ball off to colleagues who may be only five metres from them. The game's most renowned skills are being sacrificed on the altar of speed. To my mind, over-indulgence of the hand pass is the ruination of the game as a spectacle. It may be quick and smooth, as a successful possession strategy, but it is very often aesthetically displeasing. Just think of the great kickers of the ball — Maurice Fitzgerald and Kieran McDonald to name but two — and what beauty they have brought to the game. Our legislators will have to introduce rule changes that will bring more 'kicking' back into the game. If they do not, we will never see Gaelic football develop its undoubted potential as a wonderful game.'

6. 'There are far too many demands on all players but especially on the younger, more talented individuals who are expected to play at third level, county level and club level. To be asked to train for all of these teams, normally under a variety of contradictory training techniques, is quite frankly a totally unacceptable abuse of the player. At the beginning of each season, all the players' managers should meet to adopt a common strategy that primarily protects the player. Ideally that means that a player should only be asked to train for one team while being allowed to play for all his sides. This would practically eliminate the current system, as practised in most counties, where young players are asked to travel phenomenal journeys and do excessive training. No wonder so many of them suffer from 'burn-out'. The present modus operandi, which is really a self-defeating practice, has possible long-term serious consequences, both for the enjoyment of the game and the welfare of the player. Players must be protected at all times from such malpractices.'

Martin Carney made the following representative selections.

CONNACHT (1960–2005)

Eugene Lavin
(Mayo)

Harry Keegan   Noel Tierney   Dermot Flanagan
(Roscommon)   (Galway)   (Mayo)

Gerry O'Malley   John Morley   Seán Óg De Paor
(Roscommon)   (Mayo)   (Galway)

Willie Joe Padden   T.J. Kilgannon
(Mayo)   (Mayo)

Mickey Kearins   Dermot Earley   Michael Donnellan
(Sligo)   (Roscommon)   (Galway)

Jarlath Fallon   Pádraic Joyce   Tony McManus
(Galway)   (Galway)   (Roscommon)

IRELAND (1970–2005)

Billy Morgan
(Cork)

Robbie O'Malley   Mick Lyons   Paudie Lynch
(Meath)   (Meath)   (Kerry)

Tommy Drumm   Kevin Moran   Martin O'Connell
(Dublin)   (Dublin)   (Meath)

Brian Mullins   Jack O'Shea
(Dublin)   (Kerry)

Frank McGuigan   Greg Blaney   Pat Spillane
(Tyrone)   (Down)   (Kerry)

Mikey Sheehy   Seán O'Neill   Matt Connor
(Kerry)   (Down)   (Offaly)

Since those magnificent Mayo sides of the 1930s, the westerners have
won several National Football League titles. All-Ireland medals, at both
minor and U-21 levels, have also been garnered. Only last March,
Ballina Stephenites added the All-Ireland football club title to an
impressive roll of honour for the boys from the County Mayo. Under

the captaincy of the late Seán Flanagan, Mayo won successive All-Ireland senior titles in both 1950 and 1951. From that time, however, the most prestigious prize in Irish sport has eluded a football-crazy county. The names of great Mayo players like Tom Langan, Pádraic Carney, Paddy Prendergast, Willie McGee, Willie Casey, John Nallen, John Morley, Joe Corcoran, T.J. Kilgallon, Willie Joe Padden and Liam McHale are regularly recalled with fondness in the minds and hearts of GAA supporters at home and abroad. Four times (including a replay) Mayo have failed, in the last sixteen years, to cross the last hurdle on All-Ireland final day.

Martin Carney has one All-Ireland ambition. Having become a 'naturalised' Mayo man for almost the last thirty years, he would like nothing better than to see a victorious Mayo captain climb the steps of the Hogan Stand on a September Sunday.

'First and foremost, I am a Donegal man and Sam went to the hills in 1992. Now, I would love to see Mayo win a senior All-Ireland,' added Martin. In 1992 his native Donegal beat his adopted Mayo after a very close contest in the All-Ireland semi-final. On that occasion, Martin could neither win nor lose. One suspects that when Mayo do win the All-Ireland, it would be easier for him if it were not achieved at the expense of Donegal. Or perhaps, understanding Martin's penchant for diplomacy, he would look upon it as a win-win scenario. Either way, no county would deserve it more than the proud wearers of the green and red.

MARTIN CARNEY — FACT FILE

Native Place:	Bundoran/Ballyshannon, Co. Donegal
Clubs:	(a) Aodh Ruadh, Ballyshannon
	(b) St Joseph's (Amalgamation of Bundoran/ Ballyshannon)
	(c) Islandeady
	(d) Castlebar Mitchel's
College Honours:	McLarnon Cup (St Eunan's, Letterkenny) – 1968

Club Honours:	(a)	St Joseph's
		All-Ireland Club (unofficial) – 1968
		Senior Football Championship (6) – 1968, 1970, 1973, 1974, 1975, 1976
		Ulster Senior Football Championship (1) – 1975
		Senior League (1) – 1973
	(b)	Castlebar Mitchel's
		Senior Football Championship (2) – 1986, 1988
		Centenary Cup – 1984
County Honours:	(a)	Donegal
		Ulster Senior Football Championship (2) – 1972, 1974
		McKenna Cup (1) – 1975
		Special Minor Hurling Championship (1) – 1969
	(b)	Mayo
		Connacht Senior Football Championship (4) – 1981, 1985, 1988, 1989
Other Playing Honours:		Railway Cup with Combined Universities – 1973
Managerial Honours:	(a)	Connacht Minor Football Championship (1) – 1991
	(b)	Connacht U-21 Football Championship (2) – 1994, 1995
Awards:		All Star Replacement (3)
		Donegal Player of the Year 1977
		Mayo Player of the Year 1986
		Monthly Award – July 1988
		Man of the Match Awards:
		(i) Connacht Final 1985
		(ii) All-Ireland Semi-Final 1988
		Donegal Centenary Team
		Best Mayo Team (1960–1990)
Occupation:		Secondary school teacher
Family:		Married to Gina
Children:		Niamh, Eimear, Orla, Eoin

NINETEEN

Colm Browne–Laois

ON THE THRESHOLD OF THE HOLY GRAIL

There were just 15 minutes gone. A game that had drawn a record attendance of over 50,000 for an All-Ireland semi-final was, to all intents and purposes, over. A Laois team that had always promised so much had now apparently, yet again, delivered so little. Experienced Roscommon, who had won successive All-Irelands in 1943 and 1944, were in total command with the wily Jimmy Murray and the unerring Donal Keenan orchestrating every move. Then suddenly, a change overcame the Laois team. The westerners were leading by a comfortable margin of eight points when Tommy Murphy grabbed the ball near to the corner flag. The Graigecullen man steadied himself and unbelievably curled the ball over the bar for a tremendous score. Incredibly and immediately, Laois players and supporters became totally transformed. The players, to a man, responded magnificently, fetching, kicking and passing with a renewed optimism and an ever-growing sense of confidence. The battle cry of Laois supporters intensified as they sensed that perhaps, at last, their hour was about to come. After all, on that pitch stood two legends of Laois football, now at their influential best.

Bill Delaney of Stradbally and his three brothers, Jack, Chris and Mick, along with their uncle Tom, had played for Laois ten years earlier, in their county's unsuccessful appearance in the 1936 All-Ireland final against Mayo. One year later, a 16-year-old secondary school student, at Knockbeg College in Carlow, Tommy Murphy, had played for the O'Moore County against Kerry in that year's All-Ireland semi-final. Subsequent appearances by both Bill and Tommy, in the 1938 All-Ireland semi-final, confirmed their growing status as extraordinarily talented footballers. Delaney was a commanding, determined, talismanic figure. Murphy, dubbed the 'Boy wonder of football', was now at the peak of his considerable talents. By popular acclaim, it is nationally acknowledged that he was one of the most supremely gifted footballers of any generation. Now, they were leading the charge for All-Ireland supremacy.

For the last quarter of the 1946 All-Ireland semi-final, Tommy Murphy was simply majestic as he fetched magnificently, sending long, probing, angular kicks continuously into the opposition's half. Thanks to Murphy's superior aerial ability, Laois had reduced the deficit to two points with time almost up. Sensing this could be their last chance to get an All-Ireland medal, both Delaney and Murphy upped their performances to new heights of skill and commitment. Murphy passed to Delaney, who sent the ball to Stephen Hughes in the corner-forward position. The latter unleashed a rocket-like shot towards the Roscommon goal. At the last moment, Roscommon goalkeeper Gerry Dolan leapt across the goal line to save the ball and steer it to safety. Bill Delaney and Tommy Murphy looked at each other. They did not need to say anything. Laois's opportunity of a gold Celtic Cross was now gone forever. It would be a long time before a Laois side would lift a national senior title.

It was against such a background of hope, failure and tradition that every successive generation of Laois Gaelic footballers has been measured. When young Colm Browne started playing football in his back yard in Portlaoise, he, too, wanted to be the anointed one to lead the O'Moore County from the trials and tribulations of the past to the promised land of glorious achievement and much desired silverware. In that back yard, Colm and his younger brother, Gerry, honed their blossoming football skills in the early 1960s, imitating their all-time hero, Mick O'Connell, and practising the attacking attributes of Meath right half-back Pat 'Red' Collier. In deference to their mother's native county, the Royal's team of 1967 had always held a particular affection for them. When Offaly won their first two All-Ireland senior titles, in 1971 and 1972, the Faithful County took their fancy, especially the impeccable scoring exploits of star forward Tony McTague. Meanwhile, at the local primary school, the coaching skills of Br Beausang impressed the young Brownes and their pals, including future star colleagues Tom Prendergast, Liam Scully, Jimmy Bergin and Billy Bohane. At club level their team, Portlaoise, won all under age championships up to and including U-21 titles at county level. Two outstanding club officials, Billy Phelan and Jimmy Cotter, were the main driving forces behind such a comprehensive structural and coaching development, at all levels within the county.

Colm, at this stage, was now a boarder at Ballyfin College, another proverbial hotbed of GAA activity. Though he never won anything at Colleges level, Colm still enjoyed the experience of playing against strong Colleges sides like Knockbeg, St Mel's of Longford and the Franciscan College in Gormanston. In addition, future All-Ireland winning Offaly stars Richie Connor, Pat and Mick Fitzgerald as well as fellow future county man Brian Nerney, were all accomplished footballers at the famed nursery during his tenure there.

Outstanding college and club performances by Colm soon attracted the attention of Laois county selectors, and he subsequently represented the midlanders at minor level in two championship seasons, 1974 and 1975, and at U-21 level in 1976, 1977 and 1978. In 1976, the now 19-year-old trainee Garda made his first senior competitive county appearance, against Offaly at right half-forward, in that year's National Football League. His direct opponent in that initial appearance was the experienced, competent Mick Ryan, who had won All-Ireland medals with Offaly in their breakthrough years of 1971 and 1972. The following year Browne made his championship debut, against Louth. It would be four years later, in 1981, before Laois and Browne would make any significant impact in the senior championship. That year, the O'Moore men reached the Leinster final for the first time since 1968. Despite a good start against neighbours Offaly, they then conceded a very soft goal before succumbing to a 1–18 to 3–9 defeat. They were also very unfortunate to again meet the same opposition in the following year's championship, with the game following the same pattern and a similarly disappointing result.

Still, both players and management were reasonably satisfied with the side's progress on two fronts. Firstly, Offaly were a very good team with a very astute manager in Longford-born Eugene McGee. Secondly, even though long-serving star Bobby Miller was now in the twilight of a wonderful career, the nucleus of the Laois side were all individually talented athletes, whose collective skills could be developed into a very strong, vibrant, cohesive unit. Players like Pat Brophy, John Costello, Willie Brennan, Tom Prendergast, Eamon Whelan and Colm's brother, Gerry, were all men of immense ability. Colm himself had now become a team leader, whose clever anticipation and astute passing were central to the side's overall strategy.

When Laois reached another provincial decider in 1985, the outlook was promising. In that game against Dublin, however, they flopped badly, on a 0–10 to 0–4 scoreline. That result did not accurately reflect the actual quality of Laois football at that time. A combination of injuries, defections of key players and general disharmony within the county contributed to Laois fielding an under-strength side for that final. In retrospect, many people in Laois felt that a splendid opportunity of at least provincial success was lost, owing to the internal problems. Out of the trough of despair and uncertainty, a greater unity of purpose was soon achieved. New team manager Kieran Brennan, with his superb man-management skills and positive outlook, soon had a full quota of the best players within the county at his disposal.

The 1985/86 league campaign opened with unity amongst all the GAA stakeholders in the county being of paramount importance. Brennan blended the team into a well-disciplined, attacking unit with emphasis on speed, combination and support play, as well as instilling a commendable attitude of determination and selflessness throughout the side.

The league campaign began in October with a most unlikely and disappointing draw against Carlow. Thereafter, everything improved dramatically with top-class team performances being the order of the day. When they defeated Down in a quality performance, they qualified to meet Dublin in the league semi-final. The internal turmoil of the previous year was totally forgotten as they diligently prepared to meet the metropolitans on April 20, 1986, in Croke Park. Another terrific display resulted in a two-point victory for the midlanders. They were now in the National League final, for the first time since they won the inaugural league, 60 years earlier, in 1926. Furthermore, they were destined to meet Monaghan, the then current holders, who themselves had won the league for the first time when they defeated Armagh in the 1985 league final.

In front of 30,000 enthusiastic spectators, Laois began the game at full throttle, showing power, pace and panache for the first 18 minutes. With centre half-back Pat Brophy and team captain Colm Browne playing superb football, the midlanders dominated. The flawless fielding of Liam Irwin and John Costello at centre-field ensured that the Monaghan defence was continually under pressure. The impressive sight of Irwin effortlessly gaining possession and running at the beleaguered Ulstermen during the first half lifted the spirits of his fellow players and spectators alike. Twice Irwin scored from play and twice from frees to put the midlanders four points ahead, as the shouts of 'Laois, Laois' from their excited supporters rose in ever-increasing crescendo. To put more icing on the cake, Colm Browne, showing his undoubted class, cleverly intercepted a Monaghan attack. Quickly he transferred the ball to his overlapping half-back colleague, Mick Aherne. He passed to Colm's brother, Gerry, who soloed upfield before sending a defence-splitting pass to the unmarked Eamon Whelan. The Portlaoise full-forward duly dispatched the ball to the net, under the body of advancing Monaghan goalkeeper Paddy Linden.

Monaghan, however, were undaunted as they quickly regained a foothold, mainly through the tireless efforts of midfielder Kevin Carragher. The Clontibret player gained possession and, having spotted corner-forward Mick Caulfield lurking in the danger area, quickly passed the ball to him. He made no mistake as he crashed the ball to the net. It was very much 'game on' as the play ebbed and flowed for the next nine minutes. In the 29th minute came probably the most decisive moment of this thoroughly absorbing contest. Completely against the run of play, the elusive Gerry Browne sent in a high ball from near the sideline. It fell between Laois's 40 man, Willie Brennan, and the advancing Paddy Linden, just outside the parallelogram. The Graigecullen man managed to beat the unlucky Linden to the ball and he fisted it into the empty net. Shortly afterwards, the half-time whistle blew, leaving Laois ahead by 2–4 to 1–1.

It was nip and tuck in the third quarter, with Laois defending desperately against the wind. When Ray McCarron scored a penalty in the 37th minute, after colleague Nudie Hughes had been fouled in the square, the fat was really in the fire. Two points — one from a free and the other a 45 by Eamon McEneaney (he had just come on as a substitute) — and two minors from Irwin (one a free also), meant that the scoreline read 2–6 to 2–3, with ten minutes left. Monaghan then scored two further points to reduce the deficit to one point. There were only four minutes left. Now the whole Laois team, and the defence in particular, rose to Monaghan's incessant attacking in magnificent fashion. Brophy, Aherne and full-back Martin Dempsey were all very conspicuous in repelling the Monaghan men. John Costello came into his own in the middle of the park. The forwards, nevertheless, failed to turn the outfield resistance into scores, as Laois managed to kick more wides in the second half than Monaghan did in the course of the whole game. Standing out like a shining beacon of coolness under pressure in those dying minutes was the composed play of the intelligent Colm Browne. Along with Costello, the excellent Tom Prendergast and Eamon Whelan, Laois placed emphasis on retaining possession as the full-time whistle approached. Then Monaghan were awarded a free. Eamon McEneaney's well-struck kick just drifted wide at the last minute. Soon afterwards, the full-time whistle blew. Monaghan, despite a fantastic performance by corner-back Eugene Sherry and other notable displays by Gerry McCarville, Ciarán Murray, Kevin Carragher, Nudie Hughes, Ray McCarron and Eamon Murphy, had lost the league crown.

From a Laois perspective, the O'Moore County had deservedly won their first major title for forty years. Not since Bill Delaney, Tommy Murphy and company had won the Leinster provincial title in 1946 had the county's senior side experienced any worthwhile success. It was a magic moment for all Laois fans to savour. It was a particularly happy occasion for the three remaining survivors of the 1926 league success. Paddy Whelan, Jack Delaney and Chris Miller had lived to see their feat repeated. When captain fantastic himself, Colm Browne, raised aloft the National League trophy, 40 years of defeat and disappointment were immediately erased. For Colm himself, it was a special moment of joy. 'It really was a terrific team performance. We had made brilliant progress, especially considering the disappointments of the previous year's championship. The wet, slippery conditions made it difficult for the forwards to score but we held our nerve, though I was a bit concerned after they scored the penalty!'

After their historic league campaign, Laois were strong favourites to beat Wicklow in the first round of that year's Leinster senior football championship. On the day, nothing went right for them in that particular encounter at Aughrim. In a very physical contest, which saw three players sent off (two of them from Laois), the O'Moore County bowed out of the championship. Colm Browne played for three more championship seasons for Laois, without experiencing any further success. When they were knocked out of the 1989 Leinster campaign, the Portlaoise man retired. 'A lot of niggling injuries and Father Time had caught up with me. Even though there did not appear to be any immediate positive results from that league success on the future development of Laois football, later events would prove otherwise.'

Simultaneous with Colm Browne's inter-county involvement was the unprecedented success of his club, Portlaoise, during the same period. Before Colm joined the senior squad, his club had won a Leinster title in 1971/72 before being defeated by eventual All-Ireland champions Bellaghy of Derry, in a riveting encounter. That remarkable club progress was to be sustained for the course of the next 16 years when they were to reach seven further Leinster finals, winning four of them in 1976/77, 1982/83, 1985/86 and 1987/88. Colm played a central role in all those campaigns.

As Portlaoise Town had not won a county football title since 1907, it was decided in the late 1950s to concentrate on a comprehensive youth development policy. The first fruits of this were harvested when they annexed the county title for the first time in 57 years, in 1964. That 1972 All-Ireland semi-final display was another positive sign of the club's successful strategy. By the time 1976 had arrived, Bill Phelan's great work with the juveniles had manifested itself even more. Rising young stars like the Prendergasts, the Brownes, Billy Bohane, Liam Scully and Eamon Whelan were now established senior players. After winning an exciting Leinster final against Cooley Kickhams of Louth, they met Austin Stack's of Tralee in the All-Ireland semi-final. Ten thousand supporters packed O'Moore Park to see one of the best games ever played there. Brilliant scores and a fabulous atmosphere were the highlights, with the final outcome being in doubt until the last quarter. However, a strong Tralee side, powered by the great John O'Keeffe and Ger Power, won comfortably in the end. When the Kerry side beat

Ballerin of Derry in that year's final, Portlaoise knew they were not far away from ultimate success.

Nevertheless, it was to be 1982/83 before that opportunity would arise. Bill Phelan, who had been in charge of the side from 1976 to 1981, stepped down to be replaced by Colm Browne as player/manager. Phelan remained as a selector, with James O'Reilly, Paschal Delaney, Mick McDonald and Teddy Fennelly. In the 1982 county final, Portlaoise easily accounted for Annanough. Two-mile House of Wexford, St Mary's, Granard, of Longford and Sarsfields of Kildare were all defeated en route to the Leinster final against Dublin champions Ballymun Kickhams. In a devastating performance, the Town side won, thanks to stupendous performances from Eamon Whelan and the redoubtable Tom Prendergast. What made the victory all the more satisfying was the fact that it was achieved in one of the great games of the club championship.

Beating St Finbarr's of Cork in the All-Ireland semi-final at Portarlington was a marvellous feat. Though playing against a very strong breeze, the Leinster side dominated the first half to lead at the interval on a 0–5 to 0–2 scoreline. With six minutes left in the second half, the Barrs had come back to draw level at 0–6 each. As the final whistle approached, Gerry Browne secured possession and sent the ball high over the bar for the winning point. In a fantastic team performance, full-back Jimmy Bergin was outstanding. Mick Lillis, Colm Browne, Mark Kavanagh, Eamon Whelan, Mick Dooley, Pat Critchley and captain Liam Scully ably assisted him.

The final, which took place in Cloughjordan in Tipperary, was against Roscommon and Connacht champions, Clan na nGael. This resulted in a decisive triumph for Portlaoise, as they easily accounted for a Roscommon side that, uncharacteristically, failed to offer any real resistance. The final score of 0–12 to 2–0 tells its own story. Indeed, but for the inaccuracy of the Portlaoise forwards, the winning margin would have been considerably greater. They recorded 20 wides, which, in other circumstances, could have had disastrous consequences. Nevertheless, it was Portlaoise's most glorious day, in their long history, when Liam Scully raised aloft the Andy Merrigan Cup. It was also a milestone in the Laois football annals, because it was the first time that an All-Ireland senior football Cup had come to the O'Moore County. Coincidentally, 94 years earlier, in 1889, a Portlaoise club team had represented Laois in an All-Ireland senior football final. Then, they were unsuccessful against Tipperary, who were represented by the Bohercrowe team. Now, they were club champions of All-Ireland.

Brian Kavanagh, Mick Lillis and Colm Browne were again fantastic in defence. Dooley and Whelan controlled centre-field. In attack, Tom

Prendergast was in wonderful form, scoring four excellent points from play. Gerry Browne, Noel Prendergast and Pat Critchley also made notable contributions to a tremendous club achievement.

Colm described his feelings about that 1983 victory when I met him in his home in Portlaoise. 'It was the proudest moment of my club life to be involved with the players whom I grew up with. Seeing the hard work of so many people, down through the years, being rewarded was an enthralling experience. For the efforts of men like Bill Phelan who, unfortunately, died later in 1993 at a young age, we will always be eternally grateful. I was privileged to be part of a wonderful club side that went on to win two other provincial club titles within the next few years. Even though we lost in the subsequent All-Ireland semi-finals, the glow of that famous 1983 victory, even 22 years later, still shines brightly.' When Colm Browne finally retired from club football in 1993, he found it exceedingly difficult to adapt to life as a mere spectator. Shortly afterwards, he was asked to take over the management of the senior county team — a role perfectly suited to both his man-management and tactical skills. However, as many other managers have discovered, one vital ingredient — commonly known as either the 'X' factor or Lady Luck — was not on his side. Between 1993 and 2002, Colm had two prolonged management stints with Laois (1993–96 and 2000–2002) and one with Tipperary (1998–99). Despite all his determined efforts and his renowned expertise, no apparent substantial success was achieved in either county during his terms with them.

At under age level during the mid-1990s and onwards, tremendous strides were made in Laois regarding the organisation, development and promotion of Gaelic football. The midlanders, under the stewardship of Gabriel Lawlor, captured their first All-Ireland minor football title in 1996, when they defeated Kerry. They repeated this accomplishment in 1997, when they again claimed the Tom Markham Trophy. This time, with Oliver Phelan as manager, they ousted Tyrone in the final. However, the O'Neill men had their revenge when they beat the O'Moore men in the following year's decider. In 2003, with Seán Dempsey at the helm, Laois claimed their third All-Ireland minor trophy when they beat fellow Leinster side Dublin in the final. These minor successes have been a remarkable achievement by any standard.

In late 2002 the now managerless Laois, sensing that all this budding talent needed to be harnessed quickly, appointed former Kerry and Kildare manager, the legendary Mick O'Dwyer, as their supremo. The required impact was immediate and decisive. From February 2003 until their last Leinster championship game, 27 weeks later, Laois played 14 league and championship games and lost only once. In a fantastic league run, they reached the final for the first time since Colm Browne had led them to the winner's podium 17 years earlier in 1986. Even though they were well beaten by that year's eventual All-Ireland champions, Tyrone, O'Dwyer was not too despondent as he prepared his side for an assault on the Leinster championship. What a fantastic journey of enthusiasm, excitement and entertainment that campaign proved to be. When they defeated Dublin in the semi-final, they had qualified for their first provincial decider since 1991. Ironically, the final pairing was a repeat of 1946 — Laois's last Leinster trophy-final between Kildare and the O'Moore County.

Despite the controversial sendings off (two Kildare players and one Laois man got the line), the game itself was fought in a terrific atmosphere of drama, smashing individual performances and near misses. After a titanic struggle, the Laois men emerged victorious by three points. Thus 57 years of misfortune and never-ending disappointment were erased in 70 minutes of total commitment and wholehearted endeavour. Laois supporters, understandably, invaded Croke Park in their thousands to celebrate a famous victory. Once again, Mick O'Dwyer had become the oracle of success for another county.

Colm Browne has many views on the GAA's future development both within and without his native Laois.

1. 'The biggest problem in Gaelic football is the tackle. In rugby and soccer the tackle is clearly defined in theory and workable in practice. Gaelic football also has a defined tackle but it is not as easy to implement because the player in possession, in Gaelic football, has all the advantages. In order to eliminate pulling and dragging, this whole area needs to be addressed properly. Only when this is done will Gaelic football reach its full potential.'

2. 'The Railway Cup should be retained on the simple basis that the players love it. Playing with and against other great players with whom they might never get an opportunity to do so, is their main motivational factor. Unfortunately, because of our already crowded fixture list, I do not think there can be a permanent time for scheduling it. That inevitably means less marketing and less spectators. Nevertheless, if I had a chance to play for Leinster in the morning, in front of two men and a dog, I would gladly do so!'

3. 'I was on the International Rules panel in 1987. This International exchange is a wonderful outlet for social interaction amongst players, and offers a unique opportunity for Gaelic footballers to represent their country both at home and in Australia. Also, it has

given Gaelic football the free out of the hand, which is a positive development. The game itself, I feel, does nothing for me. I find it aesthetically displeasing as a so-called sporting spectacle.'

4. 'One never realises the consequences of success. After Laois won that first All-Ireland minor title, in 1996, a member of the management team told me that it was the National League success of 1986 which inspired so many of those minor stars to achieve their true potential. When Laois won the Leinster senior championship in 2003, Mick O'Dwyer deservedly received the immediate plaudits of that victory. He was the vital psychological motivating factor that propelled that achievement. However, for any county to achieve ultimate, long-lasting rewards, the solid grafting work must be done on a concerted basis over many years, within the county itself.'

5. 'On a personal level, I love reading, especially all kinds of biographies. All the explorers, particularly those of the twentieth century, appeal to me. Scott and Shackleton would be my favourites. The GAA is blessed with many very competent journalists at both local and national levels. Overall, Eugene McGee and Colm O'Rourke really have their fingers on the GAA pulse. They have a natural affinity with the real issues and how the average GAA follower feels on all topical matters.'

Colm Browne made the following representative selections:

LEINSTER (1975–2005)

John O'Leary
(Dublin)

Robbie O'Malley (Meath)	Martin Dempsey (Laois)	John Crofton (Kildare)
Tommy Drumm (Dublin)	Glen Ryan (Kildare)	Martin O'Connell (Meath)

Brian Mullins (Dublin)   Paddy Quirke (Carlow)

Gerry Browne (Laois)	Larry Tompkins (Kildare)	Ciarán Duff (Dublin)
Colm O'Rourke (Meath)	Kevin O'Brien (Wicklow)	Matt Connor (Offaly)

IRELAND (1975–2005)

Billy Morgan
(Cork)

Robbie O'Malley   John O'Keeffe   Tony Scullion
(Meath)   (Kerry)   (Derry)

Páidí Ó Sé   Glen Ryan   Paudie Lynch
(Kerry)   (Kildare)   (Kerry)

Brian Mullins   Jack O'Shea
(Dublin)   (Kerry)

Maurice Fitzgerald   Larry Tompkins   Pat Spillane
(Kerry)   (Kildare/Cork)   (Kerry)

Mickey Linden   Peter Canavan   Matt Connor
(Down)   (Tyrone)   (Offaly)

Since the halcyon days of the Delaneys and Tommy Murphy, Laois have produced many fine footballing artists. Players like Paddy Dunne, Des Connolly, Jack Kenna, Tom Browne, Bobby Miller, Tony Maher, Hugh Emerson and Denis Lalor have given the O'Moore County supporters hours of sporting pleasure. Former RTÉ GAA commentator, the late Mick Dunne, was a proud Laois man, as is the current well-respected and very competent Leinster GAA secretary, Michael Delaney. Now, men such as Fergal Byron, Joe Higgins, Tom Kelly, Brian McDonald, Colm Parkinson and Ross Munnelly carry the torch of future Laois success. The 2005 Knockbeg College All-Ireland Colleges winning captain, Donie Brennan, is also a fantastic prospect.

Three days after the 1962 All-Ireland senior football final between Roscommon and Kerry, two small boys stood to attention in their back yard in Portlaoise. One was aged five, the other just four. Standing erectly, hands by their sides, they faced an invisible tricolour and reverently hummed the National Anthem, as they re-enacted the scene in Croke Park on the previous Sunday. Nestled between their feet was a very special O'Neill's football. The boys' grandfather was a former Dublin-based Garda who had once hurled for the metropolitans. That Roscommon native, Gerry Browne, had obtained the ball that was used in the final and presented it to his two grandsons.

Even then, Colm Browne was a proud boy. In time he would become an All Star and bring national glory to both his county and club. When Laois, soon hopefully, capture the Sam Maguire Cup, all their supporters will know that no one did more than Colm Browne to prepare the way for the arrival of the Holy Grail.

COLM BROWNE – FACT FILE

Native Place:	Portlaoise, Co. Laois
Date of Birth:	May 1, 1957
Club:	Portlaoise
School Honours:	Portlaoise CBS U-12 Schools' Championship – 1968, 1969
Club Honours:	U-14 Championship – 1971
	U-16 Championship – 1973
	U-18 Championship – 1973, 1974
	U-21 Championship – 1975, 1976, 1977, 1978
	Senior Football Championship (10) – 1976, 1979, 1981, 1982, 1984, 1985, 1986, 1987, 1990, 1991
	Leinster Senior Football Championship (4) – 1976, 1982, 1985, 1987
	All-Ireland Senior Football Championship – 1983
County Honours:	National Football League – 1986
Other Playing Honours:	Railway Cup – 1985, 1986, 1987
	Member Compromise Rules Panel – 1987
Awards:	All Star 1986
	Laois Senior Football Team of the Millennium
Managerial Honours:	Senior Football Championship (4) – 1982, 1984, 1985, 1986
	Leinster Senior Football Championship (2) – 1982, 1985
	All-Ireland Senior Football Championship – 1983
	Manager Laois Senior Football Team (1993–96), (2000–2002)
	Manager Tipperary Senior Football Team (1998–1999)
Occupation:	Researcher/Analyst in Garda Research Unit at Templemore
Family:	Married to Margaret (née Frazer) from Portlaoise)
Children:	Avril, David

TWENTY

Frank McGuigan—Tyrone

TWO MOMENTOUS MINUTES, ELEVEN EXQUISITE SCORES

Forty-five times you stood on the hill of Clones on Ulster
final day.
Mick Higgins, Jim McKeever, Seán O'Neill and Frank
McGuigan
Were head and shoulders above the rest.
Watching them achieve feats of supreme athleticism, as they
fetched and kicked
A leather pigskin, amidst a plethora of talented stars.
Yes, Hugh, Gaelic football was always your number one.
And St Tiernach's Park, forever, the amphitheatre of your
dreams.

To all Ulster Gaels, nothing is as significant or as meaningful as Clones
on Ulster final day. It was my privilege to be friendly with a real, true
Gael: Hugh Shannon, who attended 45 Ulster finals. At twenty of
these I had the undoubted pleasure of being with this very affable
man. We followed a very predictable routine on these pilgrimages of
joy. As we journeyed to the games, Hugh, a former Monaghan footballer
and long-time Longford resident, recalled the exploits of the great
footballers of the past on this auspicious occasion. Three names surfaced
above all others — Mick Higgins, Jim McKeever and Seán O'Neill. As
we watched the 1984 final, one man emphatically captivated Hugh:
29-year-old Frank McGuigan became the fourth name to be
unanimously inducted into his hall of fame.

Thanks to the BBC's archive footage, Frank McGuigan's marvellous
scoring display in the 1984 Ulster final has been preserved for posterity.
Luckily, also immediately after Tyrone's All-Ireland campaign for that
year ended, Frank recalled his own views and thoughts of that
memorable season to a host of media personnel in general and in that
year's *Gaelsport Annual* in particular. In the intervening years many

esteemed writers such as Jack Mahon and Keith Duggan have encapsulated brilliantly the life and career of this superb athlete. To appreciate fully the extent of the Ardboe man's achievement and the totality of his sublime skills, I feel it is only right that those exquisite scores should be recorded in sequence. An interesting footnote is that Frank's cumulative time on the ball for those historic scores was less than two minutes in total. In the remaining 58 minutes, other Tyrone players scored four points. Yet the Ulster final of 1984 will always, and justifiably so, be known as the Frank McGuigan final. Those contrasting statistics in themselves must constitute some type of record. The following is a summary of how the *Gaelsport Annual*, in December 1984, recorded Frank's fantastic performance in the GAA's centenary year (of 1984):

1. *2ⁿᵈ Minute. McGuigan swung the ball over the bar with his left foot*
    'It's not luck. Because your luck has to change sometime and there are fellows who could be kicking away all week and they would never put the ball over the bar.' McGuigan wanted to get a couple of points early in the game, so that he would not feel under any pressure to do well. That meant that he could stop worrying about the game and play it instead.

2. *8ᵗʰ Minute. McGuigan scored with his left*
    'The local paper was giving out the week after the Ulster final because I was playing in a county championship quarter-final for my club and I only scored three points. I would not mind but I was playing centre-field. Even Jack O'Shea does not score eleven points from midfield.'

3. *9ᵗʰ Minute. McGuigan ran into position to score another left-footed point.*
    'We had a real test of our character before overcoming Derry in the first round at Ballinascreen. In the semi-final we played Down, who had beaten us earlier that year in the quarter-final of the National League. Then, the Mourne men beat us mainly because of a few late goals. Even though their winning margin in the end looked big, we knew we could improve our game for the championship. An added incentive for us to do well in this encounter was the fact that Down were real hot favourites to come out of Ulster.' Tyrone beat Down by five points to secure their place in the Ulster final for the first time since 1980. The ace talisman scored five points against Derry and two more in the Down match. All of these were from play.

For the Ulster final, shrewd Tyrone manager Art McRory, sensing the form that McGuigan was displaying, urged his team to supply McGuigan with the ball at every opportunity. Two Tyrone players, in particular, were very adept at following McRory's instructions. Midfielder and team captain Eugene McKenna and centre half-forward Damien O'Hagan – both future All Stars – were centrally involved in most of the moves which led to McGuigan's scores.

4. *20th Minute. O'Hagan found McGuigan with a probing pass from which Frank calmly lofted the ball over the bar with his right foot*
    Frank McGuigan liked to lie in on Sundays before a match: 'I go to Mass on Saturday night and get up at 10 o'clock. Before the Ulster final, you might not believe it, but I did not have any breakfast. We travelled to a hotel in Clones for a pre-match talk and I had an egg and onion sandwich there.'

5. *25th Minute. McGuigan rose high to make a spectacular catch before turning and sending the ball over the bar with his right foot*
    'Before the final we watched a video of the semi-final clash with Down and discussed how best to cope with Armagh.'
    So, to the game itself. After the third point he did not really care if he scored again. Nevertheless, during the course of the game he scored 11 points. He dummied to send the full-back the wrong way, interchanging feet to confuse the defence, winding up with seven points from his left boot, three from his right and one from his fist. Nothing went wide. 'I actually touched the ball a twelfth time but the shot dropped in to the goalkeeper's arms. Nobody remembers that now, but if we lost they would. I figure if you score a couple of points at the beginning of a game, it settles you down a wee bit.'

6. *26th Minute. McGuigan took a Séamus Daly pass and scored with his left*
    'The All-Ireland semi-final against Dublin was a more tense occasion. I think Tyrone were a bit overawed by the occasion. It was the first time for some of our boys to be in Croke Park.'

7. *33rd Minute. McGuigan's fisted point came from a Colm Donaghy lob*
    'In the match against Dublin there was no problem about playing in to the Hill 16 goal before the start.' (This was a reference to a contentious talking point before the game when Tyrone went

straight to the Hill 16 end for their warm-up. Traditionally, this end of the pitch was the preserve of the Dublin team. When Dublin manager Kevin Heffernan heard of this, he immediately sent the Dublin team to the same area. The result was that there were forty players from both sides kicking in together — a potentially dangerous cocktail. It was a psychological ploy by Tyrone to show that they had the same right to be there as Dublin.) 'Dublin were right to go down to the same goal, if they thought we were trying to intimidate them, which we weren't. We will be playing in Division One and everyone is talking about meeting this year's All-Ireland champions, Kerry, in the league. We can really go places next year.' (Little did Frank realise the awful significance of that Kerry visit when he expressed this opinion, just weeks before the accident that would irretrievably change his life forever.)

8. *43ʳᵈ Minute. McGuigan got Tyrone's second point of the second half with his left foot*
    Frank McGuigan was big for his age when he was young. He came from rural Tyrone, near Lough Neagh, where most people are either farmers or fishermen. All his family and relations before him played Gaelic football.

9. *44ᵗʰ Minute. Mc Guigan scored with his left*
    Once he left school, Frank dedicated himself to Gaelic football and was an exceptional midfielder. In 1975, he switched to full-forward. He went to the USA four times as an All Star replacement. Then came the break in his career. From late 1977 to September 1983, he lived and worked in America. During that period Frank came home twice to play for Tyrone in the Ulster championship of 1982 and 1983. He found this to be a very unsatisfactory arrangement. He had been playing very little football abroad — about seven games a year. He had only a week and a few training sessions with the other team members before he took the field with them. 'We did not know each other's style of play.' In September 1983 he got a job at home and returned for the winter, playing in the league and spending a lot of time with his team-mates. He was also fitter than usual.

10. *46ᵗʰ Minute. Again with the left McGuigan sent Tyrone nine points clear*
    'From the time I can remember, I always could kick with either foot. It never really bothered me which foot I should use. I never practised on one foot more than the other. I just kicked. It must

have been a natural ability I just had.'

Of all the points that McGuigan scored that day, his tenth point was probably the most exquisite of the lot. Two Armagh defenders ran towards their own goal, chasing after a long Tyrone kick from midfield. McGuigan flicked the ball, in mid-air, between the two surprised Armagh men. Then, he ran around their blind side and chipped the ball expertly up into his hands. Sensing that one of the Armagh defenders was about to block the ball as he prepared to kick with his right foot, he quickly changed direction with a dummy solo. He was now free from everyone. So, he casually stroked the ball over the bar with his left foot, for a truly wondrous strike.

11. *58ᵗʰ Minute. McGuigan steadied Tyrone after Armagh's goal with a right-footed point. Thus the O'Neill County claimed their first Ulster title since 1973, on a score of 0–15 to 1–7*
'Eleven points are not too hard to get, once you get the ball. I have my team-mates to thank for that.'

In the subsequent All-Ireland semi-final against Dublin, McGuigan was a marked man, both literally and metaphorically. During the first half he was subjected to a lot of personal fouling, which prompted the Tyrone manager, Art McRory, to notify the umpires prior to half-time. At the beginning of the second half, the offending Dublin player was booked but, by this time, the damage had been done. Tyrone were really only playing 'catch-up'. In the end, the Ulster men lost by nine points. McGuigan, despite getting few opportunities to exhibit his scoring prowess, still managed to score four points. Though defeated, Tyrone were far from downhearted. They had the nucleus of a good side and, most of all, they had a rejuvenated Frank McGuigan, back to his brilliant best.

Frank McGuigan was born in 1954 on the shores of Lough Neagh, the largest lake in these islands. He was one of eleven children born to Tommy and Annie. The nearby lake was renowned worldwide both for the quantity and quality of its eels. Tommy McGuigan carried on the family tradition of fishing the lake. It was very often a terribly cold and hazardous occupation, but it provided a livelihood for the McGuigans and many of their neighbours. Frank himself did not like the fishing life and only spent one year at it after he left secondary school at the age of sixteen. Instead he followed the more regular life of working from Monday to Friday as a plasterer. Here he built up the upper body strength that stood him in good stead when he indulged in his favourite hobby — Gaelic football.

In 1967 he captained his club team, Ardboe O'Donovan Rossa's, to an U-13 county championship when they defeated Coalisland in the final at Edendork. Former SDLP politician and Fine Gael TD Austin Currie had the honour of presenting Frank with his first trophy. His sparkling club performances soon drew the attention of the county minor selectors. Frank played for the O'Neill County in their successful provincial teams of 1971 and 1972, when they comprehensively defeated Fermanagh and Cavan, respectively. In the latter year, they reached the All-Ireland minor final only to be narrowly beaten by a Jimmy Barry Murphy-inspired Cork. 'That final was one of the proudest moments of my life. It was a great honour to be captain and to lead your county out in Croke Park, in front of so many people. I am a great believer in good sportsmanship. I think at the end of a game the winners should always console the losers. Cork were very gracious that day. The present Tyrone manager, Micky Harte, was our full-forward.'

Earlier that year, in the Ulster final, the new Tyrone sensation made his own little bit of history. Some fifteen minutes after collecting the Ulster minor trophy, 17-year-old McGuigan was introduced into the Tyrone senior team, who were playing Donegal in the senior decider. Though Tyrone lost the latter game, the senior career of one of the most talented footballers ever to wear a Tyrone senior jersey had commenced. 'Funnily enough, it was on the word of a club mate, Seán Coyle, that Arthur McRory first gave me a trial for Tyrone minors in early 1971 and then I made my competitive debut with them, when we played Derry in a minor league game at Ballinascreen. It all took off from there. When the Tyrone senior manager, Jody O'Neill, saw me with the minors, he obviously liked what he witnessed, so he drafted me in to the senior squad. Age had never meant anything to Jody. He himself had captained Tyrone in an All-Ireland semi-final in 1956 at the age of 19. When 1973 came around, Jody suddenly said one day, "By the way, Frank McGuigan is captain this year." It happened as simple as that.'

In 1973 18-year-old Frank McGuigan captained Tyrone to their first Ulster senior title in 16 years, when they comfortably overcame Down by eight points. In a side that also included stars like Peter Mulgrew, Séamus Donaghy and Pat King, the young Ardboe man gave an impressive display from his favoured midfield position. However, in the All-Ireland semi-final against Cork, they were heavily defeated by a very skilful Rebel fifteen who went on to claim that year's All-Ireland senior title. The physical strength of Cork posed huge problems for Tyrone.

Inexplicably, McGuigan began to lose his appetite for football.

When Tyrone failed to make an impression in the following four Ulster campaigns, McGuigan started to spend more time partying but he never drank on the morning of games. He went to bed at normal hours on the eve of matches. Nevertheless, there was one exception to this. Frank and a pal did not go to bed until six o'clock on the morning of the 1976 Ulster semi-final against Derry. Despite all of this, McGuigan continued to play superb football, both for club and county.

Another defining moment in Frank's career took place in 1977. He was selected as an All Star replacement for the trip to New York. In company with the rest of the squad, Frank had a very enjoyable time. On the night that the All Star team were due to fly home, McGuigan decided not to go on board. Despite the pleadings of his good friend, Dublin full-back Seán Doherty, the Tyrone man decided to stay. With no money, no job, no apartment, Frank was at a crossroads of his own making. Amongst others, two good Tyrone friends, Rocky Gallagher and his former minor colleague Dominic Daly, looked after him. Employment was obtained, as was accommodation. (Tragically, both Rocky and Dominic were later killed in separate road accidents.) Shortly afterwards, he met his ex-wife Geraldine, got married and settled down to a life of stability in the 'Big Apple'. Between 1977 and 1983 Frank was, to all intents and purposes, a naturalised American citizen. He played a few games of Gaelic football in Gaelic Park every summer but nothing too serious. Then, in the summer of 1983 an urgent SOS call from his home club arrived. They wanted their erstwhile star and friend to help them in a vital relegation league game. When he came home, he played tremendously well to ensure an Ardboe victory. The King was back in Ardboe. God save the King!

Other important people also had a dream of winning at least an Ulster title. Tyrone manager Art McRory, County Board officials and others tried to persuade Frank to return permanently to Ireland. Frank's wife Geraldine, who had been born in Tyrone but had lived in America for years, was in agreement. The eldest of their four children was of schoolgoing age. The hectic schedule of long working hours, huge traffic jams and the pace of city life in New York no longer appealed to Frank. He was naturally a quiet, easy-going individual who preferred the peaceful surroundings and camaraderie of his native Ardboe. When it was decided that a house would be built for Frank and his family and employment secured, the die was cast for the return of Tyrone's footballing prodigal son.

After Tyrone's impressive league and championship campaign of 1984 and Frank's wonder display on that never-to-be-forgotten day in Clones, everything appeared rosy in the garden of Tyrone's future GAA hopes. Both club and county waited in anticipation of a more prosperous sporting future. Sadly, however, the sheer uncertainty of life and its complexities was shortly to impinge negatively on Frank's footballing future.

It was three months later, in November 1984, that Frank McGuigan's life was to change irrevocably. He had been working at his house all morning. At two o'clock on that fateful Saturday afternoon, he left to play a club game. After the match he had a few drinks and then, on the way home, he had another couple. He bought a bag of chips and finally headed for home. This was his normal routine in such situations. Happily driving along, his van suddenly went out of control and hit a wall, just a short distance from his unfinished home. His leg took the whole impact and was broken, at both knee and hip. It was a long time before help arrived. When it did, he was brought to the Mid-Ulster hospital in Magherafelt, before being transferred to Altnagelvin hospital in Derry City. Being told he would never play football again did not unduly worry him, but the distressed faces of Geraldine and the children did. For twenty weeks he was confined to bed. He just kept telling himself that he would somehow survive the whole traumatic experience and that he would walk again. It was almost a year before he recovered sufficiently to be out and about again, albeit with a permanent limp.

His friends in America, Ardboe, Tyrone and many other places rallied in support to help Frank complete his house and re-establish his life. A big benefit dance was held in the Prairie Restaurant, about six miles from Cookstown. All-Ireland champions Kerry, against whom Frank was so looking forward to playing, came as guests, as did so many other GAA patrons from the neighbouring counties and indeed from all parts of Ireland. 'As well as all the Ulster-based players, I remember seeing Jimmy Keaveney and Tony Hanahoe, who came the whole way from Dublin. My favourite memory of that night is of Offaly's great Matt Connor arriving. Matt had been paralysed the year before and he drove up from Tullamore on his own. He parked his car unaided and reached the door of the function room in his wheelchair. That was a very touching gesture from a very loyal GAA person.'

In the midst of all of this, Frank McGuigan was selected at full-forward on that year's All Star team. 'A good friend, Pat Shields, who subsequently became an innocent victim of the Troubles, phoned to tell me the good news. I was delighted and it certainly boosted me, as I was bedridden at the time. I was released from hospital, my house was completed and the whole family were able to move in straight away.'

The following ten years were to bring more tragedy, sorrow and trauma for the unlucky Frank. In 1992 the whole McGuigan family were dealt two mortal blows. The youngest of his siblings, Brian, who was in America, drowned in suspicious circumstances in New Jersey. Apparently, some crank pushed him over a bridge into the raging waters below. Frank's father, Tommy, travelled to America and watched as his 23-year-old son was hauled from the dark, cold water. A few days afterwards, as Tommy and his daughter Mary were making arrangements to fly Brian's remains home, he himself unexpectedly collapsed. Mary, who was driving, was chatting away to her father when she noticed him slumping in his seat. He, too, was dead. The mortal remains of both father and son were flown home to Ireland. In one of the most poignant scenes ever witnessed, they were laid to rest in their beloved Ardboe.

During all these years and for whatever reason, Frank's drinking pattern increased and started to present domestic difficulties. Eventually, his wife and children decided to move out of the family home. It was then that Frank showed his true strength of character and his indomitable courage. Though his marriage was over, on his own initiative he decided to omit alcohol from his life. He realised that no one was to blame, including himself, for his drinking problems. Alcoholism was a disease and had to be treated as such. Now, Frank is more relaxed and has no regrets, but just believes in getting on with life. His drinking days are at an end. 'What is the point of having regrets? To have them would only make a bad situation worse.'

Speaking to me in his native Ardboe, Frank outlined his thoughts on the game's greatest players and what Gaelic football means to him.

1. 'Midfield being my favourite position, I suppose many of my best memories are of midfielders. Jack O'Shea, Brian Mullins, Eugene McKenna and Colm McAlarney would fall into this category. Jimmy Keaveney, Tony Hanahoe, Martin McHugh, Pat Spillane, Mike Sheehy, Jimmy Barry Murphy, Peter Canavan and Colm O'Rourke were top-class forwards. Seán Doherty was a wonderful full-back as well as a good personal friend. Overall, I feel that Seán O'Neill and Matt Connor were the two best footballers I ever saw. The best game I played was an Ulster club championship game against Bellaghy, after they won the All-Ireland club title. I scored 0–7 out of a total of 0–8. Supporters chaired me off the field that day, as they also did after the 1973 and 1984 Ulster final triumphs, but I was never much into that type of celebration.'

2. 'To me, football is not the be all and end all of life. I realise a lot of people get much satisfaction from it but it would not cost me a thought if the All-Ireland championship were abolished in the morning. Good health, peace of mind, peace in Ireland and

throughout the world is more important. I would really love to see everyone, everywhere, free from poverty and famine. True, football gave me much enjoyment both as a player and as a supporter. When Tyrone won the 2003 All-Ireland, as a father I was delighted that my two sons were involved. Brian was on the winning team and Frank was a sub. My only concern before the game was that Brian would not make it, as he had been very sick for the previous few weeks. Thankfully, he was able to take his place.'

3.   'Gaelic football has become very professional in terms of team preparation and the personal sacrifices that players have to make. Football management nowadays is a full-time job, so I think they should be paid like any other business people. Everyone who plays in an All-Ireland senior football or hurling final, regardless of who wins, should be financially rewarded. A holiday trip to the sun does not put food on the table. People complain about many GAA officials staying in office too long. That is not the real problem. What is most important is that those in high positions in the GAA change with the times. None of us can keep living in the past.'

On September 18, 2003, Armagh and Tyrone played in the first All-Ulster, All-Ireland senior football final. In a really exciting contest, the O'Neill County emerged victorious, to claim their first All-Ireland senior title. The disappointments of the final losses of 1986 and 1995 were forgotten, as a great GAA county gained the coveted prize. Frank McGuigan was especially happy not only for his native county, but also for his two sons, who were an integral part of the winning squad.

None of us can ever forecast the long-term significance of any of our actions. However, very often a single deed or unique occasion can have a profound effect on what happens at a future date. The words of Tyrone's All-Ireland winning captain, Peter Canavan, demonstrate the domino effect of a special magical display. 'In 1984 I followed Tyrone's Ulster championship when they defeated Derry and Down before facing Armagh in the Ulster final. That decider was to provide me with a tailor-made hero. This to me was Frank McGuigan's final. When I went home, I decided that I was going to try my best to emulate Frank McGuigan. He became my constant inspiration as I practised alone or with others.'

Of course it would be wrong to attribute Tyrone's All-Ireland solely to Frank McGuigan. All those who kept Gaelic games alive in the O'Neill County played a pivotal role. All the winning Ulster campaigns, beginning with the 1956 and 1957 successes, also were central to the capture of Sam Maguire. Individuals like supreme midfielder Jody O'Neill, the versatile Eddie Devlin and the accurate Frankie Donnelly were icons in their time. Will o' the wisp Iggy Jones and his jinking skills will never be forgotten as long as Gaelic football is played. Previous officials, coaches and managers all contributed to Tyrone annexing the ultimate prize in Irish sport. Two men in particular, Arthur McRory and Eugene McKenna, were like latter-day John the Baptists as they prepared the way for Mickey Harte and his management team in 2003.

As Hugh Shannon and I left St Tiernach's Park on that July Sunday in 1984, he turned to me with an all-embracing smile of happiness. 'Séamus, I'll tell you something. We can all die happy now because we will never again see such an individual display of pure skill and sublime accuracy.'

In December 2002, my friend Hugh passed away peacefully. Frank McGuigan's 1984 virtuoso performance had not been repeated in the interim. I have no doubt that most of us, hopefully, will join Hugh with his prophecy still intact. He would enjoy that.

FRANK McGUIGAN – FACT FILE

Native Place:	Ardboe, Co. Tyrone
Date of Birth:	November 20, 1954
Club:	Ardboe O'Donovan Rossa's
Club Honours:	U-13 Championship (Captain)
	U-14 Championship
	U-21 Championship
	Senior Football Championship (4) – 1971, 1972, 1973, 1984
	Senior Football League (3) – 1971, 1972, 1974
County Honours:	Ulster Minor Football Championship (2) – 1971, 1972 (Captain)
	Ulster U-21 Championship (2) – 1972, 1973
	Ulster Senior Football Championship (2) – 1973 (Captain), 1984
	National Football League Division Two (1) – 1973
	McKenna Cup (2) – 1973, 1984
	Gael Linn Cup (1) (With New York)

Other Honours:	Railway Cup (1) – 1984
Awards:	All Star (1) – 1984 Replacement All Star (4) – 1973, 1974, 1975, 1977 B & I Monthly Award – June 1984
Family:	Formerly married to Geraldine (née Donnelly)
Children:	Frank, Brian, Tommy, Kristin, Caitlin, and Shay

TWENTY-ONE

Joe McKenna–Limerick

OFFALY'S GENEROUS GIFT TO THE TREATYMEN

When one attempts to explore the reasons for national success in any sporting discipline, one inevitably has to go back a few years to observe how 'small acorns into tall oak trees grow'. Such is the case with Limerick's stupendous All-Ireland senior hurling team of 1973. Two years previously, in 1971, the Treatymen beat Tipperary in a wonderful National League final, by 3–12 to 3–11. In that same year they also won the Oireachtas competition and only lost to Tipperary by a point in the Munster final. Though naturally disappointed, Limerick players and supporters were quite philosophical as they looked positively towards the future. They had, after all, won their first league title since 1947 and their Munster final conquerors went on to win that year's All-Ireland final.

All and sundry reckoned that 1972 would be Limerick's year. Memories of Dermot Kelly, a wonderfully skilful hurling artist who had scored 1–12 when they had last won the Munster title in 1955, came to the fore. The supporters opined that with players of the sublime quality of team captain Eamon Grimes, Pat Hartigan, Eamon Cregan, Richie Bennis and Seán Foley, everything was pointing to a renewed resurgence that would enable them to at least emulate the 1955 side.

As it happened, 1972 turned out to be an unmitigated disaster for the Shannonsiders. Firstly, they lost their National Hurling League crown to Cork by three points. That was bad enough in itself, but when it was allied to an untimely and unexpected exit at the hands of Clare in their first game of the Munster championship, it became a crisis. Disappointment led to dissension, which quickly turned into animosity and alleged wrong training techniques. The whole unseemly situation was eventually resolved when Michael Cregan, brother of star player Eamon, who himself had retired from the playing scene after the 1972 championship, agreed to train the side.

In January 1973, Michael Cregan developed the toughest, most rigid and regimented training programme ever devised for any group of athletes. With Michael's army experience in physical education, he outlined a programme that was so intense that many players initially found it hard to cope with. As events on the playing field developed during the season, Limerick were to undergo this physical endurance and stamina work programme thrice weekly, from January to mid-August. Only then did Cregan stop so that the team could rest, as they prepared tactically and mentally for the biggest day of their lives.

They played well in the league and reached the final for the fourth successive year, only to be beaten by Wexford. This time there was no despondency, as all their preparations were geared towards a good championship campaign. Some cynics were not so sure. They maintained that Limerick's perceived allergy to winning in Croke Park was epitomised by that dismal league final performance when they lost to the Slaneysiders by nine points. Both team management and players knew that they could and would prove their detractors wrong. In addition to a coterie of well-established players, they had one ace up their sleeves which would considerably enhance the scoring potential of their forward line. A highly promising young skilful player, who had starred especially in under age ranks for another county, was about to join them. Joe McKenna, an Offaly man, was about to become a Treatyman.

Joe was born in 1951 in Shinrone, which is near the Tipperary border. He went to Dunkerrin Primary School, where he became fully immersed in hurling. Every day the young boy cycled the round trip of seven miles to the school, whose Principal, Séamus O'Riain, was later to become GAA President in 1967. The great GAA activist was also Joe's first coach, and the willing listener consequently became completely infatuated with the ancient game. Another major influencing factor was the fact that Joe's father was a Tipperary man, who had keenly followed the great exploits of the Premier County's hurlers down through the years. As a consequence, Joe became an avid follower of that wonderful All-Ireland winning team of the 1960s. In addition, one of the stars of that Tipperary team was his cousin, Mackey McKenna.

Joe followed his older brother, Michael, as a boarder to that well-known GAA college, St Flannan's of Ennis. By the time Joe was in his third year, he was acknowledged as one of the most outstanding hurling prospects in the school. Joe's impressive side won the Munster Colleges junior hurling championship (the Dean Ryan Cup). As a result, the Clare college became one of the favourites for the 1969 Harty Cup. That St Flannan's team was really a star-studded fifteen that boasted gifted players like future All-Stars Ger Loughnane and Johnny Callinan, as well as another fantastic Clare inter-county player, Seán Hehir. Their captain was none other than Joe McKenna. Joe, who played either at midfield or centre half-forward, was hopeful that he would lead his side to a Munster Colleges senior title at least. However, St Finbarr's of Farranferris, Cork, had other ideas and they narrowly defeated the Clare title aspirants by two points in a thrilling semi-final encounter. Later, the Cork side totally demolished the challenge of St Kieran's of Kilkenny to claim the most coveted national colleges hurling trophy. This added to the despair and disappointment of Joe and his secondary school colleagues.

At this time, the towering Shinrone student became a vital component in the Offaly minor team, representing them for four successive years (1966–69). For the next three years Joe, who was almost 6' 4' in height and playing superb hurling, was a central figure in the Offaly U-21 team. In the 1972 Leinster semi-final, Offaly defeated Kilkenny to qualify for the provincial final against Dublin. Having overcome a superb Cats team, they were strong favourites to win a first U-21 provincial championship for the Faithful County. With a minute to go, they were leading by four points. Then, totally against the run of play, the metropolitans notched two great opportunistic goals to score a surprise victory. Somehow, the Dublin men had snatched an unlikely victory from the jaws of defeat. When the final whistle sounded, Dublin had won by 2–11 to 0–15. 'It really was heart-breaking. We definitely thought we had it won. I will never forget the feeling of complete devastation. We had a good team, including Pádraig Horan, who captained Offaly to their first senior All-Ireland nine years later, in 1981,' Joe told me when I met him in his adopted city of Limerick.

Joe's fantastic performances at U-21 level led to a call-up to the Offaly senior hurling team. Having made his senior debut in the National League in October 1972, he played throughout the whole campaign until it ended the following spring of 1973. 'I enjoyed my introduction to senior hurling in Offaly and had the privilege of playing with two of the greatest hurlers I ever saw — Barney Moylan and Paddy Molloy. Even though Paddy was coming towards the end of his county career, he was still a fabulous hurler — one of the best I have ever seen. What I really liked about him was the way he looked after young players when they first came into the team. He was a real gentleman who gave me great advice, as well as making me feel very welcome when I joined the senior squad.'

Meanwhile, the course of Joe's future career was about to take a dramatic turn. In 1970 Joe had taken up the position of salesman in Denis Coakley's — a hardware and fertilizer firm in Limerick city. Two years later it became much more practical for him to transfer his club allegiance from his native Shinrone to the South Liberties Club in Limerick city. For the first time in the chequered history of the famed club, and with the young Offaly recruit playing a pivotal role, the city side won the county hurling championship. All hurling followers in Limerick now realised the magnificent potential of McKenna. He would be a decided acquisition to any team. Being the pragmatist that he always has been, the Offaly man transferred to Limerick County before the commencement of the 1973 Munster championship. Only time would tell whether the rich promise of McCarthy glory would be fulfilled during Joe McKenna's playing days. Neither Limerick nor he himself had long to wait for a positive answer.

Immediately, Joe was welcomed with open arms to the Limerick camp. Having overcome the internal difficulties and with a fantastic response to the new training regime, Limerick had shown a new resolve not hitherto associated with the Treatymen. This had been particularly evident in the league when they beat both Cork and Tipperary (the latter after a draw and a replay in the semi-final). Joe McKenna made his competitive Limerick debut against Clare in the semi-final of the provincial championship. The good preparatory work nearly came to nought again when Limerick could only scrape a one-point victory, thanks mainly to Eamon Grimes. Neither Limerick as a team nor Joe as a debutante played well. As a result, he was dropped for the Munster final against Tipperary.

In the final, the Premier County at first looked the more likely to take the honours. Then the Limerick selectors made a shrewd move. They asked Eamon Cregan to move out of his conventional corner-forward role to the general midfield area. This Eamon did successfully, gaining much necessary possession and moving the ball forward to considerable effect. With Ned Rea (who had moved from defence) in his new full-forward role wreaking havoc as a result of Cregan's promptings, Limerick recovered. As the game's end approached, the sides were level. Then the Treatymen were awarded a 65, which was hotly disputed by the Tipperary defence. Long-serving midfielder Richie Bennis took the puck. He sent it long, high and apparently over the bar for a sensational winning point as the referee blew the full-time whistle. Though the referee allowed the last-gasp point, many Tipperary folk still query, to this day, whether the ball went over the bar or not. Nevertheless, the score stood and the record books show that Limerick beat Tipperary to win their first Munster senior hurling title in eighteen years — the score being Limerick 6–7 to Tipperary 2–18.

In the All-Ireland semi-final, Limerick easily disposed of London 1–15 to 0–7. During that game Eamon Cregan damaged a cartilage that required intensive physiotherapy before he was pronounced fit for the greatest day of his life. Eamon's well-being was initially a source of some concern as he was such a commanding and intelligent presence in Limerick's grand plan. For the new kid on the block, Joe McKenna, this was a very trying and anxious time. 'I was unavailable for selection because I was ill for the Limerick game and unable even to go to the match. However, when I recovered and started training again, everything went well for me. I had started to perform well in our many practice sessions. The selectors then took two bold gambles. They moved Eamon Cregan to centre half-back and then selected me for the final at left corner-forward, which was an even bigger gamble. Eamon's move was really an inspirational one and everything went okay for me in the game,' Joe modestly added.

This was all part of a carefully planned strategy. Kilkenny were missing four players through injury — Eddie Keher, Jim Treacy, Eamon Morrissey and Kieran Purcell. Limerick now knew that Kilkenny would be totally relying on their captain and centre half-forward, Pat Delaney, to run at the Limerick defence. Eamon Cregan, though a recognised forward or midfielder, was earmarked as the man capable of stopping Delaney from going on his searing runs. Psychologically, Limerick were now at an advantage. Having watched Delaney play in the Leinster final, Cregan knew exactly what to expect. On the other hand, Eamon, who had played successfully at centre half-back when his club won the 1968 county senior championship final, was an unknown in that position in the eyes of the Kilkenny team. Likewise, Kilkenny were not aware of Joe McKenna's growing prowess as a superb ball-winner and accurate score-getter at senior inter-county level.

There were two distinct and specific tactics employed by Limerick for the final. Number one was that Cregan's role was to ensure that Delaney would not gain possession. It did not matter if he himself did not touch the ball. Secondly, full-back Pat Hartigan, who was famous for spectacular high catches, was instructed to forget about catching and to concentrate on the less exciting but safer policy of preventing his man from gaining possession.

Displaying fierce determination and playing scintillating, exciting hurling, Limerick seized the initiative from the moment the final began. Hartigan, Cregan and Seán Foley were phenomenal in defence. Eamon Grimes and Bernie Hartigan were dominant in the midfield sector. Full-forward Ned Rea was outstanding. The star of the forward sextet was, undoubtedly, Joe McKenna. Demonstrating craft and confidence beyond his years, he was simply flawless in his stickwork. Limerick were leading by seven points when Pat Hartigan discovered that there were only two and a half minutes left in this eighty-minute contest. Pat was in his element and wanted just one opportunity to exhibit his renowned aerial ability. Excitedly, he ran up to the more serious-minded Cregan and said, 'We have it, we have it.' Cregan advised him that anything could happen in two and a half minutes. Joe McKenna remembered the fatal minute that his Offaly U-21 side had conceded a four-point lead to lose a match they should have won the year before. Pat, nevertheless, was undeterred. Within a minute he had a chance to display his magnificence in the air. A long, high ball floated dangerously towards the Limerick square. Risking both life and limb and the possibility of conceding a goal, the mighty man soared like a bird into the air and plucked the ball from a forest of hurleys and drove the sliotar at least eighty yards downfield. Pat smirked at Cregan. Soon afterwards the full-time whistle sounded. The scoreline was both emphatic and historic. It read Limerick 1–21, Kilkenny 1–14. For the first time since the great Mick Mackey from Ahane had lifted the Liam McCarthy Cup in 1940, Limerick were All-Ireland senior hurling champions.

In a team of heroes, seven men in particular shone like beacons. Eamon Cregan was totally magnificent at centre half-back. Seán Foley gave a classical display of wing play at left-half. Jim O'Brien was immaculate in the left corner of the defence, and Richie Bennis's long striking, as ever, so often turned defence into attack. Three others, all members of the South Liberties club, were at all times marvellous in their anticipation, totally committed in their work rate and sublime in their striking. Pat Hartigan, captain Eamon Grimes and Limerick's latest icon, Joe McKenna, all put in sterling performances.

'I just could not believe how lucky I was. Over a year previously I had been very distraught by being beaten by a last-minute goal by Dublin in the U-21 Leinster final. Six months earlier I had been playing for Offaly in the National Hurling League and here I was, the holder of a senior All-Ireland hurling medal,' Joe enthused.

Having won the McCarthy Cup in 1973, Joe McKenna's performance on the playing fields improved dramatically each time he donned the green and white of Limerick. By the time the following year's Munster championship came around, he was one of the team's key figures. When they played brilliantly to overcome Clare in the Munster final by 6–14 to 3–9, excitement and euphoria enveloped this great sporting county and city. Unlike the previous year, they did not have to play an All-Ireland semi-final. The victory over Clare had guaranteed them a place on the first Sunday of September, and who was again awaiting them but a team looking for sweet revenge — Kilkenny. Still lurking in the back of the minds of many Limerick supporters, however, was their poor performance four months earlier, in the league final, when they were humiliated on their own ground by

Cork by a whopping eighteen points. When Waterford knocked out the league champions in the first round of the Munster campaign, many people thought that their semi-final opponents, All-Ireland champions Limerick, would be in trouble. For a long while it did look that way, until a Joe McKenna-inspired forward line gradually got on top and the Treatymen reached the Munster final. The supporters wondered which Limerick team would play in the All-Ireland final — the one that had succumbed so easily to Cork or the one that was so impressive in the Munster decider.

The final lacked a lot of the emotional atmosphere of their meeting one year earlier, mainly because Kilkenny never really looked like losing. Apart from a good start, the champions were struggling all through and their defence had no answer to the guile of the Kilkenny veteran trio of Eddie Keher, Kieran Purcell and Pat Delaney. Further back, Man of the Match Pat Henderson repulsed every dangerous-looking Limerick attack in glorious style, and so Kilkenny regained their title, with relative ease, when they secured victory 3–19 to 1–13. For Limerick it was a great disappointment. On a personal level 1974 heralded Joe McKenna's induction into the All Star list when the right half-forward received the first of his six national awards.

During the next eleven years Joe McKenna continued to star in the Limerick forward line. His versatility enabled him to play in all six positions but it was at full-forward that he ultimately became recognised, along with Martin Kennedy (Tipperary), Nick Rackard (Wexford) and Ray Cummins (Cork), as a supreme full-forward with amazing scoring ability. He received a further five All Star awards — in 1975 at centre half-forward and a remarkable four-in-a-row in 1978, 1979, 1980 and 1981 at full-forward. In the remainder of his career he also won two National Hurling League medals when the Treatymen defeated Wexford and Clare in the 1984 and 1985 deciders respectively.

Two further Munster senior hurling championships also came his way, in successive years, in 1980 and 1981. In 1980 they started splendidly with a fantastic run in the league, which was only ended after a replay with Cork in the final. In the championship, however, they halted Cork's bid for a record-breaking sixth-in-a-row provincial title in the Munster final. The second half of that match was a terrific, titanic struggle before Limerick emerged triumphant on a scoreline of 2–14 to 2–10. There was a fair degree of optimism amongst their supporters as they prepared to face Galway in the All-Ireland final. The whole side were playing superbly, with the marvellous Cregan and the talismanic figure of McKenna being particularly potent forces in the forward line. This achievement was all the more impressive when one considers the unfortunate loss, through injury, of their defensive anchorman, Pat Hartigan. An injury in training to an eye, in June 1979, had prematurely cut short the great hurling career of the man who had won five successive All Star awards from 1971 to 1975.

Galway, on the other hand, were mentally free of hurling's acknowledged 'Big Three', i.e. Cork, Kilkenny and Tipperary. In hurling terms they looked upon Limerick as equals. Galway got off to a dream start. By the tenth minute they led by 2–1 to 0–0. Despite repeated and relentless attacks, Limerick never really recovered from that disastrous start. When the final whistle blew, Galway had won their first senior All-Ireland since 1923 (when, incidentally, they also beat Limerick). As well as Galway's historic win, this final will also be remembered for two further reasons. One of the greatest hurlers ever to don the maroon jersey was that supreme stylist John Connolly. Now in the autumn of his playing career, he was the winners' full-forward who later was selected as Texaco Hurler of the Year. That day will also always be recalled for the magnificence of the captain's speech. The captain, Joe Connolly, a brother of John and a native Irish speaker, moved all who witnessed it, both with the fluency and quality of his address after he raised the McCarthy Cup: *'Is íontach an lá inniu a bheith mar Ghaillimheach. Tá daoine ar ais i nGaillimh agus tá gliondar ina gcroíthe, ach freisin caithfidh muid cuimhneamh ar dhaoine i Sasana, i Meiriceá, ar fud an domhain agus tá siad b'fhéidir ag caoineadh anois faoi láthair.'*

Though disappointed, Joe and his colleagues had no choice but to look forward to 1981. They would have to do so without one of Limerick's greatest ever players and the man who captained them in 1973. After a 14-year inter-county career which began in 1966, Joe's fellow clubman Eamon Grimes finally bowed out.

On the way to the 1981 All-Ireland semi-final, Limerick, powered by Joe McKenna at full-forward, left no doubt about their superiority in the replayed Munster semi-final against Tipperary when they won 3–17 to 2–12. The first game will go down in history as Joe McKenna's greatest hour. Trailing by 2–11 to 0–3, the towering McKenna lashed home 3–1 to bring Limerick back into contention and force a draw. In the Munster final McKenna was again the controlling influence as the Treatymen comfortably overcame Clare by six points.

Having been beaten by Galway in the previous year's final, Limerick were under no illusions as they faced the Tribesmen again in the All-Ireland semi-final. Luck once more was very unkind to Limerick, and after two brilliant and enthralling performances, external circumstances forced them to concede defeat after a replay. The latter game has been repeatedly documented as one of the greatest games of hurling ever witnessed. Fast and furious, it was exhilarating throughout, with the inventiveness of the Limerick attack a joy to behold. Many pundits would say that were it not for a combination of unfortunate occurrences (three injuries and a controversial sending off of Seán Foley in the drawn game), Limerick would not only have beaten Galway but would also have annexed the All-Ireland that year. Limerick had a fabulous stylist in Ollie O'Connor, the roving targetman Joe McKenna and the inimitable, evergreen Eamon Cregan. Instead, the ultimate honours in that year's hurling decider would go, ironically, to McKenna's native Offaly.

Joe McKenna continued to hurl for his adopted county until he finally retired, at the age of 34, after their Munster championship defeat to Cork in 1985. He had played for 13 championship seasons and had been one of the most esteemed full-forwards in the history of hurling. He is also one of a select group of Limerick hurlers to captain a Railway Cup team, a feat he achieved in 1981. The others are Tommy Ryan (1934 and 1935), Mick Mackey (1937) and Gary Kirby (1995).

In 2004 Joe McKenna was selected by Limerick County Board to co-ordinate affairs between the Board and the players. Using his renowned diplomatic skills, McKenna was able to harness a spirit of goodwill and a sense of proper, balanced perspective amongst all the stakeholders in the GAA in Limerick. When one of the selectors, Damian Quigley, resigned for personal reasons, the unassuming South Liberties clubman was asked to take his place. When a rift appeared in the Limerick hurling camp in early 2005, the manager, Pad Joe Whelehan, resigned. Joe McKenna was then unanimously selected to replace his fellow Offaly man as manager.

'The players are putting in a tremendous effort. Declan Nash* from my own club and the Vice-Chairman of the County Board, Liam Lenihan, are my fellow selectors. Dave Mahedy from the University of Limerick trains the team and Newtownshandrum's Ger Cunningham is our excellent coach. We have also brought back the two dual players, Stephen Lucey and Conor Fitzgerald. So there is now a very happy relationship between all units of the GAA in Limerick,' Joe told me.

Joe McKenna loves all sports, particularly rugby, soccer, Gaelic football ('I loved meeting the Gaelic footballers on our All Star trips. I think there should be much more socialising between hurlers and footballers at all levels') and horse racing. 'I was absolutely delighted to see GAA congress passing a motion to allow rugby and soccer internationals to be played in Croke Park at the discretion of Central

---

*Since I interviewed Joe, Declan Nash has resigned as a selector and Ger Cunningham has replaced him in that role.

Council. I think Limerick sports fans have a very healthy attitude towards all games. The average Limerick person supports rugby, soccer, Gaelic football, hurling and horse racing. The Munster rugby team have been fantastic ambassadors for Irish sport over the past number of years. Limerick people are also very knowledgeable about their sport, no matter what the code. Because their standards are high, their expectations are also high. In an ideal world, Limerick's attitude to sport should be replicated throughout the country,' Joe concluded.

When choosing his representative sides, Joe made the following selections:

MUNSTER (1970–1985)

Séamus Durack
(Clare)

Jackie O'Gorman   Pat Hartigan   John Horgan
(Clare)   (Limerick)   (Cork)

Denis Coughlan   Eamon Cregan   Seán Foley
(Cork)   (Limerick)   (Limerick)

Richie Bennis   John Fenton
(Limerick)   (Cork)

Johnny Callinan   Gerald McCarthy   Eamon Grimes
(Clare)   (Cork)   (Limerick)

Jimmy Barry Murphy   Ray Cummins   Seánie O'Leary
(Cork)   (Cork)   (Cork)

IRELAND (1970–1985)

Noel Skehan
(Kilkenny)

Fan Larkin   Pat Hartigan   John Horgan
(Kilkenny)   (Limerick)   (Cork)

Joe Hennessy   Pat Henderson   Seán Foley
(Kilkenny)   (Kilkenny)   (Limerick)

Frank Cummins   John Connolly
(Kilkenny)   (Galway)

Eamon Cregan	Gerald McCarthy	Eamon Grimes
(Limerick)	(Cork)	(Limerick)
Seánie O'Leary	Ray Cummins	Eddie Keher
(Cork)	(Cork)	(Kilkenny)

By universal acclaim, Mick Mackey from Ahane was not only Limerick's best ever hurler but one of the all-time greats that this ancient game of Cúchulainn has ever produced. The 1930s and 1940s were the golden eras of Limerick hurling. Between 1933 and 1947 Limerick appeared in eleven Munster finals, winning five of them and bringing home the Liam McCarthy Cup in 1934, 1936 and 1940. During all that time Mick Mackey was their star performer, winning three All-Irelands (two of them as captain in 1936 and 1940) and five consecutive National League titles (1934 to 1938).

The team of the 1970s and the 1980s may not have won as much silverware. However, they awoke in a sports-loving people an enthusiasm for all that is beautiful and much that is great about one of the world's most artistic games. In a team of craftsmen, four special hurlers made a unique contribution. Eamon Cregan from Claughaun was a highly gifted and extremely versatile hurler. Three South Liberties club men, Pat Hartigan, Eamon Grimes and Joe McKenna, were so good that racing magnate and businessman extraordinaire J.P. McManus, himself a South Liberties man, named three of his horses after the trio. Of all the great moments that Joe McKenna experienced in a Limerick jersey, one above all others is extra special. It concerns J.P. McManus, who has been an extremely generous benefactor to both South Liberties and the Limerick County Board. (For example, in July 2004 he donated five million euro towards the development of the Gaelic grounds in Limerick.)

When the newly crowned All-Ireland hurling champions of 1973 arrived back in their dressing room, in the immediate aftermath of the game, the first person there to congratulate them was J.P. McManus. It conclusively proved to Joe and his colleagues the magnetic impact that hurling has on anyone who has been involved with the game.

In the final analysis, none of us are measured by what we have. As Dr Joseph Mac Rory, Bishop of Down and Conor, said at the 1916 annual congress of the GAA: '... there is no finer game in existence than hurling, no better test of endurance, of quickness of mind and eye and of speed of hand and foot'.

Joe McKenna has played his part in carrying on that wonderful tradition of hurling excellence.

Joe McKenna – Fact File

Native Place:	Shinrone, Co. Offaly
Date of Birth:	June 10, 1951
Clubs:	(a) Shinrone, Co. Offaly (b) South Liberties, Limerick
Colleges' Honours:	Dean Ryan Cup (1968) – with St Flannan's, Ennis
Club Honours:	South Liberties Senior Hurling Championship (3) – 1972, 1976, 1978
County Honours:	(a) Offaly Played minor and U-21 with them (b) Limerick All-Ireland Senior Hurling Championship (1) – 1973 Munster Senior Hurling Championship (4) – 1973, 1974, 1980, 1981 National Hurling League (2) – 1984, 1985
Other Playing Honours:	Railway Cup (4) – 1976, 1978, 1981 (Captain), 1984
Awards:	All Stars (6) – 1974, 1975, 1978, 1979, 1980, 1981 B. & I. Award (1) – 1981
Occupation:	Businessman (hardware and plant hire)
Family:	Married to Miriam (née King, Farranshone)
Children:	Frank, Nick, Joe and Ruth

TWENTY-TWO

Jarlath Burns–Armagh/BBC/TG4

A MAN FOR ALL SEASONS

The outlooks and philosophies of all human beings are invariably fashioned by three main influencing factors: our genealogical ancestry, our experiences as we develop from infanthood to adulthood, and the oral, historical, cultural and literary traditions of our native place. No place in Ireland exemplifies more the depth of such a rich legacy than South Armagh, and no person understands or appreciates that beautiful inheritance more than former Armagh senior football captain and current TG4 analyst, Jarlath Burns. His native parish of Creggan was historically at the centre of this tradition, particularly during the eighteenth century.

Five famous poets, collectively known as 'the Creggan Poets', were instrumental in creating an embryonic love of creative writing and lyrical poetry, in the Irish language, in the eighteenth century. Séamus Dall Mac Cuarta, Pádraig Mac a Londain, Peadar Ó Doirnín and Séamus Mór Mac Murphy were all very accomplished Gaelic poets, but Art Mac Cooey was the best known of the five, and he was born in the townland of Ballinaghy, which is adjacent to Jarlath's native townland. His poem about the parish of Creggan is the 'national anthem' of the locality and his death in 1773 represented the final eclipse of the old Gaelic order. Mac Cooey's love of his native place is, appropriately, proclaimed by the epitaph inscribed on his headstone: 'That with the fragrant Gaels of Creggan, I will be put in clay under the sod.'

All of the foregoing gave Jarlath Burns a special identity. South Armagh is surrounded by mountains on one side and the political border, encompassing both Monaghan and Louth, on the other. To him, it is a nestling oasis of Irishness in music, song and story. In fact, it can also trace back its Irish language roots to time immemorial and right up to around 1950, when the last native speaker in the district died. The parish of Creggan itself also envelops two GAA catchment areas. One of these is the renowned district of thrice All-Ireland club football champions Crossmaglen Rangers. The other is Jarlath's native club area, Silverbridge. Every GAA club possesses great club people who pass on the GAA torch, and Silverbridge is no exception. Men such as Pat Trainor and the late Peter Keely were legendary in developing the GAA skills of budding stars such as Jarlath himself. Playing football in his back garden with his brothers and imitating the great GAA players of the day was a regular activity. When Armagh reached the 1977 All-Ireland senior football final, the Burns siblings had accessible icons in Jimmy Smyth, Joe Kernan, Tom McCreesh and Paddy Moriarty.

In 1971 Jarlath was enrolled as a pupil in St Patrick's Primary School in nearby Cullyhanna. There he came under the tutelage of school principal Hugh Macauley, a close personal friend of that other inspirational South Armagh Gaelgeoir, the late Cardinal Tomás Ó Fiaich. The fledgling pupil became imbued with a general love of Irish culture and the Irish language in particular. This soon manifested itself in Jarlath's participation in the annual GAA Scór competitions, in which he won an Ulster medal in Tráth na gCeist in 1984.

When Jarlath went to St Colman's College in Newry, his GAA education really took off. He came under the direct guidance of brilliant Colleges coach Ray Morgan, who had a multiplicity of Hogan Cup triumphs under his belt. In addition, future All-Ireland winning Down manager Peter McGrath was also a coach at the famed GAA nursery. Irish teachers Carol McCann, Seán Russell and Joan Higgins developed in Jarlath a greater proficiency and interest in the Irish language as a living expression of one's national identity. Success on the football field, however, eluded him. 'Unfortunately for us, we were constantly taking second place to an outstanding St Patrick's College, Maghera, side. Danny Quinn and Dermot McNicholl, who were later to win All-Ireland senior medals with Derry, were their strongest and most talented players. When I went to St Colman's, Greg Blaney, who was later to experience so much success with Down at senior inter-county level, was our icon. Even though he was behind me in Newry, I always looked up to a smaller and younger player — one James McCartan. I never ceased to be astounded by his exquisite skills. It was great to see him fulfil his undoubted potential. He was, and is, a person whom I have tremendous respect for.'

When Jarlath attended St Mary's College of Education, he encountered two other magnificent GAA coaches. 'Former Derry All-Ireland star Jim McKeever was a master tactician and great strategist. Peter Finn introduced us to new revolutionary training methods. Terminologies such as cardiovascular activity, ballistic stretching and biomechanics became the accepted norm. After Peter's sessions we never left the training ground fatigued because he always explained the reasons behind each technique which he adopted.' It was while at St Mary's that Jarlath Burns achieved his first major football success, when the small college won its first and only Sigerson Cup title, overwhelming UCC by 3–13 to 1–5 in the final. 'On that side were my future Armagh teammates, Benny Tierney, John Rafferty and Ollie Reel, as well as other future county men Pascal Canavan (Tyrone), Cathal Murray (Down), Malachy O'Rourke, our captain John Rehill of Fermanagh, Danny Quinn and Séamus Downey of Derry. Even though he was not a regular county player, Tyrone's Iggy Gallagher played a very pivotal role in our success. Downey was a particularly gifted footballer who was pacey and elusive.

'We prepared fastidiously for that Sigerson triumph. We had not the financial resources, initially, to stay overnight in Murlough House in Dundrum on Dublin's southside. Nevertheless, being the conscientious students that we were, a geography field trip was arranged, coincidentally using the same Murlough House as our headquarters. The soil samples that we were supposed to be taking just happened to be attached to the soles of our football boots! In terms of total match preparation and quality training, I have no doubt that we were at least ten years ahead of our time. It was a fantastic achievement to win such a prestigious competition when one considers our limited pool of players.' For Burns, that 1989 Sigerson success was the mechanism that the Silverbridge man needed to develop his football confidence at an even higher level.

Prior to this, Burns had played for Armagh minors in 1984 and 1985. In 1986 he made his senior debut for the Orchard County in a league game against Donegal with Anthony Molloy in direct opposition. 'He was far too strong and wily for me. I was only a rookie and did not really feature for Armagh in senior ranks for the next two years. Instead, I played with the county U-21 side in 1987 and 1988. In the 1989/90 league, I played senior again and marked Jack O'Shea (Kerry) and Declan Bolger (Dublin) in my first two games. Everything went brilliant for me and the Armagh Supporters' Club selected me as their Man of the Match in both games. This was a terrific boost to my confidence.'

Between 1991 and 1994 Armagh were unfortunate to come up against powerful Down, Donegal and Derry teams that won four All-Irelands between them. Armagh did, nevertheless, manage to reach a league decider in 1994, only to be beaten by Meath. Burns's most extraordinary memory from that period is a spellbinding performance of high catching, power and pace by Laois midfielder Tony Maher in the 1994 league semi-final. When Armagh were beaten by ten points by Derry in the 1995 Ulster senior championship, both Armagh and Burns were totally deflated. Seeing Derry centre half-back Henry Downey on the end of a move that resulted in the Lavey man sending to the net from short range was the straw that broke the camel's back. Eventually, Armagh manager Jim McCorry stepped aside to be replaced by the two Brians — McAlinden and Canavan. Initially, Burns was not selected on the squad but good club displays ensured that the 6'3" man was soon back in the fold. By summer 1996, Burns was looked upon as the man who could lead the Orchard County back to the top. In practically every game, whether in league or championship, he was the dominant figure, with his aerial skills in particular giving Armagh an increasing territorial advantage. When he was selected as team captain in 1997, he was determined to succeed. Subsequent championship near-misses against Tyrone and Derry provided Armagh with realistic hopes of senior provincial success. When 1999 came, the Orchard County were ready and waiting.

Armagh succeeded in reaching the 1999 league semi-final only to be eventually beaten by Dublin in a replay. Again, the pessimists in Armagh had a field day. When the chips were down, it was alleged that Armagh were always found wanting. On a personal level, Jarlath Burns knew that 1999 was a make or break year for him. He had a bad bout of pneumonia in the spring, and 13 years of toil in the Armagh jersey were taking their toll. 'I said to myself before that year's cham-pionship, if I manage to get through the year, regardless of what happens, I am going to take a prolonged rest and retire from inter-county football. As well, I had three young children and I did not want to miss seeing them grow up. When we failed miserably in the replayed league match with Dublin, I reckoned my permanent retirement was imminent.'

In the first game of the Ulster championship, against Donegal, they were seven points down with only two minutes gone. Then, suddenly everything seemed to go right and they trailed by only three points at the break. As the game neared its end, they were still two points behind. In injury time Armagh's Paddy McKeever scored a goal to put his side one point in front. With the last kick of an excellent game, Donegal's Michael Hegarty notched a dramatic equaliser. Once again, in the replay, Donegal started the better and by half-time they were again leading by three points. Oisín McConville, who was subsequently reinstated, had also been unfairly sent off in the first half. Things looked bleak, to say the least. Then, substitutes Cathal O'Rourke and Diarmuid Marsden instigated an Armagh revival by scoring a goal apiece. Donegal had Martin Coll sent off and a fine last quarter by the Orchard men ensured a five-point victory. The shackles were lifted and confidence was now rising, as they prepared to meet old adversaries

Derry in the Ulster semi-final.

Though Derry controlled much of the proceedings, it was the more cohesive Armagh forward line that showed the greater penetration. When Oisín McConville scored a goal in the second half, their self-belief increased a hundredfold and the whole team produced a fantastic final ten minutes to claim victory by the narrowest of margins. Buoyed by this victory, achieved in a top-quality game, Armagh now faced their nearest neighbours and old-time rivals, Down, in the Ulster final. Would it be a case of third time lucky as the same opposition had defeated Armagh in both the 1961 and 1981 Ulster finals? All Armagh were waiting in anxious expectation, as they truly believed their hour had come to fulfil their undoubted potential.

In a magnificent team performance, Armagh controlled this game effectively from start to finish. The irrepressible twin strike force of Oisín McConville and Diarmuid Marsden scored 3–9 between them as the Orchard County stormed to a 3–12 to 0–10 victory over the Mourne men. McConville, in a superb display of pinpoint accuracy, amassed the incredible total of 2–7. It was very appropriate that that wonderful servant of Armagh football, Ger Houlahan, should grace the field for the last ten minutes and finally crown a glittering career with an Ulster medal. The last time Armagh had won the Anglo Celt Cup was seventeen years earlier in 1982. Now August 1, 1999 will forever be remembered in the hearts and minds of all future generations of Armagh supporters as a momentous occasion for all concerned. When team captain Jarlath Burns hoisted aloft the Cup, there were scenes of jubilation amongst the Armagh supporters.

In a very eloquent speech, Jarlath gave due praise to his teammates, the management, officials and supporters. As he encouraged everyone to celebrate that night, he then preached caution: 'This is the best moment of my life as I watch the euphoria amongst long-suffering supporters. I also remember with pride those Armagh players like Martin McQuillan and Neil Smyth who have given such loyal service to Armagh, with no rewards. Now, I am appealing to all of you to allow us the time and dignity to let us prepare in our own way, by ourselves, for the All-Ireland semi-final. This is a beginning, not the end.'

In that semi-final against Meath, Armagh actually led by four points at one stage, and at half-time, thanks to goals from Diarmuid Marsden and the overlapping half-back Kieran Hughes, the score was 2–4 to 0–8 in the northerners' favour. Yet in the second half, many scoreable chances were missed. When full-back Gerard Reid was sent off, the result was inevitable as a Trevor Giles-inspired Meath secured a four-point win for the Royal County.

'We lost our way in the final quarter and in hindsight it is probably fair to say that we did not position our team properly. On a personal level, I felt that I had played well in Croke Park and it was nice to retire on a relative high.' Thus, the man who wore the saffron and white so gracefully and so diligently for thirteen years quietly exited after he had led Armagh back from the wilderness into its rightful place in the forefront of Gaelic football.

Three years later, as Jarlath Burns sat in the BBC sports studio in Croke Park, analysing the All-Ireland senior final between Armagh and Kerry, he just wondered and hoped. As that final was drawing to an end and it appeared that Armagh, at last, were going to be crowned All-Ireland champions, a plethora of excited hopes, interspersed with memories of past disappointments, occupied his mind. 'Out on that famous pitch were fifteen players and all the subs. I had not only played with most of them but had also been their soul mate and captain for three years. Now they were about to achieve the All-Ireland dream that every GAA player has. Just before the end of the game, I had to retire to the inner sanctum of the studio and offer my professional opinion, as Armagh led by a point with seconds to go. I feared that the jinx of Armagh's two previous All-Ireland finals, in 1953 and 1977, would return and that Kerry would score a last-minute goal. When this did not happen and the final whistle sounded, I was totally overwhelmed with uncontrolled, joyful emotion. Seeing Armagh supporters spontaneously invade Croke Park in their thousands to greet our all-conquering heroes was too much for me. I took my microphone off and banged against the window, rushed outside the studio, forgot my professional duties, with the whole country watching me. In the adjacent RTÉ studios, I believe the analyst, Tony Davis, said that in his hour of euphoria Jarlath Burns had nearly fallen off the studio podium! It was one of the finest moments that I could ever have dreamed of.'

That year, 2002, had started well for the Orchard County men. They had won six of their league games only to slump disastrously to an average Laois team in Longford's Pearse Park. In the first round of the Ulster championship against newly crowned league champions Tyrone, Armagh showed promise as they eked out a draw with the then current Ulster titleholders. A magnificent display by Oisín McConville and two points from 'rookie' full-forward Ronan Clarke enabled Armagh to deservedly achieve parity. In the replay, in a pulsating encounter, Armagh defeated the O'Neill County by three points. What impressed Jarlath and all watching Armagh supporters was not just the win but also the quality of their play. This view was further strengthened when, in a thoroughly efficient team performance with some brilliant finishing, they defeated Fermanagh by eight points in the Ulster semi-final.

When they met Donegal in the Ulster decider, expectation within the county was very high, as team manager Joe Kernan had now instilled in his side a mental toughness that blended perfectly with their renowned physical strength. Making greater use of the ball and with leaders all over the field, Armagh swept to a four-point success in a splendid display of open passing and clinical finishing. When the team captain, the redoubtable and inspirational Kieran McGeeney, lifted the Anglo Celt Cup, target number one had been accomplished. In the All-Ireland quarter-final against Sligo in Croke Park, the westerners nearly thwarted Armagh's rising All-Ireland ambition. Armagh's supporters were mightily relieved when Sligo forward Dara McGarty elected to punch an equalising point instead of trying for a match-winning goal. In the replay, another fantastic game ensued and, with ten minutes left, the Orchard men led by five points. However, a tremendous last ten minutes display from influential Sligo midfielder Eamonn O'Hara almost proved fruitful for the Yeats County. Again, Armagh were relieved to hear the final whistle as they held on grimly to an uncomfortable two-point lead.

Armagh's 1–14 to 1–13 win over Dublin in the All-Ireland semi-final was achieved after a tight, tense contest. With Armagh engaging defensively in a damage limitation exercise, their forwards were able to punish every flaw in the Dublin side. Still, Dublin were very unlucky to see their full-forward Ray Cosgrove hit his last-second 30-metres free off the post and wide. It would now appear that the vital ingredient of luck was also with Armagh as they searched for the Holy Grail. By the same token, it would also have to be stressed that Armagh's all-consuming determination, allied to their natural ability, was the main driving force as they headed for a date with destiny against Kerry in the All-Ireland final.

Kerry, with the classy Séamus Moynihan in defence and a brilliant full-forward line of Michael Frank Russell, Dara Ó Cinnéide and Colm Cooper, were favourites to shatter the dreams of Armagh's first All-Ireland senior football triumph. When Kerry led on a 0–11 to 0–7 scoreline at half-time, it appeared there was to be no romantic fairytale ending for the northerners. The fact that ace forward Oisín McConville had repeated history (Armagh had also missed a penalty in the 1953 final against the same opposition) by missing a penalty in the opening half seemed to reinforce that opinion. However, Diarmuid Marsden, who had been outstanding all through, had other ideas when he scored his third point of the game and the first of the second half, four minutes after the restart. Kerry then had three unforgivable wides, before a

Russell free again left four points between the sides. Immediately afterwards, McConville pointed a free. For the next eight minutes, the play ebbed to and fro before Liam Hassett notched what proved to be Kerry's only point from play in the second half. McConville and Ó Cinnéide then exchanged points from brilliantly struck 45's, to leave four points between the sides and 19 minutes gone on the clock. Twenty seconds later, the defining moment of this game began after an enthralling inter-passing movement between Marsden, enterprising half-back Andrew McCann and a clever one-two between McConville and superb midfielder Paul McGrane. It ended when the classy Crossmaglen Ranger shot low to the net, inside the near post. Within 42 minutes, McConville had gone from villain to hero.

The huge Armagh following now rose in cascading, resounding cheers as a sea of luminous orange colour engulfed the stadium. Armagh, led by a tour de force performance from their captain and maestro, Kieran McGeeney, drove relentlessly forward, hunting in packs, craving that elusive equaliser. Then McGeeney picked up a loose Kerry clearance, found the roving Ronan Clarke, who turned Moynihan inside out before curling the ball over the bar with an exquisitely accurate kick. Armagh supporters cheered in complete unison, as they and most neutrals hoped that Armagh's hour of glory was close at hand. With the scoreline reading Armagh 1–11, Kerry 0–14, the tension was unbearable amongst supporters of both and none as Armagh strove with all their might to create a winning opportunity. Then, eight minutes from the end, it happened. In a fabulous passing movement started by goalkeeper Benny Tierney, Armagh literally tore the Kerry defence cover apart. Impact substitute Barry O'Hagan played a series of one-twos before half-back Aidan O'Rourke released a pinpoint pass to corner-forward Stephen McDonnell. The Killeavy star, who had scored Armagh's opening point and who had earlier been injured in an accidental collision with Clarke, turned, swivelled and with the cleverest of sidesteps, sent the ball high over the bar for the lead point. During the remaining time, which, including injury time, amounted to 11 minutes, both sides had scoreable chances. With the clock registering 72.55, Armagh full-back Justin McNulty intercepted a pass and dispatched the ball to Tony McEntee. He immediately transferred it into the safe and capable hands of Kieran McGeeney. At 73.16 the long whistle sounded, with the ball tightly in the grip of Armagh's powerful talisman. A hundred years of pent-up emotions were released in that moment of glorious ecstasy for all the boys, girls, men and women from the County Armagh. 'For me it is very difficult to imagine a more happy sporting occasion for an Armagh person than that 2002 All-Ireland success,' added Jarlath Burns wistfully.

When it came to discussing current issues, Jarlath, a Pioneer, who is actively involved in promoting temperance, aired his views on four topical areas:

1. 'I agree that soccer and rugby international matches should be allowed in Croke Park during the development of rugby's headquarters at Lansdowne Road. By transferring the sanctioning powers on this from Congress to Central Council, we are not doing anything radical. In this day and age, to do otherwise is to follow a totally negative and unnecessary approach. Let us be positive about this and show the whole sporting world that the GAA is really a massive, national organisation.'

2. 'Regarding the Gaelic Players' Association, which is not officially sanctioned, I would like to state the following: First of all, there is a definite need for one cohesive national players' body. I agree totally with a lot of the GPA's aims and objectives in relation to their GAA scholarship scheme and their robust representation in getting good sponsorship for players. Nonetheless, there is one area of activity which I am doubtful about. I think their CEO or official representative should do their business like any other unit of the Association, submit their motions to Congress, and abide by its democratic decision. To be fair to them, the only way that this can be properly achieved is if they become a fully sanctioned, integrated part of the Association. In other words, if the GPA want to effect change, it can only be attained if they become an official body, subject to the same rules and regulations as all other units of the GAA.'

3. 'With regard to the experimental playing rules introduced in early 2005, I would like to say that we should not be afraid to experiment with change. I think the introduction of tees for kick-outs has two major benefits. It encourages longer kicking and so we witness higher catching. Secondly, it prevents goalkeepers developing arthritic problems in their legs in future years. I agree with a stricter interpretation of the yellow card rule, especially in its more recent amended form, where a player is suspended for one game after receiving yellow cards in two successive games. This new emphasis makes the defender think about stopping the play as opposed to the player. Many of the people who originally asked for change were the first to decry it when it appeared to detrimentally affect their own team's performance.

'I was annoyed that my own province of Ulster opted out of these experiments, for the McKenna Cup. I think the GAA is a

national organisation that should demand a national implementation system of its own rules and experiments.'

4. 'With proper marketing and a fixed time, the Railway Cup can be
a resounding success. The players want it and that is reason enough
for its retention. Just look how media hype has worked marvellously
for the Celtic and Heineken leagues in rugby. Most of all, the
huge attendances at the International Rules series in Croke Park
are proof of what can be achieved with meaningful marketing.'

For the past number of years Jarlath has acted as a GAA games analyst
on both BBC TV and TG4. He has enjoyed both experiences
immensely. 'TG4 started in 2001 doing commentaries on league and
club games, which normally would not be covered by television. This
has been a brilliant experience because it has created a wider GAA
audience, bringing our games to the very grass roots of the organisation
while at the same time promoting the Irish language in a very positive
and accessible fashion.'

It was the success of the latter which prompted Adare Productions
in 2003 to create their own GAA reality TV experience. Jarlath takes
up the story: 'Adare asked us to select a panel of players who had never
played Gaelic football, at any level, for their county, then train them
over a definite period before pairing them against Dublin in a TV
encounter. We held four provincial trials and one national trial before
making our final selection. The management team of former All-Ireland
players — Mickey 'Ned' O'Sullivan of Kerry, Brian Mullins of Dublin
and myself — were totally bowled over by the response of the players
who adopted the now familiar name 'Underdogs'. We based ourselves
in the famed Buffers Alley Club in Wexford, before taking on Dublin.
The lads played fantastic football and were unfortunate to lose by the
minimum of margins to Dublin.'

After that game, the changed management team (Mícheál Ó
Muircheartaigh replaced Brian Mullins) reviewed their selection policy
and modified their eligibility rule. Players who had represented their
counties at either minor or U-21 level were now eligible for selection.
In 2004, they played All-Ireland champions Kerry under lights, and,
after an exciting game, the Underdogs defeated the Kingdom. A new
niche in the GAA market had been created, with very worthwhile
results. The combined result of the Underdogs' team achievements
was much greater than the sum of the individual parts. Burns also
believes that their training methods, which have now been adopted by
many club sides, have wider implications for the GAA at large. 'We
first of all tested the fitness levels of our players and then gave them

individual fitness programmes. Every fortnight we recalled the players, tested them again and made whatever necessary adjustments were required in each player's individual programme. Our training sessions were confined to football skills development and tactical strategies. In order to alleviate 'burn out' caused by over-physical training, we believe this could be the way forward for all in the future.'

When it came to choosing his Ulster and Ireland teams, the U2 and Christy Moore fan made the following selections:

Ulster (1975–2005)

Brian McAlinden
(Armagh)

Kieran McKeever
(Derry)

Tony Scullion
(Derry)

Seán Lockhart
(Derry)

Paul McFlynn
(Derry)

Kieran McGeeney
(Armagh)

Martin McQuillan
(Armagh)

Anthony Tohill
(Derry)

Peter McGinnity
(Fermanagh)

James McCartan
(Down)

Greg Blaney
(Down)

Martin McHugh
(Donegal)

Peter Canavan
(Tyrone)

Frank McGuigan
(Tyrone)

Stephen McDonnell
(Armagh)

IRELAND (1975–2005)

Brian McAlinden
(Armagh)

Gay O'Driscoll   Tony Scullion   Séamus Moynihan
(Dublin)   (Derry)   (Kerry)

Páidí Ó Sé   Kieran McGeeney   Martin O'Connell
(Kerry)   (Armagh)   (Meath)

Jack O'Shea   Brian Mullins
(Kerry)   (Dublin)

Colm O'Rourke   Larry Tompkins   Pat Spillane
(Meath)   (Kildare/Cork)   (Kerry)

Mikey Sheehy   Eoin Liston   Peter Canavan
(Kerry)   (Kerry)   (Tyrone)

On the night of Armagh's triumphant success in the 2002 All-Ireland senior football final, former Armagh star full-back Jack Bratten, who played in the 1953 final against Kerry, walked into a Dublin hotel. There was an old man standing at a table with a drink at his elbow and a stick in his hand. 'He says to me, "Are you Jack Bratten?" I said I was, and with tears of joy pouring down his face, he said, "I was at the '53 final and the '77 final, but today's victory caps it all." That man was 92 years of age.' When Jarlath Burns led Armagh out of the desert and desolation of the barren years in 1999, his inspirational leadership was to prove the final catalyst for making that old man's dream come true. All of Armagh will always be eternally grateful that another 'fragrant Gael of Creggan' was destined for that honour. It can truly be said that he has been, and is, an exemplary role model for many reasons and for all seasons.

JARLATH BURNS – FACT FILE

Native Place:	Creggan, Co.Armagh
Date of Birth:	July 4, 1967
Club:	Silverbridge
Club Honours:	Armagh League – 1992, 1994
County Honours:	Ulster Championship – 1999 McKenna Cup – 1990, 1994
University Honours:	Sigerson Cup with St Mary's College, Belfast – 1989
Other Honours:	Railway Cup medals with Ulster – 1998, 1999 Represented Combined Universities – 1989, 1990
Awards:	Player of the Year (Armagh Supporters' Club) – 1997 Player of the Year (Armagh County Board) – 1996 Irish News All Star – 1998
Coaching Honours:	Various achievements at county and Ulster level with St Paul's, Bessbrook Manager of Underdogs 2003/2004
Occupation:	Irish teacher in St Paul's, Bessbrook
Family:	Married to Suzanne
Children:	Megan, Fionnan, Jarlath Óg, Conall, Ellen

TWENTY-THREE

Tony Doran–Wexford

BOOLAVOGUE'S FOLK HERO REMINISCES

At Boolavogue as the sun was setting,
O'er the bright May meadows of Shelmalier,
A rebel hand set the heather blazing,
And brought the neighbours from far and near;
Then Father Murphy from old Kilcormack,
Spurred up the rock with a warning cry:
'Arm, arm'! He cried, for I've come to lead you,
For Ireland's freedom we'll fight or die!

P.J. McCall

Until the late 1940s, long-suffering Wexford GAA supporters saw little future in their hurlers. They had contested only one Leinster final since 1918, whereas the county footballers had played in eight provincial deciders during the same period. However, one towering figure, equally adept in both codes, saw things differently. That player, Nicky Rackard of Rathnure, walked into his family homestead one autumn day in 1949 and loudly proclaimed to his startled family, 'I have no doubt but that we will win an All-Ireland senior hurling title within the next few years.' His surprising optimism was based on the amazing amount of young, talented hurlers in the county. Amongst them were his two brothers, Willie and Bobby, Nick O'Donnell, Ned Wheeler, Padge Kehoe, Jim Morrissey and Tim Flood.

Within the next thirteen years, Rackard's immortal, prophetic words rang true, as the Slaneysiders, incredibly, reached the following seven Leinster finals, winning four of them and also contesting All-Ireland finals in 1951, 1954, 1955 and 1956. In addition, in the 1960s they were in provincial finals no less than seven times. Modesty forbade him to mention himself but there is absolutely no doubt that Nicky was the real charismatic and inspirational talisman who would lead Wexford to the summit of their dreams. A goal-scorer supreme, the burly full-forward admirably blended his height, strength and awesome skill with an indomitable spirit.

When Wexford won back-to-back All-Ireland titles in 1955 and 1956, the whole neutral GAA world rejoiced. A new team of hurling heroes had arrived. This golden era of Wexford dominance immediately set alight a burning desire within every young, aspiring hurler to emulate the Rackards, Wheelers, Kehoes, O'Donnells, English's and Floods. A young, red-haired, strapping youngster from Boolavogue called Tony Doran quickly and ably rose to the challenge.

His ancestral home straddled the neighbouring parishes of Monageer/Boolavogue and Monamolin/Kilmuckridge. This geographical situation allowed Tony to claim dual citizenship, as it were. He could justifiably claim to be a resident of Boolavogue with all its historical and political connotations, and still play hurling with the Buffer's Alley club that catered for the Monamolin/Kilmuckridge areas. Tony told me about Rackard's influence when I met him in Boolavogue where he now, definitely, resides. 'Nicky Rackard was a great hurling enthusiast who promoted the game at schools level throughout the county when he founded the Rackard League in 1956. We all looked up to him and we were often very privileged when he actually came to referee our games.'

By 1962 it was becoming increasingly obvious that Tony had a special hurling talent, particularly in the art of winning the ball and then scoring decisive, match-winning goals. He starred at U-16 level with Buffer's Alley in his debut season, and the county minor selectors duly chose him for the 1963 county minor panel. With Tony playing a starring role at centre half-forward, Wexford claimed their first provincial minor title when they beat Kilkenny in the final, by two points. It was a dream first year for Doran when Wexford went on to win their first minor All-Ireland title, beating Limerick by six points in the decider.

For the next four years, Tony played at U-21 level for the Slaneysiders, as well as appearing for his last year at minor level in 1964. Alternating between centre half-forward and full-forward, Tony's scoring exploits were being very favourably compared to his boyhood hero. Like Rackard, he possessed great heart, a never-say-die spirit and, most of all, the natural ability to create a goal opportunity out of nothing. Two years later, six of those successful minors, including Tony, achieved U-21 championship glory when they defeated Tipperary in the 1965 All-Ireland U-21 final. Mick Kinsella, Vinny Staples, Pat Quigley and Tony himself were all outstanding on those two historic occasions. Incidentally, that U-21 final was played in Nowlan Park in Kilkenny, just a week after the Premier County had defeated Wexford in the All-Ireland senior final. Five Wexford players, including the outstanding Quigley brothers, Dan and Pat, had played in both games.

Having already won Leinster U-21 medals, in both 1964 and 1965, Wexford and Tony duly won their third-in-a-row provincial title in 1966. Despite having over half of their 1965 All-Ireland winning side still on duty, they lost that year's All-Ireland final to Cork, after a three-game marathon. From Doran's perspective, his personal outlook was encouraging. He had made his senior debut against Kilkenny, in a tournament game, back in the autumn of 1963, as a 17-year-old, and had played in the 1965/66 National League. In 1966, as well as his U-21 appearance, he had become a permanent member of Wexford's Intermediate championship team. Now Tony Doran had only one thing on his mind. Given his team's talent and unquenchable, determined spirit, he knew that a coveted senior All-Ireland title should come soon. When they beat Kilkenny in the 1967 National League final, Doran had won his first major competitive senior honour. He could not wait for the championship to begin.

Wexford beat Laois in the opening encounter and thus qualified to meet Kilkenny in the Leinster final. A brilliant Cats team, led by Jim Treacy, Pat Henderson, Séamus Cleere and Eddie Keher, thwarted the Slaneysiders' ambitions when they scored an easy win. Doran's initial disappointment was somewhat eased when the Marble County went on to claim that year's All-Ireland.

In 1968, Wexford accounted for Dublin in the Leinster semi-final. For the third year in a row, they met archrivals Kilkenny in the final. In a pulsating, high-scoring contest, Wexford edged out the Cats, on a 3–13 to 4–9 scoreline. Such was the exceptional quality of the play that most neutral observers did not want the game to end. The sheer tension amongst the rival supporters was clearly palpable, as first one side and then the other appeared to dominate. In the end, the laurels rested where they belonged. For the first time, Tony Doran was about to appear in a senior All-Ireland hurling final.*

Twelve years earlier, in 1956, Nicky Rackard and Padge Kehoe were All-Ireland winning stars. Young Tony Doran was then a ten-year-old boy whose only wish was to be Nicky Rackard on All-Ireland final day. Now, here he was destined to wear the same No. 14 jersey as his idol had done. To compound matters even further, Rackard was a current senior selector and Kehoe, who also had won an All-Ireland medal, in 1960, was the team's respected coach. What made the occasion

---

*There were no All-Ireland senior hurling semi-finals between 1959 and 1968 inclusively.

extra special was that, for the first time, Wexford were represented by both their minor and senior teams on hurling's greatest occasion.

That Wexford senior team of 1968 had only three survivors from the 1960 All-Ireland winning side. Top-class goalkeeper Pat Nolan (a cousin of future winning manager Liam Griffin), outstanding defender Tom Neville and wily forward Jimmy O'Brien were the three experienced stalwarts. Overall, the side contained an excellent mix of ball-winners, good man-marking defenders and accurate score-getters. In hurling terms, Wexford normally had many players who were tall and very strong. Accordingly, their style of play tended to match their physiques. Their game was based, in the main, on lift-and-strike and catch-and-strike. What endeared them to so many neutrals was their reputation for outstanding sportsmanship.

The first Sunday in September 1968 started off brightly for Wexford when their minors recorded an impressive three-point winning margin over Cork. Tony Doran's club colleagues Mick Butler and Martin Casey thus became the first two Buffer's Alley men to win All-Ireland minor medals. A further one hour would determine whether or not another gold medal would be on its way to Monamolin.

With their huge following now in full voice, Wexford faced a Tipperary side that had won five of the previous ten All-Irelands. Possessing men of the calibre of captain Mick Roche, Len Gaynor, Donie Nealon, Babs Keating, Jimmy Doyle and Liam Devaney was certainly an intimidating proposition for Wexford. When the Premier County totally controlled the first half, the omens for the Slaneysiders definitely appeared unfavourable, to say the least. The first half will always be remembered in hurling folklore for one of the best individual defensive performances ever witnessed on a hurling field. Mick Roche, at centre half-back, was simply tremendous in everything he did. In attack, Babs Keating was equally impressive as he literally tore the Wexford defence asunder. Only for some fabulous saves by goalkeeper Pat Nolan, the interval scoreline of 1–11 to 1–3 would have been much different.

At half-time, the mentors Kehoe and Rackard simply lambasted their charges for their woeful performances. Their verbal onslaught had the desired effect when, in the second period, a totally transformed Model County continually took the game to their more vaunted opponents. Their inspirational captain, Dan Quigley, and influential midfielder Phil Wilson dictated the outfield exchanges. In the forward line, Paul Lynch, Jack Berry and substitute John Quigley were very impressive in a team of stars. One player, however, stood head and shoulders above the rest. That day, all those who were privileged to witness the exciting spectacle saw, for the first time, the beginning of a true hurling legend — Tony Doran, the man from Boolavogue. One moment of hurling wizardry exemplified the budding superstar. It was halfway through the first half and Doran had already scored a goal. Then ace forward Paul Lynch scored another goal, direct from a 21-yard free, to put the sides level. For what appeared to be an eternity, the game ebbed and flowed, with no side creating a clear advantage. Suddenly, out of nowhere, the elusive Doran snatched the ball and sent it crashing to the net. The Model County were in the lead for the first time. That magical score ignited the momentum that landed an historic All-Ireland victory for Wexford, on a score of 5–8 to 3–12. Tony Doran and Wexford were overjoyed. Wexford supporters, as they did in 1955, 1956 and 1960, celebrated in style. Continuous cavalcades of joyous supporters followed their new heroes as they entered every town, village and parish during the course of the following week.

Given the double All-Ireland success, of seniors and minors, every Wexford supporter really believed that this was the beginning of another fantastic era of success for the men in purple and gold. Little did they then realise that it would be 28 years before Liam Griffin (Tony Doran's cousin) would manage a team to McCarthy Cup success, in 1996.

From 1968 to 1984, a span of 16 years, Tony Doran continued to star in the purple and gold. Despite their success in 1968, Wexford invariably struggled to emerge from Leinster, simply because they came up against one of the best Kilkenny sides in hurling history. In 1969 they were unexpectedly beaten by Offaly in the Leinster semi-final. The following season they triumphed over Kilkenny in the provincial decider before narrowly beating Galway in the All-Ireland semi-final. However, Cork overcame them in the final, in a very high-scoring contest.

For the next five years, the Noresiders appeared to have the Indian sign over the Model County, as the Cats won all five provincial finals. Though some of them were close and tense, Wexford always went home disappointed. The most frustrating of those was in 1974, when Eddie Keher scored a fantastic winning point in the dying seconds to secure a one-point triumph. When the Cats easily overcame Galway and Limerick to claim that year's All-Ireland, it was heart-rending.

Eventually, in both 1976 and 1977, Wexford broke Kilkenny's provincial dominance when they recorded convincing victories. They narrowly defeated Galway in 1976 at the penultimate stage, only to once again suffer at the hands of the Rebel County in the final. Despite a typical opportunist goal by Doran, Cork won by four points. History repeated itself in 1977 when, again, Cork took the honours at the expense of unlucky Wexford. Thus, Wexford had made three final appearances in the 1970s and were beaten by Cork each time. Sadly,

Wexford would not appear in another All-Ireland final for 19 years and that one, in 1996, would bring glorious victory. It is also hard to credit that all those who appeared for Wexford in the interim would not even win a Leinster medal.

Tony Doran played in two more Leinster finals, in 1981 and 1984. Narrow defeats were again the outcome and when Tony strode off the pitch in Croke Park in 1984, he brought the curtain down on a magnificent inter-county career. For an unbelievable 22 consecutive years, he had proudly worn the county jersey at some level. Seldom, it must be added, has any player, in any county, given so much service and provided so much happiness as Tony Doran did in his quiet, cheerful and accomplished manner. 'Those years between 1968 and 1984 were disappointing, at times, but overall the happy memories outweigh the sad ones. Beating Kilkenny in the 1976 Leinster final will always be a highlight for me. Going to Croke Park as underdogs and winning by 17 points was a great achievement. It was a great occasion for us to eventually beat Kilkenny after five years of heartbreaking defeats. On a personal level, I will never forget the 1984 Leinster semi-final against Kilkenny. The game was level and our midfielder, Billy Byrne, sent in a high ball and I beat Dick O'Hara to the catch. Then I got around him and put the ball in the net and we won the match. Some commentators, kindly, said that was the last great goal I scored as a county player.'

At club level, Buffer's Alley, which was founded in 1900, has become synonymous with wonderful hurling achievements, at both national and county level. Yet, up to the mid-1960s, the club, with its small catchment area, had never achieved senior status. It always seemed to be fluctuating between junior and intermediate grades. With the advent of Tony Doran, his brothers Joe, Billy and Colm, and many others, all this changed. In 1965, they won the Intermediate hurling championship before claiming their first senior title in 1968, having lost the previous year's final to Rathnure. Between 1968 and 1991, Doran won a total of 11 senior championship medals, ten of them on the field of play. His last winner's medal was obtained at the ripe young age of 45! Of all those tremendous county title victories, three of them stand out in Tony's mind, for different reasons. 'I will never forget the 1970 final against Shamrocks of Enniscorthy. In the first half I noticed a commotion amongst the crowd and I saw a spectator being stretchered away. When I saw Pat Nolan, a cousin of mine, walking alongside, I had this definite fear that it must be my dad. At half-time the four of us, who were playing that day, were taken to one side and told our father had a "turn". We looked at each other, said nothing but, quietly, feared the worst. We went out in the second half and played out of our skins. That's what Dad would have wanted. When the game was over, we were told the sad news, that he had passed away before half-time.

'The 1976 final was to provide another sorrowful memory. We have had many dedicated officials, like Tom Donoghue, Gerard Dempsey, Paddy Sinott and the late Tom O'Leary, over the years. Our club treasurer in the 1970s was a very hardworking official called Tom Butler. Just after we left the dressing rooms at half-time, poor Tom died suddenly from a heart attack. A happier memory concerns the 1988 county final when we beat Rathnure after six unsuccessful attempts in a final. We were not recognised by some people as proper champions because we had never beaten Rathnure. In the first game, Rathnure were the vastly superior side and went in at half time, 0–13 to 0–4 ahead. Everyone said the second half was a showpiece of flowing, fast and furious hurling. Anyhow, we fought back to draw that game. In the replay, we all really played well and we won, comfortably, by eight points. The Rathnure hoodoo was over, after 21 years of trying. If anyone had said to us, at the beginning of the year, "What's your ambition?" we would have settled for beating Rathnure in the county final.'

Subsequently, Buffer's Alley defeated Carlow Town and Seir Kieran, of Offaly, before reaching that year's Leinster club final. They were none too impressive in either contest. That particular team were now in their final provincial club decider, having been beaten by St Rynagh's of Offaly in 1982/83. Though they won the 1985/86 final against another Offaly team, Kinnity, they lost the ensuing All-Ireland final to Tipperary side Kilruane McDonagh's, by two points. They now faced Ballyhale Shamrocks of Kilkenny, who had the famed Fennelly brothers amongst their ranks. Buffer's Alley led 1–10 to 0–2 at half-time, thanks mainly to the deadly accuracy of Mick Butler from placed balls and an absolutely brilliant goal from Tony Doran. In the second half, the Fennelly-inspired Shamrocks fought back to narrow the gap to two points with three minutes remaining. However, a spectacular point from out on the sideline by the impressive Butler enabled the Alley men to win on a 1–12 to 1–9 scoreline. The outstanding Butler had amassed a personal tally of 0–10. The semi-final hurdle was crossed when the Wexford side easily disposed of Four Roads from Roscommon. Now rapidly approaching his 43rd birthday, Tony could not believe his luck. He genuinely felt that when they had lost the 1986 club final, his last chance of a club gold medal was gone.

On St Patrick's Day 1989, the final took place in Croke Park. O'Donovan Rossa of Antrim, powered by the talented Jim Close and Donal Armstrong, as well as All Star Ciarán Barr, provided the opposition. The Belfast side seized the initiative and were ahead 0–6 to 0–1 after only ten minutes. But for heroic goalkeeping by Henry Butler, the northerners would have been even further ahead. The Buffer's Alley mentors then switched Paul Gahan to centre half-back and Tom Dempsey to midfield. The move was a double success, as Gahan curtailed the threat of the strong-running Barr, and Dempsey restored parity to the midfield exchanges. After 18 minutes, the teams were level, and when Séamus O'Leary goaled, the Alley men went in at the interval leading 1–5 to 0–7. The second half totally belonged to the Wexford men. A final scoreline of 2–12 to 0–12 was a fair indication of their superiority. What was more pertinent to them was that they were now All-Ireland club champions.

The Buffer's Alley team were all heroes, especially goalkeeper Henry Butler, captain Pat Kenny at full-back and the aforementioned Gahan and Dempsey. In the forward line, Fr Martin Casey, Mick Butler and Séamus O'Leary shone, while the old warhorse himself, Tony Doran, was truly inspirational. It was really fitting that Doran's last appearance in Croke Park should be a winning one. It was hard to believe that all of 26 years earlier he had made his debut, in a minor championship game in 1963. It was also appropriate that the adoring thousands saw a cameo of the man's true greatness. Midway through the second half, he rose high to catch the ball from a sea of clutching fingers. Even though surrounded by four or five defenders, he managed to elude their despairing tackles and send the ball over the bar for a magnificent point.

There were unprecedented scenes of jubilation as captain Pat Kenny was presented with the Moore Cup. It had been 21 years since Wexford had celebrated on an All-Ireland final day. So it was proper that the remaining link with that McCarthy Cup success should be raised shoulder high in the centre of Croke Park and paraded, triumphantly, to the victory podium. Tony Doran, of the red hair and big heart, was a winner yet again. To complete that day of joyful ecstasy, there were two other links with 1968. Fr Martin Casey and Mick Butler had been on that successful minor side all those years ago. Just three weeks short of his 43rd birthday, the man from Boolavogue had won the only medal missing from his All-Ireland collection. What a fantastic achievement for a wonderful ambassador of Buffer's Alley and Wexford! 'Without doubt, this was the greatest thrill of my life, to win a medal with all the people I grew up with. Four of the team had been there from the start, in the 1960s — Henry Butler, his brother Mick, Fr Martin Casey and myself. My brother Colm had also been there from the beginning. He had come on as a sub against Carlow Town, but a recurring back injury had prevented him from taking any further part in the competition. In fact, he had a disc removed from his back just a few days before the final.'

Meeting Tony was an exceptionally pleasant experience as he recalled his career's highlights and disappointments. The great hurlers he met, his love of Gaelic football and an All Star trip formed just a fraction of those thoughts and memories.

1. 'I am a great follower of Gaelic football. I actually played U-21 and junior championship football for Wexford. My first memory of a football match was seeing Wexford playing in their last Leinster final against Kildare in 1956. Nick Redmond, Seán Turner, Paddy Kehoe, Padge Kehoe and John Ryan were all excellent players on that team. Wexford have a good side now. It was great to see them getting to the 2005 National League final. Mattie Forde winning an All Star award last year was a deserved honour. The Dublin teams of the fifties, seventies and eighties, as well as the great Kerry team, were all favourites of mine. Offaly winning All-Irelands in the 1970s and 1982 was great for the game. Willie Bryan was a magnificent fielder and Tony McTague was deadly accurate from frees. Mick O'Connell was the best Gaelic footballer I ever saw.'

2. 'There were so many brilliant hurlers from Cork, Kilkenny and Tipperary, it would be impossible to name them all. Jimmy Doyle, Babs Keating, Len Gaynor, Denis Coughlan, Ray Cummins, John Horgan, J.B. Murphy, Seán O'Leary, Gerald McCarthy and Charlie McCarthy are just some who come to mind. Pat Henderson, Ger Henderson, Fan Larkin, Ollie Walsh, Noel Skehan and Eddie Keher were all fabulous Kilkenny hurlers. John Connolly of Galway was the best midfielder I witnessed. Iggy Clarke, Seán Silke and P.J. Molloy were other very skilful hurlers. During my career, most of my direct opponents at full-back were really outstanding. Pat McDonnell and Martin Doherty of Cork, Pat Hartigan of Limerick, Pa Dillon, Brian Cody and Nicky Orr of Kilkenny were really powerful defenders. Eugene Coughlan of Offaly was a very good ball player. He was a great man to tap the ball away from you. Pat Dunny of Kildare, Paddy Molloy, Barney Moylan and Pádraig Horan of Offaly, as well as P.J. Cuddy of Laois, were great Railway Cup players. However, the greatest all-round hurler I ever met was Tipperary's Mick Roche.'

3. 'Once, when we were on an All Star trip to America, a few of us were pucking a ball around a field. Someone challenged Fan Larkin to a race, the whole length of the pitch. "Be the Lord save us, you won't. But I'll tell you what — I will race you to the 21-yard line. That is as far as I ever have to go!" said Fan.'

The following are Tony Doran's representative selections. He did not consider any Wexford player.

LEINSTER (1968–1989)

Ollie Walsh
(Kilkenny)

Fan Larkin
(Kilkenny)

Eugene Coughlan
(Offaly)

Pat Dunny
(Kildare)

Joe Hennessy
(Kilkenny)

Ger Henderson
(Kilkenny)

Martin Coogan
(Kilkenny)

Des Foley
(Dublin)

Frank Cummins
(Kilkenny)

Liam O'Brien
(Kilkenny)

Pat Delaney
(Kilkenny)

Eddie Keher
(Kilkenny)

Mick Brennan
(Kilkenny)

Pádraig Horan
(Offaly)

Kieran Purcell
(Kilkenny)

IRELAND (1968–1989)

Ollie Walsh
(Kilkenny)

Fan Larkin
(Kilkenny)

Pat Hartigan
(Limerick)

John Horgan
(Cork)

Denis Coughlan
(Cork)

Mick Roche
(Tipperary)

Iggy Clarke
(Galway)

John Connolly
(Galway)

Frank Cummins
(Kilkenny)

Jimmy Doyle
(Tipperary)

Pat Delaney
(Kilkenny)

Eddie Keher
(Kilkenny)

Babs Keating
(Tipperary)

Ray Cummins
(Cork)

Eamon Cregan
(Limerick)

As I left Boolavogue, the sun was setting, as it had done over 200 years earlier. Memories of Fr John Murphy, pikemen and yeomanry gradually surfaced out of the subconscious. Driving through the Harrow, Ferns and Bunclody, all traces of the cruelty and hardship of that era had disappeared. Peace and tranquillity now reigned over the land and its wonderful people. When Nicky Rackard walked into his parents' living room in 1949, he awoke in his county a dormant energy of hope and future glory. Nowadays, when one speaks of Wexford, one thinks of hurling and Rackard, O'Donnell, English, Quigley, Storey, Griffin and the many others who made Wexford a great hurling county. But above all others, we recall the name of one man who is indelibly linked to 200 years of history and 50 years of hurling prominence. In the barren years, Tony Doran, the maestro from Boolavogue, kept that hurling flame alive. He truly is a legend in his own lifetime.

Tony Doran – Fact File

Native Place:	Monamolin, Co. Wexford
Place of Birth:	April 4, 1946
Club:	Buffer's Alley
Club Honours:	Senior Hurling Championship (11) – 1968, 1970, 1975, 1976, 1982, 1983, 1984, 1985, 1988, 1989, and 1991
	Intermediate Hurling Championship (1) – 1965
	U-21 Hurling Championship (2) – 1965, 1966
	Intermediate Football Championship (1) – 1974
	Junior Football Championship (1) – 1972
	J.B. Football Championship (1) – 1981
	All-Ireland Club Hurling Championship (1) – 1989
	Leinster Club Hurling Championship (2) – 1985/86, 1988/89
	Senior Hurling League (7)
County Honours:	All-Ireland Senior Hurling Championship (1) – 1968
	Leinster Senior Hurling Championship (4) – 1968, 1970, 1976, 1977
	All-Ireland U-21 Hurling Championship (1) – 1965
	Leinster U-21 Hurling Championship (3) – 1964, 1965, 1966
	All-Ireland Minor Hurling Championship (1) – 1963
	Leinster Minor Hurling Championship – 1963
	National Hurling League (2) – 1967, 1973
	National Hurling League Division 1B – 1980

County Honours— contd.	Oireachtas Hurling Championship (3) – 1978, 1979, 1980 Walsh Cup Hurling Champions (3) – 1965, 1967, 1968, 1969 Wembley Hurling Champions – 1968
Other Playing Honours:	Railway Cup (7) – 1971, 1972, 1973, 1974, 1975, 1977, 1979
Awards:	Gaelic Weekly All Star 1967 All Star 1976 Texaco Hurler of the Year 1976 Bank of Ireland GAA Personality of the Month — July 1976, March 1989 Irish Independent Sports Star of the Week — March 24, 1989 Sunday Game Man of the Match — June 17, 1984 RTÉ Man of the Match Senior Hurling Final 1968 Selected on Silver Jubilee Club Hurling team Sealink Wexford Monthly Awards — April 1983, March 1989 Wexford Person of the Month — March 1989 Powers Gold Label Sports Star — 1967, 1975 Powers 21st Anniversary Award 1984 Powers Silver Anniversary (1964–1988) Hurling Winner Powers Silver Anniversary (1964–1988) Overall Sports Star 1988
Selectorial Honours:	Buffer's Alley Senior Hurling Champions – 1975, 1976, 1982 Wexford U-21 Leinster Winners 1986
Occupation:	Dairy farmer
Family:	Wife – Mary (née Hobbs), from Killena
Children:	Therese, Noelle, Tony, Pat, Marie

TWENTY-FOUR

Cormac McAnallen RIP

A PROSE POEM TRIBUTE TO A TYRONE ICON

Do Chormac

A Chormaic uasail na n-éacht; curadh réchúiseach ár n-aoise,
Cuimhneofar go deo ar do dhaonacht, d'ionracas,
D'fhearúlacht, d'uaisleacht, d'anamúlacht
Ar an bpáirc imeartha, sa seomra ranga, id' shaol laethúil.

Ar d'anam dílis Críostaí
Go ndéana Rí na bhflaitheas trócaire,
'Gus 'na fallaing imleathan bhánghorm
Go bhfille Muire chaoin tú.

Tomás Mac Aonghusa

Just before 3 a.m. on the morning of Tuesday, March 2, 2004, one of Gaelic football's finest and youngest ambassadors, Cormac McAnallen, died suddenly in his parental home in Eglish, Co. Tyrone. A rare heart condition known as Long Quiet Time (LQT) Syndrome was identified as the most probable cause of Cormac's untimely death. Eglish is both a rural parish and a tiny village where people love to live for each other and for Gaelic football. Less than six months earlier its most famous son had climaxed a marvellous sporting career. On that famous September Sunday he was the proud wearer of the No. 3 jersey when Tyrone — a great GAA county — won their first All-Ireland senior football title.

Born in 1980, Cormac's football career had, by any standards, been exceptional. He first came to prominence at that famed football nursery, St Patrick's College, Armagh, reaching a Mac Rory Cup final in 1997. That same year he also played alongside Paul McGirr on the Tyrone minor side. After the tragic and accidental death of Paul, in an Ulster championship game against Armagh, Cormac helped his teammates reach the All-Ireland final, only to be beaten by Laois. In

1998 Tyrone, now captained by the Eglish man, powered their way again to the All-Ireland minor final. This time, Tyrone and Cormac brought home the Tom Markham Trophy when they exacted sweet revenge on Laois. On that occasion Cormac displayed his natural linguistic and oratorical skills *as Gaeilge* when he received the All-Ireland minor trophy.

As Tyrone's captain fantastic he led his native county to two successive All-Ireland U-21 triumphs in 2000 and 2001, when they defeated Limerick and Mayo respectively. At the same time, he won a Sigerson Cup medal with Queen's University in 2000 and later a Dublin senior football championship medal during his time as a post-graduate student at UCD.

Undoubtedly his greatest achievement was his conversion to the full-back position in the later stages of that historic 2003 Sam Maguire Cup success. To complete that tremendous season, Cormac was selected as an All Star and represented Ireland in the three-test International series against Australia. Just prior to his untimely death, Cormac, who had been a regular on the Tyrone senior team since he made his debut in 1999, was appointed team captain in succession to Peter Canavan. The man who also won two National Football League medals in 2002 and 2003 had the honour of raising aloft the McKenna Cup in his last trophy win.

The multi-talented Cormac was also a quiz expert, who had captained his secondary school, St Patrick's, Armagh, to All-Ireland success in 1996. When he passed away, he was serving his second year as a teacher in St Catherine's College in Armagh.

Rarely has the death of a young, dedicated and gifted sportsperson touched so many people, not only in his native Tyrone but also throughout the 32 counties of Ireland. Tributes came to the McAnallen household from all sporting disciplines and right across the political spectrum as well. No one epitomised more the sense of loss of a truly remarkable human being than Armagh football captain Kieran McGeeney: 'Like all great athletes he had a lot — real courage, unbelievable focus, an unwavering dedication and commitment to his sport, true loyalty to his teammates, the ability never to give up, integrity, honesty and above all the mark of all great leaders: the ability to really listen, and the modesty to learn.'

His mother, Bridget, father Brendan, brothers Donal and Fergus, and his fiancée Ashlene Moore can all be consoled by the knowledge that they were so close to such a warm and wonderful human being. They also know that this world is but a short temporary stop on the road to where we will all meet again.

Shortly after Cormac's death, I penned the following prose poem

in his honour. In it I have used the voice of the Sam Maguire Cup as
the narrator.

Farewell Dear Cormac

In the land of O'Neill the meandering Blackwater flows
As it did in the time of Hugh and Owen Roe.
Between embattled Benburb and historic Dungannon
Lies Eglish, a haven of rural tranquillity
Where you first saw the light of day,
Just 24 years ago.

In Derrylatinee the always pensive, enquiring, scholarly
          mind
With the smiling, friendly personality,
Developed rapidly and effortlessly progressed.
When you arrived at the See of St Patrick,
On Armagh's hallowed sandy hill, a long ingrained
          tradition
Of Mac Rory excellence and scholastic achievement
          awaited you.

Those twin characteristics of that ancient seat of classical
          learning
Were greatly enhanced with your penchant for the game
          of the Gael,
And the constant thirst for the all-embracing knowledge,
Captaining SPCA to All-Ireland Quiz success
Was the first public leadership role of the budding man
We would come to love and admire.

Luck twice deserted you in 1997;
Losing Paul to a freak of nature, and your minor team
          going down
In your theatre of dreams, deeply hurt.
Recording a treble triumph in the following years
As you lifted Tom Markham and Tadhg Ó Cléirigh
Heralded you as the best young footballer in the land.

Wearing No. 3 was the catalyst
For inscribing Tír Eoghain on Gaeldom's greatest prize.
In a continuous cavalcade of euphoric, unbridled
          emotion

You traversed a county starved of success, celebrating its
 greatest achievement.
Returning to Eglish, with me, you had become Brantry's
 pride and joy;
Its most famous son, its most unassuming hero.

2004 looked ideal for a good team to become great.
Being handed the new baton
Made your sense of destiny almost inevitable.
But Divine intervention dictated that when you
Raised up the McKenna Cup to a Donegal sky
You would never again adorn the playing fields of
 Ireland.

The gracious graduate of Queen's and UCD,
The wonderful teacher at St Catherine's was now no
 more.
A leader, a talismanic figure; surely an embryonic
 statesman;
A person of loyalty, substance, spirituality, suddenly left
 us in our greatest hour.
So hard to understand, so easy to remember
'Why God's ways are not our ways.'

Never in the history of our island
Has any human being, so young in years
Yet so mature in temperament, made such a national,
 indelible impact.
That winning, laughing aura of confidence,
Though humble acquiescence enveloped a people
So desperate for real icons of transparent humanity.

For years your people craved for me to come
Amongst you and I duly, though belatedly, did.
Those last earthly days of yours, I was especially
 privileged
To be at the epicentre of a nation
Saying goodbye to a football prince
Whose deeds will inspire countless generations to come.

Still, hope springs eternal
As my alter ego, the original of the species, tells me.
When you arrived beyond Heaven's open door

You immediately sought a team meeting with all
The other GAA greats, cut down in the prime of life
So suddenly, so apparently unfairly.

Gallant John Joe, P.J. of Stradone, Pat of Coolderry
Are but a sample few who answered the latest call
Of Cormac, a true High King, to one and all.
'Always help those down below to cope with
The sheer fragility of life
And the ultimate reality of death.'

Farewell, Dear Cormac. You have served
Your family, parish, county and country well.
When our time comes, *le cúnamh Dé*, we will see you
      again
At the eternal game up in the sky.
Your nearest and dearest, as before, will once more walk
      and talk with you.
Only this time — it will be forever.

Cormac McAnallen – Fact File

Native Place:	Eglish, Co. Tyrone
Year of Birth:	1980
Clubs:	St Patrick's, Eglish Minor Football Championship (2) – 1996, 1997 Queen's University, Belfast University College, Dublin
Colleges' Honours:	Mac Rory Cup Finalist – 1997
Third Level Honours:	Sigerson Cup (Queen's University, Belfast) – 2000 Dublin Senior Football Championship (1) – UCD 2002
County Honours:	Ulster Minor Football Championship (2) – 1997, 1998 All-Ireland Minor Football Championship (1) – 1998 (Captain) Ulster U-21 Football Championship (2) – 2000, 2001 Hastings U-21 Cup (2) – 2000 (Captain), 2001 (Captain)

County Honours— *contd.*	All-Ireland U-21 Football Championship (2) – 2000 (Captain), 2001 (Captain)
	All-Ireland Senior Football Championship (1) – 2003
	Ulster Senior Football Championship (2) – 2001, 2003
	National Football League (2) – 2002, 2003
	McKenna Cup (1) – 2004 (Captain)
Other Playing Honours:	Ireland v. Australia 2003
Other Sporting Honours:	Ulster U-15 (Basketball)
Awards:	All Star (1) – 2003
	Young Player of the Year – 2001
	Scór na nÓg (County Question Time winners) (3)
	Scór na nÓg winner (All-Ireland Question Time winners) (1) – 1995
	Scór na Sinsear (County Question Time winners) (3)
	BBC Player of the Ulster Championship (1) – 2001
	Ulster GAA writers' Footballer of the Year (1) – 2001
	Queen's University Blues Sport Award – 1999
Occupation:	Secondary schoolteacher
Family:	Parents: Bridget and Brendan
	Brothers: Donal and Fergus
	Fiancée: Ashlene Moore

Index